CAMBRIDGE TEXTS IN THE HISTORY OF POLITICAL THOUGHT

Series editors

RAYMOND GEUSS
Lecturer in Social and Political Sciences, University of Cambridge

QUENTIN SKINNER
Professor of Political Science in the University of Cambridge

Cambridge Texts in the History of Political Thought is now firmly established as the major student textbook series in political theory. It aims to make available to students all the most important texts in the history of western political thought, from ancient Greece to the early twentieth century. All the familiar classic texts will be included but the series does at the same time seek to enlarge the conventional canon by incorporating an extensive range of less well-known works, many of them never before available in a modern English edition. Wherever possible, texts are published in complete and unabridged form, and translations are specially commissioned for the series. Each volume contains a critical introduction together with chronologies, biographical sketches, a guide to further reading and any necessary glossaries and textual apparatus. When completed, the series will aim to offer an outline of the entire evolution of western political thought.

For a list of titles published in the series, please see end of book.

DAVID HUME

Political Essays

EDITED BY
KNUD HAAKONSSEN
Institute for Advanced Studies
Australian National University

CAMBRIDGE
UNIVERSITY PRESS

Published by the Press Syndicate of the University of Cambridge
The Pitt Building, Trumpington Street, Cambridge, CB2 1RP
40 West 20th Street, New York, NY 10011-4211, USA
10 Stamford Road, Oakleigh, Melbourne 3166, Australia

Cambridge University Press 1994

First published 1994

Printed in Great Britain at the University Press, Cambridge

A catalogue record for this book is available from the British Library

Library of Congress cataloguing in publication data

Hume, David, 1711–1776.
Political essays / David Hume; edited by Knud Haakonssen.
p.   cm. – (Cambridge texts in the history of political thought)
Includes bibliographical references and index.
ISBN 0 521 46093X.   ISBN 0 521 46639 3 (pbk.)
1. Political science – Early works to 1800.   I. Haakonssen, Knud,
1947– .   II. Title.   III. Series.
JC176.H8971994
320'.01–dc20   93–36183   CIP

ISBN 0 521 46093 x hardback
ISBN 0 521 46639 3 paperback

For Eric

Contents

Contents

Acknowledgements

It is a pleasure to thank the people who have assisted me in preparing this volume. In particular, I thank Roger Emerson, David Norton, M. A. Stewart and Donald Winch for sharing with me their expert knowledge of Hume's texts. As always, I am indebted to my research assistant, Elizabeth Short, for her patient attention to both style and substance. Ann Smith helped me collate some of the editions of the *Essays*; Norma Chin and Wendie Woods lent their impeccable secretarial assistance; and Mary Norton subjected the introduction to a critical reading. My predecessor as editor of Hume's *Essays*, Eugene Miller, kindly kept me informed of possible corrections to his work. Several friends and colleagues took time to answer requests for specific information or references: Jeremy Black, Paul Bourke, John Cairns, Dario Castiglione, James Franklin, Karsten Friis-Johansen, Peter Groenewegen, Peter Hall, Nicholas Phillipson, Claude Rawson, Michael Silverthorn. Finally, Robert Brown and Lisbeth Haakonssen accepted the *Essays* as topics for lunchtime conversations that would have gratified the good David himself.

A number of institutions have supported my work and I gratefully acknowledge them here: most importantly, the Research School of Social Sciences within the Institute for Advanced Studies at the Australian National University; the Institute for Advanced Studies in the Humanities at the University of Edinburgh; the Max Planck Institut für Geschichte in Göttingen; and the Department of Philosophy at McGill University.

Introduction

The politics of David Hume's lifetime, 1711–76, is often seen as the 'growth of stability', as the shoring up of the complacent British *ancien régime* and the securing of the first British empire. These perceptions are by no means entirely changed if we look at the period through Hume's eyes, but they are significantly modified. Hume's writings on politics, especially his essays, convey a sense of the fragility and uncertainty of the politics that created the high-Georgian establishment of his later years. And when he died in the late summer of 1776, he had clear premonitions of the jolt that this establishment was about to receive from across the Atlantic. Hume's understanding of the transitory nature of politics was not only the result of his acute observation of Britain and Europe and his unusual historical sense; it was also based on a complex political philosophy, a crucial point of which was that public opinion is fundamental to all political authority. This convergence of political observation, historical insight and philosophical theory formed Hume's political opinion. By publishing it, he hoped to have a formative influence on the public opinion that was constitutive of politics. At the same time he presented posterity with a particularly inviting, if difficult, task of interpretation.

Hume's political situation
When Hume was born, Britain was still ruled by a daughter of the last Stuart king. Queen Anne, like her sister Mary before her, offered some comfort to those who saw the removal of James II at the Revolution in 1689 as sacrilege against the doctrine of the indefeasible hereditary right of succession in kings. It took a long time to get

rid of the idea that only direct descendants of the Stuarts could be considered kings *de jure*, and that the most Parliament could do was to provide *de facto* replacements to meet temporary difficulties, such as incurable Catholicism in the rightful heir. The Act of Settlement had already determined in 1701 that upon the death of Anne, the Elector of Hanover would succeed to the crown. But this experiment in founding a dynasty – not just an interim monarch – upon an act of Parliament began in earnest only with the succession of George I in 1714. Its experimental nature was underlined by a number of attempts by the Old Pretender, the son of James II, and, eventually, by the next Stuart, the Young Pretender, to invade Britain. While posterity can see that these attempts never provided any serious threat to the new regime, mainly because the necessary French support never came in sufficient strength, this was not so evident to contemporaries. Even the last insurrection in 1745 was considered very dangerous, and the reaction against it was so strong that Hume thought it imprudent to publish his essay 'Of the Protestant succession' in 1748.

Despite the continuing Jacobite threat, the constitutional provision of rule by the King-in-Parliament was widely accepted long before the Forty-five. But this acceptance may have derived more from the necessity of getting on with governing than from an understanding of the nature of the new government. The political nation was still divided by the party rhetoric of the seventeenth century, which made Tories pretend that England was a divine-right monarchy and Whigs that it had an ancient mixed constitution protecting the people's rights. The former had to see the Revolution settlement as a subversion of the king's rights; the latter would naturally tend to see the crown's management of business through ministerial members of Parliament as a dangerous extension of the executive prerogative. Yet these perceptions were quickly thrown into confusion by political circumstances. During the first twenty years after the Revolution, the monarchs, deterred by Whig suspicion of executive power, chose a large number of their ministers from among the Tories, thus gradually reconciling the latter to the new regime. By the same token, it was by a hitherto unimagined efficiency in executing the king's business in Parliament that the Whigs, under Sir Robert Walpole, eventually gained ascendancy in the 1720s and 1730s. The old party lines and 'principles' thus provided less and less of a clue to the conduct of politics, which was in fact dominated by the opposition between 'Court' and 'Country' interests.

Just like 'Tory' and 'Whig', the 'Court' and 'Country' labels did not denote clearly defined and organised parties. They referred to shifting constellations of interests, policies and principles represented by changing alliances of individuals and groups, often connected by family ties. At the heart of the Court-side of politics was the convergence of the interests of executive government and of commerce. Put simply, the government needed more money, mainly for the public service, public works and foreign policy, than it was politically possible to get out of Parliament in the form of taxes. But clever ministers, and especially Walpole, could manage Parliament so that the government was allowed to borrow money from its citizens. Such money was most readily available from the 'monied' (finance) sector, whose investment interests, including monopolies and overseas trading privileges, the government consequently looked after. While the Court interest thus was closely linked with city-centred monied wealth, it had to secure itself in Parliament by looking after members who often came from rural constituencies. Among many methods of doing this, a common and controversial one was the dispensation of patronage in the form of public offices.

For the Country opposition all of this was simply corruption. The people were being corrupted by the 'luxury' – consumerism – promoted by commerce. Private interest was being put above public good; patriotism was waning; and the country would soon be defensible only by the hiring of mercenary forces. Monied wealth was in itself a corrupt form of property because it, in contrast to landed wealth, could flee the country at any time and thus carried none of the responsibility for the common good of the country. Furthermore, government was being corrupted into basing its policy upon money of a merely imagined worth, namely, paper representing values still to be produced by the nation in the future. The constitution itself was being corrupted by crown manipulation of Parliament through 'placemen' and through extending each Parliament from three to seven years. During Hume's youth this Country opposition made use of an eclectic mixture of ideas; on the one hand, old or 'real' Whig notions of the ancient constitution, popular representation and rights; on the other hand, neo-republican or 'Commonwealth' ideas of civic virtue and the landed basis for proper authority. Added to these ingredients were Tory traditionalism and rural suspicions of the ways of the urban world.

While the Country opposition to some extent was a spontaneous reaction to the conduct of politics, Lord Bolingbroke in particular strove to make it into a coherent force, using his periodical the *Crafts-man* as a mouthpiece. The Court establishment also used able pens, including that of Daniel Defoe, to articulate its basic argument, namely that it was the force implementing the unique constitutional principles of the English Revolution and securing the rights of Englishmen. It was this that enabled Britons to make full use of the opportunities provided by modern commerce and created the wealth that alone would provide Britain with her security.

The question of security was not an idle one. When Hume was born, Britain was fighting the most devastating of a string of con-nected wars that had begun well before the Revolution. All of them were concerned with confining France so that a balance could be maintained between the major powers. Britons, then as later, feared more than anything else a 'universal monarchy', that is a Europe dominated directly or indirectly by one monarch in the despotical style of the East or the imperial style of ancient Rome. These fears were of course increased by the Catholicism of the contenders for European predominance. When Louis XIV was finally defeated, the Peace of Utrecht in 1714 secured Britain a quarter century of peace, the longest such period in the eighteenth century. Those were the years of Hume's childhood and youth; by contrast his middle years were darkened by major European wars, the War of the Austrian Succession, 1740–8, and the Seven Years War, 1756–63.

These wars were, of course, not only about domination of the European continent but also about control of the ocean and about colonies, that is, about trade. In the Europe which Hume observed so keenly, national fortunes were increasingly dependent upon inter-national trade, and this led not only to wars but to a rethinking of the very idea of national wealth and empire. What was the relationship between this constantly changing, ill-defined phenomenon called commerce – or 'traffick' in the contemporary phrase – and solidly earth-bound agriculture, between both and money, which in the eighteenth century meant bullion, between all of these and the highly abstract credit represented by paper bills? The common opinion, often later referred to as mercantilism, was that wealth consists in money, and that foreign trade accordingly should be aimed at creating a surplus of exports paid for in specie. The French physiocrats, in contrast, regarded wealth as reducible to the production of the soil and were generally suspicious of trade. Such ideas inevitably led to speculations about the relationship between countries with a surplus to trade with and those without, between rich commercial and poor agricultural countries.

The eighteenth century increasingly saw history in linear terms; as a matter of a progression or development through a number of social, economic and political stages. Commonly, thinkers operated with one or two pre-agricultural stages of hunters, gatherers and nomads, followed by agriculture and, mainly in recent European history, commerce. But this linear view, which has many ancient precursors, was often, so to speak, crossed by other old ideas of cycles and corruption. Put simply, the questions were whether a commercial society could continue to progress and perhaps become more and more dominant over its poorer neighbours, or whether the poorer agricultural countries would catch up and, by taking up manufacturing, would undermine an advanced commercial society by underselling it through lower wages.

This problem was very close to home for the young Hume. Having suffered starvation in the 1690s, Scotland had tried and failed disastrously to break out of poverty through a colonial trade adventure, the Darien project. When the Union of England and Scotland in 1707 created Great Britain, there was a wide-ranging public debate about the economic discrepancy between the riches of English commerce and the poverty of Scots agriculture and about the merits of a commercial society as such. The neo-republican themes of the nexus between commerce, luxury and corruption on the one hand and that between landholding, concern for the common good and patriotism on the other found a ready reception among many Scots. Andrew Fletcher of Saltoun was one of the most prominent to argue against the Unionists' vision of a Scotland riding into the modern world of commerce on the back of English trade.

The debate about the Union, both before and after, went much further than economic matters. The consideration of various forms of union brought out the conventional character and changeability of constitutional arrangements. Attention was drawn to the question of the relationship between population and Parliamentary representation. Scotland had been allocated 45 members of the House of Commons to be added to the 513 from England and Wales, and her nobility could elect 16 representatives to supplement the 220 southern peers who made up the House of Lords by right of birth. Alternatives such as a federal Europe were canvassed, and the problematic relationship between state apparatus and national community became apparent. Comparisons were invited between England's common law and Scotland's civil-law system (which remained after the Union). The relationship between church and state was put into sharp focus. After generations of conflict in England and a grudging, uncertain and limited toleration granted to dissenters from the Anglican church, the Union suddenly brought about a state with an episcopal state church south of the border and a Presbyterian one in the north.

Above all, the creation of the Union invigorated the debate, which began with the union of the English and Scottish crowns in 1603, about the relevance of the English political experience and of English political processes to Scottish life and, by doing so, it made Scotsmen reflect upon the nature of politics as such. Scotland had never had political groupings like the Whigs and Tories; her politics had largely been conducted along clannish lines of traditional allegiance to persons and families. Now, in greater numbers than ever before, her leading men were syphoned off to London as supporting cast in an alien and distant political play, leaving Scotland and her national capital with an empty political stage. The vacancy was filled to a remarkable extent by a kind of replacement politics that expressed itself in developing and supplementing older schemes for economic development and educational renewal, as well as in the life of the law and the politics of church government – for Scotland preserved her own legal system and her Kirk. It was, in short, the politics of culture. Forced by circumstances, Scotland thus delivered dramatic proof that issues such as these could make up a *public* life, could be dealt with in a public process not unlike the political process but with a measure of independence from politics in the narrower sense. In short, Scotland's position as a nationally coherent province on the political periphery, while common in early modern Europe, was assumed under circumstances that made her reflect publicly on the advent of the modern world and her place in it in a way that might otherwise have taken much longer and been even more difficult. This public reflection is now commonly referred to as the Scottish

Enlightenment, and Hume's writings on public issues are to be seen, at least in their inception, as a contribution to it.

Hume's politics

Such was, in brief compass, the political situation whose logic Hume intended to analyse and repair. All the issues catalogued above were discussed or, at least, referred to when Hume presented his politics to the world in the 1740s and 1750s. As indicated earlier, he dealt with politics in three different genres; as political philosophy, especially in *A Treatise of Human Nature*, Book III, and in *An Enquiry Concerning the Principles of Morals*, but also in some of the *Essays*; as political observation in many of the *Essays*; and as political history in the *History of England*, but also in several of the *Essays*. The *Essays* thus function both as a political supplement to the *Treatise* and as an extension of the *History* from 1689 to 1740. Several of them may in fact have been intended for the volume on politics Hume mentions in the advertisement to the *Treatise* in 1739. Yet, when Hume published the first collection in 1741, he explained in the preface that these essays had been written for a projected journal. Hume's ideal was clearly the polite essay of Addison and Steele, but his overall project was equally clearly wider and more ambitious. He not only wanted to introduce into Scotland elegant conversation pieces on moral and, as we would say, cultural topics, he wanted to make politics itself a topic of such conversation. With the switch from an Edinburgh journal to a book form, this undoubtedly became an ambition not only for the Scottish, but for the greater British stage. This is to say that Hume wanted to show that political debate need not be the usual divisive, sectarian assertion of irreconcilable positions, but that it could indeed be the collective formulation of public opinion. Behind this project lay the idea that there is no such thing as a right political arrangement inherent in history, as in the ancient constitution of Whig lore, or in nature, as in natural-rights theories, or in the divine dispensation, as in divine-right monarchism. As long as such beliefs prevailed, political debate could be nothing but pointless assertion and counter-assertion. For Hume, political arrangements were not given; they were, in a complex sense, made by people acting on their beliefs. If people could be persuaded to reflect upon this, the political process, whether of conservation or reform, would become a matter of self-consciously forming opinions.

Hume approached his task in three ways; he showed by example how to make politics into polite conversation; he refuted the claims of the political sects or parties for an empirical, especially historical, foundation; and he provided a metaphysics of politics as convention. We will look at each in turn.

To political partisans, one of the most provocative aspects of Hume's political writings was his ability to find something to be said on both sides of most public questions, that is, to identify something to talk about. He juxtaposed opposing standpoints, often in semi-dialogue form, in order to make this explicit. Similarly he imitated ancient models of character drawing in order to convey the complexity of political personalities and thus get away from one-sided panegyric and denunciation. In the *Essays* the most striking example of this is the character of Sir Robert Walpole; and the *History* presents a large number of character sketches.

The basis for Hume's independence was his thorough analysis of British politics which, given the nature of that politics, had to involve a revaluation of English political history. All sides in the English political debate relied on a prescriptive use of history to justify their standpoints. Hume's critical intervention in the debate had three sides to it. He tried to show that the rival historical interpretations generally were wrong; and, second, that the associated understandings of contemporary politics were mistaken, with errors concerning the past reinforcing those concerning the present, and vice versa. Third, the implication of his critique is that the prescriptive use of history is quite misguided. These points are best appreciated by looking at Hume's own analysis of the political situation indicated in the first section above.

According to Hume, contemporary Britain was characterised by five striking features. First, it provided its citizens with an extraordinary degree of personal freedom which included religious liberty, safety of property and, at least in principle, guarantees against arbitrary taxation. Second, it secured this freedom through a mixed constitution in which the component powers were linked in a most peculiar way. Third, British politics was to a significant degree dominated by institutional arrangements rather than by individuals. Fourth, Britain, or at least England, was, along with the Netherlands, the first major country to base a large part of its wealth upon commerce, hitherto the preserve of – generally republican – city-states.

Fifth, in trying to keep its competitive edge in the increasingly commercial society of Europe, Britain was in effect engaged in empire-building based upon trade and only secondarily on conquest.

While many of Hume's contemporaries agreed that these were the characteristic features of modern Britain, Britons were, in his eyes, generally mistaken in their understanding of them. This applied in particular to the first three points.

Those who appreciated the freedom of the English constitution saw it as a genius that was inherent in that constitution but which, disastrously, had been trapped by despotic Stuart kings in the seventeenth century. The events in 1688–9 were thus truly a revolution that returned Englishmen to their ancient freedom. On such an interpretation the Revolution was seen either as a revival of the ancient constitution or as a new political contract in imitation of the original contract implied by earlier instruments of freedom, such as Magna Charta. In Hume's eyes all of this was simply Whig fantasy. For him Britain's system of freedom was brand new; it was a creation or, rather, an effect of the Revolution settlement. Rather than the certainty of antiquity, the system of liberty had all the uncertainty of novelty; and if things went wrong, it would be disastrously misguided to see the calamity as a corruption of tradition.

In order to underscore this thesis, Hume provided a grandiose interpretation of English history, of which we can indicate only one or two central features. He argued that there was no evidence for the much vaunted ancient free constitution. The revered charters of freedom were on the whole catalogues of special privileges forced upon despotically inclined monarchs by groups of power-hungry feudal lords. And despite such limitations, the concentration of power in the crown began early, grew steadily and had reached absolutist proportions of the common European kind well before the first Stuart king. Like his European peers, James I simply followed a pattern of absolutist kingship and his son, Charles I, tried to do likewise. They faced unusual opposition, however, and they proved to have very little talent for coping with this. Because of England's geographic position, there was no tradition for her monarchs to maintain a standing army; when the need for arms arose, special funds were granted the king by Parliament. While the king certainly was the richest person in the realm, he was far from rich enough to maintain an establishment, particularly a standing army, which would threaten the independence of the nobility and the gentry. This relative dependence upon Parliament created great difficulties whenever English kings wanted, or needed, to play a significant role in European politics, for example, in their attempts to restrain first the Spanish and then the French Bourbon ambitions of universal monarchy. The Parliaments upon which the Stuarts, and especially Charles I, were dependent, fell under the influence of puritans, that is, Presbyterians who would tolerate no hierarchy of authority in religious matters and who accordingly rejected the Anglican episcopal church with the king as head. The mixture of religious fervour – enthusiasm, as Hume called it – and political self-assertion dressed in the mythology of ancient liberties became an uncontrollable force. It was spurred on by the inability of Charles I to understand the situation and to appreciate the need for compromise with his own divine-right idea of kingship.

Hume's suggestion was, in other words, that the early Stuarts were more misguided than evil, and that Parliament, while striving for freedom and balance in the constitution, did so on grounds that were historically false, theoretically confused and politically dangerous. He extended this thesis to the later Stuarts and in particular to James II, whose misguidedness extended to the ambition of re-imposing the 'superstitious' system of Catholicism upon the country.

There was no ancient free constitution for the Revolution to revive or return to. But nor was the Revolution, in Hume's eyes, a dissolution of government and a contract of the people to form a new one. One element of the government, the king, had left the country, and the residue, the Convention Parliament, was not a meeting of the people to constitute a new government but a scramble of the small political elite to rescue what could be rescued of existing institutions. Furthermore, conferring James's crown on his daughter and her foreign husband, the Prince of Orange, was plainly unconstitutional.

The freedom enjoyed by modern Britons was thus neither ancient, nor based upon popular contractual consent. It was an unenvisaged outcome of the messy power politics of the Revolution and of the subsequent years, during which crown and Parliament were forced into a mutual dependency that put limitations upon the power of both. The mixed constitution that had resulted was not the noble separation of powers sometimes pretended by Court apologists and idealised out of recognition in Montesquieu's *Spirit of Laws*. But nor was it a corruption fatal to decent government, as alleged by republican Commonwealthmen and the Country opposition. The novelty of post-Revolution politics was that the crown through patronage and through influence on the election of many members of Parliament had created a dependency of parliamentarians as individuals and as groups that could match the budgetary dependency of the crown upon Parliament as an institution. This was, on Hume's analysis, a delicate balance vital to the very survival of the British constitution, and it was not helped by the charged language, bogus theory and false history of the political factions.

An important element in Hume's analysis of modern British politics which sets him further apart from his contemporaries is his emphasis on the institutional character of that politics. In any political system with more than one centre of power, the conduct of politics will tend to be dominated by the formal relations between these centres. When there is, in addition, provision for frequent change of personnel in at least one of these centres, much will depend on the conventions and rules governing the exercise of power. This was obviously happening in Britain. It set her apart from monarchies proper and made her into a semi-republic, monarchies being characterised by administration – as opposed to politics – dependent on one person. The emphasis on the office rather than the office-holder was especially important in relations between government and citizen, and Hume saw the impartial administration of justice as fundamental to a modern commercial society. But while he thought that a regular system of justice could develop only in a 'free' constitution like Britain's, he irreverently suggested that it could be, and was being, imitated by modern monarchies, such as France. The adoption of such a system of justice by monarchies happened especially once they began to take up commerce and to imitate the arts and sciences which would also emerge first in free societies. In other words, not only were the liberties under a free government increasingly dependent upon institutional arrangements rather than upon personal qualities or 'virtues', but absolutist monarchy, the incarnation of 'vice' in republican and traditional Whig demonology, was itself adopting such arrangements.

If Britain's freedom, mixed constitution and institutional politics were novel, so was her commerce. And, like these, commerce was in some respects a fragile growth and not without its dangers. There had of course been commercial societies before, but these had been confined city-states which in effect acted as large merchant houses and brokers between the real political powers. The novelty of the Dutch and the English experiments was to support big-power status with commerce and, especially in the case of the English, to combine commerce with agriculture. The Humean thesis was that these two tasks were indeed possible, provided they were properly understood. First, it was important to see that the defence of a large trading nation did not consist in conquest and empire but in maintaining a balance of power through alliances and treaties and in protecting trade routes. Second, commerce and agriculture were not rival but complementary sectors of the economy. Commerce created large cities, and these provided agriculture with markets and therefore with capital and ideas for improvement. Not least, availability of land as an object of investment for commercial capital was an important means of tying commerce to the country, and this was enhanced by the social and political status conferred by landownership.

This thesis was supported by a basic point about wealth. For Hume, wealth was not primarily about having, but about doing. More particularly, wealth did not consist in money, which was simply a measure of the productive capacity at the disposal of the owner of the money (though Hume remained a hard-currency man as far as this measure was concerned). This applied not only to individuals but to whole countries. It was on this basis that Hume's view differed from the mercantile system, which he regarded as self-defeating if pursued as a policy. The problem was that if the foreign trade of a nation succeeded in creating a net inflow of specie, the greater quantity of money would, generally, increase prices in the country, thus making its exports dearer and attracting increased imports. This so-called specie-flow theory, which is Hume's most famous contribution to modern economics, was closely connected with his suggestion that in a world of mercantile trade policy, nations will be pitted against each other in a 'jealousy of trade', since one nation's gain inevitably must be seen as others' loss. For Hume the productivity that determines wealth was a matter of ideas, namely ideas of what to produce, and such ideas are derived from the market-place. The wider and more varied the market-place, the better the chance of riches in ideas. One nation's riches ought therefore to be seen as an opportunity rather than a danger by others. Rich neighbours are good customers if you supply them with ideas of how to spend their wealth.

This is the core of Hume's case for free trade and for the expansion of commerce.

As for land, Hume certainly agrees with the physiocrats that it has a very special status. But for Hume this is not because land is in some sense the ultimate source of all surplus, but because possession of land is and, in Hume's opinion, ought to be socially and politically enabling. Furthermore, he always saw a lively interplay between city and country – both economic and social – as the backbone of a healthy society. It was the city that generated new ideas and new tastes and thus created employment for both hand and mind, thus alleviating the tedium of country life.

Contemporary Britain was, on Hume's analysis, a world of novel opportunities. It provided unprecedented individual liberty under a limited government and with the security of a regular system of law and justice. In competition with and emulation of neighbouring states, especially France, it saw a flourishing of arts and sciences, which was closely connected with the international world of trade that also created the wealth of the modern world. Hume's modernist interpretation of his time is further deepened by his engagement in the long-standing debates about the relative merits of the ancient and the modern world, especially with regard to literature and politeness, government and institutions, growth of population and the character of labour (whether slave or free). The *Essays* are full of such contrasts, but they are particularly concentrated in the essay 'Of the populousness of ancient nations', an essay that, because of its great length (nearly 100 pages, of which many are devoted to detailed discussions of population figures) had to be left out of the present edition.

In this essay Hume undertook a comparison of ancient and modern society that in effect debunked republican romance about antiquity. He pointed out, first, that the economic basis for ancient society was slavery and that this was not only a cruel institution but also, when compared to free wage-labour detrimental to the growth of population. Ancient economies were further hampered by the lack of significant manufacture and commerce, which were the necessary stimulants to agricultural development. He acknowledged that as long as the ancient states remained city-republics, they had some advantages. Their small size prevented the accumulation of great individual riches and the creation of widespread poverty among citizens (as opposed to slaves); it also made for greater political participation ('liberty') by those who were citizens. The latter was also a great weakness, however, since every institutional structure could fall prey to populist whimsy. Regular government was further made precarious and often impossible because the small communities tended to be divided into family factions and politics to be replaced by often bloody faction-fighting. Similarly ancient warfare was particularly ferocious because it involved the whole of the citizenry, who tended to see enemy cities and citizens as prey. By contrast, the modern army did not consist of the citizenry as a whole but of men taken from among the poor who had to be kept under discipline. If indiscriminate murder and plunder were allowed, as in ancient warfare, such discipline would break down. Modern warfare thus had to be conducted according to certain rules because the armies themselves were rule-governed.

In short, the ancient world ought to teach the modern that it was disastrous to base social life on people's personal qualities. Virtue unassisted by institutional structures was commonly no match for vice. Fortunately, the modern world, pressured by commerce and urban life, was developing a genius for institutional living, that is, for extending the artificial virtues of rule-following to more and more areas of life and making individuals more predictable and safer company for each other.

It was, however, also an important part of Hume's analysis to show the ways in which the modern world was fraught with the dangers and insecurity of novelty. A high degree of individual freedom could easily turn to licence and anarchy, for the bulk of the population was necessarily uneducated and consequently easy prey for both religious and political 'enthusiasm' (fanaticism). It was in response to such problems that Hume's great friend, Adam Smith, developed his ideas of upward social mobility in commercial society and of general education as safety valves for social unrest. While Hume was getting at the former point, he concentrated on the idea of pacifying potential leaders of unrest. Priests in the pay of a state church with leisure to pursue literary and scholarly ambitions and politicians with prospects of public jobs and pensions would have their energy deflected from rabble-rousing. Hume was far from optimistic, however, that such arrangements would always suffice: he was, for instance, greatly disturbed by the public unrest among the London mob supporting John Wilkes in the 1760s.

As for the balance of the mixed constitution, the principal point of Hume's historical analysis was to show that this was largely a precarious accidental and recent development which could be preserved only if it was understood in terms of his realistic analysis. In order for this to happen, the antiquated cant of party ideology had to cease and a culture of proper political debate had to be developed.

Hume's greatest and most persistent fears concerned the public debt. The surplus of commerce made available easy loans that were irresistible for governments keen to expand their domestic and foreign agenda without alienating their electorate through corresponding tax increases. But the public debt in effect represented a confiscation of the productive power and hence the freedom of action of future generations, and Hume feared that a point would soon be reached where this practice would have intolerable effects.

Finally, Hume grew apprehensive of traditional colonialism in the form of conquest and ownership of foreign lands. If governments would understand that commercial wealth was about doing, namely exchange, and not having, then they would see that colonies were to be treated as partners in exchange and had to be granted corresponding freedom. This might be as full members of the mother country or it might, in the fullness of time, be as independent countries. It was in this light that Hume appreciated the situation of the North American colonies.

Hume's political philosophy

Hume's analysis of the balance between opportunity and danger characterising the modern world was based on a philosophical theory of culture which treated morals and politics as artifacts. The human mind is not equipped to discern the rules and institutions of morals and politics as eternal and universal verities in either history, nature or supernatural religion. We can empirically ascertain, however, that there are certain permanent features of human nature which lead to great regularities in human behaviour. These regularities include the emergence of moral and political institutions supervenient upon human individuals. But since the supervenience of such phenomena is also dependent upon something as fickle as human beliefs, change, and hence uncertainty, are generally the lot of humanity. We therefore have to combine understanding of such regularities as we can find with historically informed observations of our particular situation. This was how Hume understood his science of politics.

The most general features we observe in human nature include, according to Hume, a modified self-interest and a confined benevolence, that is, a self-interest modified by concern for those dependent upon us and a benevolence largely confined to people we know. Like moralists before him, notably the great natural-law philosopher Samuel Pufendorf, Hume thus combined Hugo Grotius's idea of sociability and Thomas Hobbes's idea of unsociability as the fundamental characteristics of the active side of human nature. Self-interest and benevolence, thus understood, spontaneously regulate a large part of direct personal relationships. The forms they assume in doing so Hume calls, in his complex moral theory, *natural* virtues. A large number of human relations cannot, however, be understood in terms of personal attitudes of goodness and badness. Whenever we need to ask whether an act was right or wrong, *irrespective of its goodness or badness*, we implicitly refer to something beyond the attitudes or virtues of the individuals involved, namely to some kind of rule. Such rules are quite different from those pertaining to the natural virtues. The rule that you should love your neighbour is encouraging you to show goodness, a natural virtue. The rule that you should pay your debt is not concerned with your motives but with the performance of a certain action irrespective of your attitude. The latter kind of rules are not given us by nature as part of our spontaneous reactions to other people, but they do evolve spontaneously as a result of our interaction with others. Such rules of right and wrong, which are not concerned with the goodness or badness of the agent, Hume calls artificial and our observance of them artificial virtues.

A number of these rules are virtually universal and can be traced with great certainty by the science of human nature. This applies in particular to rules arising from the most common parts of the human condition, namely our inability as individuals or in small family groups to find security and satisfaction of our needs and ambitions in nature. This inability is remedied by rules of coordination that ensure that we do not claim the same fruits of nature as others and that we seek leadership and cooperation in emergencies. The former are the basic rules of justice pertaining to the holding, to the acquisition and to the transfer of property. Such rules arise from experiments in mutual trust between groups and the subsequent imitation of such behaviour.

Once a regular pattern of behaviour has emerged, it will seem like a deficiency of character not to stick to it, just as lack of a natural virtue like benevolence is condemned as a moral failure. The internalisation of fears of such deficiency becomes the basis for the obligation of the rules of justice and consequently for a large part of their moral character. Similarly the emergence of patterns of obeisance to leadership in warfare and in private disputes provides the basis for morally obligatory rules of allegiance and thus for political society. In his early work, Hume thought that such patterns of deference could only arise in the first instance through mutual agreement, though he was adamant that such an original contract had no continuing influence, or, more specifically, that it had no prescriptive force, as alleged in traditional contractarianism. Later he denied the existence of any original contract, thus bringing this part of his thought into line with the emergence theory he generally proffered. It should be noted, however, that philosophers today still try to translate this theory into contractarian terms.

The basis for government is a combination of two factors: a people's perception of the public interest in security, especially through the maintenance of a regular system of justice, and their perception of their obligation to allegiance. Playing upon the trope that the world is governed by opinion, Hume formulates the point provocatively by saying that government is founded on opinion, namely opinion of interest and opinion of right. People are generally born into and continue to live in societies that are under some form of government. The opinions of these subjects that their government can care for the public interest, and has the right to exercise authority, are the foundation of this government. Consequently, a central task of the science of politics is to account for the formation and transformation of these fundamental opinions.

The formation of sound political opinions is the most basic political activity, and Hume's political theorising was such an activity. There is often a sense of urgency in Hume's political writings, for he was keenly aware that people's opinions are liable to change. Under the influence of passions – of avarice, of factional or dynastic or confessional allegiances, of utopian dreams of perfection – our understanding of our situation and that of our society too often becomes clouded, particularly when we are faced with uncertainty and instability. When there is uncertainty about who has authority or about what those in authority may do, our habitual ways of thinking and behaving are broken. Under such circumstances opinions and actions are much more likely to be influenced by *imagined* situations than by *actual* conditions, and passionate flights of fancy tend to take over. Since opinions are formed by experience, we can only have empirically well-founded opinions about who is doing what in society if there is a certain regularity of behaviour. The message of Hume's theory concerning the basic features of society is that such regularity cannot come from individual minds and wills alone; it depends upon something outside the individual, namely regular or rule-bound institutions that can guide our behaviour and consequently our expectations of each other. If such institutions, once acquired, are lightly given up, we lose habit and regularity; we lose, that is, the most important means of orienting ourselves to others. Consequently we cannot know what we ourselves may do with success, and we will have lost our most elementary freedom. This is the rationale for the enormous emphasis Hume placed on institutional stability.

Stability can be seen from two perspectives: the stability of what those in authority *do*, and the stability of who they *are*. These two topics are fundamental to Hume's political thought. The conduct of government is only stable and predictable if it follows publicly known general rules – only if it is government in accordance with law. Government must therefore be concerned with issues that are suitable subjects of law. These are primarily forms of behaviour that are in the public interest, but not necessarily in the interest of each individual concerned in the particular instance. They are, in other words, forms of behaviour falling under the rules of justice, especially those pertaining to property and contract.

Hume has no doubt about the necessity of a governmental agenda in defence and foreign affairs as well as in economics and culture, but priority is given to maintaining those two basic institutions of justice – property and contract – which make social life possible. In so far as the populace has a clear opinion that this balance of priorities constitutes the public interest and that the government protects this interest as well as any possible government could, to that extent the government has a secure source of allegiance. It follows that Hume must reject policies that significantly break the rules of justice. He rejects, for example, the suggestion that governments should treat individual citizens according to their natural merit. Such a policy would create the greatest uncertainty. Merit is so dependent on each particular situation that it is impossible to formulate general rules or standards for it. Consequently no orderly allocation of goods could be based on merit. The same criticism applies to all other schemes for the distribution of goods or status on the basis of personal charac- teristics or virtues. In so far as government adheres to the rules of justice, it abstains from interfering with the natural qualities of individuals, with their virtues and vices and with their personal free- dom. Since the most obvious and most endangered expression of one's individuality is productivity and exchange, in the widest sense of these words, justice is centrally concerned with property and con- tractual relations and, by protecting these, government is therefore protecting the integrity of the individual person. It should here be noted that Hume eschews using the language of natural rights to express his point, probably because the commonly accepted notions of rights were religiously infested and, on one understanding, bound up with contractarianism.

Having seen what Hume means by stability of governmental action, we are left with a second question about stability, the question of who governs. All governments, Hume says, are founded on two opinions, opinion of right and opinion of interest. We have discussed opinion of interest in terms of the regular administration of justice as the ideal of what good government should do and what citizens should seek from their government. Opinion of right is concerned with whom the people think should rule, and it is divided into two kinds, right to power and right to property. A government generally held by the people to have a right to power and to serve the public interest will be stable, unless its constitution allows for some popular influence, as in a republican or mixed constitution. In these cases people's opinion of the right to govern normally includes the idea that there should be *some* proportionality between property and political influence. But Hume rejects James Harrington's radical claim that the balance of political power is directly dependent upon the balance of property. There is a certain tendency for power to gravitate towards the proper- tied, but this process is normally influenced by several other factors, such as reverence for settled constitutional forms – that is, it is influ- enced by the opinion of right to power. Otherwise the British govern- ment would have become republican, given the weight of the proper- tied gentry represented in the House of Commons. In constitutions where property can have influence, there is always a danger that this may conflict with beliefs about the right to power, and consequently there is a danger of instability. This is the framework of Hume's analysis of factionalism in 'free' government in general and in that of Britain in particular. The danger of instability is not great in governments, such as absolute monarchies, that rest primarily on the opinion of right to power, but monarchies are fraught with other dangers which we cannot go into here.

Hume thought social life with political liberty highly precarious. As we have seen, he feared the tendency of free constitutions to breed factions and the tendency of factionalism to degenerate into fanaticism, disorder and anarchy, out of which would grow tyranny. In other words, the very engine of civilised living, namely freedom under law, found its most refined protection in a system of political liberty which inevitably harboured forces that could become destructive of that engine. This was, as we have indicated, the situation in which contemporary Britain found itself, and the anatomy of factionalism was consequently a central concern in Hume's literary intervention in public life.

The new and difficult point Hume had to impress on his readers was that in a free constitution political differences could not be *about* the constitution; they had to be *within* the constitution. Factionalism was, on his analysis, inconsistent with this. The general danger in factionalism was that it would lead to fragmentation by pitting group interests against each other at the expense of the public interest. Even worse, it tended to transform the recurring question of who should discharge the offices of government into a question of the balance between the powers of the constitution itself. This was particularly dangerous in a mixed constitution such as the British, where the main factions naturally would form around two different principles of government, the monarchical and the republican. The extraordinary thing was that Britain, as Hume saw it, was in the process of breaking away from this division. But his contemporaries did not appreciate this and, by continuing the old factional rant, they endangered the precarious constitutional and political balance that was emerging. Hume's political theory and historical analysis gave him the means of enlightening them.

Chronology

1745–6	In London and at Weldehall, St Albans, as tutor to the insane Marquess of Annandale.
1746–8	Secretary to General St Clair, first during an incursion on the French coast, subsequently on a diplomatic mission to Vienna and Turin.
1748	Publishes *Philosophical Essays Concerning Human Understanding*, later entitled *Enquiry Concerning Human Understanding*.
1749–51	At Ninewells with brother John.
1751–63	In Edinburgh, living with sister Katherine. Is rejected for the chair of logic at Glasgow (1752).
1751	Publishes *Enquiry Concerning the Principles of Morals*.
1752	Publishes *Political Discourses*.
1752–7	Keeper of the Advocates' Library, Edinburgh.
1754–62	Publishes *The History of England* (vol. 1 was *of Great Britain*).
1757	Publishes *Four Dissertations*.
1763–6	In Paris as secretary to the British ambassador, Lord Hertford; for six months in 1765–6 as chargé d'affaires. Becomes well connected in the salons and among men of letters.
1766–7	In Edinburgh.
1767–9	In London; as Under-Secretary of State for the Northern Department (minister for Scottish affairs), 1768–9.
1769–76	In Edinburgh with sister Katherine.
1776	Dies 25 August in his new house in New Town, suffering from a bowel disorder (cancer?).
1777	*My Own Life*.
1779	*Dialogues Concerning Natural Religion*.

Bibliographical notes

Bibliography

The Hume literature is very extensive and only a few pointers for further study can be offered here. The most useful bibliographical tools are T. E. Jessop, *A Bibliography of David Hume and of Scottish Philosophy from Francis Hutcheson to Lord Balfour*, London, 1938; William B. Todd, 'David Hume: A preliminary bibliography', in Todd, ed., *Hume and the Enlightenment*, Edinburgh and Austin, Tex., 1974, pp. 189–205; and Roland Hall, *Fifty Years of Hume Scholarship*, Edinburgh, 1978. From 1975 to 1985, the last was updated annually by Hall in *Hume Studies*, a journal devoted to Hume scholarship.

Biography

The most important documents are Hume's letters, of which more are frequently discovered. Roughly one hundred have been identified since the two most comprehensive collections were published, namely, *The Letters of David Hume*, ed. J. Y. T. Greig, 2 vols., Oxford, 1932; and *New Letters of David Hume*, ed. R. Klibansky and E. C. Mossner, Oxford, 1954. The letters should be read with the brief autobiography, *The Life of David Hume, Esq., Written by Himself*, London, 1777 (commonly known as *My Own Life*) which included Adam Smith's moving account of Hume in a letter to their publisher, William Strahan; both are often included in modern editions of the *Essays*. Of the huge amount of eighteenth-century literature that bears upon Hume's life, there is a significant (but unreliable) collection of letters to Hume in *Letters of Eminent Persons Addressed to David Hume*, ed. J. Hill Burton, Edinburgh and London, 1849. See also, John

Home, *A Sketch of the Character of Mr Hume and Diary of a Journey from Morpeth to Bath*, ed. David Fate Norton, Edinburgh, 1976.

The two major studies of Hume's life are J. Hill Burton, *Life and Correspondence of David Hume*, 2 vols., Edinburgh, 1846, and Ernest C. Mossner, *The Life of David Hume*, Edinburgh, 1954, but a most readable short book is J. Y. T. Greig, *The Philosophy of David Hume*, New York, 1931.

Works

There is no scholarly critical edition of Hume's works, but one is in preparation for Oxford University Press under the editorship of Tom Beauchamp, David Fate Norton and M. A. Stewart. The best general collection is still *The Philosophical Works of David Hume*, ed. T. H. Green and T. H. Grose, 4 vols., London, 1874–5, available in a reprint, Aalen, 1964. The best editions of the *Treatise* and the two *Enquiries* are *A Treatise of Human Nature*, ed. L. A. Selby-Bigge, 2nd revised edn, P. H. Nidditch, Oxford, 1978, and *Enquiries Concerning Human Understanding and Concerning the Principles of Morals*, ed. L. A. Selby-Bigge, 3rd revised edn, P. H. Nidditch, Oxford, 1975. The two main works on religion are in *The Natural History of Religion* and *Dialogues Concerning Natural Religion*, ed. (respectively) by A. W. Colver and J. V. Price, Oxford, 1976. There is an important older edition of the *Dialogues* by Norman Kemp Smith, Edinburgh, 1935. A convenient edition of all the *Essays* is *Essays, Moral, Political, and Literary*, ed. Eugene F. Miller, Indianapolis, revised edn, 1987. Two pamphlets are of importance; one was published anonymously by Hume to draw attention to the *Treatise*, *An Abstract of a Book Lately Published; Entituled, A Treatise of Human Nature, &c*, Edinburgh, 1740, now included in the Selby-Bigge/Nidditch edition of the *Treatise*. The other pamphlet, likewise anonymous but commonly ascribed to Hume, is *A Letter from a Gentleman to His Friend in Edinburgh*, Edinburgh, 1745; it is a response to the charges of irreligion raised by Hume's opponents when he was a candidate for the chair of moral philosophy at Edinburgh. It has been edited by E. C. Mossner and J. V. Price, Edinburgh, 1967. An anonymous work entitled *The History of the Proceedings in the Case of Margaret, Commonly Called Peg, only Lawful Sister to John Bull, Esq.*, Edinburgh, 1761, is commonly thought to be by Adam Ferguson. This has recently been ascribed to David Hume in a new edition with a useful introduction, *Sister*

Peg: A Pamphlet Hitherto Unknown by David Hume, ed. D. Raynor, Cambridge, 1982. As for *The History of England, From the Invasion of Julius Caesar to the Revolution in 1688*, it has lived a life separate from the collections of Hume's other works, including that of Green and Grose, and the text has never received serious critical editing. The most accessible edition was issued, with a foreword by W. B. Todd, in Indianapolis, 1983, 6 vols. This should be supplemented by *The History of Great Britain, Containing the Reigns of James I and Charles I*, ed. Duncan Forbes, Harmondsworth, 1970; this presents the first edition of the volume of the *History* that Hume published first. It varies significantly from the final version incorporated into the full *History*.

Commentary

General For important discussions of the general nature of Hume's philosophical enterprise and its coherence, see Annette C. Baier, *A Progress of Sentiments. Reflections on Hume's Treatise*, Cambridge, Mass., 1991; Norman Kemp Smith, *The Philosophy of David Hume*, London, 1941; David Fate Norton, *David Hume: Common Sense Moralist, Sceptical Metaphysician*, Princeton, NJ, 1982; John Passmore, *Hume's Intentions*, Cambridge, 1952; John P. Wright, *The Sceptical Realism of David Hume*, Minneapolis, 1983. M. A. Box, *The Suasive Art of David Hume*, Princeton, NJ, 1990, is a fine study of Hume as a writer.

Political thought For general interpretations of Hume's political thought, see Duncan Forbes, *Hume's Philosophical Politics*, Cambridge, 1975; Knud Haakonssen, 'The structure of Hume's political thought', in David Fate Norton, ed., *The Cambridge Companion to Hume*, Cambridge, 1993; Donald W. Livingston, *Hume's Philosophy of Common Life*, Chicago, 1984; David Miller, *Philosophy and Ideology in Hume's Political Philosophy*, Oxford, 1981; John B. Stewart, *Opinion and Reform in Hume's Political Philosophy*, Princeton, NJ, 1992; Frederic G. Whelan, *Order and Artifice in Hume's Political Philosophy*, Princeton, NJ, 1985. Concerning justice, see Jonathan Harrison, *Hume's Theory of Justice*, Oxford, 1981; concerning justice and obligation, Knud Haakonssen, *The Science of a Legislator. The Natural Jurisprudence of David Hume and Adam Smith*, Cambridge, 1981, ch. 1.

On property, Stephen Buckle, *Natural Law and the Theory of Property. Grotius to Hume*, Oxford, 1991, ch. 5. On Hume and contractarianism, see David Gauthier, 'David Hume: Contractarian', *Philosophical Review*, 89 (1979): 3–38; Stephen Buckle and Dario Castiglione, 'Hume's critique of the contract theory', *History of Political Thought*, 12 (1991): 457–80. Concerning Hume and eighteenth-century political debate, see J. G. A. Pocock, *Virtue, Commerce, and History*, Cambridge, 1985; John Robertson, *The Scottish Enlightenment and the Militia Issue*, Edinburgh, 1985, ch. 3.

Economics　Guidance to Hume's economic ideas is to be found in Istvan Hont, 'The "rich country–poor country" debate in Scottish classical political economy', in Istvan Hont and Michael Ignatieff, eds., *Wealth and Virtue. The Shaping of Political Economy in the Scottish Enlightenment*, Cambridge, 1983, pp. 271–315; Eugene Rotwein's introduction to David Hume, *Writings on Economics*, Edinburgh, 1954; Andrew S. Skinner, 'David Hume: Principles of Political Economy', in Norton, ed., *Companion to David Hume*.

History　Hume's historical work is studied in Nicholas Capaldi and Donald W. Livingston, eds., *Liberty in Hume's 'History of England'*, Dordrecht, 1990; Nicholas Phillipson, *Hume*, London, 1990; V. Wexler, *David Hume and the History of England*, Philadelphia, 1979; David Wootton, 'David Hume: "the Historian" ', in Norton, ed., *Companion to David Hume*. David Fate Norton and Richard H. Popkin, eds., *David Hume: Philosophical Historian*, Indianapolis, 1965.

Hume and America　For bibliography, see R. B. Sher, 'Introduction: Scottish–American studies, past and present', in Sher and J. R. Smitten, eds., *Scotland and America in the Age of Enlightenment*, Princeton, NJ, 1990, pp. 1–27. Three important contributions are Douglas Adair, 'That politics may be reduced to a science: David Hume, James Madison and the Tenth "Federalist" ', in Adair, *Fame and the Founding Fathers*, New York, 1974, pp. 93–106; J. G. A. Pocock, 'Hume and the American Revolution: The dying thoughts of a North Briton', in Pocock, *Virtue, Commerce, and History*, pp. 125–41; and Gary Wills, *Inventing America: Jefferson's Declaration of Independence*, New York, 1978.

Hume and Europe   See, for example, Laurence L. Bongie, *David Hume. Prophet of the Counter-Revolution*, Oxford, 1965; G. Gawlick and L. Kreimendahl, *Hume in der deutschen Aufklärung*, Stuttgart-Bad Cannstatt, 1987; and Marialuisa Baldi, *David Hume nel settecento italiano: filosofia ed economia*, Florence, 1983.

A note on the text and the edition

The copy text for the essays in this edition is the *Essays and Treatises on Several Subjects. In two Volumes*, vol. I, 'Containing Essays, Moral, Political, and Literary', London and Edinburgh, 1772. To these essays have been added the essay 'Of the origin of government', which first appeared in the edition of 1777. The edition of 1772 was the last to appear in Hume's lifetime, but we know that he was working on revisions of this text until shortly before his death in August 1776. He did not live, however, to see the new edition through the press; it only appeared the following year. Although all subsequent editions of the *Essays* have been based upon this posthumous edition, no attempt has been made to establish which of the changes introduced in it were made by Hume and which may stem from his publishers and printers. Since this is a technical task inappropriate for an edition like the present one, it was decided to use the last edition for which we can be sure that Hume had full responsibility, that of 1772.

There is no critical edition of any of Hume's essays. Many of the essays appeared in eleven editions in his lifetime, and most of them underwent constant and considerable revisions. T. H. Green and T. H. Grose made a fairly comprehensive but still incomplete collation of the 1777 edition with the lifetime editions, and their work has been the basis for all subsequent editions that have included any variant readings. The most significant addition to Green and Grose is the work of Eugene F. Miller in his revised edition of the *Essays* (1987). Using the 1777 edition as copy-text, Miller provides a full collation with the 1772 edition. But for the earlier editions, we are still dependent upon the impressionistic work of Green and Grose.

In preparing the present edition, I have compared the 1772 copy-text with the first editions and with the 1777 edition of the essays included. Due to restrictions on space, I have included only substantial variants that are indispensable for our understanding of Hume as a political thinker.

The brief excerpts from Hume's *History*, printed as an appendix, are reproduced from the text as it was in the last edition on which Hume worked, that which appeared in 1778.

Hume's punctuation and spelling (including the use of capital letters and italics) have been followed, except for his extensive use of capitals in the titles of the essays.

The footnotes are Hume's, while all editorial notes, indicated by inserted numerals, are collected at the end of the volume. Biographical notes and a bibliography are to be found before the main text. When supplying English translations of Hume's quotations from foreign languages, I have generally used eighteenth-century translations. The year in which each essay first appeared is indicated in brackets after the title in the endnotes.

Editions of the Essays *during Hume's lifetime*[a]

Essays, Moral and Political, Edinburgh, 1741.
Essays, Moral and Political, 2nd edn, Edinburgh, 1742.
Essays, Moral and Political, vol. II, Edinburgh, 1742.
Essays, Moral and Political, 3rd edn, London, Edinburgh, 1748.
Three Essays, Moral and Political, Edinburgh, 1748.
Political Discourses, Edinburgh, 1752.
Political Discourses, 2nd edn, Edinburgh, 1752.
Essays and Treatises on Several Subjects, 4 vols., London, Edinburgh, 1753–4.
Four Dissertations, London, 1757.
Essays and Treatises on Several Subjects, London, Edinburgh, 1758.
Essays and Treatises on Several Subjects, 4 vols., London, Edinburgh, 1760.
Essays and Treatises on Several Subjects, 2 vols., London, Edinburgh, 1764.

[a] The first posthumous edition is included since Hume was working on it before he died.

Essays and Treatises on Several Subjects, 2 vols., London, Edinburgh,
1767.
Essays and Treatises on Several Subjects, 2 vols., London, Edinburgh,
1768.
Essays and Treatises on Several Subjects, 4 vols., London, Edinburgh,
1770.
Essays and Treatises on Several Subjects, 2 vols., London, Edinburgh,
1772.
Essays and Treatises on Several Subjects, 2 vols., London, Edinburgh,
1777.

Biographical notes

ADDISON, Joseph (1672–1719), English essayist, poet, classicist and politician. Friend of Swift and, notably, Steele with whom he collaborated in the *Tatler* (1709–11) and the *Spectator* (1711–12 and 1714). He published the newspaper the *Freeholder* (1715–16).

AESCHINES (*c.*390–*c.*322 BC), Athenian orator and politician.

ALBINUS, D. Clodius, governor of Britain when Commodus was killed in AD 192. Tried to become emperor but was killed in 197.

ALCIBIADES (*c.*450–404 BC), Athenian politician and general.

ALEXANDER the Great (III) (356–23 BC), king of Macedon 336–23; son of Philip II. Educated by Aristotle. A series of famous victories over the Persians secured an empire stretching beyond the Indus and annexing Egypt.

ANACHARSIS (b. *c.*600), Scythian prince, later sometimes counted among the Seven Sages.

ANGRIA, Tulagee (first half of eighteenth century), Indian pirate 'prince' of significant power and possessions.

ANNE (1665–1714), queen of England and Scotland (from 1707, Great Britain).

ANTIGONUS (d. 310 BC), one of Alexander the Great's generals and would-be successors as ruler over the Macedonian empire.

ANTIOCHUS III (the Great, d. 187 BC), king of the Seleucid empire in Syria and Asia Minor 223–187 BC.

ANTONIUS, Marcus (Mark Antony) (*c.*83–30 BC), Roman general and triumvir, friend and champion of Caesar, after whose assassination he joined with Octavian and Lepidus in oppressive government of Rome.

APPIAN of Alexandria (flourished in the middle of the second century), author of 'ethnographic' histories of Rome, written in Greek.

ARATUS of Sicyon (d. 213 BC), general of the Achaean League.

ARCHIMEDES (*c.*287–12 BC), born in Syracuse; the greatest of ancient mathematicians, he was also an astronomer and inventor.

ARIOSTO, Ludovico (1474–1535). In the service of Duke Alfonso of Este, whose family he celebrated in *Orlando Furioso* (1532).

ARISTOTLE (384–22 BC), the great philosopher who contributed to logic, metaphysics, physics, biology, psychology, ethics, politics, rhetoric and poetics.

ARRIAN (Flavius Arrianus) (first half of second century), Greek-born Roman officer who governed Cappadocia 131–7. Apart from his important *Anabasis [Expedition] of Alexander [the Great]*, his great significance, not least in the eighteenth century, is that he preserved Epictetus' lectures and wrote a famous *Encheiridion* (manual) to Epictetus' philosophy.

ATTALUS I (Soter) (269–197 BC), king of Pergamum 241–197.

AUGUSTUS (63 BC–AD 14), the first Roman emperor.

BACON, Francis, first baron Verulam and viscount St Albans (1561–1626), English philosopher and statesman; author of *The Advancement of Learning* (1605), *Novum Organum* (1620), *History of Henry VII* (1622), *Essays* (1597–1625), etc.

BOILEAU-DESPREAUX, Nicolas (1636–1711), French critic and poet, one of the most influential neo-classicists of his day and proponent of the ancients in 'the quarrel of ancients and moderns'. Works include *Satires* (1660–66), *Epîtres* (1669–77), *L'Art poétique* (1674) which influenced Pope's *Essay on Criticism*, *Réflexions sur Longin* (1701) and translation of *On the Sublime*, still believed to be by Longinus.

BOLINGBROKE, Henry St John, first viscount (1678–1751), English statesman and writer. With the accession of George I he fell from power (Secretary of State) because of Jacobite links; after exile, he played a leading role in using Tory ideas to formulate a Country opposition to Walpole. Author of *A Dissertation upon Parties* (1735), *The Idea of a Patriot King* (1743), etc.

BORGIA, Cesare (1476–1507), Italian prince, at one time ruler over Romagna, Perugia, Siena, Piombino and Urbino. Commonly taken to be the inspiration for Machiavelli's *The Prince*.

BOULAINVILLIERS, Henri, comte de (1658–1722), was the most prominent defender in his generation of the 'thèse nobiliaire' according to which the French constitution properly – namely historically – understood was mixed. *Pace* the absolutist 'thèse royale', a reinstatement of the aristocracy to prominence was therefore required to balance the French government.

BRAHE, Tycho (1546–1601), Danish astronomer.

BRUTUS, Lucius Junius; according to tradition, he founded the Roman republic when he overthrew the Etruscan kings of Rome and became the first consul in 509 BC (cf. Lucretia).

BRUTUS, Marcus Junius (c.85–42 BC), leader in the conspiracy against Caesar – his former patron – and hailed in republican lore as a heroic tyrannicide. Object of the famous line attributed to the dying Caesar, *Et tu, Brute!* ('Even you, Brutus.' Cf. Shakespeare, *Julius Caesar*, III.i.76).

CALIGULA (AD 12–41), emperor of Rome (37–41).

CAMDEN, William (1551–1623), English historian and antiquary, author of *Britannia* (1586) and *Annales rerum Anglicorum et Hibernicarum, regnante Elizabetha*, I (1615) and II (1629) (English trans. by R. Norton in 1635).

CAMILLUS, Marcus Furius (early fourth century BC), Roman statesman and general. The great hero who fought off the Gauls after the sack of Rome in 390 BC and re-established patrician forms of government by defeating a popular uprising.

CAPET, Hugh (c.938–96), king of France 987–96; while he himself was elected, he did much to weaken the principle of elective kingship.

CAPITOLINUS, Julius (end of the third century), author of a number of biographies of emperors – and pretenders – forming part of the biographical collection called the *Historia Augusta*.

CATILINE (Lucius Sergius Catilina) (d. 62 BC), governor of the Roman province of Africa 67–6 BC; prosecuted for extortion in office, but acquitted; defeated in consular elections in 63 (by Cicero) and in 62, he conspired to make a *coup* which Cicero revealed in his famous speeches (*In Catilinam* I and II) in the senate, and one of the consuls for 62, Gaius Antonius, defeated his army and killed him.

CATO, Marcus Porcius ('Uticensis' or the Younger) (95–46 BC), Roman senator of strict stoic principles.

CATULLUS, Gaius Valerius (*c.*84–*c.*54 BC), Roman poet.

CERVANTES SAAVEDRA, Miguel de (1547–1616), Spanish author, mainly famous for *Don Quixote* (1605–15).

CHARLES I (1600–49), king of England, Scotland and Ireland 1625–49; beheaded in Whitehall on 30 January 1649.

CHARLES II (1630–85), king of England, Scotland and Ireland 1660–85.

CHARLES II, king of Spain 1665–1700.

CHARLES V, Holy Roman Emperor 1519–56 (as Charles I, king of Spain from 1516).

CHARLES VIII (1470–98), king of France 1483–98.

CHARPENTIER, François (1620–1702), French man of letters and secretary to the Académie Française. Proponent of the 'moderns' side in 'the quarrel of ancients and moderns'. Author of *L'Excellence de la langue française* (1683).

CICERO, Marcus Tullius (106–43 BC), Roman statesman, orator and philosophical and literary writer. Legal and political career destroyed by republican opposition to Caesar and Antony. Works such as *De officiis, De finibus bonorum et malorum, De natura deorum, Academica, Tusculanae disputationes* were hugely influential in the eighteenth century with their eclectic presentation of the ancient philosophical schools.

CLEOMENES III (*c.*260–219 BC), king of Sparta 235–19 BC.

COLLINS, Anthony (1676–1729), English deist and philosopher.

COLUMBUS, Christopher (1451–1506), Italian-born explorer who, in the service of the court of Castile, sailed to Latin America in 1492.

COMMODUS, Lucius Aelius Aurelius (AD 161–92), Roman emperor AD 180–92.

CONDE, Louis, prince de (1621–86), French general.

CONFUCIUS (K'ung Fu-tse) (551–479 BC), Chinese philosopher.

CONSTANTINE I, the Great (Flavius Valerius Constantinus Augustus) (*c.*AD 285–337), Roman emperor who made Christianity a state religion (324) and relocated the capital of the empire from Rome to Byzantium (renamed Constantinople).

CORNEILLE, Pierre (1606–84), French dramatist. Of a large oeuvre that was fundamental to classic French theatre's heroic tragedy, some of the most important plays are: *Le Cid*; *Horace*; *Cinna*; *Polyeucte*; *La Mort de Pompée*; *Le Menteur*; *Rodogune*; all produced between 1636 and 1646 and followed by many more.

CTESIPHON, contemporary and ally of Demosthenes.

CURTIUS RUFUS, Quintus (first century AD), historian and rhetorician.

CYRUS the Great, founder-king of the Persian Empire, 559–29 BC.

DACIER, Anne Lefebvre (*c.*1654–1720), French classicist and translator of many works of ancient literature. Her dispute with La Motte over proper respect for the original *Iliad*, which she had translated, was a major contribution to 'the quarrel of ancients and moderns'.

DEMOSTHENES (382–22 BC), great Athenian orator and statesman; vigorous spokesman for a strong response to the expansionism of Philip of Macedon.

DESCARTES, René (1596–1650), one of the most influential modern philosophers, author of *Discours de la méthode* (1637), *Meditationes de prima philosophiae* (1641), *Principia philosophiae* (1644), etc.

DIDIUS JULIANUS, Marcus, bought the post as Roman emperor at a mock auction after Pertinax and ruled for less than three months in AD 193 until executed by order of the Senate.

DIODORUS SICULUS, Greek historian from Sicily, who between *c.* 60 and 30 BC wrote a history of the world.

DIONYSIUS I (431–367 BC), tyrant of Syracuse 405–367.

DIONYSIUS of Halicarnassus (first century BC), Greek-born critic, historian and rhetor in Rome.

DOMITIAN (AD 51–96), emperor of Rome AD 81–96.

DRAKE, Sir Francis (*c.* 1540–96), English naval explorer and admiral; he sailed through the Strait of Magellan into the Pacific and returned home via Java and the Cape of Good Hope (1578–80). Assisted by appropriate storms, he beat off the Spanish Armada in 1588.

DRUSUS, Julius Caesar (*c.* 13 BC–AD 23) (Drusus the Younger), son of Tiberius.

DUBOS, Jean-Baptiste, abbé (1670–1742), historian, diplomat and theoretician of taste. Friend of Bayle and Locke. In politics he used history to defend the absolutist 'thèse royale' (cf. Boulainvilliers); in matters of taste he was a restrained proponent of the 'moderns' against the 'ancients', emphasising sentiment and physical factors in questions of art. Works include *Les Intérêts d'Angleterre mal-entendus dans la présente guerre* (1703); *Réflexions critiques sur la poésie et la peinture* (1719; trans. *Critical Reflexions on Poetry and Painting*, 1748); *Histoire critique de la monarchie française* (1734).

EDWARD III (1312–77), king of England 1327–77.

ELIZABETH I (1533–1603), queen of England and Ireland 1558–1603.

EPAMINONDAS (d. 362 BC), great Theban general who led Thebes to victory over Sparta at Leuctra (371), invaded the Peloponnese repeatedly, and was killed in the indecisive battle against the Athenian–Spartan alliance at Mantinea (362).

EUBULUS (*c.*405–*c.*335 BC), Athenian statesman; opponent of Demosthenes' war policy towards Macedonia.

FABIUS Maximus Verrucosus, Cunctator, Quintus (*c.*275–203 BC), Roman general and consul during second Punic War, dictator 221 and 217 BC.

FLEURY, André-Hercule, cardinal de (1653–1743), 'first minister' of France under Louis XV 1726–43.

FONTENELLE, Bernard le Bovier, sieur de (1657–1757), French man of letters. A protagonist of science and of a naturalistic outlook, he aroused the scorn of 'ancients' like Boileau and Racine. Author of *Dialogue des morts* (1683); *Entretiens sur la pluralité des mondes* (1686); *Histoire des oracles* (1687; *The History of Oracles and the Cheats of the Pagan Priests*, 1688); *Digression sur les anciens et les modernes* (1688); *Réflexions sur la poétique* (*c.* 1695, publ. 1742).

GALBA, Servius Sulpicius (*c.* 3 BC–AD 69), succeeded Nero as Roman emperor for half a year before being murdered by Otho and the praetorian guard.

GALILEO (Galilei) (1564–1642), Italian astronomer and natural philosopher.

GERMANICUS, Nero Claudius (15 BC–AD 19), adopted son of Tiberius.

GORDIAN I (M. Antonius Africanus) (AD 158–238), Roman emperor for twenty-two days in AD 238.

GORDIAN II (M. Antonius Gordianus) (AD 193–238), son of and co-ruler with Gordian I.

GORDIAN III (Antonius Gordianus Pius) (AD 225–44), Roman emperor 238–44.

GUICCIARDINI, Francesco (1483–1540), Florentine historian and jurist; diplomat in papal service; assisted election of Cosimo de' Medici as duke of Florence; author of *Storia d'Italia* (1494–1532).

HAMPDEN, John (1594–1643), leader in the Parliamentary opposition to Charles I and member of the Long Parliament. Killed in the Civil War.

HANNIBAL (247–182 BC), Carthage's great general in the second Punic War with Rome.

HARRINGTON, James (1611–77), English republican theorist, author of *Commonwealth of Oceana* (1656), *The Prerogative of Popular Government* (1657–8), *The Art of Law-giving* (1659), etc. His ideas of property as the basis for political power, of elections by ballot, rotation of offices, etc. were very influential in the eighteenth century.

HENRI III (1551–89), king of France 1575–89. Reign dominated by civil war between Huguenots and Catholics.

HENRI IV (1553–1610), king of Navarre and, 1589–1610, of France. Brought up as a Protestant, he professed Catholicism after his accession to the French throne but by the Edict of Nantes (1598) secured freedom of conscience for Protestants.

HENRY IV (1367–1413), king of England 1399–1413.

HENRY VII (1457–1509), first Tudor king of England 1485–1509.

HIERO II (d. 216 BC), king of Syracuse 269–16 BC.

HOADLEY, Benjamin (1676–1761), bishop of Bangor (1715), Hereford (1721), Salisbury (1723) and Winchester (1734). A low-church, Whig polemicist.

HOMER (eighth century BC?), Greek epic poet, according to tradition author of the *Iliad* and the *Odyssey*.

HORACE (Quintus Horatius Flaccus) (65–8 BC), Roman poet and satirist, author of *Odes*, *Satires*, *Essays* and *Ars poetica*–all very influential in early modern Europe.

JAMES I/VI (1566–1625), king of Scots (as James VI) 1567–1625, king of England (as James I) 1603–25.

JAMES II (1633–1701), king of England, Scotland and Ireland 1685–8.

JUSTINIAN (Flavius Petrus Sabbatius Justinianus) (AD *c.*483–565), emperor of the East Roman or Byzantine empire 527–65; great codifier and systematiser of Roman law.

JUVENAL (Decimus Junius Juvenalis) (*c.*AD 60–*c.*136), commonly considered the greatest Roman satirical poet, his *Satires*, with their stoic background, have had a significant influence on English literature; in the eighteenth century especially on Pope, Swift and Johnson. Important translation by Dryden.

LAW, John (1671–1729), Scottish-born financial adventurer *par excellence*, monetary theorist and comptroller-general of finance in France. Introduced banking and paper currency into France; concentrated the French public trading companies into one large company and amalgamated this with the Banque Royale. Pursued a grand colonial plan known as the Mississippi Scheme. Law's financial empire collapsed with a run on the bank in 1720.

LEPTINES, mid-fourth century BC Athenian, known from Demosthenes' speech against him.

LIVY (Titus Livius) (59 BC–AD 17), author of 142-book history of Rome; since the Renaissance the 35 surviving books have been among the most widely read accounts of Rome.

LOCKE, John (1632–1704), great English philosopher; author of *An Essay Concerning Human Understanding* (1690), *Two Treatises of Government* (1690), *The Reasonableness of Christianity* (1695), several *Letters* on toleration, etc.

LONGINUS, Cassius (*c.* AD 213–73), Greek Neoplatonist philosopher and rhetorician. In the eighteenth century Longinus was still generally supposed to be the author of *On the Sublime*, which we now know must stem from an earlier period, probably the first century AD. This treatise was hugely influential in the eighteenth century, especially through Boileau's French translation.

LOUIS XIII (1601–43), king of France 1610–43.

LOUIS XIV (1638–1715), king of France 1643–1715.

LUCIAN (*c.*AD 115), Greek prose author of works in several genres.

LUCRETIUS (Titus Lucretius Carus) (*c.*98–55 BC), Roman poet and philosopher who followed Epicurus closely in his main work, *De rerum naturae*.

LYCURGUS, according to tradition, the great legislator of Sparta.

LYTTLETON, George, first baron Lyttleton (1709–73), politician in opposition to Walpole; patron of literature, friend of Pope, Fielding, Thomson, Mrs Montagu; author of a history of Henry II (1767–71) and of *Dialogues of the Dead* (1760).

MACHIAVELLI, Niccolò di Bernardo dei (1469–1527), Florentine state official and republican political theorist.

MARCHMONT, Hugh Hume, Lord Polworth, later third earl of (1708–94), Scots politician.

MARK ANTONY, *see* ANTONIUS, Marcus.

MASSINISSA (*c.*240–149 BC), Numidian ruler and ally of Rome against Carthage.

MAXIMILIAN I (1459–1519), Holy Roman Emperor 1493–1519.

MAZARIN, Jules, cardinal (1602–61), Italian-born French churchman and statesman, protégé of Richelieu, first minister under Louis XIV.

MENANDER (342/1–291/0 BC), Athenian comic playwright.

MICHELANGELO (Buonarroti) (1475–1564), Florentine painter, sculptor, architect and poet.

MILTON, John (1608–74), English poet and defender of religious and civil liberties. Attacks episcopacy (*The reason of Church Government*, 1642); defends divorce (*The Doctrine and Discipline of Divorce*, 1643); defends liberty of the press (*Areopagitica*, 1644); defends popular right to depose tyrants (*The Tenure of Kings and Magistrates*, 1649). His three epic masterpieces are *Paradise Lost* (1667), *Paradise Regained* (1671) and *Samson Agonistes* (1671).

MOLIERE, pseudonym of Jean-Baptiste Poquelin (1622–73), French comic playwright and actor. Most famous for *Le Bourgeois Gentilhomme* (1660), *L'Ecole des maris* (1661), *L'Ecole des femmes* (1662), *Tartuffe* (1664), *Le Mariage forcé* (1664), *Don Juan* (1665), *Le Misanthrope* (1666), *L'Avare* (1669), *Les Femmes savantes* (1672), *Le Malade imaginaire* (1673).

MORE, Sir (Saint) Thomas (1478–1535), English statesman, Lord Chancellor (1529–32), and author. Resisted Henry VIII's break with the Roman church and was executed for high treason. Author of *Utopia* (1516) and *History of Richard III* (1543/57).

NERO (AD 37–68), emperor of Rome AD 54–68.

NIGER (C. Pescennius Niger Justus), declared Roman emperor in Antioch in 193, but ousted and killed by Severus.

OTHO, Marcus Salvius (AD 32–69), governor of Lusitania and friend of Nero who, in the hope of becoming emperor himself, conspired with the praetorian guard to murder Nero's successor, Galba. He was soon defeated and committed suicide.

OVID (Publius Ovidius Naso) (43 BC–AD 17), Roman poet, author of the *Heroides*, the *Amores, Ars Amatoria*, the *Metamorphoses*, the *Tristia* and the *Fasti*. Augustus banished him from Rome for his 'immoral' poetry.

PAULUS, Lucius Aemilius (*c.* 230–160 BC), Roman consul in 182 and 168.

PERSEUS (*c.*213/2–168 BC), king of Macedon, elder son of Philip V.

PERTINAX, Publius Helvius, Roman emperor for three months in AD 193 after the murder of Commodus.

PETRONIUS ARBITER (d. AD 65), Latin satirist, author of the *Satyricon*.

PHAEDRUS, Gaius Julius (*c.*15BC–*c.*AD 50), freed slave in the household of Augustus; author of a collection of fables based in part on Aesop.

PHILIP II (1527–98), king of Spain 1556–98.

PHILIP III, king of Spain 1598–1621.

PHILIP IV, king of Spain 1621–65.

PHILIP V (238–179 BC), king of Macedon.

PHILIP VI, of Valois (1293–1350), king of France 1328–50.

PLATO (427–347 BC), the great Athenian philosopher, pupil of Socrates, teacher of Aristotle, founder of the Academy. In a large number of dialogues, the most famous of which is the *Republic*, he developed one of the most influential philosophies of all time.

PLAUTUS, Titus Maccius (*c*.250–184 BC), Roman author of comedies.

PLINY the Elder (Gaius Plinius Secundus) (AD 23/4–79), Roman author of the large *Historia naturalis*.

PLINY the Younger (Gaius Plinius Caecilius Secundus) (AD *c*.62–*c*.113), nephew of Pliny the Elder. Roman lawyer and official; author of essay-style *Epistles* in ten books.

PLUTARCH (*c*.AD 46–*c*. 120), Greek biographer, historian and moral philosopher.

POLYBIUS (*c*.203–*c*.120 BC), Greek historian of Rome.

POPE, Alexander (1688–1744), English poet and satirist. He published verse translations of Homer, imitations of Horace and an edition of Shakespeare but is chiefly remembered for *The Rape of the Lock*, *Essay on Man* and the *Dunciad*.

PRUSIAS I, king of Bithynia *c*.230–*c*.182 BC.

PRUSIAS II, king of Bithynia *c*.182–149 BC.

PTOLEMIES, Egyptian dynasty descended from one of Alexander the Great's generals; ruled Egypt from Alexander's death in 323 BC until the Roman conquest in 30 BC.

PYRRHUS (319–272 BC), king of Epirus in Greece 307–2 and 297–272 BC.

QUINTILIAN (Marcus Fabius Quintilianus) (b. *c*. AD 35), Spanish-born teacher of rhetoric at Rome; main work is *Institutio oratoria* (*c*. AD 95).

RAPHAEL (Raffaello Sanzio) (1483–1520), Italian painter; born in Urbino, active in Florence and Rome.

RETZ, Jean-François Paul de Gondi, cardinal de (1614–79), French churchman–politician; a leader in one of the many rebellions against absolutist developments, known collectively as the Fronde (1648–53).

RICHELIEU, Armand Jean Duplessis, cardinal, duc de (1588–1642), from 1629 'first minister' and virtual ruler of France.

ROCHESTER, John Wilmot, earl of (1647–80), poet, satirist, member of the 'Court Wits' at the court of Charles II.

RUBENS, Peter Paul (1577–1640), Flemish baroque painter.

SALLUST (Gaius Sallustius Crispus) (86–34 BC), Roman historian, famous for his *Bellum Catilinae* and *Bellum Iugurthinum*.

SCIPIO (Publius Cornelius Scipio Africanus Maior) (236–183 BC), the Roman consul and general who conquered Spain and won the second Punic War.

SENECA, Lucius Annaeus ('the Younger' or 'the philosopher') (*c.*4 BC–AD 65), Roman politician, adviser to Nero and prolific author. In addition to his ethical writings which were important in the Enlightenment's concern with stoicism, he wrote extensively on natural history as well as poetry.

SEVERUS, Lucius Septimius, Roman emperor AD 193–211.

SHAFTESBURY, Anthony Ashley Cooper, third earl of (1671–1713), English philosopher; author of *Characteristics of Men, Manners, Opinions and Times* (1711; enlarged edn 1714).

SPRAT, Thomas (1635–1713), bishop of Rochester, dean of Westminster. Author of well-known history of the Royal Society (1667), a life of Abraham Cowley and the poem *The Plague of Athens*.

STRABO (64 BC–AD 21 or later), Greek geographer.

SUETONIUS (Gaius Suetonius Tranquillus) (b. *c.*AD 70), Roman author, mainly known for his biographies of the emperors.

SWIFT, Jonathan (1667–1745), Anglo-Irish churchman, poet, pamphleteer, satirist and Tory supporter. In a large oeuvre the most well known are the *Battle of the Books* (1704), *A Tale of a Tub* (1704), *Gulliver's Travels* (1726).

TACITUS, Publius (or Gaius) Cornelius (AD 56 or 57–117 or later), Roman historian; since early modern times considered the greatest historian of the Empire, especially through his *Annals* and *Histories*.

TASSO, Torquato (1544–95), served in the court of Duke Alfonso II of Este at Ferrara. Main works: *Rinaldo* (1562) an epic; the play *Aminta* (1573); and the epic *Jerusalem Delivered* (1580–1). His theoretical writings on epic poetry were influential in the seventeenth and eighteenth centuries. He is celebrated, for example, in Goethe's *Torquato Tasso*, Byron's *The Lament of Tasso*, and Donizetti's opera *Torquato Tasso*.

TEMPLE, Sir William (1628–99), English diplomat and essayist, writing especially on political and economic matters.

THUCYDIDES (b. *c.* 460–55; d. *c.* 400–399 BC), Greek historian of the Peloponnesian War between Athens and Sparta 431–404 BC.

TIBERIUS (Tiberius Claudius Nero Caesar) (42 BC–AD 37), Roman emperor AD 14–37.

TINDAL, Matthew (1655–1733), English deist.

TITUS Flavius Vespasianus, Roman emperor AD 79–81.

TRAJANUS, Marcus Ulpius, Roman emperor AD 98–117.

TURGOT, Anne Robert Jacques (1727–81), French financier and statesman. A leading physiocrat who, as comptroller-general of finance to Louis XVI, tried to implement his economic theories.

VELLEIUS PATERCULUS, Gaius (*c.*19 BC–after AD 31), Roman historian.

VERRES, Gaius (career from 84 to 43 BC), governor of Sicily, made notorious for his extortion through Cicero's speeches at his trial.

VESPASIAN (Titus Flavius Sabinus Vespasianus) (AD 9–79), Roman emperor 69–79.

VIRGIL (Publius Vergilius Maro) (70–19 BC), commonly considered the greatest Roman poet, thanks in particular to the *Eclogues*, the *Georgics* and the *Aeneid*.

VITELLIUS, Aulus, Roman emperor April–December AD 69. Backed by legions in Germany, he expelled Otho, but several other parts of the army promoted Vespasianus, sacked Rome and killed Vitellius.

VOLTAIRE, pseudonym of François-Marie Arouet (1694–1778), French author who wrote in many of the genres and fields central to the Enlightenment–satires, novels, poetry, drama, criticism, history, moral essays, polemics, plus a huge correspondence.

WALPOLE, Sir Robert, first earl of Orford (1676–1745), leader of the Whigs and prime minister 1715–17 and 1721–42.

WILLIAM III (1650–1702), king of England, Scotland and Ireland 1689–1702, stadtholder of the Netherlands 1672–1702.

WOLSEY, Thomas (*c.* 1475–1530), English cardinal; arraigned for high treason after refusing support for Henry VIII's divorce of Catharine of Aragon, he died on his way to London.

XENOPHON (*c.*430–*c.*354 BC), Athenian writer and disciple of Socrates. The *Anabasis* and the *Hellenica* are historical works, while the *Memorabilia* and the *Symposium* are memoirs of Socrates. The *Oeconomicus*, on household economy, was influential in early modern Europe, as was the biographical fiction *Cyropaedia*, on King Cyrus of Persia.

Bibliography

Addison, Joseph, *Cato. A Tragedy*, in *The Works*, ed. R. Hurd, 4 vols., London 1854, vol. I, pp. 162–229

The Freeholder, ed. J. Leheney, Oxford, 1979

Addison, Joseph and Richard Steele, eds., *The Spectator* (1711–12, 1714), ed. D. F. Bond, 5 vols., Oxford, 1965

Aeschines, *The Speeches of Aeschines*, with an English translation by C. D. Adams, Loeb Classical Library, London and Cambridge, Mass., 1948, pp. 308–511

Anon. *Confucius Sinarum philosophus, sive scientia Sinensis*, Paris, 1687

Anon. *The False Accusers Accus'd, or the Undeceived Englishman*, etc., London, 1741

Appian, *Roman History*, with an English translation by H. White, 4 vols, Loeb Classical Library, London and Cambridge, Mass., 1972

Arbuthnot, John, *Tables of Ancient Coins, Weights and Measures* ... [1705], London, 1727

Aristotle, *Politics*, trans. B. Jowett, in *The Complete Works of Aristotle*, ed. J. Barnes, 2 vols., Princeton, NJ, 1984, vol. II, pp. 1986–2129

The Constitution of Athens, trans. F. G. Kenyon, in *The Complete Works of Aristotle*, ed. J. Barnes, 2 vols., Princeton, NJ, 1984, vol. II, pp. 2341–83

Arrian, *Anabasis of Alexander*, in *Arrian*, with an English translation by P. A. Brunt, 2 vols., Loeb Classical Library, Cambridge, Mass. and London, 1976

Asconius Pedianus, Quintus, Commentary on Cicero, 'Pro T. Annus Milone', in Cicero, *The Speeches*, pp. 124–36

Athenaeus of Naucratis, *The Deipnosophists*, with an English translation by C. B. Gulick, 7 vols., Loeb Classical Library, Cambridge,
Mass. and London, 1969, vol. IV

Bacon, Francis, *The Advancement of Learning*, ed. G. W. Kitchin,
London and New York, 1965

Essayes or Counsels, Civill and Morall, ed. M. Kiernan, Oxford, 1985

Barclay, Robert, *An Apology for the True Christian Divinity* (Latin,
London [?] 1676; English, London [?] 1678

Beaufort, Louis de, *Dissertation sur l'incertitude des cinq premiers siècles
de l'histoire romaine*, Paris, 1738.

Bentivoglio, Guido, *Relazioni in tempo delle sue nunziature* (1629) trans.
in part as *Historicall Relations of the United Provinces and of Flanders*, London, 1652

Della guerra di Fiandra (1632–9) trans. *The Compleat History of the
Warrs of Flanders*, London, 1654

Berkeley, George, *Alciphron, or the Minute Philosopher*, in *The Works*,
ed. A. A. Luce and T. E. Jessop, 9 vols., London, 1948–57, vol.
III (1950)

Bolingbroke, Henry St John, Viscount, *A Dissertation upon Parties*, in
Works, 5 vols., ed. D. Mallet, London, 1754, vol. II, pp. 1–256

Boswell, James, *The Journal of a Tour to Corsica: Memoirs of Pascal
Paoli*, ed. with an introduction by S. C. Roberts, Cambridge,
1923

Boulainvilliers, Henri, comte de, *Etat de la France, Contenant XIV
Lettres sur les Anciens Parlements de France. Avec l'Histoire de ce
Royaume depuis le Commencement de la Monarchie jusqu'à Charles
VIII. On y a joint des Memoires présentés à M. le Duc d'Orleans.*
3 vols., London, 1728

Brandt, Gerard, *The History of the Reformation and other Ecclesiastical
Transactions in and about the Low-Countries, from the Beginning of
the Eighth Century, down to the Famous Synod of Dort, inclusive.* 2
vols., London, 1720–2

Burmann, Pieter, *De vectigalibus populi Romani dissertatio*, Utrecht,
1694

Burton, Robert, *The Anatomy of Melancholy*, London, 1621

Caesar, Julius, *The Gallic War*, with an English translation by H. J.
Edwards, Loeb Classical Library, London and New York, 1917

Camden, William, *Annales rerum Anglicarum et Hibernicarum, regnante
Elizabetha* (1615–25); trans. *The Historie of the most renowned and
victorious princesse Elizabeth, late Queen of England*, London, 1635

Capitolinus, Julius, *Maximus and Balbinus*, in *Scriptores Historiae Augustae*, with an English translation by D. Magie, 3 vols., Loeb Classical Library, Cambridge, Mass. and London, 1960, vol. I, pp. 448–85

Cicero, Marcus Tullius, *De finibus bonorum et malorum*, with an English translation by H. Rackham, Loeb Classical Library, Cambridge, Mass. and London, 1971

De natura deorum. Academica, with an English translation by H. Rackham, Loeb Classical Library, London and Cambridge, Mass., 1967

De officiis, with an English translation by W. Miller, Loeb Classical Library, Cambridge, Mass. and London, 1975

De re publica. De legibus, with an English translation by W. Keyes, Loeb Classical Library, Cambridge, Mass. and London, 1977

The Five Days Debate at Cicero's House in Tusculum ... Between Master and Sophister [*Tusculan Disputations*], London, 1683

'In G. Verrem actio prima', in *The Verrine Orations*, with an English translation by L. H. G. Greenwood, Loeb Classical Library, 2 vols., London and New York, 1928

'Pro T. Annio Milone oratio'/'The Speech on Behalf of Titus Annius Milo', in *The Speeches*, with an English translation by N. H. Watts, Loeb Classical Library, London, New York, 1931, pp. 6–123

Letters to Atticus, with an English translation by E. O. Winstedt, 3 vols., Loeb Classical Library, Cambridge, Mass. and London, 1970

Columella, Lucius Junius Moderatus, *De re rustica. De arboribus*, with an English translation by H. B. Ash, E. S. Forster and E. Heffner, 3 vols., Loeb Classical Library, London and Cambridge, Mass., 1960

Curtius Rufus, Quintus, *History of Alexander*, in *Quintus Curtius*, with an English translation by J. C. Rolfe, 2 vols., Loeb Classical Library, London and Cambridge, Mass., 1956

Defoe, Daniel, *A General History of the Pyrates*, ed. M. Schonhorn, London, 1972

Demosthenes, *Demosthenes* I–III, with English translations by C. A. and J. H. Vince, Loeb Classical Library, London and Cambridge, Mass., 1954

Dio Cassius, *Roman History*, with an English translation by E. Cary, 9 vols., Loeb Classical Library, London and Cambridge, Mass., 1955, vol. VI

Diodorus Siculus, *Library of History*, in *Diodorus of Sicily*, with an English translation by C. H. Oldfather, C. L. Sherman, C. B. Welles, R. M. Geer, F. Walton, 12 vols., Loeb Classical Library, Cambridge, Mass. and London, 1933–67

Dionysius of Halicarnassus, *Roman Antiquities*, with an English translation by E. Cary, 7 vols., Loeb Classical Library, London and Cambridge, Mass., 1950, vol. VII

Dubos, Jean Baptiste, *Les Intérêts de l'Angleterre mal-entendus dans la présente guerre* (1703), Amsterdam, 1704

Du Halde, Jean Baptiste, *Description géographique, historique, chronologique et physique de l'Empire de la Chine et de la Tartarie Chinoise*, Paris 1735, Eng. trans. 1736, 3rd edn 1741: *The General History of China . . .* , 4 vols., London, 1741

Dutot, *Réflexions politiques sur les finances, et le commerce . . .*, La Haye, 1738

   Political Reflections upon the Finances and Commerce of France . . ., London, 1739

Encyclopaedia Britannica; Or, a Dictionary of Arts and Sciences, Compiled upon a New Plan . . . By a Society of Gentlemen in Scotland, 3 vols., Edinburgh, 1771

Erasmus, Desiderius, *In Praise of Folly/Moriae Encomium*, translated by B. Radice, in *The Collected Works of Erasmus*, Toronto, 1974– , vol. XXVII, ed. A. H. T. Levy, Toronto, 1986, pp. 83–153

   Witt against Wisdom: Or a Panegyrick upon Folly, rendered into English by [White Kennet], Oxford, 1683

Fiddes, Richard, *Life of Cardinal Wolsey*, London, 1724

Folkes Martin, *A Table of English Silver Coins from the Norman Conquest to the Present Time*, London, 1745

Forbes, D., *Hume's Philosophical Politics*, Cambridge, 1975

Gee, Joshua, *The Trade and Navigation of Great Britain Considered*, London, 1729

Gibbon, Edward, *Decline and Fall of the Roman Empire*, ed. J. B. Bury, 6th edn, 7 vols., London, 1912

   'Essai sur l'étude de la littérature', in *The Miscellaneous Works of Edward Gibbon . . .* , ed. John, Lord Sheffield, 5 vols., London, 1814, vol. IV

Grotius, Hugo, *The Rights of War and Peace . . .*, translated into English. To which are added . . . the . . . notes of J. Barbeyrac, 3 vols., London 1738

Guicciardini, Francesco, *The History of Italy from the Year 1490 to 1532*, trans. A. P. Goddard, 10 vols., London, 1753

Harrington, James, *Commonwealth of Oceana*, in *The Political Works
. . . , ed. J. G. A. Pocock, Cambridge, 1977
The Prerogative of Popular Government, in *The Political Works*
Herodian, *History*, in *Herodian*, 2 vols., with an English translation
by C. R. Whittaker, Loeb Classical Library, London and Cam-
bridge, Mass., 1969
Herodotus, *Histories*, in *Herodotus*, with an English translation by
A. D. Godley, 4 vols., Loeb Classical Library, Cambridge, Mass.
and London, 1920–5
Hobbes, Thomas, *Leviathan*, ed. R. Tuck, Cambridge, 1991
Horace, *The Odes, Satyrs, and Epistles*, trans. Thomas Creech, 6th
edn, London, 1737
Ars Poetica, in *Satires, Epistles and Ars Poetica*, with an English trans-
lation by H. Rushton Fairclough, Loeb Classical Library,
London and Cambridge, Mass., 1942
Houssaie, Amelott de la, *The History of the Government of Venice.
Wherein the Policies, Councils, Magistrates, and Laws of that State
are fully related; and the use of the Balloting Box exactly described*,
London 1677
Hume, David, *Enquiries Concerning Human Understanding and Con-
cerning the Principles of Morals*, reprinted from the . . . edition of
1777 and edited . . . by L. A. Selby-Bigge, revised edition P. H.
Nidditch, Oxford, 1975
Essays Moral and Political, 2 vols., Edinburgh, 1741–2
Essays Moral, Political, and Literary, ed. E. F. Miller, Indianapolis,
Ind., 1987
*The History of England from the Invasion of Julius Caesar to the Revolu-
tion in 1688*, 6 vols., Indianapolis, Ind., 1983
The Letters of David Hume, ed. J. Y. T. Greig, 2 vols., Oxford, 1969
Political Discourses, Edinburgh, 1752
A Treatise of Human Nature, ed. L. A. Selby-Bigge, 2nd edn, revised
by P. H. Nidditch, Oxford, 1978
Hutcheson, Archibald, *A Collection of Treatises Relating to National
Debts and Funds*, London, 1721
Hutcheson, Francis, *A Short Introduction to Moral Philosophy*, (trans.
from the Latin); facsimile of first edn, 1747, *Collected Works*, 7
vols., Hildesheim, 1969–71, vol. IV
A System of Moral Philosophy. Facsimile of first edn, 1755, *Collected
Works*, Hildesheim, 1969, vols. V–VI

Isocrates, 'Busiris', in *Isocrates*, with an English translation by L. van Hook, 3 vols., Loeb Classical Library, London and Cambridge, Mass., 1968, vol. I, pp. 102–31

Janiçon, François Michel, *Etat présent de la République des Provinces-Unies et des Pais qui en dépendent*, 2 vols., La Haye, 1729

Johnson, Samuel, *A Dictionary of the English Language*, 2 vols., London 1819

Juvenal, *The Satires of Juvenal*. Anon. trans., Dublin, 1741

Korb, Johann-Georg, *Diarium itineris in Moscoviam perillustris ac magnifici domini Ignatii Christophori . . . anno MDCXCVIII . . .* (1700); English translation, *Diary of the Journey into Muscovy of the Right Illustrious and Magnificent Sir Ignatius Christopher . . . in the Year 1698*, 2 vols. in one, Vienna, 1863

Law, John, *The Present State of the French Revenues and Trade and of the Controversy betwixt the Parliament of Paris and Mr. Law*, London, 1720

Le Clerc, Jean, *Histoire des Provinces-Unies des Pays Bas*, 3 vols., Amsterdam, 1723–8

Leibniz, Gottfried Wilhelm, *Das neueste von China (1697), Novissima Sinica*, ed. H.-G. Nesselrath and H. Reinbothe, Cologne, 1979

Lemprière, John, *Classical Dictionary of Proper Names Mentioned in Ancient Authors Writ Large* [1788], London, 1987

Limojon de Saint Didier, Alexandre Toussaint, *La Ville et la République de Venise*, Paris, 1680, trans. into English as *The City and Republic of Venice*. In Three Parts. Originally Written in French by Monsieur De S. Desdier [*sic*], London, 1699

Livy [Livius], Titus, *The Roman History* . . . with the Entire Supplement by John Freinsheim. 6 vols., London, 1744–5

Locke, John, *Some Considerations of the Consequences of the Lowering of Interest and Raising the Value of Money. In a Letter to a Member of Parliament*, London, 1692

Two Treatises of Government, ed. P. Laslett, Cambridge, 1960

Longinus, *On the Sublime*. Trans. with commentary by James A. Arieti and John M. Crossett, New York and Toronto, 1985

Lucian, *Dialogues of the Courtesans*, in *Lucian*, with an English translation by M. D. Macleod, 8 vols., Loeb Classical Library, London and Cambridge, Mass., 1961, vol. VII

On Salaried Posts in Great Houses, in *Lucian*, with an English translation by A. M. Harmon, 8 vols., Loeb Classical Library, London and Cambridge, Mass., 1971, vol. III

Saturnalia, in *Lucian*, with an English translation by K. Kilburn, 8 vols., Loeb Classical Library, Cambridge, Mass. and London, 1959, vol. VI

Lucretius Carus, T., *De rerum natura*, with an English translation by W. H. O. Rouse, revised by M. Ferguson, Loeb Classical Library, Cambridge, Mass. and London, 1975

Lucretius, His Six Books of Epicurean Philosophy, London, 1683

Machiavelli, Niccolò, *The Discourses [on the First Ten Books of Titus Livius]*, ed., introd. B. Crick; trans. L. J. Walker, revised B. Richardson, Harmondsworth, 1970

The Florentine History, trans. Thomas Bedingfeld [1595], London, 1905

The Prince, ed. Q. Skinner, Cambridge, 1989

Malebranche, Nicolas, *Entretien d'un philosophe chrétien et d'un philosophe chinois*, Paris, 1708

Mandeville, Bernard, *The Fable of the Bees: Or, Private Vices, Publick Benefits*, ed. F. B. Kaye, 2 vols., Oxford, 1966

Melon, Jean-François, *Essai politique sur le commerce* (1734), new edn, n.p., 1736

A Political Essay upon Commerce, trans. D. Bindon, Dublin, 1739

Menander, *Menandri quae supersunt*, ed. A. Koerte (Bibliotheca Scriptorum Graecorum Teubneriana), 2 vols., Leipzig, 1959

[Miège, Guy], *A Relation of Three Embassies from His Sacred Majestie Charles II to the Great Duke of Muscovie, the King of Sweden, and the King of Denmark. Performed by the Right Honble. the Earle of Carlisle in the Years 1663 & 1664*, London, 1669

Molesworth, Robert, *The Principles of a Real Whig*, 1711

Montesquieu, Charles-Louis de Secondat, baron de La Brède et de, *Considérations sur les causes de la grandeur des Romains et de leur décadence*, in *Oeuvres complètes . . .*, ed. A. Masson, 3 vols., Paris 1950, vol. I

The Spirit of the Laws, trans. and ed. A. M. Cohler, B. C. Miller, H. S. Stone, Cambridge, 1989

More, Henry, *Enthusiasmus Triumphatus, or, A Brief Discourse of the Nature, Causes, Kinds, and Cure of Enthusiasm*, London, 1662

Morgan, Thomas, *The Moral Philosopher. In a Dialogue between Phila-lethes a Christian Deist, and Theophanes a Christian Jew*, London, 1737

Nepos, Cornelius, 'Datames', (*The Books on the Great Generals of For-eign Nations*, XIV), in *Lucius Annaeus Florus, Epitome of Roman History; Cornelius Nepos*, with an English translation by E. S. Forster and J. C. Rolfe, Loeb Classical Library, London and New York, 1929

Ovid (Publius Ovidius Naso), *Fasti*, with an English translation by J. G. Frazer, Loeb Classical Library, London and Cambridge, Mass., 1951

Paris Duverney, Joseph, *Examen du livre intitulé Réflexions politiques sur les finances et le commerce* [by Dutot], 2 vols., La Haye, 1740

Plato, *Crito*, translated by H. Tredennick, in *The Collected Dialogues of Plato*, ed. E. Hamilton and H. Cairns, New York, 1966
Laws, translated by A. E. Taylor, in *The Collected Dialogues*
[attrib.] *Alcibiades I*, in *Plato*, trans. W. R. M. Lamb, Loeb Classical Library, London and Cambridge, Mass., 1955, vol. VIII

Pliny the Elder, *Natural History*, with an English translation by H. Rackham and W. H. S. Jones, 10 vols., Loeb Classical Library, London and Cambridge, Mass., 1938–62

Pliny the Younger, *Letters and Panegyricus*, with an English translation by B. Radice, 2 vols., Loeb Classical Library, London and Cam-bridge, Mass., 1969

Plutarch, *Lives*, with an English translation by B. Perrin. 11 vols., Loeb Classical Library, New York and London, 1914–21, vols. I, II, V, VIII, IX
Moralia, with an English translation by F. C. Babbitt, W. C. Helmbold, H. N. Fowler, *et al.*, 16 vols., Loeb Classical Library, Cambridge, Mass. and London, 1970, vols. I, VI, X
Symposiaca Problemata, in *Moralia*, vol. 8, with an English transla-tion by P. A. Clement and H. B. Hoffleit, Loeb Classical Lib-rary, London and Cambridge, Mass., 1969

Polybius, *The Histories*, with an English translation by W. R. Paton, 6 vols., Loeb Classical Library, Cambridge, Mass. and London, 1922–7

Pope, Alexander, *An Essay on Man . . .* , Scolar Press facsimile reprint of 1734 London edn, Menston, 1969

[Pope, Alexander] *The First Epistle of the Second Book of Horace, Imitated*, London, 1737

Procopius of Caesarea, *History of the Wars of Justinian*, trans. H. B. Dewing, Loeb Classical Library, 7 vols.

Pufendorf, Samuel von, *The Compleat History of Sweden*, London, 1702

    Of the Law of Nature and Nations . . . Done into English by Basil Kennet . . . To which are . . . added . . . the notes of Mr. Barbeyrac translated from his last edition . . . 1712, 5th edn, London, 1749

Quintilian, *The Institutio Oratoria*, with an English translation by H. E. Butler, 4 vols., Loeb Classical Library, London and Cambridge, Mass., 1969

Ralegh, Walter, *The History of the World in Five Books* (1614), 6 vols., Edinburgh, 1820

Rapin-Thoyras, Paul de, *Histoire d'Angleterre*, 10 vols., The Hague, 1723–7

    The History of England, translated by N. Tindal, 2 vols., 2nd edn, London, 1732

Retz, Jean-François Paul de Gondi, cardinal de, *Mémoires*, in *Oeuvres*, nouv. édn, 10 vols., Paris, 1870–96, vol. II

Rousseau, Jean-Baptiste, *Poésies diverses*, in *Oeuvres*, 5 vols., Paris, 1820, vol. II, pp. 321–75

Rousseau, Jean-Jacques, *Considerations on the Government of Poland and on its Proposed Reformation* (completed 1772; pub. 1782) in *Political Writings*, trans., ed. F. Watkins, Edinburgh, 1953, pp. 157–274

    The Social Contract and Discourses, trans. and ed. G. D. H. Cole, revised J. H. Brumfitt and J. C. Hall, London, 1973

Sallust, Gaius Sallustius Crispus, *Bellum Catilinarium et Jugurthinum* . . . *I.E. The History of the Wars of Catiline and Jugurtha*. With a Free Translation . . . A large Dissertation upon the Usefulness of Translations of Classick Authors . . . As also the Life of Sallust by . . . Le Clerk. By John Clarke. London, 1734

Sewel, William, *History of the Rise, Increase and Progress of the Christian People call'd Quakers*, London [?] 1717

Shaftesbury, Anthony Ashley Cooper (third earl of), *Characteristics of Men, Manners, Opinions, Times*, ed. J. M. Robertson, introd. S. Grean, Indianapolis, 1964

Simmons, R. C., *The American Colonies. From Settlement to Independence*, London, 1976

Smith, Adam, *An Inquiry into the Nature and Causes of the Wealth of Nations*, ed. R. H. Campbell, A. S. Skinner, 2 vols., Oxford, 1976

Smollett, Tobias, *The History of England from the Revolution to the Death of George the Second*, 5 vols., London, 1812

Spenser, Edmund, *A View of the Present State of Ireland*, ed. W. L. Renwick, Oxford, 1970

Stanyan, Abraham, *An Account of Switzerland Written in the Year 1714*, London, 1714

Steele, Richard, ed., *The Tatler* (1709–11), ed. D. F. Bond, 3 vols., Oxford, 1987

Strabo, *The Geography*, with an English translation by H. L. Jones, 8 vols., Loeb Classical Library, London, 1917–32

Suetonius, *The Lives of the Caesars*, in *Suetonius*, with an English translation by J. C. Rolfe, 2 vols., Loeb Classical Library, London and Cambridge, Mass., 1970

Swift, Jonathan, *A Short View of the State of Ireland* (1727–8), in *Prose Works*, vol. XII: *Irish Tracts 1728–1733*, ed. H. Davis, Oxford, 1955

    An Answer to a Paper called A Memorial of the Poor Inhabitants, Tradesmen and Labourers of the Kingdom of Ireland (1728), in *Prose Works*, vol. XII: *Irish Tracts 1728–1733*, ed. H. Davis, Oxford, 1955

Tacitus, Publius Cornelius, *The Works of Tacitus*, 2 vols., London, 1728 and 1731

    Annals, with an English translation by J. Jackson, and *Histories*, with an English translation by C. H. Moore. In *Tacitus*, 5 vols., Loeb Classical Library, Cambridge, Mass., 1914–37, vols. II–V

    A Dialogue on Oratory, in *Dialogus, Agricola, Germania*, with an English translation by W. Peterson, Loeb Classical Library, London and New York, 1914

Temple, Sir William, *Observations upon the United Provinces of the Netherlands* (1673), in *The Works*, 2 vols., London, 1740, vol. I

Thucydides, *History of the Peloponnesian War*, in *Thucydides*, with an English translation, 4 vols., Loeb Classical Library, London and New York, 1923

Vanderlint, Jacob, *Money Answers all Things: Or an Essay to make Money sufficiently Plentiful among all Ranks of People. . .* , London 1734

Vauban, Sébastien le Prestre, seigneur de, *Projet d'une dixme royale*, n.p., 1707

A Project for a Royal Tythe or General Tax, London, 1708

Vega, Garcilaso de la, *The Royal Commentaries of Peru, in Two Parts*, London, 1688

Velleius Paterculus, Gaius, *Historiae Romanae*, in *Compendium of Roman History . . .* , with an English translation by F. W. Shipley, Loeb Classical Library, London and Cambridge, Mass., 1961

Virgil, *Georgics*, in *Virgil*, with an English translation by H. Rushton Fairclough, 2 vols., Loeb Classical Library, London and Cambridge, Mass., 1932, vol. I

Voltaire (François-Marie Arouet), *Essai sur les mœurs et l'esprit des nations*, in *Oeuvres complètes* . . . Second edn, 75 vols., Paris, 1825–8, vols. xx–xxv

La Henriade. An Epick Poem. In Ten Cantos, London, 1732

Histoire de Charles XII, roi de Suède, in *Oeuvres complètes* . . . Second edn, 75 vols., Paris, 1825–8, vol. xxx

Letters on England, translated with an introduction by L. Tancock. Harmondsworth, 1980

Lettres philosophiques, Paris, 1733

Waller, Edmund, *Poems, &c. Written upon several Occasions, and to several persons.* 8th edn with Additions, to which is Prefix'd the Author's Life. London, 1711

Wolff, Christian, Freiherr von, *Oratio de Sinarum philosophia practica* [1721], with German translation by M. Albrecht, Hamburg, 1985

Xenophon, *Cyropaedia*, in *Xenophon*, with an English translation by W. Miller, 7 vols., Loeb Classical Library, London and New York, 1914, vols. I–II

Hellenica, Anabasis, Apology, and Symposium, with an English translation by C. L. Brownson and O. J. Todd, 3 vols., Loeb Classical Library, London and Cambridge, Mass., 1950

Hiero; *Ways and Means*; in *Xenophon*, *Scripta Minora*, with an English translation by E. C. Marchant, 7 vols., Loeb Classical Library, London and Cambridge, Mass., 1971, vol. VII

Symposium (or *Banquet*), in *Xenophon*, with an English translation by O. J. Todd, 7 vols., Loeb Classical Library, London and Cambridge, Mass., 1947, vol. III

ESSAY ONE

Of the liberty of the press

NOTHING is more apt to surprize a foreigner, than the extreme liberty, which we enjoy in this country, of communicating whatever we please to the public, and of openly censuring every measure, entered into by the king or his ministers. If the administration resolve upon war, it is affirmed, that, either wilfully or ignorantly, they mistake the interest of the nation, and that peace, in the present situation of affairs, is infinitely preferable. If the passion of the ministers lie towards peace, our political writers breathe nothing but war and devastation, and represent the pacific conduct of the government as mean and pusillanimous. As this liberty is not indulged in any other government, either republican or monarchical; in HOLLAND and VENICE, more than in FRANCE or SPAIN; it may very naturally give occasion to a question, *How it happens that* GREAT BRITAIN *alone enjoys this peculiar privilege?*[1]

The Reason, why the laws indulge us in such a liberty seems to be derived from our mixed form of government, which is neither wholly monarchical, nor wholly republican. It will be found, if I mistake not, a true observation in politics, that the two extremes in government, liberty and slavery, commonly approach nearest to each other; and that, as you depart from the extremes, and mix a little of monarchy with liberty, the government becomes always the more free; and on the other hand, when you mix a little of liberty with monarchy, the yoke becomes always the more grievous and intolerable. In a government, such as that of FRANCE, which is absolute, and where laws, custom, and religion concur, all of them, to make the people fully satisfied with their condition, the monarch cannot entertain any

I

jealousy against his subjects, and therefore is apt to indulge them in great *liberties* both of speech and action. In a government altogether republican, such as that of HOLLAND, where there is no magistrate so eminent as to give *jealousy* to the state, there is no danger in intrusting the magistrates with large discretionary powers; and though many advantages result from such powers, in preserving peace and order, yet they lay a considerable restraint on men's actions, and make every private citizen pay a great respect to the government. Thus it seems evident that the two extremes of absolute monarchy and of a republic, approach near to each other in some material circumstances. In the *first*, the magistrate has no jealousy of the people: in the *second*, the people have none of the magistrate: Which want of jealousy begets a mutual confidence and trust in both cases, and produces a species of liberty in monarchies, and of arbitrary power in republics.

To justify the other part of the foregoing observation, that, in every government, the means are most wide of each other, and that the mixtures of monarchy and liberty render the yoke either more easy or more grievous; I must take notice of a remark in TACITUS with regard to the ROMANS under the emperors, that they neither could bear total slavery nor total liberty, *Nec totam servitutem, nec totam libertatem pati possunt.*[2] This remark a celebrated poet has translated and applied to the ENGLISH, in his lively description of queen ELIZAB-ETH's policy and government,

> *Et fit aimer son joug a l'Anglois indompté,*
> *Qui ne peut ni servir, ni vivre en liberté.*
> HENRIADE, *liv.* I.[3]

According to these remarks, we are to consider the ROMAN government under the emperors as a mixture of despotism and liberty, where the despotism prevailed; and the ENGLISH government as a mixture of the same kind, where the liberty predominates. The consequences are conformable to the foregoing observation; and such as may be expected from those mixed forms of government, which beget a mutual watchfulness and jealousy. The ROMAN emperors were, many of them, the most frightful tyrants that ever disgraced human nature; and it is evident, that their cruelty was chiefly excited by their *jealousy*, and by their observing that all the great men of ROME bore with impatience the dominion of a family, which, but a little before, was no wise superior to their own. On the other hand, as the republican part of the government prevails in ENGLAND, although with a great mixture of monarchy, it is obliged, for its own preservation, to maintain a watchful *jealousy* over the magistrates, to remove all discretionary powers, and to secure every one's life and fortune by general and inflexible laws. No action must be deemed a crime but what the law has plainly determined to be such: No crime must be imputed to a man but from a legal proof before his judges; and even these judges must be his fellow-subjects, who are obliged, by their own interest, to have a watchful eye over the encroachments and violence of the ministers. From these causes it proceeds, that there is as much liberty, and even, perhaps, licentiousness in BRITAIN, as there were formerly slavery and tyranny in ROME.

These principles account for the great liberty of the press in these kingdoms, beyond what is indulged in any other government. It is apprehended, that arbitrary power would steal in upon us, were we not careful to prevent its progress, and were there not an easy method of conveying the alarm from one end of the kingdom to the other. The spirit of the people must frequently be rouzed, in order to curb the ambition of the court; and the dread of rouzing this spirit must be employed to prevent that ambition. Nothing so effectual to this purpose as the liberty of the press, by which all the learning, wit and genius of the nation may be employed on the side of freedom, and every one be animated to its defence. As long, therefore, as the republican part of our government can maintain itself against the monarchical, it will naturally be careful to keep the press open, as of importance to its own preservation.

It must however be allowed, that the unbounded liberty of the press, though it be difficult to propose a suitable remedy for it, is one of the evils, attending those mixt forms of government.[4]

ESSAY TWO

That politics may be reduced to a science

IT is a question with several, whether there be any essential difference between one form of government and another? and, whether every form may not become good or bad, according as it is well or ill administered?[a] Were it once admitted, that all governments are alike, and that the only difference consists in the character and conduct of the governors, most political disputes would be at an end, and all *Zeal* for one constitution above another, must be esteemed mere bigotry and folly. But, though a friend to moderation, I cannot forbear condemning this sentiment, and should be sorry to think, that human affairs admit of no greater stability, than what they receive from the casual humours and characters of particular men.

It is true; those who maintain, that the goodness of all government consists in the goodness of the administration, may cite many particular instances in history, where the very same government, in different hands, has varied suddenly into the two opposite extremes of good and bad. Compare the FRENCH government under HENRY III. and under HENRY IV. Oppression, levity, artifice on the part of the rulers; faction, sedition, treachery, rebellion, disloyalty on the part of the subjects: these compose the character of the former miserable aera. But when the patriot and heroic prince, who succeeded, was once firmly seated on the throne, the government, the people, every thing seemed to be totally changed; and all from the difference of the temper and sentiments of these two sovereigns. Instances of this kind

---

[a] *For forms of government let fools contest,*
Whate'er is best administer'd is best.
ESSAY on Man, Book 3[1]

4

may be multiplied, almost without number, from ancient as well as modern history, foreign as well as domestic.[2]

But here it may be proper to make a distinction. All absolute governments must very much depend on the administration; and this is one of the great inconveniences attending that form of government. But a republican and free government would be an obvious absurdity, if the particular checks and controuls, provided by the constitution, had really no influence, and made it not the interest, even of bad men, to act for the public good. Such is the intention of these forms of government, and such is their real effect, where they are wisely constituted: As on the other hand, they are the source of all disorder, and of the blackest crimes, where either skill or honesty has been wanting in their original frame and institution.

So great is the force of laws, and of particular forms of government, and so little dependence have they on the humours and tempers of men, that consequences almost as general and certain may sometimes be deduced from them, as any which the mathematical sciences afford us.

The constitution of the ROMAN republic gave the whole legislative power to the people, without allowing a negative voice either to the nobility or consuls. This unbounded power they possessed in a collective, not in a representative body. The consequences were: When the people, by success and conquest, had become very numerous, and had spread themselves to a great distance from the capital, the city-tribes, though the most contemptible, carried almost every vote: They were, therefore, most cajoled by every one that affected popularity: They were supported in idleness by the general distribution of corn, and by particular bribes, which they received from almost every candidate: by this means, they became every day more licentious, and the CAMPUS MARTIUS[3] was a perpetual scene of tumult and sedition: Armed slaves were introduced among these rascally citizens; so that the whole government fell into anarchy, and the greatest happiness, which the ROMANS could look for, was the despotic power of the CAESARS. Such are the effects of democracy without a representative.

A Nobility may possess the whole, or any part of the legislative power of a state, in two different ways. Either every nobleman shares the power as part of the whole body, or the whole body enjoys the power as composed of parts, which have each a distinct power and authority. The VENETIAN aristocracy is an instance of the first kind of government: The POLISH of the second. In the VENETIAN government the whole body of nobility possesses the whole power, and no nobleman has any authority which he receives not from the whole. In the POLISH government every nobleman, by means of his fiefs, has a distinct hereditary authority over his vassals, and the whole body has no authority but what it receives from the concurrence of its parts. The different operations and tendencies of these two species of government might be made apparent even *a priori*. A VENETIAN nobility is preferable to a POLISH, let the humours and education of men be ever so much varied. A nobility, who possess their power in common, will preserve peace and order, both among themselves, and their subjects; and no member can have authority enough to controul the laws for a moment. The nobles will preserve their authority over the people, but without any grievous tyranny, or any breach of private property; because such a tyrannical government promotes not the interest of the whole body, however it may that of some individuals. There will be a distinction of rank between the nobility and people, but this will be the only distinction in the state. The whole nobility will form one body, and the whole people another, without any of those private feuds and animosities, which spread ruin and desolation every where. It is easy to see the disadvantages of a POLISH nobility in every one of these particulars.

It is possible so to constitute a free government, as that a single person, call him doge, prince, or king, shall possess a large share of power, and shall form a proper balance or counterpoise to the other parts of the legislature. This chief magistrate may be either *elective* or *hereditary*; and though the former institution may, to a superficial view, appear the most advantageous; yet a more accurate inspection will discover in it greater inconveniencies than in the latter, and such as are founded on causes and principles eternal and immutable. The filling of the throne, in such a government, is a point of too great and too general interest, not to divide the whole people into factions: Whence a civil war, the greatest of ills, may be apprehended, almost with certainty, upon every vacancy. The prince elected must be either a *Foreigner* or a *Native*: the former will be ignorant of the people whom he is to govern; suspicious of his new subjects, and suspected by them; giving his confidence entirely to strangers, who will have no other care but of enriching themselves in the quickest manner, while their master's favour and authority are able to support them.

A native will carry into the throne all his private animosities and friendships, and will never be viewed in his elevation, without exciting the sentiment of envy in those, who formerly considered him as their equal. Not to mention, that a crown is too high a reward ever to be given to merit alone, and will always induce the candidates to employ force, or money, or intrigue, to procure the vote of the electors: So that such an election will give no better chance for superior merit in the prince, than if the state had trusted to birth alone for determining their sovereign.

It may therefore be pronounced as an universal axiom in politics, *That an hereditary prince, a nobility without vassals, and a people voting by their representatives, form the best* MONARCHY, ARISTOCRACY, *and* DEMOCRACY. But in order to prove more fully, that politics admit of general truths, which are invariable by the humour or education either of subject or sovereign, it may not be amiss to observe some other principles of this science, which may seem to deserve that character.

It may easily be observed, that, though free governments have been commonly the most happy for those who partake of their freedom; yet are they the most ruinous and oppressive to their provinces: And this observation may, I believe, be fixed as a maxim of the kind we are here speaking of. When a monarch extends his dominions by conquest, he soon learns to consider his old and his new subjects as on the same footing; because, in reality, all his subjects are to him the same, except the few friends and favourites, with whom he is personally acquainted. He does not, therefore, make any distinction between them in his *general* laws; and, at the same time, is careful to prevent all *particular* acts of oppression on the one as well as on the other. But a free state necessarily makes a great distinction, and must always do so, till men learn to love their neighbours as well as themselves. The conquerors, in such a government, are all legislators, and will be sure to contrive matters, by restrictions of trade, and by taxes, so as to draw some private, as well as public, advantage from their conquests. Provincial governors have also a better chance, in a republic, to escape with their plunder, by means of bribery or intrigue; and their fellow-citizens, who find their own state to be enriched by the spoils of the subject provinces, will be the more inclined to tolerate such abuses. Not to mention, that it is a necessary precaution in a free state to change the governors frequently; which obliges these temporary tyrants to be more expeditious and rapacious, that they may accumulate sufficient wealth before they give place to their successors. What cruel tyrants were the ROMANS over the world during the time of their commonwealth! It is true they had laws to prevent oppression in their provincial magistrates; but CICERO informs us, that the ROMANS could not better consult the interest of the provinces than by repealing these very laws. For, in that case, says he, our magistrates, having entire impunity, would plunder no more than would satisfy their own rapaciousness; whereas, at present, they must also satisfy that of their judges, and of all the great men in ROME, of whose protection they stand in need.[4] Who can read of the cruelties and oppressions of VERRES without horror and astonishment? And who is not touched with indignation to hear, that, after CICERO had exhausted on that abandoned criminal all the thunders of his eloquence, and had prevailed so far as to get him condemned to the utmost extent of the laws; yet that cruel tyrant lived peaceably to old age, in opulence and ease, and, thirty years afterwards, was put into the proscription by MARK ANTHONY, on account of his exorbitant wealth, where he fell with CICERO himself, and all the most virtuous men of ROME?[5] After the dissolution of the commonwealth, the ROMAN yoke became easier upon the provinces, as TACITUS informs us;[b] and it may be observed, that many of the worst emperors, DOMITIAN,[c] for instance, were careful to prevent all oppression on the provinces. In[d] TIBERIUS's time, GAUL was esteemed richer than ITALY itself: Nor, do I find, during the whole time of the ROMAN monarchy, that the empire became less rich or populous in any of its provinces; though indeed its valour and military discipline were always upon the decline. The oppression and tyranny of the CARTHAGINIANS over their subject states in AFRICA went so far, as we learn from POLYBIUS,[e] that, not content with exacting the half of all the produce of the ground, which of itself was a very high rent, they also loaded them with many other taxes. If we pass from ancient to modern times, we shall still find the observation to hold. The provinces of absolute monarchies are always better treated than those of free states. Com-

---

[b] Ann. lib. I. cap. 2.
[c] SUET. in vita DOMIT.
[d] *Egregium resumendae libertati tempus, si ipsi florentes, quam inops* ITALIA, *quam imbellis urbana plebs, nihil validum in exercitibus, nisi quod externum cogitarent.* TACIT. Ann. lib. 3.
[e] Lib. I. cap. 72.

pare the *Païs conquis*[6] of FRANCE with IRELAND, and you will be convinced of this truth; though this latter kingdom, being, in a good measure, peopled from ENGLAND, possesses so many rights and privileges as should naturally make it challenge better treatment than that of a conquered province. CORSICA is also an obvious instance to the same purpose.[7]

There is an observation in MACHIAVEL, with regard to the conquests of ALEXANDER the Great, which I think, may be regarded as one of those eternal political truths, which no time nor accidents can vary. It may seem strange, says that politician, that such sudden conquests, as those of ALEXANDER, should be possessed so peaceably by his successors, and that the PERSIANS, during all the confusions and civil wars among the GREEKS, never made the smallest efforts towards the recovery of their former independent government.[8] To satisfy us concerning the cause of this remarkable event, we may consider, that a monarch may govern his subjects in two different ways. He may either follow the maxims of the eastern princes, and stretch his authority so far as to leave no distinction of rank among his subjects, but what proceeds immediately from himself; no advantages of birth; no hereditary honours and possessions; and, in a word, no credit among the people, except from his commission alone. Or a monarch may exert his power after a milder manner, like our EUROPEAN princes; and leave other sources of honour, beside his smile and favour: Birth, titles, possessions, valour, integrity, knowledge, or great and fortunate atchievements. In the former species of government, after a conquest, it is impossible ever to shake off the yoke; since no one possesses, among the people, so much personal credit and authority as to begin such an enterprize: Whereas, in the latter, the least misfortune, or discord among the victors, will encourage the vanquished to take arms, who have leaders ready to prompt and conduct them in every undertaking.[f]

---

[f] I Have taken it for granted, according to the supposition of MACHIAVEL, that the ancient PERSIANS had no nobility; though there is reason to suspect, that the FLORENTINE secretary, who seems to have been better acquainted with the ROMAN than the GREEK authors, was mistaken in this particular. The more ancient PERSIANS, whose manners are described by XENOPHON, were a free people, and had nobility. Their homotimoi were preserved even after the extending of their conquests and the consequent change of their government. ARRIAN mentions them in DARIUS's time, *De exped.* ALEX. lib. ii. Historians also speak often of the persons in command as men of family. TYGRANES, who was general of the MEDES under XERXES, was of the race of

Such is the reasoning of MACHIAVEL, which seems solid and con-
clusive; though I wish he had not mixed falsehood with truth, in
asserting, that monarchies, governed according to eastern policy,
though more easily kept when once subdued, yet are the most difficult
to subdue; since they cannot contain any powerful subject, whose discontent and faction may facilitate the enterprizes of an enemy. For
besides, that such a tyrannical government enervates the courage of
men, and renders them indifferent towards the fortunes of their sovereign; besides this, I say, we find by experience, that even the temporary
and delegated authority of the generals and magistrates; being always,
in such governments, as absolute within its sphere, as that of the prince
himself; is able, with barbarians, accustomed to a blind submission, to
produce the most dangerous and fatal revolutions. So that, in every
respect, a gentle government is preferable, and gives the greatest security to the sovereign as well as to the subject.

Legislators, therefore, ought not to trust the future government of
a state entirely to chance, but ought to provide a system of laws to

ACHMAENES, HEROD. lib. vii. cap. 62. ARTACHAEAS, who directed the cutting of the
canal about mount ATHOS, was of the same family. Id. cap. 117. MEGABYZUS was one
of the seven eminent PERSIANS who conspired against the MAGI. His son, ZOPYRUS,
was in the highest command under DARIUS, and delivered BABYLON to him. His
grandson, MEGABYZUS, commanded the army, defeated at MARATHON. His great-
grandson, ZOPYRUS, was also eminent, and was banished PERSIA. HEROD. lib. iii.
THUC. lib. i. ROSACES, who commanded an army in EGYPT under ARTAXERXES, was
also descended from one of the seven conspirators, DIOD. SIC. lib. xvi. AGESILAUS,
in XENOPHON, Hist. GRAEC. lib. iv. being desirous of making a marriage betwixt king
COTYS his ally, and the daughter of SPITHRIDATES, a PERSIAN of rank, who had
deserted to him, first asks COTYS what family SPITHRIDATES is of. One of the most
considerable in PERSIA, says COTYS. ARIAEUS, when offered the sovereignty by CLE-
ARCHUS and the ten thousand GREEKS, refused it as of too low a rank, and said, that
so many eminent PERSIANS would never endure his rule. *Id. de exped.* lib. ii. Some of
the families descended from the seven PERSIANS abovementioned remained during
all ALEXANDER's successors; and MITHRIDATES, in ANTIOCHUS's time, is said by
POLYBIUS to be descended from one of them, lib. v. cap. 43. ARTABAZUS was esteemed,
as ARRIAN says, en tois protois Person. lib. iii. And when ALEXANDER married in
one day 80 of his captains to PERSIAN women, his intention plainly was to ally the
MACEDONIANS with the most eminent PERSIAN families. Id. lib. vii. DIODORUS SIC-
ULUS says they were of the most noble birth in PERSIA, lib. xvii. The government of
PERSIA was despotic, and conducted, in many respects, after the eastern manner, but
was not carried so far as to extirpate all nobility, and confound all ranks and orders.
It left men who were still great, by themselves and their family, independent of their
office and commission. And the reason why the MACEDONIANS kept so easily dominion
over them was owing to other causes easy to be found in the historians; though it
must be owned that MACHIAVEL's reasoning is, in itself, just, however doubtful its
application to the present case.[9]

regulate the administration of public affairs to the latest posterity. Effects will always correspond to causes; and wise regulations in any commonwealth are the most valuable legacy that can be left to future ages. In the smallest court or office, the stated forms and methods, by which business must be conducted, are found to be a considerable check on the natural depravity of mankind. Why should not the case be the same in public affairs? Can we ascribe the stability and wisdom of the VENETIAN government, through so many ages, to any thing but the form of government? And is it not easy to point out those defects in the original constitution, which produced the tumultuous governments of ATHENS and ROME, and ended at last in the ruin of these two famous republics? And so little dependance has this affair on the humours and education of particular men, that one part of the same republic may be wisely conducted, and another weakly, by the very same men, merely on account of the difference of the forms and institutions, by which these parts are regulated. Historians inform us that this was actually the case with GENOA. For while the state was always full of sedition, and tumult, and disorder, the bank of St. GEORGE, which had become a considerable part of the people, was conducted, for several ages, with the utmost integrity and wisdom.[g]

The ages of greatest public spirit are not always most eminent for private virtue. Good laws may beget order and moderation in the government, where the manners and customs have instilled little humanity or justice into the tempers of men. The most illustrious period of the ROMAN history, considered in a political view, is that between the beginning of the first and end of the last PUNIC war; the due balance between the nobility and people being then fixed by the contests of the tribunes, and not being yet lost by the extent of conquests. Yet at this very time, the horrid practice of poisoning was so common, that, during part of a season, a Praetor punished capitally for this crime above three thousand[h] persons in a part of ITALY; and found informations of this nature still multiplying upon him.[11] There

---

[g] *Essempio veramente raro, & da Filosofi intante loro imaginate & vedute Republiche mai non trovato, vedere dentro ad un medesimo cerchio, fra medesimi cittadini, la liberta, & la tirannide, la vita civile & la corotta, la giustitia & la licenza; perche quello ordine solo mantiere quella citta piena di costumi antichi & venerabili. E s'egli auvenisse (che col tempo in ogni modo auverra) que* SAN GIORGIO *tutta quel la citta occupasse, sarrebbe quella una Republica piu dalla* VENETIANA *memorabile.* Della Hist. Florentinè, lib. 8.[10]

[h] T. LIVII, lib. 40. cap. 43.

is a similar, or rather a worse instance,[i] in the more early times of the commonwealth.[12] So depraved in private life were that people, whom in their histories we so much admire. I doubt not but they were really more virtuous during the time of the two *Triumvirates*; when they were tearing their common country to pieces, and spreading slaughter and desolation over the face of the earth, merely for the choice of tyrants.[j][13]

Here, then, is a sufficient inducement to maintain, with the utmost ZEAL, in every free state, those forms and institutions, by which liberty is secured, the public good consulted, and the avarice or ambition of particular men restrained and punished. Nothing does more honour to human nature, than to see it susceptible of so noble a passion; as nothing can be a greater indication of meanness of heart in any man, than to see him destitute of it. A man who loves only himself, without regard to friendship and desert, merits the severest blame; and a man, who is only susceptible of friendship, without public spirit, or a regard to the community, is deficient in the most material part of virtue.

But this is a subject which needs not be longer insisted on at present. There are enow of zealots on both sides who kindle up the passions of their partizans, and under pretence of public good, pursue the interests and ends of their particular faction. For my part, I shall always be more fond of promoting moderation than zeal; though perhaps the surest way of producing moderation in every party is to increase our zeal for the public. Let us therefore try, if it be possible, from the foregoing doctrine, to draw a lesson of moderation with regard to the parties, into which our country is at present divided; at the same time, that we allow not this moderation to abate the industry and passion, with which every individual is bound to pursue the good of his country.

Those who either attack or defend a minister in such a government as ours, where the utmost liberty is allowed, always carry matters to an extreme, and exaggerate his merit or demerit with regard to the public. His enemies are sure to charge him with the greatest enormities, both in domestic and foreign management; and there is no mean-

---

[i] *Id.* lib. 8. cap. 18.
[j] *L'Aigle contre L'Aigle*, ROMAINS *contre* ROMAINS,
Combatans seulement pour le choix de tyrans.
CORNEILLE

ness nor crime, of which, in their account, he is not capable. Unne-
cessary wars, scandalous treaties, profusion of public treasure,
oppressive taxes, every kind of mal-administration is ascribed to him.
To aggravate the charge, his pernicious conduct, it is said, will extend
its baleful influence even to posterity, by undermining the best constitution in the world, and disordering that wise system of laws, institutions, and customs, by which our ancestors, during so many centuries,
have been so happily governed. He is not only a wicked minister
in himself, but has removed every security provided against wicked
ministers for the future.

On the other hand, the partizans of the minister make his panegyric
run as high as the accusation against him, and celebrate his wise,
steady and moderate conduct in every part of his administration. The
honour and interest of the nation supported abroad, public credit
maintained at home, persecution restrained, faction subdued; the
merit of all these blessings is ascribed solely to the minister. At the
same time, he crowns all his other merits by a religious care of the
best constitution in the world, which he has preserved in all its parts,
and has transmitted entire, to be the happiness and security of the
latest posterity.

When this accusation and panegyric are received by the partizans
of each party, no wonder they beget an extraordinary ferment on
both sides, and fill the nation with violent animosities. But I would
fain persuade these party-zealots, that there is a flat contradiction
both in the accusation and panegyric, and that it were impossible
for either of them to run so high, were it not for this contradiction.
If our constitution be really *that noble fabric, the pride of* BRITAIN,
the envy of our neighbours, raised by the labour of so many centuries,
repaired at the expence of so many millions, and cemented by such a
profusion of blood;[k] I say, if our constitution does in any degree
deserve these eulogies, it would never have suffered a wicked and
weak minister to govern triumphantly for a course of twenty years,
when opposed by the greatest geniuses in the nation, who exercised
the utmost liberty of tongue and pen, in parliament, and in their
frequent appeals to the people. But, if the minister be wicked and
weak, to the degree so strenuously insisted on, the constitution
must be faulty in its original principles, and he cannot consistently

[k] *Dissertation on parties*, Letter 10.[14]

be charged with undermining the best constitution in the world. A constitution is only so far good, as it provides a remedy against mal-administration; and if the BRITISH constitution, when in its greatest vigour, and repaired by two such remarkable events, as the *Revolution* and *Accession*, by which our ancient royal family was sacrificed to it;[15] if our constitution, I say, with so great advantages, does not, in fact, provide any such remedy, we are rather beholden to any minister who undermines it, and affords us an opportunity of erecting in its place a better constitution.

I would employ the same topics to moderate the zeal of those who defend the minister. *Is our constitution so excellent?* Then a change of ministry can be no such dreadful event; since it is essential to such a constitution, in every ministry, both to preserve itself from violation, and to prevent all enormities in the administration. *Is our constitution very bad?* Then so extraordinary a jealousy and apprehension, on account of changes, is ill-placed; and a man should no more be anxious in this case, than a husband, who had married a woman from the stews, should be watchful to prevent her infidelity. Public affairs, in such a constitution, must necessarily go to confusion, by whatever hands they are conducted; and the zeal of *patriots* is in that case much less requisite than the patience and submission of *philosophers*. The virtue and good intentions of CATO and BRUTUS are highly laudable; but, to what purpose did their zeal serve? To nothing, but to hasten the fatal period of the ROMAN government, and render its convulsions and dying agonies more violent and painful.[16]

I would not be understood to mean, that public affairs deserve no care and attention at all. Would men be moderate and consistent, their claims might be admitted; at least might be examined. The *country-party* might still assert, that our constitution, though excellent, will admit of mal-administration to a certain degree; and therefore, if the minister be bad, it is proper to oppose him with a *suitable* degree of zeal. And, on the other hand, the *court-party* may be allowed, upon the supposition that the minister were good, to defend, and with *some* zeal too, his administration. I would only persuade men not to con-tend, as if they were fighting *pro aris & focis*,[17] and change a good constitution into a bad one, by the violence of their factions.[18]

I have not here considered any thing that is personal in the present controversy. In the best civil constitution, where every man is restrained by the most rigid laws, it is easy to discover either the good or bad intentions of a minister, and to judge, whether his personal character deserve love or hatred. But such questions are of little importance to the public, and lay those, who employ their pens upon them, under a just suspicion either of malevolence or of flattery.

ESSAY THREE

Of the first principles of government

NOTHING appears more surprizing to those, who consider human affairs with a philosophical eye, than the easiness with which the many are governed by the few; and the implicit submission, with which men resign their own sentiments and passions to those of their rulers. When we enquire by what means this wonder is effected, we shall find, that, as FORCE is always on the side of the governed, the governors have nothing to support them but opinion. It is therefore, on opinion only that government is founded; and this maxim extends to the most despotic and most military governments, as well as to the most free and most popular. The soldan of EGYPT, or the emperor of ROME, might drive his harmless subjects, like brute beasts, against their sentiments and inclination: but he must, at least, have led his *mamalukes*, or *praetorian bands*, like men, by their opinion.[1]

Opinion is of two kinds, to wit, opinion of INTEREST, and opinion of RIGHT. By opinion of interest, I chiefly understand the sense of the general advantage which is reaped from government; together with the persuasion, that the particular government, which is established, is equally advantageous with any other that could easily be settled. When this opinion prevails among the generality of a state, or among those who have the force in their hands, it gives great security to any government.

Right is of two kinds, right to POWER and right to PROPERTY. What prevalence opinion of the first kind has over mankind, may easily be understood, by observing the attachment which all nations have to their ancient government, and even to those names, which have had the sanction of antiquity. Antiquity always begets the opinion of right;

16

and whatever disadvantageous sentiments we may entertain of mankind, they are always found to be prodigal both of blood and treasure in the maintenance of public justice. There is, indeed, no particular, in which, at first sight, there may appear a greater contradiction in the frame of the human mind than the present. When men act in a faction, they are apt, without shame or remorse, to neglect all the ties of honour and morality, in order to serve their party; and yet, when a faction is formed upon a point of right or principle, there is no occasion, where men discover a greater obstinacy, and a more determined sense of justice and equity. The same social disposition of mankind is the cause of these contradictory appearances.

It is sufficiently understood, that the opinion of right to property is of moment in all matters of government. A noted author has made property the foundation of all government; and most of our political writers seem inclined to follow him in that particular.[2] This is carrying the matter too far; but still it must be owned, that the opinion of right to property has a great influence in this subject.

Upon these three opinions, therefore, of public *interest*, of *right to power*, and of *right to property*, are all governments founded, and all authority of the few over the many. There are indeed other principles, which add force to these, and determine, limit, or alter their operation; such as *self-interest, fear*, and *affection*: But still we may assert, that these other principles can have no influence alone, but suppose the antecedent influence of those opinions above-mentioned. They are, therefore, to be esteemed the secondary, not the original principles of government.

For, *first*, as to *self-interest*, by which I mean the expectation of particular rewards, distinct from the general protection which we receive from government, it is evident that the magistrate's authority must be antecedently established, or, at least be hoped for, in order to produce this expectation. The prospect of reward may augment his authority with regard to some particular persons; but can never give birth to it, with regard to the public. Men naturally look for the greatest favours from their friends and acquaintance; and therefore, the hopes of any considerable number of the state would never center in any particular set of men, if these men had no other title to magistracy, and had no separate influence over the opinions of mankind. The same observation may be extended to the other two principles of *fear* and *affection*. No man would have any reason to *fear* the fury of a tyrant, if he had no authority over any but from fear; since, as a single man, his bodily force can reach but a small way, and all the farther power he possesses must be founded either on our own opinion, or on the presumed opinion of others. And though *affection* to wisdom and virtue in a *sovereign* extends very far, and has great influence; yet he must antecedently be supposed invested with a public character, otherwise the public esteem will serve him in no stead, nor will his virtue have any influence beyond a narrow sphere.

A Government may endure for several ages, though the balance of power, and the balance of property do not coincide. This chiefly happens, where any rank or order of the state has acquired a large share in the property; but from the original constitution of the government, has no share in the power. Under what pretence would any individual of that order assume authority in public affairs? As men are commonly much attached to their ancient government, it is not to be expected, that the public would ever favour such usurpations. But where the original constitution allows any share of power, though small, to an order of men, who possess a large share of the property, it is easy for them gradually to stretch their authority, and bring the balance of power to coincide with that of property. This has been the case with the house of commons in ENGLAND.

Most writers, that have treated of the BRITISH government, have supposed, that as the lower house represents all the commons of GREAT BRITAIN, its weight in the scale is proportioned to the property and power of all whom it represents. But this principle must not be received as absolutely true. For though the people are apt to attach themselves more to the house of commons, than to any other member of the constitution; that house being chosen by them as their representatives, and as the public guardians of their liberty; yet are there instances where the house, even when in opposition to the crown, has not been followed by the people; as we may particularly observe of the *tory* house of commons in the reign of king WILLIAM.[3] Were the members obliged to receive instructions from their constituents, like the DUTCH deputies, this would entirely alter the case; and if such immense power and riches, as those of the whole commons of BRITAIN, were brought into the scale, it is not easy to conceive, that the crown could either influence that multitude of people, or withstand that overbalance of property. It is true, the crown has great influence over the collective body of BRITAIN in the elections of members; but were this influence, which at present is only exerted once in seven years,[4] to be employed in bringing over the people to every vote, it would soon be wasted; and no skill, popularity, or revenue, could support it. I must, therefore, be of opinion, that an alteration in this particular would introduce a total alteration in our government, and would soon reduce it to a pure republic; and, perhaps, to a republic of no inconvenient form. For though the people, collected in a body like the ROMAN tribes, be quite unfit for government, yet when dispersed in small bodies, they are more susceptible both of reason and order; the force of popular currents and tides is, in a great measure, broken; and the public interest may be pursued with some method and constancy. But it is needless to reason any farther concerning a form of government, which is never likely to have place in BRITAIN, and which seems not to be the aim of any party amongst us. Let us cherish and improve our ancient government as much as possible, without encouraging a passion for such dangerous novelties.[5]

ESSAY FOUR

Of the origin of government

MAN, born in a family, is compelled to maintain society, from necessity, from natural inclination, and from habit. The same creature, in his farther progress, is engaged to establish political society, in order to administer justice; without which there can be no peace among them, nor safety, nor mutual intercourse. We are, therefore, to look upon all the vast apparatus of our government, as having ultimately no other object or purpose but the distribution of justice, or, in other words, the support of the twelve judges. Kings and parliaments, fleets and armies, officers of the court and revenue, ambassadors, ministers, and privy-counsellors, are all subordinate in their end to this part of administration. Even the clergy, as their duty leads them to inculcate morality, may justly be thought, so far as regards this world, to have no other useful object of their institution.

All men are sensible of the necessity of justice to maintain peace and order; and all men are sensible of the necessity of peace and order for the maintenance of society. Yet, notwithstanding this strong and obvious necessity, such is the frailty or perverseness of our nature! it is impossible to keep men, faithfully and unerringly, in the paths of justice. Some extraordinary circumstances may happen, in which a man finds his interests to be more promoted by fraud or rapine, than hurt by the breach which his injustice makes in the social union. But much more frequently, he is seduced from his great and important, but distant interests, by the allurement of present, though often very frivolous temptations. This great weakness is incurable in human nature.

Men must, therefore, endeavour to palliate what they cannot cure. They must institute some persons, under the appellation of magistrates, whose peculiar office it is, to point out the decrees of equity, to punish transgressors, to correct fraud and violence, and to oblige men, however reluctant, to consult their own real and permanent interests. In a word, OBEDIENCE is a new duty which must be invented to support that of JUSTICE; and the tyes of equity must be corroborated by those of allegiance.

But still, viewing matters in an abstract light, it may be thought, that nothing is gained by this alliance, and that the factitious duty of obedience, from its very nature, lays as feeble a hold of the human mind, as the primitive and natural duty of justice. Peculiar interests and present temptations may overcome the one as well as the other. They are equally exposed to the same inconvenience. And the man, who is inclined to be a bad neighbour, must be led by the same motives, well or ill understood, to be a bad citizen and subject. Not to mention, that the magistrate himself may often be negligent, or partial, or unjust in his administration.

Experience, however, proves, that there is a great difference between the cases. Order in society, we find, is much better maintained by means of government; and our duty to the magistrate is more strictly guarded by the principles of human nature, than our duty to our fellow-citizens. The love of dominion is so strong in the breast of man, that many, not only submit to, but court all the dangers, and fatigues, and cares of government; and men, once raised to that station, though often led astray by private passions, find, in ordinary cases, a visible interest in the impartial administration of justice. The persons, who first attain this distinction by the consent, tacit or express, of the people, must be endowed with superior personal qualities of valour, force, integrity, or prudence, which command respect and confidence: and after government is established, a regard to birth, rank, and station has a mighty influence over men, and enforces the decrees of the magistrate. The prince or leader exclaims against every disorder, which disturbs his society. He summons all his partizans and all men of probity to aid him in correcting and redressing it: and he is readily followed by all indifferent persons in the execution of his office. He soon acquires the power of rewarding these services; and in the progress of society, he establishes subordinate ministers and often a military force, who find an immediate and a visible interest, in supporting his authority. Habit soon consolidates what other principles of human nature had imperfectly founded; and men, once accustomed to obedience, never think of departing from that path, in which they and their ancestors have constantly trod, and to which they are confined by so many urgent and visible motives.

But though this progress of human affairs may appear certain and inevitable, and though the support which allegiance brings to justice, be founded on obvious principles of human nature, it cannot be expected that men should beforehand be able to discover them, or foresee their operation. Government commences more casually and more imperfectly. It is probable, that the first ascendant of one man over multitudes began during a state of war; where the superiority of courage and of genius discovers itself most visibly, where unanimity and concert are most requisite, and where the pernicious effects of disorder are most sensibly felt. The long continuance of that state, an incident common among savage tribes, enured the people to submission; and if the chieftain possessed as much equity as prudence and valour, he became, even during peace, the arbiter of all differences, and could gradually, by a mixture of force and consent, establish his authority. The benefit sensibly felt from his influence, made it be cherished by the people, at least by the peaceable and well disposed among them; and if his son enjoyed the same good qualities, government advanced the sooner to maturity and perfection; but was still in a feeble state, till the farther progress of improvement procured the magistrate a revenue, and enabled him to bestow rewards on the several instruments of his administration, and to inflict punishments on the refractory and disobedient. Before that period, each exertion of his influence must have been particular, and founded on the peculiar circumstances of the case. After it, submission was no longer a matter of choice in the bulk of the community, but was rigorously exacted by the authority of the supreme magistrate.

In all governments, there is a perpetual intestine struggle, open or secret, between AUTHORITY and LIBERTY; and neither of them can ever absolutely prevail in the contest. A great sacrifice of liberty must necessarily be made in every government; yet even the authority, which confines liberty, can never, and perhaps ought never, in any constitution, to become quite entire and uncontroulable. The sultan is master of the life and fortune of any individual; but will not be permitted to impose new taxes on his subjects: a French monarch can impose taxes at pleasure; but would find it dangerous to attempt the lives and fortunes of individuals.[1] Religion also, in most countries, is commonly found to be a very intractable principle; and other principles or prejudices frequently resist all the authority of the civil magistrate; whose power, being founded on opinion, can never subvert other opinions, equally rooted with that of his title to dominion. The government, which, in common appellation, receives the appellation of free, is that which admits of a partition of power among several members, whose united authority is no less, or is commonly greater than that of any monarch; but who, in the usual course of administration, must act by general and equal laws, that are previously known to all the members and to all their subjects. In this sense, it must be owned, that liberty is the perfection of civil society; but still authority must be acknowledged essential to its very existence: and in those contests, which so often take place between the one and the other, the latter may, on that account, challenge the preference. Unless perhaps one may say (and it may be said with some reason) that a circumstance, which is essential to the existence of civil society, must always support itself, and needs be guarded with less jealousy, than one that contributes only to its perfection, which the indolence of men is so apt to neglect, or their ignorance to overlook.

ESSAY FIVE

Of the independency of Parliament[1]

POLITICAL writers have established it as a maxim, that, in contriving any system of government, and fixing the several checks and controuls of the constitution, every man ought to be supposed a *knave*, and to have no other end, in all his actions, but private interest. By this interest we must govern him, and, by means of it, make him co-operate to public good, notwithstanding his insatiable avarice and ambition. Without this, say they, we shall in vain boast of the advantages of any constitution, and shall find, in the end, that we have no security for our liberties or possessions, except the good-will of our rulers; that is, we shall have no security at all.

It is, therefore, a just *political* maxim, *that every man must be supposed a knave:* Though at the same time, it appears somewhat strange, that a maxim should be true in *politics*, which is false in *fact*. But to satisfy us on this head, we may consider, that men are generally more honest in their private than in their public capacity, and will go greater lengths to serve a party, than when their own private interest is alone concerned. Honour is a great check upon mankind: But where a considerable body of men act together, this check is, in a great measure, removed; since a man is sure to be approved of by his own party, for what promotes the common interest; and he soon learns to despise the clamours of adversaries. To which we may add, that every court or senate is determined by the greater number of voices; so that, if self-interest influences only the majority, (as it will always do) the whole senate follows the allurements of this separate interest, and acts as if it contained not one member, who had any regard to public interest and liberty.

When there offers, therefore, to our censure and examination, any plan of government, real or imaginary, where the power is distributed among several courts, and several orders of men, we should always consider the separate interest of each court, and each order; and, if we find, that, by the skillful division of power, this interest must necessarily, in its operation, concur with public, we may pronounce that government to be wise and happy. If, on the contrary, separate interest be not checked, and be not directed to the public, we ought to look for nothing but faction, disorder, and tyranny from such a government. In this opinion I am justified by experience, as well as by the authority of all philosophers and politicians, both ancient and modern.

How much, therefore, would it have surprized such a genius as CICERO, or TACITUS, to have been told, that, in a future age, there should arise a very regular system of *mixed* government, where the authority was so distributed, that one rank, whenever it pleased, might swallow up all the rest, and engross the whole power of the constitution. Such a government, they would say, will not be a mixed government. For so great is the natural ambition of men, that they are never satisfied with power; and if one order of men, by pursuing its own interest, can usurp upon every other order, it will certainly do so, and render itself, as far as possible, absolute and uncontroulable.

But, in this opinion, experience shews they would have been mistaken. For this is actually the case with the BRITISH constitution. The share of power, allotted by our constitution to the house of commons, is so great, that it absolutely commands all the other parts of the government. The king's legislative power is plainly no proper check to it. For though the king has a negative in framing laws; yet this, in fact, is esteemed of so little moment, that whatever is voted by the two houses, is always sure to pass into a law, and the royal assent is little better than a form. The principal weight of the crown lies in the executive power. But besides that the executive power in every government is altogether subordinate to the legislative; besides this, I say, the exercise of this power requires an immense expence; and the commons have assumed to themselves the sole right of granting money. How easy, therefore, would it be for that house to wrest from the crown all these powers, one after another; by making every grant conditional, and choosing their time so well, that their refusal of subsidies should only distress the government, without giving foreign powers any advantage over us? Did the house of commons depend in the same manner on the king, and had none of the members any property but from his gift, would not he command all their resolutions, and be from that moment absolute? As to the house of lords, they are a very powerful support to the crown, so long as they are, in their turn, supported by it; but both experience and reason shew, that they have no force or authority sufficient to maintain themselves alone, without such support.

How, therefore, shall we solve this paradox? And by what means is this member of our constitution confined within the proper limits; since, from our very constitution, it must necessarily have as much power as it demands, and can only be confined by itself? How is this consistent with our experience of human nature? I answer, that the interest of the body is here restrained by that of the individuals, and that the house of commons stretches not its power, because such an usurpation would be contrary to the interest of the majority of its members. The crown has so many offices at its disposal, that, when assisted by the honest and disinterested part of the house, it will always command the resolutions of the whole; so far, at least, as to preserve the ancient constitution from danger. We may, therefore, give to this influence what name we please; we may call it by the invidious appellations of *corruption* and *dependence*; but some degree and some kind of it are inseparable from the very nature of the constitution, and necessary to the preservation of our mixed government.

Instead then of asserting[a] absolutely, that the dependence of parliament, in every degree, is an infringement of BRITISH liberty, the country-party should have made some concessions to their adversaries, and have only examined what was the proper degree of this dependence, beyond which it became dangerous to liberty. But such a moderation is not to be expected in party-men of any kind. After a concession of this nature, all declamation must be abandoned; and a calm enquiry into the proper degree of court-influence and parliamentary dependence would have been expected by the readers. And though the advantage, in such a controversy, might possibly remain to the *country-party*; yet the victory would not be so compleat as they wish for, nor would a true patriot have given an entire loose to his

----

[a] See *Dissertation on Parties*, throughout.[2]

zeal, for fear of running matters into a contrary extreme, by diminishing too[b] far the influence of the crown. It was, therefore, thought best to deny, that this extreme could ever be dangerous to the constitution, or that the crown could ever have too little influence over members of parliament.

All questions concerning the proper medium between extremes are difficult to be decided; both because it is not easy to find *words* proper to fix this medium, and because the good and ill, in such cases, run so gradually into each other, as even to render our *sentiments* doubtful and uncertain. But there is a peculiar difficulty in the present case, which would embarrass the most knowing and most impartial examiner. The power of the crown is always lodged in a single person, either king or minister; and as this person may have either a greater or less degree of ambition, capacity, courage, popularity, or fortune, the power, which is too great in one hand, may become too little in another. In pure republics, where the power is distributed among several assemblies or senates, the checks and controuls are more regular in their operation; because the members of such numerous assemblies may be presumed to be always nearly equal in capacity and virtue; and it is only their number, riches, or authority, which enter into consideration. But a limited monarchy admits not of any such stability; nor is it possible to assign to the crown such a determinate degree of power, as will, in every hand, form a proper counterbalance to the other parts of the constitution. This is an unavoidable disadvantage, among the many advantages, attending that species of government.

---

[b] BY that *influence of the crown*, which I would justify, I mean only that arising from the offices and honours which are at the disposal of the crown. As to private *bribery*, it may be considered in the same light as the practice of employing spies, which is scarcely justifiable in a good minister, and is infamous in a bad one: But to be a spy, or to be corrupted, is always infamous under all ministers, and is to be regarded as a shameless prostitution. POLYBIUS justly esteems the pecuniary influence of the senate and censors to be one of the regular and constitutional weights, which preserved the balance of the ROMAN government. Lib. vi. cap. 15.[3]

ESSAY SIX

Whether the British government inclines more to absolute monarchy, or to a republic

It affords a violent prejudice against almost every science, that no prudent man, however sure of his principles, dares prophesy concerning any event, or foretel the remote consequences of things. A physician will not venture to pronounce concerning the condition of his patient a fortnight or month after: And still less dares a politician foretel the situation of public affairs a few years hence. Harrington thought himself so certain of his general principle, *that the balance of power depends on that of property*, that he ventured to pronounce it impossible ever to re-establish monarchy in England: But his book was scarcely published when the king was restored; and we see, that monarchy has ever since subsisted upon the same footing as before.[1] Notwithstanding this unlucky example, I will venture to examine an important question, *viz. Whether the* British *government inclines more to absolute monarchy, or to a republic; and in which of these two species of government it will most probably terminate?* As there seems not to be any great danger of a sudden revolution either way, I shall at least escape the shame attending my temerity, if I should be found to have been mistaken.

Those who assert, that the balance of our government inclines towards absolute monarchy, may support their opinion by the following reasons. That property has a great influence on power cannot possibly be denied; but yet the general maxim, *that the balance of one depends on the balance of the other*, must be received with several limitations. It is evident, that much less property in a single hand will be able to counterbalance a greater property in several; not only because it is difficult to make many persons combine in the same

28

views and measures; but because property, when united, causes much greater dependence, than the same property, when dispersed. A hundred persons, of 1000 *l.* a year a-piece, can consume all their income, and no body shall ever be the better for them, except their servants and tradesmen, who justly regard their profits as the product of their own labour. But a man possessed of 100,000 *l.* a year, if he has either any generosity or any cunning, may create a great dependence by obligations, and still a greater by expectations. Hence we may observe, that, in all free governments, any subject exorbitantly rich has always created jealousy, even though his riches bore no proportion to those of the state. CRASSUS's fortune, if I remember well, amounted only to about sixteen hundred thousand pounds in our money; and yet we find, that, though his genius was nothing extraordinary, he was able, by means of his riches alone, to counterbalance, during his lifetime, the power of POMPEY as well as that of CAESAR, who afterwards became master of the world. The wealth of the MEDICI made them masters of FLORENCE; though, it is probable, it was not considerable, compared to the united property of that opulent republic.[2]

These considerations are apt to make one entertain a magnificent idea of the BRITISH spirit and love of liberty; since we could maintain our free government, during so many centuries, against our sovereigns, who, besides the power and dignity and majesty of the crown, have always been possessed of much more property than any subject has ever enjoyed in any commonwealth. But it may be said, that this spirit, however great, will never be able to support itself against that immense property, which is now lodged in the king, and which is still encreasing. Upon a moderate computation, there are near three millions at the disposal of the crown. The civil list amounts to near a million; the collection of all taxes to another; and the employments in the army and navy, together with ecclesiastical preferments, to above a third million: An enormous sum, and what may fairly be computed to be more than a thirtieth part of the whole income and labour of the kingdom. When we add to this great property, the encreasing luxury of the nation, our proneness to corruption, together with the great power and prerogatives of the crown, and the command of military force, there is no one but must despair of being able, without extraordinary efforts, to support our free government much longer under these disadvantages.

On the other hand, those who maintain, that the byass of the BRITISH government leans towards a republic, may support their opinion by specious arguments. It may be said, that, though this immense property in the crown, be joined to the dignity of first magistrate, and to many other legal powers and prerogatives, which should naturally give it greater influence; yet it really becomes less dangerous to liberty upon that very account. Were BRITAIN a republic, and were any private man possessed of a revenue, a third, or even a tenth part as large as that of the crown, he would very justly excite jealousy; because he would infallibly have great authority in the government: And such an irregular authority, not avowed by the laws, is always more dangerous than a much greater authority, derived from them. A man, possessed of usurped power, can set no bounds to his pretensions: His partizans have liberty to hope for every thing in his favour: His enemies provoke his ambition, with his fears, by the violence of their opposition: And the government being thrown into a ferment, every corrupted humour in the state naturally gathers to him. On the contrary, a legal authority, though great, has always some bounds, which terminate both the hopes and pretensions of the person possessed of it: The laws must have provided a remedy against its excesses: Such an eminent magistrate has much to fear, and little to hope from his usurpations: And as his legal authority is quietly submitted to, he has small temptation and small opportunity of extending it farther. Besides, it happens, with regard to ambitious aims and projects, what may be observed with regard to sects of philosophy and religion. A new sect excites such a ferment, and is both opposed and defended with such vehemence, that it spreads always faster, and multiplies its partizans with greater rapidity, than any old established opinion, recommended by the sanction of the laws and of antiquity. Such is the nature of novelty, that, where any thing pleases, it becomes doubly agreeable, if new; but if it displeases, it is doubly displeasing, upon that very account. And, in most cases, the violence of enemies is favourable to ambitious projects, as well as the zeal of partizans.

It may further be said, that, though men be much governed by interest; yet even interest itself, and all human affairs, are entirely governed by *opinion*. Now, there has been a sudden and sensible change in the opinions of men within these last fifty years, by the progress of learning and of liberty. Most people, in this island, have divested themselves of all superstitious reverence to names and authority: The clergy have much lost their credit: Their pretensions and doctrines have been ridiculed; and even religion can scarcely support itself in the world. The mere name of *king* commands little respect; and to talk of a king as GOD's viceregent on earth, or to give him any of those magnificent titles, which formerly dazzled mankind, would but excite laughter in every one. Though the crown, by means of its large revenue, may maintain its authority in times of tranquillity, upon private interest and influence; yet, as the least shock or convulsion must break all these interests to pieces, the royal power, being no longer supported by the settled principles and opinions of men, will immediately dissolve. Had men been in the same disposition at the *revolution*, as they are at present, monarchy would have run a great risque of being entirely lost in this island.

Durst I venture to deliver my own sentiments amidst these opposite arguments, I would assert, that, unless there happen some extraordinary convulsion, the power of the crown, by means of its large revenue, is rather upon the encrease; though, at the same time I own, that its progress seems very slow, and almost insensible. The tide has run long, and with some rapidity, to the side of popular government, and is just beginning to turn towards monarchy.

It is well known, that every government must come to a period, and that death is unavoidable to the political as well as to the animal body. But, as one kind of death may be preferable to another, it may be enquired, whether it be more desirable for the BRITISH constitution to terminate in a popular government, or in absolute monarchy? Here I would frankly declare, that, though liberty be preferable to slavery, in almost every case; yet I should rather wish to see an absolute monarch than a republic in this island. For, let us consider, what kind of republic we have reason to expect. The question is not concerning any fine imaginary republic, of which a man may form a plan in his closet. There is no doubt, but a popular government may be imagined more perfect than absolute monarchy, or even than our present constitution. But what reason have we to expect that any such government will ever be established in BRITAIN, upon the dissolution of our monarchy? If any single person acquire power enough to take our constitution to pieces, and put it up a-new, he is really an absolute monarch; and we have already had an instance of this kind, sufficient to convince us, that such a person will never resign his power, or establish any free government.[3] Matters, therefore, must be trusted to their natural progress and operation; and the house of commons, according to its present constitution, must be the only legislature in such a popular government. The inconveniencies attending such a situation of affairs, present themselves by the thousands. If the house of commons, in such a case, ever dissolve itself, which is not to be expected, we may look for a civil war every election. If it continue itself, we shall suffer all the tyranny of a faction, subdivided into new factions. And, as such a violent government cannot long subsist, we shall, at last, after many convulsions, and civil wars, find repose in absolute monarchy, which it would have been happier for us to have established peaceably from the beginning. Absolute monarchy, therefore, is the easiest death, the true *Euthanasia* of the BRITISH constitution.

Thus, if we have reason to be more jealous of monarchy, because the danger is more imminent from that quarter; we have also reason to be more jealous of popular government, because that danger is more terrible. This may teach us a lesson of moderation in all our political controversies.

ESSAY SEVEN

Of parties in general

OF all men, that distinguish themselves by memorable atchievements, the first place of honour seems due to LEGISLATORS and founders of states, who transmit a system of laws and institutions to secure the peace, happiness, and liberty of future generations. The influence of useful inventions in the arts and sciences may, perhaps, extend farther than that of wise laws, whose effects are limited both in time and place; but the benefit arising from the former, is not so sensible as that which results from the latter. Speculative sciences do, indeed, improve the mind; but this advantage reaches only to a few persons, who have leisure to apply themselves to them. And as to practical arts, which encrease the commodities and enjoyments of life, it is well known, that men's happiness consists not so much in an abundance of these, as in the peace and security with which they possess them; and those blessings can only be derived from good government. Not to mention, that general virtue and good morals in a state, which are so requisite to happiness, can never arise from the most refined precepts of philosophy, or even the severest injunctions of religion; but must proceed entirely from the virtuous education of youth, the effect of wise laws and institutions. I must, therefore, presume to differ from Lord BACON in this particular, and must regard antiquity as somewhat unjust in its distribution of honours, when it made gods of all the inventors of useful arts, such as CERES, BACCHUS, AESCULA-PIUS; and dignified legislators, such as ROMULUS and THESEUS, only with the appellation of demigods and heroes.[1]

As much as legislators and founders of states ought to be honoured and respected among men, as much ought the founders of sects and factions to be detested and hated; because the influence of faction is directly contrary to that of laws. Factions subvert government, render laws impotent, and beget the fiercest animosities among men of the same nation, who ought to give mutual assistance and protection to each other. And what should render the founders of parties more odious is, the difficulty of extirpating these weeds, when once they have taken root in any state. They naturally propagate themselves for many centuries, and seldom end but by the total dissolution of that government, in which they are sown. They are, besides, plants which grow most plentifully in the richest soil; and though absolute governments be not entirely free from them, it must be confessed, that they rise more easily, and propagate themselves faster in free governments, where they always infect the legislature itself, which alone could be able, by the steady application of rewards and punishments, to eradicate them.

Factions may be divided into PERSONAL and REAL; that is, into factions, founded on personal friendship or animosity among such as compose the contending parties, and into those founded on some real difference of sentiment or interest. The reason of this distinction is obvious; though I must acknowledge, that parties are seldom found pure and unmixed, either of the one kind or the other. It is not often seen, that a government divides into factions, where there is no difference in the views of the constituent members, either real or apparent, trivial or material: And in those factions, which are founded on the most real and most material difference, there is always observed a great deal of personal animosity or affection. But notwithstanding this mixture, a party may be denominated either personal or real, according to that principle which is predominant, and is found to have the greatest influence.

Personal factions arise most easily in small republics. Every domestic quarrel, there, becomes an affair of state. Love, vanity, emulation, any passion, as well as ambition and resentment, begets public division. The NERI and BIANCHI of FLORENCE, the FREGOSI and ADORNI of GENOA, the COLONESI and ORSINI of modern ROME, were parties of this kind.[2]

Men have such a propensity to divide into personal factions, that the smallest appearance of real difference will produce them. What can be imagined more trivial than the difference between one colour of livery and another in horse races? Yet this difference begat two

most inveterate factions in the GREEK empire, the PRASINI and
VENETI, who never suspended their animosities, till they ruined that
unhappy government.[3]

We find in the ROMAN history a remarkable dissension between
two tribes, the POLLIA and PAPIRIA, which continued for the space
of near three hundred years, and discovered itself in their suffrages
at every election of magistrates.[a] This faction was the more remarkable, as it could continue for so long a tract of time; even though it
did not spread itself, nor draw any of the other tribes into a share of
the quarrel. If mankind had not a strong propensity to such divisions,
the indifference of the rest of the community must have suppressed
this foolish animosity, that had not any aliment of new benefits and
injuries, of general sympathy and antipathy, which never fail to take
place, when the whole state is rent into two equal factions.[5]

Nothing is more usual than to see parties, which have begun upon
a real difference, continue even after that difference is lost. When
men are once inlisted on opposite sides, they contract an affection to
the persons with whom they are united, and an animosity against
their antagonists: And these passions they often transmit to their
posterity. The real difference betwee GUELF and GHIBBELLINE was
long lost in ITALY, before these factions were extinguished. The
GUELFS adhered to the pope, the GHIBBELLINES to the emperor; and
yet the family of SFORZA, who were in alliance with the emperor,
though they were GUELFS, being expelled MILAN by the king[b] of
FRANCE, assisted by JACOMO TRIVULZIO and the GHIBBELLINES, the
pope concurred with the latter, and they formed leagues with the
pope against the emperor.[6]

The civil wars which arose some few years ago in MOROCCO,
between the *blacks* and *whites*, merely on account of their complexion,

---

[a] As this fact has not been much observed by antiquaries or politicians, I shall deliver
it in the words of the ROMAN historian. *Populus* TUSCULANUS *cum conjugibus ac* liberis
ROMAM venit: Ea multitudo, veste mutata, & specie reorum tribus circuit, genibus se
omnium advolvens. Plus itaque misericordia ad poenae veniam impetrandam, quam
causa ad crimen purgandum valuit. Tribus omnes praeter POLLIAM, antiquarunt
legem. POLLIAE sententia fuit, puberes verberatos necari, liberos conjugesque sub
corona lege belli venire: Memoriamque ejus irae TUSCULANIS in poenae tam atrocis
auctores mansisse ad patris aetatem constat; nec quemquam fere ex POLLIA tribu
candidatum PAPIRAM ferre solitam, T. LIVII, lib. 8. The CASTELANI and NICOLLOTI
are two mobbish factions in VENICE, who frequently box together, and then lay aside
their quarrels presently.[4]
[b] Lewis XII.

are founded on a pleasant difference. We laugh at them; but I believe, were things rightly examined, we afford much more occasion of ridicule to the MOORS. For, what are all the wars of religion, which have prevailed in this polite and knowing part of the world? They are certainly more absurd than the MOORISH civil wars. The difference of complexion is a sensible and a real difference: But the controversy about an article of faith, which is utterly absurd and unintelligible, is not a difference in sentiment, but in a few phrases and expressions, which one party accepts of, without understanding them; and the other refuses in the same manner.[7]

Real factions may be divided into those from *interest*, from *principle*, and from *affection*. Of all factions, the first are the most reasonable, and the most excusable. Where two orders of men, such as the nobles and people, have a distinct authority in a government, not very accurately balanced and modelled, they naturally follow a distinct interest; nor can we reasonably expect a different conduct, considering that degree of selfishness implanted in human nature. It requires great skill in a legislator to prevent such parties; and many philosophers are of opinion, that this secret, like the *grand elixir*,[8] or *perpetual motion*, may amuse men in theory, but can never possibly be reduced to practice. In despotic governments, indeed, factions often do not appear; but they are not the less real; or rather, they are more real and more pernicious, upon that very account. The distinct orders of men, nobles and people, soldiers and merchants, have all a distinct interest; but the more powerful oppresses the weaker with impunity, and without resistance; which begets a seeming tranquillity in such governments.

There has been an attempt in ENGLAND to divide the *landed* and *trading* part of the nation; but without success. The interest of these two bodies are not really distinct, and never will be so, till our public debts encrease to such a degree, as to become altogether oppressive and intolerable.

Parties from *principle*, especially abstract speculative principle, are known only to modern times, and are, perhaps, the most extraordinary and unaccountable *phaenomenon*, that has yet appeared in human affairs. Where different principles beget a contrariety of conduct, which is the case with all different political principles, the matter may be more easily explained. A man, who esteems the true right of government to lie in one man, or one family, cannot easily agree with his fellow citizen, who thinks that another man or family is possessed of this right. Each naturally wishes that right may take place, according to his own notions of it. But where the difference of principle is attended with no contrariety of action, but every one may follow his own way, without interfering with his neighbour, as happens in all religious controversies; what madness, what fury can beget such unhappy and such fatal divisions?

Two men, travelling on the highway, the one east, the other west, can easily pass each other, if the way be broad enough: But two men, reasoning upon opposite principles of religion, cannot so easily pass, without shocking; though one should think, that the way were also, in that case, sufficiently broad, and that each might proceed, without interruption, in his own course. But such is the nature of the human mind, that it always lays hold on every mind that approaches it; and as it is wonderfully fortified by an unanimity of sentiments, so is it shocked and disturbed by any contrariety. Hence the eagerness, which most people discover in a dispute; and hence their impatience of opposition, even in the most speculative and indifferent opinions.

This principle, however frivolous it may appear, seems to have been the origin of all religious wars and divisions. But as this principle is universal in human nature, its effects would not have been confined to one age, and to one sect of religion, did it not there concur with other more accidental causes, which raise it to such a height, as to produce the greatest misery and devastation. Most religions of the ancient world arose in the unknown ages of government, when men were as yet barbarous and uninstructed, and the prince, as well as peasant, was disposed to receive, with implicit faith, every pious tale or fiction, which was offered him. The magistrate embraced the religion of the people, and entering cordially into the care of sacred matters, naturally acquired an authority in them, and united the ecclesiastical with the civil power. But the *Christian* religion arising, while principles directly opposite to it were firmly established in the polite part of the world, who despised the nation that first broached this novelty; no wonder, that, in such circumstances, it was but little countenanced by the civil magistrate, and that the priesthood was allowed to engross all the authority in the new sect. So bad a use did they make of this power, even in those early times, that the primitive ersecutions may, perhaps, *in part*,[c] be ascribed to the violence instilled by them into their followers. And the same principles of priestly government continuing, after Christianity became the established religion, they have engendered a spirit of persecution, which has ever since been the poison of human society, and the source of the most inveterate factions in every government. Such divisions, therefore, on the part of the people, may justly be esteemed factions of *principle*; but, on the part of the priests, who are the prime movers, they are really factions of *interest*.

There is another cause (beside the authority of the priests, and the separation of the ecclesiastical and civil powers) which has contributed to render CHRISTENDOM the scene of religious wars and divisions. Religions, that arise in ages totally ignorant and barbarous, consist mostly of traditional tales and fictions, which may be different in every sect, without being contrary to each other; and even when they are contrary, every one adheres to the tradition of his own sect, without much reasoning or disputation. But as philosophy was widely spread over the world, at the time when Christianity arose, the teachers of the new sect were obliged to form a system of speculative opinions; to divide, with some accuracy, their articles of faith; and to explain, comment, confute, and defend with all the subtilty of argument and science. Hence naturally arose keenness in dispute, when the Christian religion came to be split into new divisions and heresies: And this keenness assisted the priests in their policy, of begetting a

---

[c] I SAY, *in part*; For it is a vulgar error to imagine, that the ancients were as great friends to toleration as the ENGLISH or DUTCH are at present. The laws against external superstition, amongst the ROMANS, were as ancient as the time of the twelve tables; and the JEWS as well as CHRISTIANS were sometimes punished by them; though, in general, these laws were not rigorously executed. Immediately after the conquest of GAUL, they forbad all but the natives to be initiated into the religion of the DRUIDS; and this was a kind of persecution. In about a century after this conquest, the emperor, CLAUDIUS, quite abolished that superstition by penal laws; which would have been a very grievous persecution, if the imitation of the ROMAN manners had not, before-hand, weaned the GAULS from their ancient prejudices. SUETONIUS in *vita* CLAUDII. PLINY ascribes the abolition of the Druid superstitions to TIBERIUS, probably because that emperor had taken some steps towards restraining them (lib. xxx. cap. i.). This is an instance of the usual caution and moderation of the ROMANS in such cases; and very different from their violent and sanguinary method of treating the *Christians*. Hence we may entertain a suspicion, that those furious persecutions of *Christianity* were, in some measure, owing to the imprudent zeal and bigotry of the first propagators of that sect; and Ecclesiastical history affords us many reasons to confirm this suspicion.[9]

mutual hatred and antipathy among their deluded followers. Sects of philosophy, in the ancient world, were more zealous than parties of religion; but in modern times, parties of religion are more furious and enraged than the most cruel factions that ever arose from interest and ambition.

I have mentioned parties from *affection* as a kind of *real* parties, beside those from *interest* and *principle*. By parties from affection, I understand those which are founded on the different attachments of men towards particular families and persons, whom they desire to rule over them. These factions are often very violent; though, I must own, it may seem unaccountable, that men should attach themselves so strongly to persons, with whom they are no wise acquainted, whom perhaps they never saw, and from whom they never received, nor can ever hope for any favour. Yet this we often find to be the case, and even with men, who, on other occasions, discover no great generosity of spirit, nor are found to be easily transported by friendship beyond their own interest. We are apt to think the relation between us and our sovereign very close and intimate. The splendor of majesty and power bestows an importance on the fortunes even of a single person. And when a man's good-nature does not give him this imaginary interest, his ill-nature will, from spite and opposition to persons whose sentiments are different from his own.

ESSAY EIGHT

Of the parties of Great Britain

Were the British government proposed as a subject of speculation, one would immediately perceive in it a source of division and party, which it would be almost impossible for it, under any administration, to avoid. The just balance between the republican and monarchical part of our constitution is really, in itself, so extremely delicate and uncertain, that, when joined to men's passions and prejudices, it is impossible but different opinions must arise concerning it, even among persons of the best understanding. Those of mild tempers, who love peace and order, and detest sedition and civil wars, will always entertain more favourable sentiments of monarchy, than men of bold and generous spirits, who are passionate lovers of liberty, and think no evil comparable to subjection and slavery. And though all reasonable men agree in general to preserve our mixed government; yet, when they come to particulars, some will incline to trust larger powers to the crown, to bestow on it more influence, and to guard against its encroachments with less caution, than others who are terrified at the most distant approaches of tyranny and despotic power. Thus are there parties of PRINCIPLE involved in the very nature of our constitution, which may properly enough be denominated those of COURT and COUNTRY. The strength and violence of each of these parties will much depend upon the particular administration. An administration may be so bad, as to throw a great majority into the opposition; as a good administration will reconcile to the court many of the most passionate lovers of liberty. But however the nation may fluctuate between them, the parties themselves will always subsist, so long as we are governed by a limited monarchy.

But, besides this difference of *Principle*, those parties are very much fomented by a difference of INTEREST, without which they could scarcely ever be dangerous or violent. The crown will naturally bestow all trust and power upon those, whose principles, real or pretended, are most favourable to monarchical government; and this temptation will naturally engage them to go greater lengths than their principles would otherwise carry them. Their antagonists, who are disappointed in their ambitious aims, throw themselves into the party whose sentiments incline them to be most jealous of royal power, and naturally carry those sentiments to a greater height than sound politics will justify. Thus *Court* and *Country*, which are the genuine offspring of the BRITISH government, are a kind of mixed parties, and are influenced both by principle and by interest. The heads of the factions are commonly most governed by the latter motive; the inferior members of them by the former.

As to ecclesiastical parties, we may observe, that, in all ages of the world, priests have been enemies to liberty; and it is certain, that this steady conduct of theirs must have been founded on fixed reasons of interest and ambition. Liberty of thinking, and of expressing our thoughts, is always fatal to priestly power, and to those pious frauds, on which it is commonly founded; and, by an infallible connexion, which prevails among all kinds of liberty, this privilege can never be enjoyed, at least, has never yet been enjoyed, but in a free government. Hence it must happen, in such a constitution as that of BRITAIN, that the established clergy, while things are in their natural situation, will always be of the *Court*-party; as, on the contrary, dissenters of all kinds will be of the *Country*-party; since they can never hope for that toleration, which they stand in need of, but by means of our free government. All princes, that have aimed at despotic power, have known of what importance it was to gain the established clergy: As the clergy, on their side, have shewn a great facility of entering into the views of such princes.[a] GUSTAVUS VAZA was, perhaps, the only ambitious monarch, that ever depressed the church, at the same time that he discouraged liberty. But the exorbitant power of the bishops in SWEDEN, who, at that time, overtopped the crown

[a] Judaei sibi ipsi reges imposuere; qui mobilitate vulgi expulsi, resumpta per arma dominatione; fugas civium, urbium eversiones, fratrum, conjugum, parentum neces, aliaque solita regibus ausi, superstitionem fovebant; quia honor sacerdotii firmamentum potentiae assumebatur. TACIT. *hist. lib.* v.[1]

itself, together with their attachment to a foreign family, was the reason of his embracing such an unusual system of politics.[2]

This observation, concerning the propensity of priests to the government of a single person, is not true with regard to one sect only. The *Presbyterian* and *Calvinistic* clergy in HOLLAND were professed friends to the family of ORANGE; as the *Arminians*, who were esteemed heretics, were of the LOUVESTEIN faction, and zealous for liberty.[3] But if a prince has the choice of both, it is easy to see, that he will prefer the episcopal to the presbyterian form of government, both because of the greater affinity between monarchy and episcopacy, and because of the facility, which a prince finds, in such a government, of ruling the clergy, by means of their ecclesiastical superiors.[b]

If we consider the first rise of parties in ENGLAND, during the great rebellion, we shall find, that it was conformable to this general theory, and that the species of government gave birth to them, by a regular and infallible operation. The ENGLISH constitution, before that time, had lain in a kind of confusion; yet so, as that the subjects possessed many noble privileges, which, though not exactly bounded and secured by law, were universally deemed, from long possession, to belong to them as their birth-right. An ambitious, or rather a misguided, prince arose, who deemed all these privileges to be concessions of his predecessors, revokeable at pleasure; and, in prosecution of this principle, he openly acted in violation of liberty, during the course of several years. Necessity, at last, constrained him to call a parliament: The spirit of liberty arose and spread itself: The prince, being without any support, was obliged to grant every thing required of him: And his enemies, jealous and implacable, set no bounds to their pretensions. Here then began those contests, in which it was no wonder, that men of that age were divided into different parties; since, even at this day, the impartial are at a loss to decide concerning the justice of the quarrel. The pretensions of the parliament, if yielded to, broke the balance of the constitution, by rendering the government almost entirely republican. If not yielded to, the nation was, perhaps, still in danger of absolute power, from the settled principles and inveterate habits of the king, which had plainly appeared

[b] Populi imperium juxta libertatem; paucorum dominatio regiae libidini proprior est. TACIT. *Ann. lib.* vi.[4]

42

in every concession that he had been constrained to make to his people. In this question, so delicate and uncertain, men naturally fell to the side which was most conformable to their usual principles; and the more passionate favourers of monarchy declared for the king, as the zealous friends of liberty sided with the parliament. The hopes of success being nearly equal on both sides, *interest* had no general influence in this contest: So that ROUND-HEAD and CAVALIER were merely parties of principle; neither of which disowned either monarchy or liberty; but the former party inclined most to the republican part of our government, the latter to the monarchical. In this respect, they may be considered as court and country-party, enflamed into a civil war, by an unhappy concurrence of circumstances, and by the turbulent spirit of the age. The commonwealth's men, and the partizans of absolute power, lay concealed in both parties, and formed but an inconsiderable part of them.[5]

The clergy had concurred with the king's arbitrary designs; and, in return, were allowed to persecute their adversaries, whom they called heretics and schismatics. The established clergy were episcopal; the non-conformists presbyterian: So that all things concurred to throw the former, without reserve, into the king's party; and the latter into that of the parliament.[6]

Every one knows the event of this quarrel; fatal to the king first, to the parliament afterwards. After many confusions and revolutions, the royal family was at last restored, and the ancient government re-established. CHARLES II was not made wiser by the example of his father; but prosecuted the same measures, though at first, with more secrecy and caution. New parties arose, under the appellation of *Whig* and *Tory*, which have continued ever since to confound and distract our government.[7] To determine the nature of these parties is, perhaps, one of the most difficult problems, that can be met with, and is a proof that history may contain questions, as uncertain as any to be found in the most abstract sciences.[8] We have seen the conduct of the two parties, during the course of seventy years, in a vast variety of circumstances, possessed of power, and deprived of it, during peace, and during war: Persons, who profess themselves of one side or other, we meet with every hour, in company, in our pleasures, in our serious occupations: We ourselves are constrained, in a manner, to take party; and living in a country of the highest liberty, every one may openly declare all his sentiments and opinions: Yet are we at a loss to tell the nature, pretensions, and principles of the different factions.

When we compare the parties of WHIG and TORY, to those of ROUND-HEAD and CAVALIER, the most obvious difference, that appears between them, consists in the principles of *passive obedience*, and *indefeasible right*, which were but little heard of among the CAVALIERS, but became the universal doctrine, and were esteemed the true characteristic of a TORY. Were these principles pushed into their most obvious consequences, they imply a formal renunciation of all our liberties, and an avowal of absolute monarchy; since nothing can be a greater absurdity than a limited power, which must not be resisted, even when it exceeds its limitations. But as the most rational principles are often but a weak counterpoise to passion; it is no wonder that these absurd principles[9] were found too weak for that effect. The TORIES, as men, were enemies to oppression; and also as ENGLISHMEN, they were enemies to arbitrary power. Their zeal for liberty was, perhaps, less fervent than that of their antagonists; but was sufficient to make them forget all their general principles, when they saw themselves openly threatened with a subversion of the ancient government. From these sentiments arose the *revolution*; an event of mighty consequence, and the firmest foundation of BRITISH liberty. The conduct of the TORIES, during that event, and after it, will afford us a true insight into the nature of that party.

In the *first* place, they appear to have had the genuine sentiments of BRITONS in their affection for liberty, and in their determined resolution not to sacrifice it to any abstract principle whatsoever, or to any imaginary rights of princes. This part of their character might justly have been doubted of before the *revolution*, from the obvious tendency of their avowed principles, and from their compliances with a court, which seemed to make little secret of its arbitrary designs. The *revolution* shewed them to have been, in this respect, nothing, but a genuine *court-party*, such as might be expected in a BRITISH government: That is, *Lovers of liberty, but greater lovers of monarchy*. It must, however, be confessed, that they carried their monarchical principles farther, even in practice, but more so in theory, than was, in any degree, consistent with a limited government.

Secondly, Neither their principles nor affections concurred, entirely or heartily, with the settlement made at the *revolution*, or with that which has since taken place. This part of their character may seem opposite to the former; since any other settlement, in those circumstances of the nation, must probably have been dangerous, if not fatal to liberty. But the heart of man is made to reconcile contradictions; and this contradiction is not greater than that between *passive obedience*, and the *resistance* employed at the *revolution*. A TORY, therefore, since the *revolution*, may be defined in a few words, to be *a lover of monarchy, though without abandoning liberty; and a partizan of the family of* STUART. As a WHIG may be defined to be *a lover of liberty though without renouncing monarchy; and a friend to the settlement in the* PROTESTANT *line*.

These different views, with regard to the settlement of the crown, were accidental, but natural additions to the principles of the *court* and *country* parties, which are the genuine divisions in the BRITISH government. A passionate lover of monarchy is apt to be displeased at any change of the succession; as favouring too much of a commonwealth: A passionate lover of liberty is apt to think that every part of the government ought to be subordinate to the interests of liberty.

Some, who will not venture to assert, that the *real* difference between WHIG and TORY was lost at the *revolution*, seem inclined to think, that the difference is now abolished, and that affairs are so far returned to their natural state, that there are at present no other parties among us but *court* and *country*; that is, men, who by interest or principle, are attached either to monarchy or liberty. The TORIES have been so long obliged to talk in the republican stile, that they seem to have made converts of themselves by their hypocrisy, and to have embraced the sentiments, as well as language of their adversaries. There are, however, very considerable remains of that party in ENGLAND, with all their old prejudices; and a proof that *court* and *country* are not our only parties, is, that almost all the dissenters side with the court, and the lower clergy, at least, of the church of ENGLAND, with the opposition. This may convince us, that some biass still hangs upon our constitution, some extrinsic weight, which turns it from its natural course, and causes a confusion in our parties.[c10]

---

[c] Some of the opinions delivered in these Essays, with regard to the public transactions in the last century, the Author, on more accurate examination, found reason to retract in his *History of* GREAT BRITAIN. And as he would not enslave himself to the systems of either party, neither would he fetter his judgment by his own preconceived opinions and principles; nor is he ashamed to acknowledge his mistakes. These mistakes were indeed, at that time, almost universal in this kingdom.

Of superstition and enthusiasm

THAT *the corruption of the best things produces the worst*, is grown into a maxim, and is commonly proved, among other instances, by the pernicious effects of *superstition* and *enthusiasm*, the corruptions of true religion.

These two species of false religion, though both pernicious, are yet of a very different, and even of a contrary nature. The mind of man is subject to certain unaccountable terrors and apprehensions, proceeding either from the unhappy situation of private or public affairs, from ill health, from a gloomy and melancholy disposition, or from the concurrence of all these circumstances. In such a state of mind, infinite unknown evils are dreaded from unknown agents; and where real objects of terror are wanting, the soul, active to its own prejudice, and fostering its predominant inclination, finds imaginary ones, to whose power and malevolence it sets no limits. As these enemies are entirely invisible and unknown, the methods taken to appease them are equally unaccountable, and consist in ceremonies, observances, mortifications, sacrifices, presents, or in any practice, however absurd or frivolous, which either folly or knavery recommends to a blind and terrified credulity. Weakness, fear, melancholy, together with ignorance, are, therefore, the true sources of SUPERSTITION.

But the mind of man is also subject to an unaccountable elevation and presumption, arising from prosperous success, from luxuriant health, from strong spirits, or from a bold and confident disposition. In such a state of mind, the imagination swells with great, but confused conceptions, to which no sublunary beauties or enjoyments can

46

correspond. Every thing mortal and perishable vanishes as unworthy of attention. And a full range is given to the fancy in the invisible regions or world of spirits, where the soul is at liberty to indulge itself in every imagination, which may best suit its present taste and disposition. Hence arise raptures, transports, and surprising flights of fancy; and confidence and presumption still encreasing, these raptures, being altogether unaccountable, and seeming quite beyond the reach of our ordinary faculties, are attributed to the immediate inspiration of that Divine Being, who is the object of devotion. In a little time, the inspired person comes to regard himself as a distinguished favourite of the Divinity; and when this frenzy once takes place, which is the summit of enthusiasm, every whimsy is consecrated: Human reason, and even morality are rejected as fallacious guides: And the fanatic madman delivers himself over, blindly, and without reserve, to the supposed illapses of the spirit, and to inspiration from above. Hope, pride, presumption, a warm imagination, together with ignorance, are, therefore, the true sources of ENTHUSIASM.

These two species of false religion might afford occasion to many speculations; but I shall confine myself, at present, to a few reflections concerning their different influence on government and society.

My first reflection is, *That superstition is favourable to priestly power, and enthusiasm not less or rather more contrary to it, than sound reason and philosophy.* As superstition is founded on fear, sorrow, and a depression of spirits, it represents the man to himself in such despicable colours, that he appears unworthy, in his own eyes, of approaching the divine presence, and naturally has recourse to any other person, whose sanctity of life, or, perhaps, impudence and cunning, have made him be supposed more favoured by the Divinity. To him the superstitious entrust their devotions: To his care they recommend their prayers, petitions, and sacrifices: And by his means, they hope to render their addresses acceptable to their incensed Deity. Hence the origin of PRIESTS, who may justly be regarded as an invention of a timorous and abject superstition, which, ever diffident of itself, dares not offer up its own devotions, but ignorantly thinks to recommend itself to the Divinity, by the mediation of his supposed friends and servants. As superstition is a considerable ingredient in almost all religions, even the most fanatical; there being nothing but philosophy able entirely to conquer these unaccountable terrors; hence it proceeds, that in almost every sect of religion there are priests to be found: But the stronger mixture there is of superstition, the higher is the authority of the priesthood.

On the other hand, it may be observed, that all enthusiasts have been free from the yoke of ecclesiastics, and have expressed great independence in their devotion; with a contempt of forms, ceremonies, and traditions. The *quakers* are the most egregious, though, at the same time, the most innocent enthusiasts that have yet been known; and are, perhaps, the only sect, that have never admitted priests amongst them. The *independents*, of all the ENGLISH sectaries, approach nearest to the *quakers* in fanaticism, and in their freedom from priestly bondage. The *presbyterians* follow after, at an equal distance in both particulars.[1] In short, this observation is founded in experience; and will also appear to be founded in reason, if we consider, that, as enthusiasm arises from a presumptuous pride and confidence, it thinks itself sufficiently qualified to *approach* the Divinity, without any human mediator. Its rapturous devotions are so fervent, that it even imagines itself *actually* to *approach* him by the way of contemplation and inward converse; which makes it neglect all those outward ceremonies and observances, to which the assistance of the priests appears so requisite in the eyes of their superstitious votaries. The fanatic consecrates himself, and bestows on his own person a sacred character, much superior to what forms and ceremonious institutions can confer on any other.

My *second* reflection with regard to these species of false religion is, *that religions, which partake of enthusiasm are, on their first rise, more furious and violent than those which partake of superstition; but in a little time become more gentle and moderate.* The violence of this species of religion, when excited by novelty, and animated by opposition, appears from numberless instances; of the *anabaptists* in GERMANY, the *camisars* in FRANCE, the *levellers* and other fanatics in ENGLAND, and the *covenanters* in SCOTLAND.[2] Enthusiasm being founded on strong spirits, and a presumptuous boldness of character, it naturally begets the most extreme resolutions; especially after it rises to that height as to inspire the deluded fanatic with the opinion of divine illuminations, and with a contempt for the common rules of reason, morality, and prudence.

It is thus enthusiasm produces the most cruel disorders in human society; but its fury is like that of thunder and tempest, which exhaust themselves in a little time, and leave the air more calm and serene than before. When the first fire of enthusiasm is spent, men naturally, in all fanatical sects, sink into the greatest remissness and coolness in sacred matters; there being no body of men among them, endowed with sufficient authority, whose interest is concerned to support the religious spirit: No rites, no ceremonies, no holy observances, which may enter into the common train of life, and preserve the sacred principles from oblivion. Superstition, on the contrary, steals in gradually and insensibly; renders men tame and submissive; is acceptable to the magistrate, and seems inoffensive to the people: Till at last the priest, having firmly established his authority, becomes the tyrant and disturber of human society, by his endless contentions, persecutions, and religious wars. How smoothly did the ROMISH church advance in her acquisition of power? But into what dismal convulsions did she throw all EUROPE, in order to maintain it? On the other hand, our sectaries, who were formerly such dangerous bigots, are now become very free reasoners; and the *quakers* seem to approach nearly the only regular body of *deists* in the universe, the *literati*, or the disciples of CONFUCIUS in CHINA.[a3]

My *third* observation on this head is, *that superstition is an enemy to civil liberty, and enthusiasm a friend to it.* As superstition groans under the dominion of priests, and enthusiasm is destructive of all ecclesiastical power, this sufficiently accounts for the present observation. Not to mention, that enthusiasm, being the infirmity of bold and ambitious tempers, is naturally accompanied with a spirit of liberty; as superstition, on the contrary, renders men tame and abject, and fits them for slavery. We learn from the ENGLISH history, that, during the civil wars, the *independents* and *deists*, though the most opposite in their religious principles; yet were united in their political ones, and were alike passionate for a commonwealth. And since the origin of *whig* and *tory*, the leaders of the *whigs* have either been *deists* or profest *latitudinarians* in their principles; that is, friends to toleration, and indifferent to any particular sect of *christians*: While the sectaries, who have all a strong tincture of enthusiasm, have always, without exception, concurred with that party, in defence of civil liberty. The resemblance in their superstitions long united the high-church *tories*, and the *Roman catholics*, in support of prerogative and kingly power; though experience of the tolerating spirit of the *whigs* seems of late to have reconciled the *catholics* to that party.

[a] The CHINESE Literati have no priests or ecclesiastical establishment.

The *molinists* and *jansenists* in FRANCE have a thousand unintelligible disputes, which are not worthy the reflection of a man of sense: But what principally distinguishes these two sects, and alone merits attention, is the different spirit of their religion. The *molinists*, conducted by the *jesuits*, are great friends to superstition, rigid observers of external forms and ceremonies, and devoted to the authority of the priests, and to tradition. The *jansenists* are enthusiasts, and zealous promoters of the passionate devotion, and of the inward life; little influenced by authority; and, in a word, but half catholics. The consequences are exactly conformable to the foregoing reasoning. The *jesuits* are the tyrants of the people, and the slaves of the court: And the *jansenists* preserve alive the small sparks of the love of liberty, which are to be found in the FRENCH nation.[4]

Of civil liberty[1]

THOSE who employ their pens on political subjects, free from party-rage, and party-prejudices, cultivate a science, which, of all others, contributes most to public utility, and even to the private satisfaction of those who addict themselves to the study of it. I am apt, however, to entertain a suspicion, that the world is still too young to fix many general truths in politics, which will remain true to the latest posterity. We have not as yet had experience of three thousand years; so that not only the art of reasoning is still defective in this science, as in all others, but we even want sufficient materials upon which we can reason. It is not fully known, what degree of refinement, either in virtue or vice, human nature is susceptible of; nor what may be expected of mankind from any great revolution in their education, customs, or principles. MACHIAVEL was certainly a great genius; but having confined his study to the furious and tyrannical governments of ancient times, or to the little disorderly principalities of ITALY, his reasonings, especially upon monarchical government, have been found extremely defective; and there scarcely is any maxim in his *prince*, which subsequent experience has not entirely refuted. *A weak prince*, says he, *is incapable of receiving good counsel; for if he consult with several, he will not be able to choose among their different counsels. If he abandon himself to one, that minister may, perhaps, have capacity; but he will not long be a minister: He will be sure to dispossess his master, and place himself and his family upon the throne.*[2] I mention this, among many instances of the errors of that politician, proceeding, in a great measure, from his having lived in too early an age of the world, to be a good judge of political truth. Almost all the princes of EUROPE are at present governed by their ministers; and have been so for near two centuries; and yet no such event has ever happened, or can possibly happen. SEJANUS might project dethroning the CAESARS; but FLEURY, though ever so vicious, could not, while in his senses, entertain the least hopes of dispossessing the BOURBONS.[3]

Trade was never esteemed an affair of state till the last century; and there scarcely is any ancient writer on politics, who has made mention of it.[a] Even the ITALIANS have kept a profound silence with regard to it, though it has now engaged the chief attention, as well of ministers of state, as of speculative reasoners. The great opulence, grandeur, and military atchievements of the two maritime powers seem first to have instructed mankind in the importance of an extensive commerce.

Having, therefore, intended in this essay to make a full comparison of civil liberty and absolute government, and to show the great advantages of the former above the latter; I began to entertain a suspicion, that no man in this age was sufficiently qualified for such an undertaking; and that whatever any one should advance on that head would, in all probability, be refuted by further experience, and be rejected by posterity. Such mighty revolutions have happened in human affairs, and so many events have arisen contrary to the expectation of the ancients, that they are sufficient to beget the suspicion of still further changes.

It had been observed by the ancients, that all the arts and sciences arose among free nations; and, that the PERSIANS and EGYPTIANS, notwithstanding their ease, opulence, and luxury, made but faint efforts towards a relish in those finer pleasures, which were carried to such perfection by the GREEKS, amidst continual wars, attended with poverty, and the greatest simplicity of life and manners. It had also been observed, that, when the GREEKS lost their liberty, though they increased mightily in riches, by means of the conquests of ALEXANDER; yet the arts, from that moment, declined among them, and have never since been able to raise their head in that climate. Learning was transplanted to ROME, the only free nation at that time in the universe; and having met with so favourable a soil, it made prodigious shoots for above a century; till the decay of liberty produced

---

[a] XENOPHON mentions it; but with a doubt if it be of any advantage to a state. Ei de kai emporia ophelei ti polin, *&c.* XEN. HIERO. PLATO totally excludes it from his imaginary republic. De legibus, lib. iv.[4]

also the decay of letters, and spread a total barbarism over the world. From these two experiments, of which each was double in its kind, and shewed the fall of learning in absolute governments, as well as its rise in popular ones, LONGINUS thought himself sufficiently justified, in asserting, that the arts and sciences could never flourish, but in a free government: And in this opinion, he has been followed by several eminent writers[b] in our own country, who either confined their view merely to ancient facts, or entertained too great a partiality in favour of that form of government, established amongst us.[5]

But what would these writers have said, to the instances of modern ROME and of FLORENCE? Of which the former carried to perfection all the finer arts of sculpture, painting, and music, as well as poetry, though it groaned under tyranny, and under the tyranny of priests: While the latter made its chief progress in the arts and sciences, after it began to lose its liberty by the usurpation of the family of MEDICI. ARIOSTO, TASSO, GALILEO, more than RAPHAEL, and MICHAEL ANGELO, were not born in republics. And though the LOMBARD school was famous as well as the ROMAN, yet the VENETIANS have had the smallest share in its honours, and seem rather inferior to the other ITALIANS, in their genius for the arts and sciences. RUBENS established his school at ANTWERP, not at AMSTERDAM: DRESDEN, not HAMBURGH, is the centre of politeness in GERMANY.[6]

But the most eminent instance of the flourishing of learning in absolute governments, is that of FRANCE, which scarcely ever enjoyed any established liberty, and yet has carried the arts and sciences as near perfection as any other nation. The ENGLISH are, perhaps, greater philosophers; the ITALIANS better painters and musicians; the ROMANS were greater orators: But the FRENCH are the only people, except the GREEKS, who have been at once philosophers, poets, orators, historians, painters, architects, sculptors, and musicians. With regard to the stage, they have excelled even the GREEKS, who far excelled the ENGLISH. And, in common life, they have, in a great measure, perfected that art, the most useful and agreeable of any, *l'Art de Vivre*, the art of society and conversation.

If we consider the state of the sciences and polite arts in our own country, HORACE's observation, with regard to the ROMANS, may, in a great measure, be applied to the BRITISH.

[b] Mr. ADDISON and LORD SHAFTESBURY.

. . . Sed in longum tamen aevum
Manserunt, hodieque manent vestigia ruris.[7]

The elegance and propriety of style have been very much neglected among us. We have no dictionary of our language, and scarcely a tolerable grammar. The first polite prose we have, was writ by a man who is still alive.[c] As to SPRAT, LOCKE, and even TEMPLE, they knew too little of the rules of art to be esteemed elegant writers. The prose of BACON, HARRINGTON, and MILTON, is altogether stiff and pedantic; though their sense be excellent.[8] Men, in this country, have been so much occupied in the great disputes of *Religion, Politics,* and *Philosophy*, that they had no relish for the seemingly minute observations of grammar and criticism. And though this turn of thinking must have considerably improved our sense and our talent of reasoning; it must be confessed, that, even in those sciences abovementioned, we have not any standard-book, which we can transmit to posterity: And the utmost we have to boast of, are a few essays towards a more just philosophy; which, indeed, promise well, but have not, as yet, reached any degree of perfection.

It has become an established opinion, that commerce can never flourish but in a free government; and this opinion seems to be founded on a longer and larger experience than the foregoing, with regard to the arts and sciences. If we trace commerce in its progress through TYRE, ATHENS, SYRACUSE, CARTHAGE, VENICE, FLORENCE, GENOA, ANTWERP, HOLLAND, ENGLAND, *&c.* we shall always find it to have fixed its seat in free governments. The three greatest trading towns now in the world, are LONDON, AMSTERDAM, and HAMBURGH; all free cities, and protestant cities; that is, enjoying a double liberty. It must, however, be observed, that the great jealousy entertained of late, with regard to the commerce of FRANCE, seems to prove, that this maxim is no more certain and infallible than the foregoing, and that the subjects of an absolute prince may become our rivals in commerce, as well as in learning.

Durst I deliver my opinion in an affair of so much uncertainty, I would assert, that, notwithstanding the efforts of the FRENCH, there is something hurtful to commerce inherent in the very nature of absolute government, and inseparable from it: Though the reason I should assign for this opinion, is somewhat different from that which

[c] Dr. SWIFT.

is commonly insisted on. Private property seems to me almost as secure in a civilized EUROPEAN monarchy, as in a republic; nor is danger much apprehended in such a government, from the violence of the sovereign; more than we commonly dread harm from thunder, or earthquakes, or any accident the most unusual and extraordinary. Avarice, the spur of industry, is so obstinate a passion, and works its way through so many real dangers and difficulties, that it is not likely to be scared by an imaginary danger, which is so small, that it scarcely admits of calculation. Commerce, therefore, in my opinion, is apt to decay in absolute governments, not because it is there less *secure*, but because it is less *honourable*. A subordination of ranks is absolutely necessary to the support of monarchy. Birth, titles, and place, must be honoured above industry and riches. And while these notions prevail, all the considerable traders will be tempted to throw up their commerce, in order to purchase some of those employments, to which privileges and honours are annexed.

Since I am upon this head, of the alterations which time has produced, or may produce in politics, I must observe, that all kinds of government, free and absolute, seem to have undergone, in modern times, a great change for the better, with regard both to foreign and domestic management. The *balance of power* is a secret in politics, fully known only to the present age; and I must add, that the internal POLICE of states has also received great improvements within the last century.[9] We are informed by SALLUST, that CATILINE's army was much augmented by the accession of the highwaymen about ROME; though I believe, that all of that profession, who are at present dispersed over EUROPE, would not amount to a regiment.[10] In CICERO's pleadings for MILO, I find this argument, among others, made use of to prove, that his client had not assassinated CLODIUS. Had MILO, said he, intended to have killed CLODIUS, he had not attacked him in the day-time, and at such a distance from the city: He had way-laid him at night, near the suburbs, where it might have been pretended, that he was killed by robbers; and the frequency of the accident would have favoured the deceit. This is a surprizing proof of the loose police of ROME, and of the number and force of these robbers; since CLODIUS[d] was at that time attended by thirty slaves, who were compleatly armed, and sufficiently accustomed to blood and danger in the frequent tumults excited by that seditious tribune.[11]

[d] *Vide Asc. Ped. in Orat. pro Milone.*

55

But though all kinds of government be improved in modern times, yet monarchical government seems to have made the greatest advances towards perfection. It may now be affirmed of civilized monarchies, what was formerly said in praise of republics alone, *that they are a government of Laws, not of Men.*[12] They are found susceptible of order, method, and constancy, to a surprizing degree. Property is there secure; industry encouraged; the arts flourish; and the prince lives secure among his subjects, like a father among his children. There are, perhaps, and have been for two centuries, near two hundred absolute princes, great and small, in EUROPE; and allowing twenty years to each reign, we may suppose, that there have been in the whole two thousand monarchs or tyrants, as the GREEKS would have called them: Yet of these there has not been one, not even PHILIP II. of SPAIN, so bad as TIBERIUS, CALIGULA, NERO, or DOMITIAN, who were four in twelve amongst the ROMAN emperors.[13] It must, however, be confessed, that, though monarchical governments have approached nearer to popular ones, in gentleness and stability; they are still inferior. Our modern education and customs instil more humanity and moderation than the ancient; but have not as yet been able to overcome entirely the disadvantages of that form of government.

But here I must beg leave to advance a conjecture, which seems probable, but which posterity alone can fully judge of. I am apt to think, that, in monarchical governments there is a source of improvement, and in popular governments a source of degeneracy, which in time will bring these species of civil polity still nearer an equality. The greatest abuses, which arise in FRANCE, the most perfect model of pure monarchy, proceed not from the number or weight of the taxes, beyond what are to be met with in free countries; but from the expensive, unequal, arbitrary, and intricate method of levying them, by which the industry of the poor, especially of the peasants and farmers, is, in a great measure, discouraged, and agriculture rendered a beggarly and slavish employment. But to whose advantage do these abuses tend? If to that of the nobility, they might be esteemed inherent in that form of government; since the nobility are the true supports of monarchy; and it is natural their interest should be more consulted, in such a constitution, than that of the people. But the nobility are, in reality, the principal losers by this oppression; since it ruins their estates, and beggars their tenants. The only gainers by it are the *Financiers*, a race of men rather odious to the nobility and the whole kingdom.[14] If a prince or minister, therefore, should arise, endowed with sufficient discernment to know his own and the public interest, and with sufficient force of mind to break through ancient customs, we might expect to see these abuses remedied; in which case, the difference between that absolute government and our free one, would not appear so considerable as at present.

The source of degeneracy, which may be remarked in free governments, consists in the practice of contracting debt, and mortgaging the public revenues, by which taxes may, in time, become altogether intolerable, and all the property of the state be brought into the hands of the public. This practice is of modern date. The ATHENIANS, though governed by a republic, paid near two hundred *per Cent.* for those sums of money, which any emergence made it necessary for them to borrow; as we learn from XENOPHON.[e] Among the moderns, the DUTCH first introduced the practice of borrowing great sums at low interest, and have well nigh ruined themselves by it. Absolute princes have also contracted debt; but as an absolute prince may make a bankruptcy when he pleases, his people can never be oppressed by his debts. In popular governments, the people, and chiefly those who have the highest offices, being commonly the public creditors, it is difficult for the state to make use of this remedy, which, however it may be sometimes necessary, is always cruel and barbarous. This, therefore, seems to be an inconvenience, which nearly threatens all free governments; especially our own, at the present juncture of affairs. And what a strong motive is this, to encrease our frugality of public money; lest, for want of it, we be reduced, by the multiplicity of taxes, or what is worse, by our public impotence and inability for defence, to curse our very liberty, and wish ourselves in the same state of servitude with all the nations that surround us?

---

[e] Ktesin de ap'oudenos an houto kalen ktesainto hosper aph'hou an protelesosin eis ten aphormen ... hoi de ge pleistoi Athenaion pleiona lepsontai kat'eniauton e hosa an eisenenkosin, hoi gar mnan protelesantes, engus dyoin mnain prosodon hexousi ... ho dokei ton anthropinon asphalestaton te kai polychroniotaton einai. XEN. POROI.[15]

ESSAY ELEVEN

Of the rise and progress of the arts and sciences

NOTHING requires greater nicety, in our enquiries concerning human affairs, than to distinguish exactly what is owing to *chance*, and what proceeds from *causes*; nor is there any subject, in which an author is more liable to deceive himself by false subtilties and refinements. To say, that any event is derived from chance, cuts short all farther enquiry concerning it, and leaves the writer in the same state of ignorance with the rest of mankind. But when the event is supposed to proceed from certain and stable causes, he may then display his ingenuity, in assigning these causes; and as a man of any subtilty can never be at a loss in this particular, he has thereby an opportunity of swelling his volumes, and discovering his profound knowledge, in observing what escapes the vulgar and ignorant.

The distinguishing between chance and causes must depend upon every particular man's sagacity, in considering every particular incident. But, if I were to assign any general rule to help us in applying this distinction, it would be the following, *What depends upon a few persons is, in a great measure, to be ascribed to chance, or secret and unknown causes: What arises from a great number, may often be accounted for by determinate and known causes.*

Two natural reasons may be assigned for this rule. *First*, If you suppose a dye to have any biass, however small, to a particular side, this biass, though, perhaps, it may not appear in a few throws, will certainly prevail in a great number, and will cast the balance entirely to that side. In like manner, when any *causes* beget a particular inclination or passion, at a certain time, and among a certain people; though many individuals may escape the contagion, and be ruled by passions peculiar to themselves; yet the multitude will certainly be seized by the common affection, and be governed by it in all their actions.

Secondly, Those principles or causes, which are fitted to operate on a multitude, are always of a grosser and more stubborn nature, less subject to accidents, and less influenced by whim and private fancy, than those which operate on a few only. The latter are commonly so delicate and refined, that the smallest incident in the health, education, or fortune of a particular person, is sufficient to divert their course, and retard their operation; nor is it possible to reduce them to any general maxims or observations. Their influence at one time will never assure us concerning their influence at another; even though all the general circumstances should be the same in both cases.

To judge by this rule, the domestic and the gradual revolutions of a state must be a more proper subject of reasoning and observation, than the foreign and the violent, which are commonly produced by single persons, and are more influenced by whim, folly, or caprice, than by general passions and interests. The depression of the lords, and rise of the commons in ENGLAND, after the statutes of alienation and the encrease of trade and industry,[1] are more easily accounted for by general principles, than the depression of the SPANISH, and rise of the FRENCH monarchy, after the death of CHARLES QUINT. Had HARRY IV. Cardinal RICHLIEU, and LOUIS XIV. been SPANIARDS; and PHILIP II. III. and IV. and CHARLES II. been FRENCHMEN, the history of these two nations had been entirely reversed.[2]

For the same reason, it is more easy to account for the rise and progress of commerce in any kingdom, than for that of learning; and a state, which should apply itself to the encouragement of the one, would be more assured of success, than one which should cultivate the other. Avarice, or the desire of gain, is an universal passion, which operates at all times, in all places, and upon all persons: But curiosity, or the love of knowledge, has a very limited influence, and requires youth, leisure, education, genius, and example, to make it govern any person. You will never want booksellers, while there are buyers of books: But there may frequently be readers where there are no authors. Multitudes of people, necessity and liberty, have begot commerce in HOLLAND: But study and application have scarcely produced any eminent writers.

We may, therefore, conclude, that there is no subject, in which we must proceed with more caution, than in tracing the history of the arts and sciences; lest we assign causes which never existed, and reduce what is merely contingent to stable and universal principles. Those who cultivate the sciences in any state, are always few in number: The passion, which governs them, limited: Their taste and judgment delicate and easily perverted: And their application disturbed with the smallest accident. Chance, therefore, or secret and unknown causes, must have a great influence on the rise and progress of all the refined arts.

But there is a reason, which induces me not to ascribe the matter altogether to chance. Though the persons, who cultivate the sciences with such astonishing success, as to attract the admiration of posterity, be always few, in all nations and all ages; it is impossible but a share of the same spirit and genius must be antecedently diffused throughout the people among whom they arise, in order to produce, form, and cultivate, from their earliest infancy, the taste and judgment of those eminent writers. The mass cannot be altogether insipid, from which such refined spirits are extracted. *There is a God within us*, says OVID, *who breathes that divine fire, by which we are animated.*[a] Poets, in all ages, have advanced this claim to inspiration. There is not, however, any thing supernatural in the case. Their fire is not kindled from heaven. It only runs along the earth; is caught from one breast to another; and burns brightest, where the materials are best prepared, and most happily disposed. The question, therefore, concerning the rise and progress of the arts and sciences, is not altogether a question concerning the taste, genius, and spirit of a few, but concerning those of a whole people; and may, therefore, be accounted for, in some measure, by general causes and principles. I grant, that a man, who should enquire, why such a particular poet, as HOMER, for instance, existed, at such a place, in such a time, would throw himself headlong into chimæra, and could never treat of such a subject, without a multitude of false subtilties and refinements. He might as well pretend to give a reason, why such particular generals, as FABIUS and SCIPIO, lived in ROME at such a time, and why FABIUS

---

[a] Est Deus in nobis; agitante calescimus illo:
Impetus hic, sacræ semina mentis habet.
OVID, *Fast. lib.* i[3]

came into the world before Scipio. For such incidents as these, no other reason can be given than that of Horace.

> Scit genius, natale comes, qui temperat astrum,
>> Naturæ Deus humanæ, mortalis in unum ...
> ... Quodque caput, vultu mutabilis, albus & ater.[4]

But I am persuaded, that in many cases good reasons might be given, why such a nation is more polite and learned, at a particular time, than any of its neighbours. At least, this is so curious a subject, that it were a pity to abandon it entirely, before we have found whether it be susceptible of reasoning, and can be reduced to any general principles.

My first observation on this head is, *That it is impossible for the arts and sciences to arise, at first, among any people unless that people enjoy the blessing of a free government.*

In the first ages of the world, when men are as yet barbarous and ignorant, they seek no farther security against mutual violence and injustice, than the choice of some rulers, few or many, in whom they place an implicit confidence, without providing any security, by laws or political institutions, against the violence and injustice of these rulers. If the authority be centered in a single person, and if the people, either by conquest, or by the ordinary course of propagation, encrease to a great multitude, the monarch, finding it impossible, in his own person, to execute every office of sovereignty, in every place, must delegate his authority to inferior magistrates, who preserve peace and order in their respective districts. As experience and education have not yet refined the judgments of men to any considerable degree, the prince, who is himself unrestrained, never dreams of restraining his ministers, but delegates his full authority to every one, whom he sets over any portion of the people. All general laws are attended with inconveniencies, when applied to particular cases; and it requires great penetration and experience, both to perceive that these inconveniencies are fewer than what result from full discretionary powers in every magistrate; and also to discern what general laws are, upon the whole, attended with fewest inconveniencies. This is a matter of so great difficulty, that men may have made some advances, even in the sublime arts of poetry and eloquence, where a rapidity of genius and imagination assists their progress, before they have arrived at any great refinement in their municipal laws, where frequent trials and diligent observation can alone direct their improvements. It is not, therefore, to be supposed, that a barbarous monarch, unrestrained and uninstructed, will ever become a legislator, or think of restraining his *Bashaws*, in every province, or even his *Cadis* in every village.[5] We are told, that the late *Czar*, though actuated with a noble genius, and smit with the love and admiration of EUROPEAN arts; yet professed an esteem for the TURKISH policy in this particular, and approved of such summary decisions of causes, as are practised in that barbarous monarchy, where the judges are not restrained by any methods, forms, or laws. He did not perceive, how contrary such a practice would have been to all his other endeavours for refining his people.[6] Arbitrary power, in all cases, is somewhat oppressive and debasing; but it is altogether ruinous and intolerable, when contracted into a small compass; and becomes still worse, when the person, who possesses it, knows that the time of his authority is limited and uncertain. *Habet subjectos tanquam suos; viles, ut alienos.*[b] He governs the subjects with full authority, as if they were his own; and with negligence or tyranny, as belonging to another. A people, governed after such a manner, are slaves in the full and proper sense of the word; and it is impossible they can ever aspire to any refinements of taste or reason. They dare not so much as pretend to enjoy the necessaries of life in plenty or security.

To expect, therefore, that the arts and sciences should take their first rise in a monarchy, is to expect a contradiction. Before these refinements have taken place, the monarch is ignorant and uninstructed; and not having knowledge sufficient to make him sensible of the necessity of balancing his government upon general laws, he delegates his full power to all inferior magistrates. This barbarous policy debases the people, and for ever prevents all improvement. Were it possible, that, before science were known in the world, a monarch could possess so much wisdom as to become a legislator, and govern his people by law, not by the arbitrary will of their fellow-subjects, it might be possible for that species of government to be the first nursery of arts and sciences. But in that supposition there seems to be a manifest contradiction.

It may happen, that a republic, in its infant state, may be supported by as few laws as a barbarous monarchy, and may entrust as unlimited

[b] TACIT. hist. lib. i.[7]

an authority to its magistrates or judges. But, besides that the frequent elections by the people, are a considerable check upon authority; it is impossible, but, in time, the necessity of restraining the magistrates, in order to preserve liberty, must at last appear, and give rise to general laws and statutes. The ROMAN Consuls, for some time, decided all causes, without being confined by any positive statutes, till the people, bearing this yoke with impatience, created the *decemvirs*, who promulgated the *twelve tables*;[8] a body of laws, which, though, perhaps, they were not equal in bulk to one ENGLISH act of parliament, were almost the only written rules, which regulated property and punishment, for some ages, in that famous republic. They were, however, sufficient, together with the forms of a free government, to secure the lives and properties of the citizens; to exempt one man from the dominion of another; and to protect every one against the violence or tyranny of his fellow-citizens. In such a situation the sciences may raise their heads and flourish: But never can have being amidst such a scene of oppression and slavery, as always results from barbarous monarchies, where the people alone are restrained by the authority of the magistrates, and the magistrates are not restrained by any law or statute. An unlimited despotism of this nature, while it exists, effectually puts a stop to all improvements, and keeps men from attaining that knowledge, which is requisite to instruct them in the advantages, arising from a better police, and more moderate authority.

Here then are the advantages of free states. Though a republic should be barbarous, it necessarily, by an infallible operation, gives rise to LAW, even before mankind have made any considerable advances in the other sciences. From law arises security: From security curiosity: And from curiosity knowledge. The latter steps of this progress may be more accidental; but the former are altogether necessary. A republic without laws can never have any duration. On the contrary, in a monarchical government, law arises not necessarily from the forms of government. Monarchy, when absolute, contains even something repugnant to law. Great wisdom and reflexion can alone reconcile them. But such a degree of wisdom can never be expected, before the greater refinements and improvements of human reason. These refinements require curiosity, security, and law. The *first* growth, therefore, of the arts and sciences can never be expected in despotic governments.

There are other causes, which discourage the rise of the refined arts in despotic governments; though I take the want of laws, and the delegation of full powers to every petty magistrate, to be the principal. Eloquence certainly springs up more naturally in popular governments: Emulation too in every accomplishment must there be more animated and enlivened: And genius and capacity have a fuller scope and career. All these causes render free governments the only proper *nursery* for the arts and sciences.

The next observation, which I shall make on this head, is, *That nothing is more favourable to the rise of politeness and learning, than a number of neighbouring and independent states, connected together by commerce and policy.* The emulation, which naturally arises among those neighbouring states, is an obvious source of improvement: But what I would chiefly insist on is the stop, which such limited territories give both to *power* and to *authority*.

Extended governments, where a single person has great influence, soon become absolute; but small ones change naturally into commonwealths. A large government is accustomed by degrees to tyranny; because each act of violence is at first performed upon a part, which, being distant from the majority, is not taken notice of, nor excites any violent ferment. Besides, a large government, though the whole be discontented, may, by a little art, be kept in obedience; while each part, ignorant of the resolutions of the rest, is afraid to begin any commotion or insurrection. Not to mention, that there is a superstitious reverence for princes, which mankind naturally contract when they do not often see the sovereign, and when many of them become not acquainted with him so as to perceive his weaknesses. And as large states can afford a great expence, in order to support the pomp of majesty; this is a kind of fascination on men, and naturally contributes to the enslaving of them.

In a small government, any act of oppression is immediately known throughout the whole: The murmurs and discontents, proceeding from it, are easily communicated: And the indignation rises the higher, because the subjects are not apt to apprehend in such states, that the distance is very wide between themselves and their sovereign. 'No man,' said the prince DE CONDE, 'is a hero to his *Valet de Chambre*.'[9] It is certain that admiration and acquaintance are altogether incompatible towards any mortal creature. Sleep and love convinced even ALEXANDER himself that he was not a God:[10] But I suppose, that such as daily attended him could easily, from the numberless weaknesses to which he was subject, have given him many still more convincing proofs of his humanity.

But the divisions into small states are favourable to learning, by stopping the progress of *authority* as well as that of *power*. Reputation is often as great a fascination upon men as sovereignty, and is equally destructive to the freedom of thought and examination. But where a number of neighbouring states have a great intercourse of arts and commerce, their mutual jealousy keeps them from receiving too lightly the law from each other, in matters of taste and of reasoning, and makes them examine every work of art with the greatest care and accuracy. The contagion of popular opinion spreads not so easily from one place to another. It readily receives a check in some state or other, where it concurs not with the prevailing prejudices. And nothing but nature and reason, or, at least, what bears them a strong resemblance, can force its way through all obstacles, and unite the most rival nations into an esteem and admiration of it.

GREECE was a cluster of little principalities, which soon became republics; and being united both by their near neighbourhood, and by the ties of the same language and interest, they entered into the closest intercourse of commerce and learning. There concurred a happy climate, a soil not unfertile, and a most harmonious and comprehensive language; so that every circumstance among that people seemed to favour the rise of the arts and sciences. Each city produced its several artists and philosophers, who refused to yield the preference to those of the neighbouring republics: Their contention and debates sharpened the wits of men: A variety of objects was presented to the judgment, while each challenged the preference to the rest: and the sciences, not being dwarfed by the restraint of authority, were enabled to make such considerable shoots, as are, even at this time, the objects of our admiration. After the ROMAN *christian*, or *catholic* church had spread itself over the civilized world, and had engrossed all the learning of the times; being really one large state within itself, and united under one head; this variety of sects immediately disappeared, and the PERIPATETIC philosophy was alone admitted into all the schools, to the utter depravation of every kind of learning.[11] But mankind, having at length thrown off this yoke, affairs are now returned nearly to the same situation as before, and EUROPE is at present a copy at large, of what GREECE was formerly a pattern in miniature. We have seen the advantage of this situation in several instances. What checked the progress of the CARTESIAN philosophy, to which the FRENCH nation shewed such a strong propensity towards the end of the last century, but the opposition made to it by the other nations of EUROPE, who soon discovered the weak sides of that philosophy?[12] The severest scrutiny, which NEWTON's theory has undergone, proceeded not from his own countrymen, but from foreigners; and if it can overcome the obstacles, which it meets with at present in all parts of EUROPE, it will probably go down triumphant to the latest posterity. The ENGLISH are become sensible of the scandalous licentiousness of their stage, from the example of the FRENCH decency and morals.[13] The FRENCH are convinced, that their theatre has become somewhat effeminate, by too much love and gallantry; and begin to approve of the more masculine taste of some neighbouring nations.

In CHINA, there seems to be a pretty considerable stock of politeness and science, which, in the course of so many centuries, might naturally be expected to ripen into something more perfect and finished, than what has yet arisen from them. But CHINA is one vast empire, speaking one language, governed by one law, and sympathizing in the same manners. The authority of any teacher, such as CONFUCIUS, was propagated easily from one corner of the empire to the other. None had courage to resist the torrent of popular opinion. And posterity was not bold enough to dispute what had been universally received by their ancestors. This seems to be one natural reason, why the sciences have made so slow a progress in that mighty empire.[c]

---

[c] IF it be asked how we can reconcile to the foregoing principles the happiness, riches, and good police of the CHINESE, who have always been governed by a sole monarch, and can scarcely form an idea of a free government; I would answer, that though the CHINESE government be a pure monarchy, it is not, properly speaking, absolute. This proceeds from a peculiarity in the situation of that country: They have no neighbours, except the TARTARS, from whom they were, in some measure, secured, at least seemed to be secured, by their famous wall, and by the great superiority of their numbers. By this means, military discipline has always been much neglected amongst them; and their standing forces are mere militia, of the worst kind; and unfit to suppress any general insurrection in countries so extremely populous. The sword, therefore, may properly be said to be always in the hands of the people, which is a sufficient restraint upon the monarch, and obliges him to lay his *mandarins* or governors of provinces under the restraint of general laws, in order to prevent those rebellions, which we learn from history to have been so frequent and dangerous in that government. Perhaps, a pure monarchy of this kind, were it fitted for defence against foreign

If we consider the face of the globe, Europe, of all the four parts of the world, is the most broken by seas, rivers, and mountains; and Greece of all countries of Europe. Hence these regions were naturally divided into several distinct governments. And hence the sciences arose in Greece; and Europe has been hitherto the most constant habitation of them.

I have sometimes been inclined to think, that interruptions in the periods of learning, were they not attended with such a destruction of ancient books, and the records of history, would be rather favourable to the arts and sciences, by breaking the progress of authority, and dethroning the tyrannical usurpers over human reason. In this particular, they have the same influence, as interruptions in political governments and societies. Consider the blind submission of the ancient philosophers to the several masters in each school, and you will be convinced, that little good could be expected from an hundred centuries of such a servile philosophy. Even the Eclectics, who arose about the age of Augustus, notwithstanding their professing to chuse freely what pleased them from every different sect, were yet, in the main, as slavish and dependent as any of their brethren; since they sought for truth, not in nature, but in the several schools; where they supposed she must necessarily be found, though not united in a body, yet dispersed in parts.[15] Upon the revival of learning, those sects of Stoics and Epicureans, Platonists and Pythagoricians, could never regain any credit or authority; and, at the same time, by the example of their fall, kept men from submitting, with such blind deference, to those new sects, which have attempted to gain an ascendant over them.[16]

The *third* observation, which I shall form on this head, of the rise and progress of the arts and sciences, is, *That though the only proper Nursery of these noble plants be a free state; yet may they be transplanted into any government; and that a republic is most favourable to the growth of the sciences, a civilized monarchy to that of the polite arts.*

To balance a large state or society, whether monarchical or republican, on general laws, is a work of so great difficulty, that no human genius, however comprehensive, is able, by the mere dint of reason and reflection, to effect it. The judgments of many must unite in this

enemies, would be the best of all governments, as having both the tranquillity attending kingly power, and the moderation and liberty of popular assemblies.[14]

work: Experience must guide their labour: Time must bring it to perfection: And the feeling of inconveniencies must correct the mistakes, which they inevitably fall into, in their first trials and experiments. Hence appears the impossibility, that this undertaking should be begun and carried on in any monarchy; since such a form of government, ere civilized, knows no other secret or policy, than that of entrusting unlimited powers to every governor or magistrate, and subdividing the people into so many classes and orders of slavery. From such a situation, no improvement can ever be expected in the sciences, in the liberal arts, in laws, and scarcely in the manual arts and manufactures. The same barbarism and ignorance, with which the government commences, is propagated to all posterity, and can never come to a period by the efforts or ingenuity of such unhappy slaves.

But though law, the source of all security and happiness, arises late in any government, and is the slow product of order and of liberty, it is not preserved with the same difficulty, with which it is produced; but when it has once taken root, is a hardy plant, which will scarcely ever perish through the ill culture of men, or the rigour of the seasons. The arts of luxury, and much more the liberal arts, which depend on a refined taste or sentiment, are easily lost; because they are always relished by a few only, whose leisure, fortune, and genius fit them for such amusements. But what is profitable to every mortal, and in common life, when once discovered, can scarcely fall into oblivion, but by the total subversion of society, and by such furious inundations of barbarous invaders, as obliterate all memory of former arts and civility. Imitation also is apt to transport these coarser and more useful arts from one climate to another, and make them precede the refined arts in their progress; though perhaps they sprang after them in their first rise and propagation. From these causes proceed civilized monarchies; where the arts of government, first invented in free states, are preserved to the mutual advantage and security of sovereign and subject.

However perfect, therefore, the monarchical form may appear to some politicians, it owes all its perfection to the republican; nor is it possible, that a pure despotism, established among a barbarous people, can ever, by its native force and energy, refine and polish itself. It must borrow its laws, and methods, and institutions, and consequently its stability and order, from free governments. These advantages are the sole growth of republics. The extensive despotism of a barbarous monarchy, by entering into the detail of the government, as well as into the principal points of administration, for ever prevents all such improvements.

In a civilized monarchy, the prince alone is unrestrained in the exercise of his authority, and possesses alone a power, which is not bounded by any thing but custom, example, and the sense of his own interest. Every minister or magistrate, however eminent, must submit to the general laws, which govern the whole society, and must exert the authority delegated to him after the manner, which is prescribed. The people depend on none but their sovereign, for the security of their property. He is so far removed from them, and is so much exempt from private jealousies or interests, that this dependence is scarcely felt. And thus a species of government arises, to which, in a high political rant, we may give the name of *Tyranny*, but which, by a just and prudent administration, may afford tolerable security to the people, and may answer most of the ends of political society.

But though in a civilized monarchy, as well as in a republic, the people have security for the enjoyment of their property; yet in both these forms of government, those who possess the supreme authority have the disposal of many honours and advantages, which excite the ambition and avarice of mankind. The only difference is, that, in a republic, the candidates for office must look downwards, to gain the suffrages of the people; in a monarchy, they must turn their attention upwards, to court the good graces and favour of the great. To be successful in the former way, it is necessary for a man to make himself *useful*, by his industry, capacity, or knowledge: To be prosperous in the latter way, it is requisite for him to render himself *agreeable*, by his wit, complaisance, or civility. A strong genius succeeds best in republics: A refined taste in monarchies. And consequently the sciences are the more natural growth of the one, and the polite arts of the other.

Not to mention, that monarchies, receiving their chief stability from a superstitious reverence to priests and princes, have commonly abridged the liberty of reasoning, with regard to religion and politics, and consequently metaphysics and morals. All these form the most considerable branches of science. Mathematics and natural philosophy, which only remain, are not half so valuable.

Among the arts of conversation, no one pleases more than mutual deference or civility, which leads us to resign our own inclinations to those of our companion, and to curb and conceal that presumption and arrogance, so natural to the human mind. A good-natured man, who is well educated, practices this civility to every mortal, without premeditation or interest. But in order to render that valuable quality general among any people, it seems necessary to assist the natural disposition by some general motive. Where power rises upwards from the people to the great, as in all republics, such refinements of civility are apt to be little practised, since the whole state is, by that means, brought near to a level, and every member of it is rendered, in a great measure, independent of another. The people have the advantage, by the authority of their suffrages: The great, by the superiority of their station. But in a civilized monarchy, there is a long train of dependence from the prince to the peasant, which is not great enough to render property precarious, or depress the minds of the people; but is sufficient to beget in every one an inclination to please his superiors, and to form himself upon those models, which are most acceptable to people of condition and education. Politeness of manners, therefore, arises most naturally in monarchies and courts; and where that flourishes, none of the liberal arts will be altogether neglected or despised.

The republics in EUROPE are at present noted for want of politeness. *The good-manners of a* SWISS *civilized in* HOLLAND,[d] is an expression for rusticity among the FRENCH.[17] The ENGLISH, in some degree, fall under the same censure, notwithstanding their learning and genius. And if the VENETIANS be an exception to the rule, they owe it, perhaps, to their communication with the other ITALIANS, most of whose governments beget a dependence more than sufficient for civilizing their manners.

It is difficult to pronounce any judgment concerning the refinements of the ancient republics in this particular: But I am apt to suspect, that the arts of conversation were not brought so near to perfection among them as the arts of writing and composition. The scurrility of the ancient orators, in many instances, is quite shocking, and exceeds all belief. Vanity too is often not a little offensive in authors of that age;[e] as well as the common licentiousness and

---

[d] C'est la politesse d'un Suisse
En HOLLANDE civilisé.
ROUSSEAU

[e] It is needless to cite CICERO or PLINY on this head: They are too much noted: But one is a little surprised to find ARRIAN, a very grave, judicious writer, interrupt the

immodesty of their stile; *quicunque impudicus, adulter, ganeo, manu, ventre, pene, bona patria laceraverat*, says SALLUST in one of the gravest and most moral passages of his history.[19] *Nam fuit ante Helenam Cunnus teterrima belli Causa*, is an expression of HORACE, in tracing the origin of moral good and evil.[20] OVID and LUCRETIUS[f] are almost as licentious in their stile as Lord ROCHESTER; though the former were fine gentlemen and delicate writers, and the latter, from the corruptions of that court, in which he lived, seems to have thrown off all regard to shame and decency.[21] JUVENAL inculcates modesty with great zeal; but sets a very bad example of it, if we consider the impudence of his expressions.

I shall also be bold to affirm, that, among the ancients, there was not much delicacy of breeding, or that polite deference and respect, which civility obliges us either to express or counterfeit towards the persons with whom we converse. CICERO was certainly one of the finest gentlemen of his age; yet I must confess I have frequently been shocked with the poor figure under which he represents his friend ATTICUS, in those dialogues, where he himself is introduced as a speaker. That learned and virtuous ROMAN, whose dignity, though he was only a private gentleman, was inferior to that of no one in ROME, is there shewn in rather a more pitiful light than PHILALE-THES's friend in our modern dialogues. He is a humble admirer of the orator, pays him frequent compliments, and receives his instructions, with all the deference which a scholar owes to his master.[g] Even CATO is treated in somewhat of a cavalier manner in the dialogues *de finibus*.[23]

One of the most particular details of a real dialogue, which we meet with in antiquity, is related by POLYBIUS;[h] when PHILIP, king of MACEDON, a prince of wit and parts, met with TITUS FLAMININUS, one of the politest of the ROMANS, as we learn from PLUTARCH,[i]

---

thread of his narration all of a sudden, to tell his readers that he himself is as eminent among the GREEKS for eloquence as ALEXANDER was for arms. Lib. i.[18]

[f] This poet (See lib. iv. 1165.) recommends a very extraordinary cure for love, and what one expects not to meet with in so elegant and philosophical a poem. It seems to have been the original of some of Dr. SWIFT's images. The elegant CATULLUS and PHAEDRUS fall under the same censure.

[g] ATT. Non mihi videtur ad beate vivendum satis esse virtutem. MAR. At hercule BRUTO meo videtur; cujus ego judicium, pace tua dixerim, longe antepono tuo. TUSC. Quaest. lib. v.[22]

[h] Lib. xvii.

[i] In vita FLAMIN.

accompanied with ambassadors from almost all the GREEK cities. The AETOLIAN ambassador very abruptly tells the king, that he talked like a fool or a madman (lerein). *That's evident*, says his majesty, *even to a blind man*; which was a raillery on the blindness of his excellency. Yet all this did not pass the usual bounds: For the conference was not disturbed; and FLAMININUS was very well diverted with these strokes of humour. At the end, when PHILIP craved a little time to consult with his friends, of whom he had none present, the ROMAN general, being desirous also to shew his wit, as the historian says, tells him, *that perhaps the reason, why he had none of his friends with him, was because he had murdered them all*; which was actually the case. This unprovoked piece of rusticity is not condemned by the historian; caused no farther resentment in PHILIP, than to excite a SARDONIAN smile, or what we call a grin; and hindered him not from renewing the conference next day. PLUTARCH[j] too mentions this raillery amongst the witty and agreeable sayings of FLAMININUS.[24]

Cardinal WOLSEY apologized for his famous piece of insolence, in saying, EGO ET REX MEUS, *I and my king* by observing, that this expression was conformable to the *Latin* idiom, and that a ROMAN always named himself before the person to whom, or of whom he spake.[25] Yet this seems to have been an instance of want of civility among that people. The ancients made it a rule, that the person of the greatest dignity should be mentioned first in the discourse; insomuch, that we find the spring of a quarrel and jealousy between the ROMANS and AETOLIANS, to have been a poet's naming the AETOLIANS before the ROMANS, in celebrating a victory gained by their united arms over the MACEDONIANS.[k] Thus LIVIA disgusted TIBERIUS by placing her own name before his in an inscription.[l]

No advantages in this world are pure and unmixed. In like manner, as modern politeness, which is naturally so ornamental, runs often into affectation and foppery, disguise and insincerity; so the ancient simplicity, which is naturally so amiable and affecting, often degenerates into rusticity and abuse, scurrility and obscenity.

If the superiority in politeness should be allowed to modern times, the modern notions of *gallantry*, the natural produce of courts and monarchies, will probably be assigned as the causes of this refine-

---

[j] PLUT. in vita FLAMIN.
[k] Ibid.[26]
[l] TACIT. Ann. lib. iii. cap. 64.

ment. No one denies this invention to be modern:[m] But some of the most zealous partizans of the ancients, have asserted it to be foppish and ridiculous, and a reproach, rather than a credit to the present age.[n] It may here be proper to examine this question.

Nature has implanted in all living creatures an affection between the sexes, which, even in the fiercest and most rapacious animals, is not merely confined to the satisfaction of the bodily appetite, but begets a friendship and mutual sympathy, which runs through the whole tenor of their lives. Nay, even in those species, where nature limits the indulgence of this appetite to one season and to one object, and forms a kind of marriage or association between a single male and female, there is yet a visible complacency and benevolence, which extends farther, and mutually softens the affections of the sexes towards each other. How much more must this have place in man, where the confinement of the appetite is not natural; but either is derived accidentally from some strong charm of love, or arises from reflections on duty and convenience? Nothing, therefore, can proceed less from affectation than the passion of gallantry. It is *natural* in the highest degree. Art and education, in the most elegant courts, make no more alteration on it, than on all the other laudable passions. They only turn the mind more towards it; they refine it; they polish it; and give it a proper grace and expression.

But gallantry is as *generous* as it is *natural*. To correct such gross vices, as lead us to commit real injury on others, is the part of morals, and the object of the most ordinary education. Where *that* is not attended to, in some degree, no human society can subsist. But in order to render conversation, and the intercourse of minds more easy and agreeable, good-manners have been invented, and have carried the matter somewhat farther. Whereever nature has given the mind a propensity to any vice, or to any passion disagreeable to others, refined breeding has taught men to throw the biass on the opposite side, and to preserve, in all their behaviour, the appearance of sentiments different from those to which they naturally incline. Thus, as we are commonly proud and selfish, and apt to assume the preference above others, a polite man learns to behave with deference towards his companions, and to yield the superiority to them in all the

---

[m] In the *Self-Tormentor* of TERENCE, CLINIAS, whenever he comes to town, instead of waiting on his mistress, sends for her to come to him.
[n] Lord SHAFTESBURY, see his *Moralists*.[27]

common incidents of society. In like manner, wherever a person's situation may naturally beget any disagreeable suspicion in him, it is the part of good-manners to prevent it, by a studied display of sentiments, directly contrary to those of which he is apt to be jealous. Thus, old men know their infirmities, and naturally dread contempt from the youth: Hence, well-educated youth redouble the instances of respect and deference to their elders. Strangers and foreigners are without protection: Hence, in all polite countries, they receive the highest civilities, and are entitled to the first place in every company. A man is lord in his own family, and his guests are, in a manner, subject to his authority: Hence, he is always the lowest person in the company; attentive to the wants of every one; and giving himself all the trouble, in order to please, which may not betray too visible an affectation, or impose too much constraint on his guests.° Gallantry is nothing but an instance of the same generous attention. As nature has given *man* the superiority above *woman* by endowing him with greater strength both of mind and body; it is his part to alleviate that superiority, as much as possible, by the generosity of his behaviour, and by a studied deference and complaisance for all her inclinations and opinions. Barbarous nations display this superiority, by reducing their females to the most abject slavery; by confining them, by beating them, by selling them, by killing them. But the male sex, among a polite people, discover their authority in a more generous, though not a less evident manner; by civility, by respect, by complaisance, and, in a word, by gallantry. In good company, you need not ask, Who is the master of the feast? The man, who sits in the lowest place, and who is always industrious in helping everyone, is certainly the person. We must either condemn all such instances of generosity, as foppish and affected, or admit of gallantry among the rest. The ancient MUSCOVITES wedded their wives with a whip, instead of a ring.[29] The same people, in their own houses, took always the precedency above foreigners, even[p] foreign ambassadors.[30] These two instances of their generosity and politeness are much of a piece.

° The frequent mention in ancient authors of that ill-bred custom of the master of the family's eating better bread or drinking better wine at the table, than he afforded his guests, is but an indifferent mark of the civility of those ages. See JUVENAL, sat. 5. PLINII lib. xiv. cap. 13. Also PLINII *Epist. Lucian de mercede conductis, Saturnalia* &c. There is scarcely any part of EUROPE at present so uncivilized as to admit of such a custom.[28]

[p] See *Relation of three Embassies*, by the Earl of CARLISLE.

Gallantry is not less consistent with *wisdom* and *prudence*, than with *nature* and *generosity*; and when under proper regulations, contributes more than any other invention, to the *entertainment* and *improvement* of the youth of both sexes. Among every species of animals, nature has founded on the love between the sexes their sweetest and best enjoyment. But the satisfaction of the bodily appetite is not alone sufficient to gratify the mind; and even among brute-creatures, we find, that their play and dalliance, and other expressions of fondness, form the greatest part of the entertainment. In rational beings, we must certainly admit the mind for a considerable share. Were we to rob the feast of all its garniture of reason, discourse, sympathy, friendship, and gaiety, what remains would scarcely be worth acceptance, in the judgment of the truly elegant and luxurious.

What better school for manners, than the company of virtuous women; where the mutual endeavour to please must insensibly polish the mind, where the example of the female softness and modesty must communicate itself to their admirers, and where the delicacy of that sex puts every one on his guard, lest he give offence by any breach of decency?[31]

Among the ancients, the character of the fair-sex was considered as altogether domestic; nor were they regarded as part of the polite world or of good company. This, perhaps, is the true reason why the ancients have not left us one piece of pleasantry, that is excellent, (unless one may except the Banquet of XENOPHON, and the Dialogues of LUCIAN)[32] though many of their serious compositions are altogether inimitable. HORACE condemns the coarse railleries and cold jests of PLAUTUS:[33] But, though the most easy, agreeable, and judicious writer in the world, is his own talent for ridicule very striking or refined? This, therefore, is one considerable improvement, which the polite arts have received from gallantry, and from courts, where it first arose.[34]

But, to return from this digression, I shall advance it as a *fourth* observation on this subject, of the rise and progress of the arts and sciences, *That when the arts and sciences come to perfection in any state, from that moment they naturally, or rather necessarily decline, and seldom or never revive in that nation, where they formerly flourished.*

It must be confessed, that this maxim, though conformable to experience, may, at first sight, be esteemed contrary to reason. If the natural genius of mankind be the same in all ages, and in almost all countries, (as seems to be the truth) it must very much forward and cultivate this genius, to be possessed of patterns in every art, which may regulate the taste, and fix the objects of imitation. The models left us by the ancients gave birth to all the arts about 200 years ago, and have mightily advanced their progress in every country of EUROPE: Why had they not a like effect during the reign of TRAJAN and his successors; when they were much more entire, and were still admired and studied by the whole world? So late as the emperor JUSTINIAN, the POET, by way of distinction, was understood, among the GREEKS, to be HOMER; among the ROMANS, VIRGIL. Such admiration still remained for these divine geniuses; though no poet had appeared for many centuries, who could justly pretend to have imitated them.

A man's genius is always, in the beginning of life, as much unknown to himself as to others, and it is only after frequent trials, attended with success, that he dares think himself equal to those undertakings, in which those, who have succeeded, have fixed the admiration of mankind. If his own nation be already possessed of many models of eloquence, he naturally compares his own juvenile exercises with these; and being sensible of the great disproportion, is discouraged from any farther attempts, and never aims at a rivalship with those authors, whom he so much admires. A noble emulation is the source of every excellence. Admiration and modesty naturally extinguish this emulation. And no one is so liable to an excess of admiration and modesty as a truly great genius.

Next to emulation, the greatest encourager of the noble arts is praise and glory. A writer is animated with new force, when he hears the applauses of the world for his former productions; and, being roused by such a motive, he often reaches a pitch of perfection, which is equally surprizing to himself and to his readers. But when the posts of honour are all occupied, his first attempts are but coldly received by the public; being compared to productions, which are both in themselves more excellent, and have already the advantage of an established reputation. Were MOLIERE and CORNEILLE to bring upon the stage at present their early productions, which were formerly so well received, it would discourage the young poets, to see the indifference and disdain of the public. The ignorance of the age alone could have given admission to the *Prince of* TYRE; but it is to that we owe *the Moor*: Had *Every man in his humour* been rejected, we had never seen VOLPONE.[35]

Perhaps, it may not be for the advantage of any nation to have the arts imported from their neighbours in too great perfection. This extinguishes emulation, and sinks the ardour of the generous youth. So many models of ITALIAN painting brought into BRITAIN, instead of exciting our artists, is the cause of their small progress in that noble art. The same, perhaps, was the case of ROME, when it received the arts from GREECE. That multitude of polite productions in the FRENCH language, dispersed all over GERMANY and the NORTH, hinder these nations from cultivating their own language, and keep them still dependent on their neighbours for those elegant entertainments.

It is true, the ancients had left us models in every kind of writing, which are highly worthy of admiration. But besides that they were written in languages, known only to the learned; besides this, I say, the comparison is not so perfect or entire between modern wits, and those who lived in so remote an age. Had WALLER been born in ROME, during the reign of TIBERIUS, his first productions had been despised, when compared to the finished odes of HORACE.[36] But in this island the superiority of the ROMAN poet diminished nothing from the fame of the ENGLISH. We esteemed ourselves sufficiently happy, that our climate and language could produce but a faint copy of so excellent an original.

In short, the arts and sciences, like some plants, require a fresh soil; and however rich the land may be, and however you may recruit it by art or care, it will never, when once exhausted, produce any thing that is perfect or finished in the kind.

ESSAY TWELVE

Of national characters

THE vulgar are apt to carry all *national characters* to extremes; and having once established it as a principle, that any people are knavish, or cowardly, or ignorant, they will admit of no exception, but comprehend every individual under the same censure. Men of sense condemn these undistinguishing judgments: Though at the same time, they allow, that each nation has a peculiar set of manners, and that some particular qualities are more frequently to be met with among one people than among their neighbours. The common people in SWITZERLAND have probably more honesty than those of the same rank in IRELAND; and every prudent man will, from that circumstance alone, make a difference in the trust which he reposes in each. We have reason to expect greater wit and gaiety in a FRENCHMAN than in a SPANIARD; though CERVANTES was born in SPAIN. An ENGLISHMAN will naturally be supposed to have more knowledge than a DANE; though TYCHO BRAHE was a native of DENMARK.

Different reasons are assigned for these *national characters*; while some account for them from *moral*, others from *physical* causes. By *moral* causes, I mean all circumstances which are fitted to work on the mind as motives or reasons, and which render a peculiar set of manners habitual to us. Of this kind are, the nature of the government, the revolutions of public affairs, the plenty or penury in which the people live, the situation of the nation with regard to its neighbours, and such like circumstances. By *physical* causes, I mean those qualities of the air and climate, which are supposed to work insensibly on the temper, by altering the tone and habit of the body, and giving a particular complexion, which, though reflexion and reason may

78

sometimes overcome it, will yet prevail among the generality of mankind, and have an influence on their manners.

That the character of a nation will much depend on *moral* causes, must be evident to the most superficial observer; since a nation is nothing but a collection of individuals, and the manners of individuals are frequently determined by these causes. As poverty and hard labour debase the minds of the common people, and render them unfit for any science and ingenious profession; so where any government becomes very oppressive to all its subjects, it must have a proportional effect on their temper and genius, and must banish all the liberal arts from among them.

The same principle of moral causes fixes the character of different professions, and alters even that disposition, which the particular members receive from the hand of nature. A *soldier* and a *priest* are different characters, in all nations, and all ages; and this difference is founded on circumstances, whose operation is eternal and unalterable.

The uncertainty of their life makes soldiers lavish and generous, as well as brave: Their idleness, together with the large societies, which they form in camps or garrisons, inclines them to pleasure and gallantry: By their frequent change of company, they acquire good breeding and an openness of behaviour: Being employed only against a public and an open enemy, they become candid, honest, and undesigning: And as they use more the labour of the body than that of the mind, they are commonly thoughtless and ignorant.[a]

It is a trite, but not altogether a false maxim, that *priests of all religions are the same*; and though the character of the profession will not, in every instance, prevail over the personal character, yet is it sure always to predominate with the greater number. For as chymists observe, that spirits, when raised to a certain height, are all the same, from whatever materials they be extracted; so these men, being elevated above humanity, acquire a uniform character, which is entirely their own, and which, in my opinion, is, generally speaking, not the

---

[a] IT is a saying of MENANDER, Kompsos stratiotes, oud'an ei plattei [sic] theos Outheis genoit'an. MEN. apud STOBAEUM. *It is not in the power even of God to make a polite soldier*. The contrary observation with regard to the manners of soldiers takes place in our days. This seems to me a presumption, that the ancients owed all their refinement and civility to books and study; for which, indeed, a soldier's life is not so well calculated. Company and the world is their sphere. And if there be any politeness to be learned from company, they will certainly have a considerable share of it.[1]

most amiable that is to be met with in human society. It is, in most points, opposite to that of a soldier; as is the way of life, from which it is derived.[b]

As to *physical causes*, I am inclined to doubt altogether of their operation in this particular; nor do I think, that men owe any thing

[b] THOUGH all mankind have a strong propensity to religion at certain times and in certain dispositions; yet are there few or none, who have it to that degree, and with that constancy, which is requisite to support the character of this profession. It must, therefore, happen, that clergymen, being drawn from the common mass of mankind, as people are to other employments, by the views of profit, the greatest part, though no atheists or free-thinkers, will find it necessary, on particular occasions, to feign more devotion than they are, at that time, possessed of, and to maintain the appearance of fervor and seriousness, even when jaded with the exercises of their religion, or when they have their minds engaged in the common occupations of life. They must not, like the rest of the world, give scope to their natural movements and sentiments: They must set a guard over their looks and words and actions: And in order to support the veneration paid them by the ignorant vulgar, they must not only keep a remarkable reserve, but must promote the spirit of superstition, by a continued grimace and hypocrisy. This dissimulation often destroys the candor and ingenuity of their temper, and makes an irreparable breach in their character.

If by chance any of them be possessed of a temper more susceptible of devotion than usual, so that he has but little occasion for hypocrisy to support the character of his profession; it is so natural for him to overrate this advantage, and to think that it atones for every violation of morality, that frequently he is not more virtuous than the hypocrite. And though few dare openly avow those exploded opinions, *that every thing is lawful to the saints*, and *that they alone have property in their goods*; yet may we observe, that these principles lurk in every bosom, and represent a zeal for religious observances as so great a merit, that it may compensate for many vices and enormities. This observation is so common, that all prudent men are on their guard, when they meet with any extraordinary appearance of religion; though at the same time, they confess, that there are many exceptions to this general rule, and that probity and superstition, or even probity and fanaticism, are not altogether and in every instance incompatible.

Most men are ambitious; but the ambition of other men may commonly be satisfied, by excelling in their particular profession, and thereby promoting the interests of society. The ambition of the clergy can often be satisfied only by promoting ignorance and superstition and implicit faith and pious frauds. And having got what ARCHIMEDES only wanted, (*viz.* another world on which he could fix his engines) no wonder they move this world at their pleasure.

Most men have an overweaning conceit of themselves; but *these* have a particular temptation to that vice, who are regarded with such veneration, and are even deemed sacred, by the ignorant multitude.

Most men are apt to bear a particular regard for members of their own profession; but as a lawyer, or physician, or merchant, does, each of them, follow out his business apart, the interests of these professions are not so closely united as the interests of clergymen of the same religion; where the whole body gains by the veneration, paid to their common tenets, and by the suppression of antagonists.

Few men can bear contradiction with patience; but the clergy too often proceed even to a degree of fury on this head: Because all their credit and livelihood depend of their temper or genius to the air, food, or climate. I confess, that the contrary opinion may justly, at first sight, seem probable; since we find, that these circumstances have an influence over every other animal, and that even those creatures, which are fitted to live in all climates, such as dogs, horses, &c. do not attain the same perfection in all. The courage of bull-dogs and game-cocks seems peculiar to ENGLAND. FLANDERS is remarkable for large and heavy horses: SPAIN for horses light, and of good mettle. And any breed of these creatures, transplanted from one country to another, will soon lose the qualities, which they derived from their native climate. It may be asked, why not the same with men?[c]

upon the belief, which their opinions meet with; and they alone pretend to a divine and supernatural authority, or have any colour for representing their antagonists as impious and prophane. The *Odium Theologicum*, or Theological Hatred, is noted even to a proverb, and means that degree of rancour, which is the most furious and implacable.

Revenge is a natural passion to mankind; but seems to reign with the greatest force in priests and women: Because, being deprived of the immediate exertion of anger, in violence and combat, they are apt to fancy themselves despised on that account; and their pride supports their vindictive disposition.

Thus many of the vices of human nature are, by fixed moral causes, inflamed in that profession; and though several individuals escape the contagion, yet all wise governments will be on their guard against the attempts of a society, who will for ever combine into one faction, and while it acts as a society, will for ever be actuated by ambition, pride, revenge, and a persecuting spirit.

The temper of religion is grave and serious; and this is the character required of priests, which confines them to strict rules of decency, and commonly prevents irregularity and intemperance amongst them. The gaiety, much less the excesses of pleasure, is not permitted in that body; and this virtue is perhaps, the only one which they owe to their profession. In religions, indeed, founded on speculative principles, and where public discourses make a part of religious service, it may also be supposed that the clergy will have a considerable share in the learning of the times; though it is certain that their taste in eloquence will always be better than their skill in reasoning and philosophy. But whoever possesses the other noble virtues of humanity, meekness, and moderation, as very many of them, no doubt, do, is beholden for them to nature or reflection, not to the genius of his calling.

It was no bad expedient in the old ROMANS, for preventing the strong effect of the priestly character, to make it a law that no one should be received into the sacerdotal office, till he was past fifty years of age, DION. *Hal.* lib. i. The living a layman till that age, it is presumed, would be able to fix the character.[2]

[c] CAESAR (*de Bello* GALLICO, lib. i) says, that the GALLIC horses were very good; the GERMAN very bad. We find in lib. vii. that he was obliged to remount some GERMAN cavalry with GALLIC horses. At present, no part of EUROPE has so bad horses of all kinds as FRANCE: But GERMANY abounds with excellent war horses. This may beget a little suspicion, that even animals depend not on the climate; but on the different breeds, and on the skill and care in rearing them. The north of ENGLAND abounds in the best horses of all kinds which are in the world. In the neighbouring counties,

There are few questions more curious than this, or which will occur oftener in our enquiries concerning human affairs; and therefore it may be proper to give it a full examination.

The human mind is of a very imitative nature; nor is it possible for any set of men to converse often together, without acquiring a similitude of manners, and communicating to each other their vices as well as virtues. The propensity to company and society is strong in all rational creatures; and the same disposition, which gives us this propensity, makes us enter deeply into each other's sentiments, and causes like passions and inclinations to run, as it were, by contagion, through the whole club or knot of companions. Where a number of men are united into one political body, the occasions of their intercourse must be so frequent, for defence, commerce, and government, that, together with the same speech or language, they must acquire a resemblance in their manners, and have a common or national character, as well as a personal one, peculiar to each individual. Now though nature produces all kinds of temper and understanding in great abundance, it does not follow, that she always produces them in like proportions, and that in every society the ingredients of industry and indolence, valour and cowardice, humanity and brutality, wisdom and folly, will be mixed after the same manner. In the infancy of society, if any of these dispositions be found in greater abundance than the rest, it will naturally prevail in the composition, and give a tincture to the national character. Or should it be asserted, that no species of temper can reasonably be presumed to predominate, even in those contracted societies, and that the same proportions will always be preserved in the mixture; yet surely the persons in credit and authority, being still a more contracted body, cannot always be presumed to be of the same character; and their influence on the manners of the people, must, at all times, be very considerable. If on the first establishment of a republic, a BRUTUS should be placed in authority, and be transported with such an enthusiasm for liberty and public good, as to overlook all the ties of nature, as well as private interest, such an illustrious example will naturally have an effect on

north side the TWEED, no good horses of any kind are to be met with. STRABO, lib. ii. rejects, in a great measure, the influence of climates upon men. All is custom and education, says he. It is not from nature, that the ATHENIANS are learned, the LACEDEMONIANS ignorant, and the THEBANS too, who are still nearer neighbours to the former. Even the difference of animals, he adds, depends not on climate.[3]

the whole society, and kindle the same passion in every bosom.[4] Whatever it be that forms the manners of one generation, the next must imbibe a deeper tincture of the same dye; men being more susceptible of all impressions during infancy, and retaining these impressions as long as they remain in the world. I assert, then, that all national characters, where they depend not on fixed *moral* causes, proceed from such accidents as these, and that physical causes have no discernable operation on the human mind. It is a maxim in all philosophy, that causes, which do not appear, are to be considered as not existing.

If we run over the whole globe, or revolve all the annals of history, we shall discover every where signs of a sympathy or contagion of manners, none of the influence of air or climate.

First. We may observe, that, where a very extensive government has been established for many centuries, it spreads a national character over the whole empire, and communicates to every part a similarity of manners. Thus the CHINESE have the greatest uniformity of character imaginable; though the air and climate, in different parts of those vast dominions, admit of very considerable variations.

Secondly. In small governments, which are contiguous, the people have notwithstanding a different character, and are often as distinguishable in their manners as the most distant nations. ATHENS and THEBES were but a short day's journey from each other; though the ATHENIANS were as remarkable for ingenuity, politeness, and gaiety, as the THEBANS for dulness, rusticity, and a phlegmatic temper. PLUTARCH, discoursing of the effects of air on the minds of men, observes, that the inhabitants of the PIRAEUM possessed very different tempers from those of the higher town of ATHENS, which was distant about four miles from the former: But I believe no one attributes the difference of manners in WAPPING and St. JAMES's, to a difference of air or climate.[5]

Thirdly. The same national character commonly follows the authority of government to a precise boundary; and upon crossing a river or passing a mountain, one finds a new set of manners, with a new government. The LANGUEDOCIANS and GASCONS are the gayest people in FRANCE; but whenever you pass the PYRENEES, you are among SPANIARDS. Is it conceivable, that the qualities of the air should change exactly with the limits of an empire, which depend so much on the accidents of battles, negociations, and marriages?

Fourthly. Where any set of men, scattered over distant nations, maintain a close society or communication together, they acquire a similitude of manners, and have but little in common with the nations amongst whom they live. Thus the Jews in Europe, and the Armenians in the east, have a peculiar character; and the former are as much noted for fraud, as the latter for probity.[d] The *Jesuits*, in all *Roman-catholic* countries, are also observed to have a character peculiar to themselves.[6]

Fifthly. Where any accident, as a difference in language or religion, keeps two nations, inhabiting the same country, from mixing with each other, they will preserve, during several centuries, a distinct and even opposite set of manners. The integrity, gravity, and bravery of the Turks, form an exact contrast to the deceit, levity, and cowardice of the modern Greeks.

Sixthly. The same set of manners will follow a nation, and adhere to them over the whole globe, as well as the same laws and language. The Spanish, English, French and Dutch colonies are all distinguishable even between the tropics.

Seventhly. The manners of a people change very considerably from one age to another; either by great alterations in their government, by the mixtures of new people, or by that inconstancy, to which all human affairs are subject. The ingenuity, industry, and activity of the ancient Greeks have nothing in common with the stupidity and indolence of the present inhabitants of those regions. Candour, bravery, and love of liberty formed the character of the ancient Romans; as subtilty, cowardice, and a slavish disposition do that of the modern. The old Spaniards were restless, turbulent, and so addicted to war, that many of them killed themselves, when deprived of their arms by the Romans.[e] One would find an equal difficulty, at present, (at least one would have found it fifty years ago) to rouze up the modern Spaniards to arms. The Batavians were all soldiers of fortune, and hired themselves into the Roman armies. Their posterity make use of foreigners for the same purpose that the Romans

---

[d] A Small sect or society amidst a greater are commonly most regular in their morals; because they are more remarked, and the faults of individuals draw dishonour on the whole. The only exception to this rule is, when the superstition and prejudices of the large society are so strong as to throw an infamy on the smaller society, independent of their morals. For in that case, having no character either to save or gain, they become careless of their behaviour, except among themselves.

[e] Tit. Livii, lib. xxxiv, cap. 17.[7]

did their ancestors. Though some few strokes of the FRENCH character be the same with that which CAESAR has ascribed to the GAULS; yet what comparison between the civility, humanity, and knowledge of the modern inhabitants of that country, and the ignorance, barbarity, and grossness of the ancient?[8] Not to insist upon the great difference between the present possessors of BRITAIN, and those before the ROMAN conquest; we may observe that our ancestors, a few centuries ago, were sunk into the most abject superstition, last century they were inflamed with the most furious enthusiasm, and are now settled into the most cool indifference with regard to religious matters, that is to be found in any nation of the world.

Eighthly. Where several neighbouring nations have a very close communication together, either by policy, commerce, or travelling, they acquire a similitude of manners, proportioned to the communication. Thus all the FRANKS appear to have a uniform character to the eastern nations. The differences among them are like the peculiar accents of different provinces, which are not distinguishable, except by an ear accustomed to them, and which commonly escape a foreigner.

Ninthly. We may often remark a wonderful mixture of manners and characters in the same nation, speaking the same language, and subject to the same government: And in this particular the ENGLISH are the most remarkable of any people, that perhaps ever were in the world. Nor is this to be ascribed to the mutability and uncertainty of their climate, or to any other *physical* causes; since all these causes take place in the neighbouring country of SCOTLAND, without having the same effect. Where the government of a nation is altogether republican, it is apt to beget a particular set of manners. Where it is altogether monarchical, it is more apt to have the same effect; the imitation of superiors spreading the national manners faster among the people. If the governing part of a state consists altogether of merchants, as in HOLLAND, their uniform way of life will fix their character. If it consists chiefly of nobles and landed gentry, like GERMANY, FRANCE, and SPAIN, the same effect follows. The genius of a particular sect or religion is also apt to mould the manners of a people. But the ENGLISH government is a mixture of monarchy, aristocracy, and democracy. The people in authority are composed of gentry and merchants. All sects of religion are to be found among them. And the great liberty and independency, which every man enjoys, allows him to display the manners peculiar to him. Hence the ENGLISH, of any people in the universe, have the least of a national character; unless this very singularity may pass for such.

If the characters of men depended on the air and climate, the degrees of heat and cold should naturally be expected to have a mighty influence; since nothing has a greater effect on all plants and irrational animals. And indeed there is some reason to think, that all the nations, which live beyond the polar circles or between the tropics, are inferior to the rest of the species, and are incapable of all the higher attainments of the human mind. The poverty and misery of the northern inhabitants of the globe, and the indolence of the southern, from their few necessities, may, perhaps, account for this remarkable difference, without our having recourse to *physical* causes. This however is certain, that the characters of nations are very promiscuous in the temperate climates, and that almost all the general observations, which have been formed of the more southern or more northern people in these climates, are found to be uncertain and fallacious.[f]

Shall we say, that the neighbourhood of the sun inflames the imagination of men, and gives it a peculiar spirit and vivacity. The FRENCH, GREEKS, EGYPTIANS, and PERSIANS are remarkable for gaiety. The SPANIARDS, TURKS, and CHINESE are noted for gravity and a serious deportment, without any such difference of climate, as to produce this difference of temper.

The GREEKS and ROMANS, who called all other nations barbarians, confined genius and a fine understanding to the more southern climates, and pronounced the northern nations incapable of all know-

---

[f] I am apt to suspect the negroes, and in general all the other species of men (for there are four or five different kinds) to be naturally inferior to the whites. There scarcely ever was a civilized nation of any other complexion than white, nor even any individual eminent either in action or speculation. No ingenious manufactures amongst them, no arts, no sciences. On the other hand, the most rude and barbarous of the whites such as the ancient GERMANS, the present TARTARS, have still something eminent about them, in their valour, form of government, or some other particular. Such a uniform and constant difference could not happen, in so many countries and ages, if nature had not made an original distinction between these breeds of men. Not to mention our colonies, there are NEGROE slaves dispersed all over EUROPE, of whom none ever discovered any symptoms of ingenuity; though low people, without education, will start up amongst us, and distinguish themselves in every profession. In JAMAICA, indeed, they talk of one negro as a man of parts and learning; but it is likely he is admired for slender accomplishments, like a parrot, who speaks a few words plainly.

ledge and civility. But BRITAIN has produced as great men, either for action or learning, as GREECE or ITALY has to boast of.

It is pretended, that the sentiments of men become more delicate as the country approaches nearer the sun; and that the taste of beauty and elegance receives proportional improvements in every latitude; as we may particularly observe of the languages, of which the more southern are smooth and melodious, the northern harsh and untuneable. But this observation holds not universally. The ARABIC is uncouth and disagreeable: The MUSCOVITE soft and musical. Energy, strength, and harshness form the character of the LATIN tongue: The ITALIAN is the most liquid, smooth, and effeminate language that can possibly be imagined. Every language will depend somewhat on the manners of the people; but much more on that original stock of words and sounds, which they received from their ancestors, and which remain unchangeable, even while their manners admit of the greatest alterations. Who can doubt, but the ENGLISH are at present a more polite and knowing people than the GREEKS were for several ages after the siege of TROY? Yet is there no comparison between the language of MILTON and that of HOMER. Nay, the greater are the alterations and improvements, which happen in the manners of a people, the less can be expected in their language. A few eminent and refined geniuses will communicate their taste and knowledge to a whole people, and produce the greatest improvements; but they fix the tongue by their writings, and prevent, in some degree, its farther changes.

Lord BACON has observed, that the inhabitants of the south are, in general, more ingenious than those of the north; but that, where the native of a cold climate has genius, he rises to a higher pitch than can be reached by the southern wits. This observation a late writer[g] confirms, by comparing the southern wits to cucumbers, which are commonly all good in their kind; but at best are an insipid fruit: While the northern geniuses are like melons, of which not one in fifty is good; but when it is so, it has an exquisite relish.[9] I believe this remark may be allowed just, when confined to the EUROPEAN nations, and to the present age, or rather to the preceding one: But I think it may be accounted for from moral causes. All the sciences and liberal arts have been imported to us from the south; and it is

[g] Dr. Berkeley: Minute Philosopher.

easy to imagine, that, in the first ardor of application, when excited by emulation and by glory, the few, who were addicted to them, would carry them to the greatest height, and stretch every nerve, and every faculty, to reach the pinnacle of perfection. Such illustrious examples spread knowledge every where, and begot an universal esteem for the sciences: After which, it is no wonder, that industry relaxes; while men meet not with suitable encouragement, nor arrive at such distinction by their attainments. The universal diffusion of learning among a people, and the entire banishment of gross ignorance and rusticity, is, therefore, seldom attended with any remarkable perfection in particular persons. It seems to be taken for granted in the dialogue *de Oratoribus*, that knowledge was much more common in VESPASIAN's age than in that of CICERO and AUGUSTUS.[10] QUINTILIAN also complains of the profanation of learning, by its becoming too common. 'Formerly,' says JUVENAL, 'science was confined to GREECE and ITALY. Now the whole world emulates ATHENS and ROME. Eloquent GAUL has taught BRITAIN, knowing in the laws. Even THULE entertains thoughts of hiring rhetoricians for its instruction'.[h] This state of learning is remarkable; because JUVENAL is himself the last of the ROMAN writers, that possessed any degree of genius. Those, who succeeded, are valued for nothing but the matters of fact, of which they give us information. I hope the late conversion of MUSCOVY to the study of the sciences will not prove a like prognostic to the present period of learning.

Cardinal BENTIVOGLIO gives the preference to the northern nations above the southern with regard to candour and sincerity; and mentions, on the one hand, the SPANIARDS and ITALIANS, and on the other, the FLEMINGS and GERMANS.[12] But I am apt to think, that this has happened by accident. The ancient ROMANS seem to have been a candid sincere people, as are the modern TURKS. But if we must needs suppose, that this event has arisen from fixed causes, we may only conclude from it, that all extremes are apt to concur, and are commonly attended with the same consequences. Treachery is the

---

[h] "Sed Cantaber unde
Stoicus? antiqui praesertim aetate Metelli.
Nunc totus GRAIAS, nostrasque habet orbis ATHENAS.
GALLIA causidicos docuit facunda BRITANNOS:
De conducendo loquitor jam rhetore THULE."
Sat. 15[11]

usual concomitant of ignorance and barbarism; and if civilized nations ever embrace subtle and crooked politics, it is from an excess of refinement, which makes them disdain the plain direct path to power and glory.

Most conquests have gone from north to south; and it has hence been inferred, that the northern nations possess a superior degree of courage and ferocity. But it would have been juster to have said, that most conquests are made by poverty and want upon plenty and riches. The SARACENS, leaving the deserts of ARABIA, carried their conquests northwards upon all the fertile provinces of the ROMAN empire; and met the TURKS half way, who were coming southwards from the deserts of TARTARY.

An eminent writer[i] has remarked, that all courageous animals are also carnivorous, and that greater courage is to be expected in a people, such as the ENGLISH, whose food is strong and hearty, than in the half-starved commonalty of other countries. But the SWEDES, notwithstanding their disadvantages in this particular, are not inferior, in martial courage, to any nation that ever was in the world.

In general, we may observe, that courage, of all national qualities, is the most precarious; because it is exerted only at intervals, and by a few in every nation; whereas industry, knowledge, civility, may be of constant and universal use, and for several ages, may become habitual to the whole people. If courage be preserved, it must be by discipline, example, and opinion. The tenth legion of CAESAR, and the regiment of PICARDY in FRANCE were formed promiscuously from among the citizens; but having once entertained a notion, that they were the best troops in the service, this very opinion really made them such.[14]

As a proof how much courage depends on opinion, we may observe, that, of the two chief tribes of the GREEKS, the DORIANS, and IONIANS, the former were always esteemed, and always appeared more brave and manly than the latter; though the colonies of both the tribes were interspersed and intermingled through all the extent of GREECE, the Lesser ASIA, SICILY, ITALY, and the islands of the AEGEAN sea. The ATHENIANS were the only IONIANS that ever had any reputation for valour or military atchievements; though even these were esteemed inferior to the LACEDEMONIANS, the bravest of the DORIANS.

---

[i] Sir WILLIAM TEMPLE's account of the Netherlands.[13]

The only observation, with regard to the difference of men in different climates, on which we can rest any weight, is the vulgar one, that people in the northern regions have a greater inclination to strong liquors, and those in the southern to love and women. One can assign a very probable *physical* cause for this difference. Wine and distilled spirits warm the frozen blood in the colder climates, and fortify men against the injuries of the weather: As the genial heat of the sun, in the countries exposed to his beams, inflames the blood, and exalts the passion between the sexes.

Perhaps too, the matter may be accounted for by *moral* causes. All strong liquors are rarer in the north, and consequently are more coveted. DIODORUS SICULUS[j] tells us, that the GAULS in his time were great drunkards, and much addicted to wine; chiefly, I suppose, from its rarity and novelty. On the other hand, the heat in the southern climates, obliging men and women to go half naked, thereby renders their frequent commerce more dangerous, and inflames their mutual passion. This makes parents and husbands more jealous and reserved; which still farther inflames the passion. Not to mention, that, as women ripen sooner in the southern regions, it is necessary to observe greater jealousy and care in their education; it being evident, that a girl of twelve cannot possess equal discretion to govern this passion, with one who feels not its violence till she be seventeen or eighteen.

Perhaps too, the fact is false, that nature has, either from moral or physical causes, distributed these respective inclinations to the different climates. The ancient GREEKS, though born in a warm climate, seem to have been much addicted to the bottle; nor were their parties of pleasure any thing but matches of drinking among men, who passed their time altogether apart from the fair. Yet when ALEXANDER led the GREEKS into PERSIA, a still more southern climate, they multiplied their debauches of this kind, in imitation of the PERSIAN manners.[k] So honourable was the character of a drunkard among the PERSIANS, that CYRUS the younger,

---

[j] *Lib. v.* The same author ascribes taciturnity to that people; a new proof that national characters may alter very much. Taciturnity, as a national character, implies unsociableness. ARISTOTLE in his Politics, book ii. chap 2. says, that the GAULS are the only warlike nation, who are negligent of women.[15]

[k] BABYLONII *maxime in vinum, & quae ebrietatem sequuntur, effusi sunt.* QUINT. CUR. lib. v. cap. 1.[16]

soliciting the sober LACEDEMONIANS for succour against his brother ARTAXERXES, claims it chiefly on account of his superior endowments, as more valorous, more bountiful, and a better drinker.[1] DARIUS HYSTASPES made it be inscribed on his tomb-stone, among his other virtues and princely qualities, that no one could bear a greater quantity of liquor.[18] You may obtain any thing of the NEGROES by offering them strong drink; and may easily prevail with them to sell, not only their parents, but their wives and mistresses, for a cask of brandy. In FRANCE and ITALY few drink pure wine, except in the greatest heats of summer; and indeed, it is then almost as necessary, in order to recruit the spirits, evaporated by heat, as it is in SWEDEN, during the winter, in order to warm the bodies congealed by the rigour of the season.

If jealousy be regarded as a proof of an amorous disposition, no people were more jealous than the MUSCOVITES, before their communication with EUROPE had somewhat altered their manners in this particular.

But supposing the fact true, that nature, by physical principles, has regularly distributed these two passions, the one to the northern, the other to the southern regions; we can only infer, that the climate may affect the grosser and more bodily organs of our frame; not that it can work upon those finer organs, on which the operations of the mind and understanding depend. And this is agreeable to the analogy of nature. The races of animals never degenerate when carefully tended; and horses, in particular, always show their blood in their shape, spirit, and swiftness: But a coxcomb may beget a philosopher; as a man of virtue may leave a worthless progeny.

I shall conclude this subject with observing, that though the passion for liquor be more brutal and debasing than love, which, when properly managed, is the source of all politeness and refinement; yet this gives not so great an advantage to the southern climates, as we may be apt, at first sight, to imagine. When love goes beyond a certain pitch, it renders men jealous, and cuts off the free intercourse between the sexes, on which the politeness of a nation will commonly much depend. And if we would subtilize and refine upon this point, we might observe, that the people, in very temperate climates, are the most likely to attain all sorts of improvement; their blood not

---

[1] PLUT. SYMP. lib. i. quaest. 4.[17]

being so inflamed as to render them jealous, and yet being warm enough to make them set a due value on the charms and endowments of the fair sex.

Of commerce

THE greatest part of mankind may be divided into two classes; that of *shallow* thinkers, who fall short of the truth; and that of *abstruse* thinkers, who go beyond it. The latter class are by far the most uncommon; and I may add, by far the most useful and valuable. They suggest hints, at least, and start difficulties, which they want, perhaps, skill to pursue; but which may produce fine discoveries, when handled by men who have a more just way of thinking. At worst, what they say is uncommon; and if it should cost some pains to comprehend it, one has, however, the pleasure of hearing something that is new. An author is little to be valued, who tells us nothing but what we can learn from every coffeehouse conversation.

All people of *shallow* thought are apt to decry even those of *solid* understanding, as *abstruse* thinkers, and metaphysicians, and refiners; and never will allow any thing to be just which is beyond their own weak conceptions. There are some cases, I own, where an extraordinary refinement affords a strong presumption of falsehood, and where no reasoning is to be trusted but what is natural and easy. When a man deliberates concerning his conduct in any *particular* affair, and forms schemes in politics, trade, oeconomy, or any business in life, he never ought to draw his arguments too fine, or connect too long a chain of consequences together. Something is sure to happen, that will disconcert his reasoning, and produce an event different from what he expected. But when we reason upon *general* subjects, one may justly affirm, that our speculations can scarcely ever be too fine, provided they be just; and that the difference between a common man and a man of genius is chiefly seen in the shallowness or depth of the principles upon which they proceed. General reasonings seem intricate, merely because they are general; nor is it easy for the bulk of mankind to distinguish, in a great number of particulars, that common circumstance in which they all agree, or to extract it, pure and unmixed, from the other superfluous circumstances. Every judgment or conclusion, with them, is particular. They cannot enlarge their view to those universal propositions, which comprehend under them an infinite number of individuals, and include a whole science in a single theorem. Their eye is confounded with such an extensive prospect; and the conclusions, derived from it, even though clearly expressed, seem intricate and obscure. But however intricate they may seem, it is certain, that general principles, if just and sound, must always prevail in the general course of things, though they may fail in particular cases; and it is the chief business of philosophers to regard the general course of things. I may add, that it is also the chief business of politicians; especially in the domestic government of the state, where the public good, which is, or ought to be their object, depends on the concurrence of a multitude of causes; not, as in foreign politics, on accidents and chances, and the caprices of a few persons. This therefore makes the difference between *particular* deliberations and *general* reasonings, and renders subtilty and refinement much more suitable to the latter than to the former.

I thought this introduction necessary before the following discourses on *commerce, money, interest, balance of trade, &c.* where, perhaps, there will occur some principles which are uncommon, and which may seem too refined and subtile for such vulgar subjects. If false, let them be rejected: But no one ought to entertain a prejudice against them, merely because they are out of the common road.

The greatness of a state, and the happiness of its subjects, how independent soever they may be supposed in some respects, are commonly allowed to be inseparable with regard to commerce; and as private men receive greater security, in the possession of their trade and riches, from the power of the public, so the public becomes powerful in proportion to the opulence and extensive commerce of private men. This maxim is true in general; though I cannot forbear thinking, that it may possibly admit of exceptions, and that we often establish it with too little reserve and limitation. There may be some circumstances, where the commerce and riches and luxury of individuals, instead of adding strength to the public, will serve only to thin its armies, and diminish its authority among the neighbouring nations. Man is a very variable being, and susceptible of many different opinions, principles, and rules of conduct. What may be true, while he adheres to one way of thinking, will be found false, when he has embraced an opposite set of manners and opinions.

The bulk of every state may be divided into *husbandmen* and *manufacturers*. The former are employed in the culture of the land; the latter work up the materials furnished by the former, into all the commodities which are necessary or ornamental to human life. As soon as men quit their savage state, where they live chiefly by hunting and fishing, they must fall into these two classes; though the arts of agriculture employ *at first* the most numerous part of the society.[a] Time and experience improve so much these arts, that the land may easily maintain a much greater number of men, than those who are immediately employed in its cultivation, or who furnish the more necessary manufactures to such as are so employed.

If these superfluous hands apply themselves to the finer arts, which are commonly denominated the arts of *luxury*, they add to the happiness of the state; since they afford to many the opportunity of receiving enjoyments, with which they would otherwise have been unacquainted. But may not another scheme be proposed for the employment of these superfluous hands? May not the sovereign lay claim to them, and employ them in fleets and armies, to encrease the dominions of the state abroad, and spread its fame over distant nations? It is certain that the fewer desires and wants are found in the proprietors and labourers of land, the fewer hands do they employ; and consequently the superfluities of the land, instead of maintaining tradesmen and manufacturers, may support fleets and armies to a much greater extent, than where a great many arts are required to minister to the luxury of particular persons. Here therefore seems to be a kind of opposition between the greatness of the state and the happiness of the subject. A state is never greater than when all its superfluous hands are employed in the service of the

---

[a] Mons. MELON, in his political essay on commerce, asserts, that even at present, if you divide FRANCE into 20 parts, 16 are labourers or peasants; 2 only artizans; one belonging to the law, church, and military; and one merchants, financiers, and bourgeois. This calculation is certainly very erroneous. In FRANCE, ENGLAND, and indeed most parts of EUROPE, half of the inhabitants live in cities; and even of those who live in the country, a great number are artizans, perhaps above a third.[1]

public. The ease and convenience of private persons require, that these hands should be employed in their service. The one can never be satisfied, but at the expence of the other. As the ambition of the sovereign must entrench on the luxury of individuals; so the luxury of individuals must diminish the force, and check the ambition of the sovereign.

Nor is this reasoning merely chimerical; but is founded on history and experience. The republic of SPARTA was certainly more powerful than any state now in the world, consisting of an equal number of people; and this was owing entirely to the want of commerce and luxury. The HELOTES were the labourers: The SPARTANS were the soldiers or gentlemen. It is evident that the labour of the HELOTES could not have maintained so great a number of SPARTANS, had these latter lived in ease and delicacy, and given employment to a great variety of trades and manufactures. The like policy may be remarked in ROME. And indeed, throughout all ancient history, it is observable, that the smallest republics raised and maintained greater armies, than states consisting of triple the number of inhabitants, are able to support at present. It is computed, that, in all EUROPEAN nations, the proportion between soldiers and people does not exceed one to a hundred. But we read, that the city of ROME alone, with its small territory, raised and maintained, in early times, ten legions against the LATINS.[2] ATHENS, the whole of whose dominions was not larger than YORKSHIRE, sent to the expedition against SICILY near forty thousand men.[b] DIONYSIUS the elder, it is said, maintained a standing army of a hundred thousand foot and ten thousand horse, besides a large fleet of four hundred sail;[c] though his territories extended no farther than the city of SYRACUSE, about a third of the island of SICILY, and some sea-port towns and garrisons on the coast of ITALY and ILLYRICUM.[5] It is true, the ancient armies, in time of war, subsisted much upon plunder: But did not the enemy plunder in their turn? which was a more ruinous way of levying a tax, than any other that could be devised. In short, no probable reason can be assigned for the great power of the more ancient states above the modern, but their want of commerce and luxury. Few artizans were maintained by the labour of the farmers, and therefore more soldiers might live

[b] THUCYDIDES, lib. vii.[3]
[c] DIOD. SIC. lib. vii. This account, I own, is somewhat suspicious, not to say worse; chiefly because this army was not composed of citizens, but of mercenary forces.[4]

upon it. Titus Livius says, that Rome, in his time, would find it difficult to raise as large an army as that which, in her early days, she sent out against the Gauls and Latins.[d] Instead of those soldiers who fought for liberty and empire in Camillus's time, there were, in Augustus's days, musicians, painters, cooks, players, and tailors; and if the land was equally cultivated at both periods, it could certainly maintain equal numbers in the one profession as in the other. They added nothing to the mere necessaries of life, in the latter period more than in the former.

It is natural on this occasion to ask, whether sovereigns may not return to the maxims of ancient policy, and consult their own interest in this respect, more than the happiness of their subjects? I answer, that it appears to me, almost impossible; and that because ancient policy was violent, and contrary to the more natural and usual course of things. It is well known with what peculiar laws Sparta was governed, and what a prodigy that republic is justly esteemed by every one, who has considered human nature as it has displayed itself in other nations, and other ages. Were the testimony of history less positive and circumstantial, such a government would appear a mere philosophical whim or fiction, and impossible ever to be reduced to practice. And though the Roman and other ancient republics were supported on principles somewhat more natural, yet was there an extraordinary concurrence of circumstances to make them submit to such grievous burthens. They were free states; they were small ones; and the age being martial, all their neighbours were continually in arms. Freedom naturally begets public spirit, especially in small states; and this public spirit, this *amor patriae*, must encrease, when the public is almost in continual alarm, and men are obliged, every moment, to expose themselves to the greatest dangers for its defence. A continual succession of wars makes every citizen a soldier: He takes the field in his turn: And during his service he is chiefly maintained by himself. This service is indeed equivalent to a heavy tax; yet is it less felt by a people addicted to arms, who fight for honour and revenge more than pay, and are unacquainted with gain and industry as well as pleasure.[e] Not to mention the great equality of fortunes among

---

[d] Titi Livii, lib. vii. cap. 24. 'Adeo in quae laboramus,' says he, 'sola crevimus, divitias luxuriemque.'[6]

[e] The more ancient Romans lived in perpetual war with all their neighbours: And in old Latin, the term *hostis*, expressed both a stranger and an enemy. This is remarked

the inhabitants of the ancient republics, where every field, belonging to a different proprietor, was able to maintain a family, and rendered the numbers of citizens very considerable, even without trade and manufactures.

But though the want of trade and manufactures, among a free and very martial people, may *sometimes* have no other effect than to render the public more powerful, it is certain, that, in the common course of human affairs, it will have a quite contrary tendency. Sovereigns must take mankind as they find them, and cannot pretend to introduce any violent change in their principles and ways of thinking. A long course of time, with a variety of accidents and circumstances, are requisite to produce those great revolutions, which so much diversify the face of human affairs. And the less natural any set of principles are, which support a particular society, the more difficulty will a legislator meet with in raising and cultivating them. It is his best policy to comply with the common bent of mankind, and give it all the improvements of which it is susceptible. Now, according to the most natural course of things, industry and arts and trade encrease the power of the sovereign as well as the happiness of the subjects; and that policy is violent, which aggrandizes the public by the poverty of individuals. This will easily appear from a few considerations, which will present to us the consequences of sloth and barbarity.

Where manufactures and mechanic arts are not cultivated, the bulk of the people must apply themselves to agriculture; and if their skill and industry encrease, there must arise a great superfluity from their labour beyond what suffices to maintain them. They have no temptation, therefore, to encrease their skill and industry; since they cannot exchange that superfluity for any commodities, which may serve either to their pleasure or vanity. A habit of indolence naturally pre-

by Cicero; but by him is ascribed to the humanity of his ancestors, who softened, as much as possible, the denomination of an enemy, by calling him by the same appellation which signified a stranger. *De Off.* lib. ii. It is however much more probable, from the manners of the times, that the ferocity of those people was so great as to make them regard all strangers as enemies, and call them by the same name. It is not, besides, consistent with the most common maxims of policy or of nature, that any state should regard its public enemies with a friendly eye, or preserve any such sentiments for them as the Roman orator would ascribe to his ancestors. Not to mention, that the early Romans really exercised piracy, as we learn from their first treaties with Carthage, preserved by Polybius, lib. iii. and consequently, like the Sallee and Algerine rovers, were actually at war with most nations, and a stranger and an enemy were with them almost synonimous.[7]

vails. The greater part of the land lies uncultivated. What is cultivated, yields not its utmost for want of skill and assiduity in the
farmers. If at any time the public exigencies require, that great numbers should be employed in the public service, the labour of the
people furnishes now no superfluities, by which these numbers can
be maintained. The labourers cannot encrease their skill and industry
on a sudden. Lands uncultivated cannot be brought into tillage for
some years. The armies, mean while, must either make sudden and
violent conquests, or disband for want of subsistence. A regular attack
or defence, therefore, is not to be expected from such a people, and
their soldiers must be as ignorant and unskilful as their farmers and
manufacturers.

Every thing in the world is purchased by labour; and our passions
are the only causes of labour. When a nation abounds in manufactures and mechanic arts, the proprietors of land, as well as the
farmers, study agriculture as a science, and redouble their industry
and attention. The superfluity, which arises from their labour, is not
lost; but is exchanged with manufacturers for those commodities,
which men's luxury now makes them covet. By this means, land
furnishes a great deal more of the necessaries of life, than what
suffices for those who cultivate it. In times of peace and tranquillity,
this superfluity goes to the maintenance of manufacturers, and the
improvers of liberal arts. But it is easy for the public to convert
many of these manufacturers into soldiers, and maintain them by that
superfluity, which arises from the labour of the farmers. Accordingly
we find, that this is the case in all civilized governments. When the
sovereign raises an army, what is the consequence? He imposes a
tax. This tax obliges all the people to retrench what is least necessary
to their subsistence. Those, who labour in such commodities, must
either enlist in the troops, or turn themselves to agriculture, and
thereby oblige some labourers to enlist for want of business. And to
consider the matter abstractedly, manufactures encrease the power
of the state only as they store up so much labour, and that of a kind
to which the public may lay claim, without depriving any one of the
necessaries of life. The more labour, therefore, is employed beyond
mere necessaries, the more powerful is any state; since the persons
engaged in that labour may easily be converted to the public service.
In a state without manufactures, there may be the same number of
hands; but there is not the same quantity of labour, nor of the same

kind. All the labour is there bestowed upon necessaries, which can admit of little or no abatement.

Thus the greatness of the sovereign and the happiness of the state are, in a great measure, united with regard to trade and manufactures. It is a violent method, and in most cases impracticable, to oblige the labourer to toil, in order to raise from the land more than what subsists himself and family. Furnish him with manufactures and commodities, and he will do it of himself. Afterwards you will find it easy to seize some part of his superfluous labour, and employ it in the public service, without giving him his wonted return. Being accustomed to industry, he will think this less grievous, than if, at once, you obliged him to an augmentation of labour without any reward. The case is the same with regard to the other members of the state. The greater is the stock of labour of all kinds, the greater quantity may be taken from the heap, without making any sensible alteration in it.

A public granary of corn, a storehouse of cloth, a magazine of arms; all these must be allowed real riches and strength in any state. Trade and industry are really nothing but a stock of labour, which, in times of peace and tranquillity, is employed for the ease and satisfaction of individuals; but in the exigencies of state, may, in part, be turned to public advantage. Could we convert a city into a kind of fortified camp, and infuse into each breast so martial a genius, and such a passion for public good, as to make every one willing to undergo the greatest hardships for the sake of the public; these affections might now, as in ancient times, prove alone a sufficient spur to industry, and support the community. It would then be advantageous, as in camps, to banish all arts and luxury; and, by restrictions on equipage and tables, make the provisions and forage last longer than if the army were loaded with a number of superfluous retainers. But as these principles are too disinterested and too difficult to support, it is requisite to govern men by other passions, and animate them with a spirit of avarice and industry, art and luxury. The camp is, in this case, loaded with a superfluous retinue; but the provisions flow in proportionably larger. The harmony of the whole is still supported; and the natural bent of the mind being more complied with, individuals, as well as the public, find their account in the observance of those maxims.

The same method of reasoning will let us see the advantage of *foreign* commerce, in augmenting the power of the state, as well as the riches and happiness of the subject. It encreases the stock of labour in the nation; and the sovereign may convert what share of it he finds necessary to the service of the public. Foreign trade, by its imports, furnishes materials for new manufactures; and by its exports, it produces labour in particular commodities, which could not be consumed at home. In short, a kingdom, that has a large import and export, must abound more with industry, and that employed upon delicacies and luxuries, than a kingdom which rests contented with its native commodities. It is, therefore, more powerful, as well as richer and happier. The individuals reap the benefit of these commodities, so far as they gratify the senses and appetites. And the public is also a gainer, while a greater stock of labour is, by this means, stored up against any public exigency; that is, a greater number of laborious men are maintained, who may be diverted to the public service, without robbing any one of the necessaries, or even the chief conveniencies of life.

If we consult history, we shall find, that, in most nations, foreign trade has preceded any refinement in home manufactures, and given birth to domestic luxury. The temptation is stronger to make use of foreign commodities, which are ready for use, and which are entirely new to us, than to make improvements on any domestic commodity, which always advance by slow degrees, and never affect us by their novelty. The profit is also very great, in exporting what is superfluous at home, and what bears no price, to foreign nations, whose soil or climate is not favourable to that commodity. Thus men become acquainted with the *pleasures* of luxury and the *profits* of commerce; and their *delicacy* and *industry*, being once awakened, carry them on to farther improvements, in every branch of domestic as well as foreign trade. And this perhaps is the chief advantage which arises from a commerce with strangers. It rouses men from their indolence; and presenting the gayer and more opulent part of the nation with objects of luxury, which they never before dreamed of, raises in them a desire of a more splendid way of life than what their ancestors enjoyed. And at the same time, the few merchants, who possess the secret of this importation and exportation, make great profits; and becoming rivals in wealth to the ancient nobility, tempt other adventurers to become their rivals in commerce. Imitation soon diffuses all those arts; while domestic manufacturers emulate the foreign in their improvements, and work up every home commodity to the utmost perfection of which it is susceptible. Their own steel and iron, in such laborious hands, become equal to the gold and rubies of the INDIES.

When the affairs of the society are once brought to this situation, a nation may lose most of its foreign trade, and yet continue a great and powerful people. If strangers will not take any particular commodity of ours, we must cease to labour in it. The same hands will turn themselves towards some refinement in other commodities, which may be wanted at home. And there must always be materials for them to work upon; till every person in the state, who possesses riches, enjoys as great plenty of home commodities, and those in as great perfection, as he desires; which can never possibly happen. CHINA is represented as one of the most flourishing empires in the world; though it has very little commerce beyond its own territories.

It will not, I hope, be considered as a superfluous digression, if I here observe, that, as the multitude of mechanical arts is advantageous, so is the great number of persons to whose share the productions of these arts fall. A too great disproportion among the citizens weakens any state. Every person, if possible, ought to enjoy the fruits of his labour, in a full possession of all the necessaries, and many of the conveniencies of life. No one can doubt, but such an equality is most suitable to human nature, and diminishes much less from the *happiness* of the rich than it adds to that of the poor. It also augments the *power of the state*, and makes any extraordinary taxes or impositions be paid with more chearfulness. Where the riches are engrossed by a few, these must contribute very largely to the supplying of the public necessities. But when the riches are dispersed among multitudes, the burthen feels light on every shoulder, and the taxes make not a very sensible difference on any one's way of living.

Add to this, that, where the riches are in few hands, these must enjoy all the power, and will readily conspire to lay the whole burthen on the poor, and oppress them still farther, to the discouragement of all industry.

In this circumstance consists the great advantage of ENGLAND above any nation at present in the world, or that appears in the records of any story. It is true, the ENGLISH feel some disadvantages in foreign trade by the high price of labour, which is in part the effect of the riches of their artisans, as well as of the plenty of money: But as foreign trade is not the most material circumstance, it is not to be put in competition with the happiness of so many millions. And if there were no more to endear to them that free government under which they live, this alone were sufficient. The poverty of the common people is a natural, if not an infallible effect of absolute monarchy; though I doubt, whether it be always true, on the other hand, that their riches are an infallible result of liberty. Liberty must be attended with particular accidents, and a certain turn of thinking, in order to produce that effect. Lord BACON, accounting for the great advantages obtained by the ENGLISH in their wars with FRANCE, ascribes them chiefly to the superior ease and plenty of the common people amongst the former; yet the government of the two kingdoms was, at that time, pretty much alike.[8] Where the labourers and artisans are accustomed to work for low wages, and to retain but a small part of the fruits of their labour, it is difficult for them, even in a free government, to better their condition, or conspire among themselves to heighten their wages. But even where they are accustomed to a more plentiful way of life, it is easy for the rich, in an arbitrary government, to conspire against *them*, and throw the whole burthen of the taxes on their shoulders.

It may seem an odd position, that the poverty of the common people in FRANCE, ITALY, and SPAIN, is, in some measure, owing to the superior riches of the soil and happiness of the climate; yet there want not reasons to justify this paradox. In such a fine mould or soil as that of those more southern regions, agriculture is an easy art; and one man, with a couple of sorry horses, will be able, in a season, to cultivate as much land as will pay a pretty considerable rent to the proprietor. All the art, which the farmer knows, is to leave his ground fallow for a year, as soon as it is exhausted; and the warmth of the sun alone and temperature of the climate enrich it, and restore its fertility. Such poor peasants, therefore, require only a simple maintenance for their labour. They have no stock or riches, which claim more; and at the same time, they are for ever dependant on their landlord, who gives no leases, nor fears that his land will be spoiled by the ill methods of cultivation. In ENGLAND, the land is rich, but coarse; must be cultivated at a great expence; and produces slender crops, when not carefully managed, and by a method which gives not the full profit but in a course of several years. A farmer, therefore, in ENGLAND must have a considerable stock, and a long lease; which beget proportional profits. The fine vineyards of CHAMPAGNE and BURGUNDY, that often yield to the landlord above five pounds *per* acre, are cultivated by peasants, who have scarcely bread: The reason is, that such peasants need no stock but their own limbs, with instruments of husbandry, which they can buy for twenty shillings. The farmers are commonly in some better circumstances in those countries. But the grasiers are most at their ease of all those who cultivate the land. The reason is still the same. Men must have profits proportionable to their expence and hazard. Where so considerable a number of the labouring poor as the peasants and farmers are in very low circumstances, all the rest must partake of their poverty, whether the government of that nation be monarchical or republican.

We may form a similar remark with regard to the general history of mankind. What is the reason, why no people, living between the tropics, could never yet attain to any art or civility, or reach even any police in their government, and any military discipline; while few nations in the temperate climates have been altogether deprived of these advantages? It is probable that one cause of this phaenomenon is the warmth and equality of weather in the torrid zone, which render clothes and houses less requisite for the inhabitants, and thereby remove, in part, that necessity, which is the great spur to industry and invention. *Curis acuens mortalia corda.*[9] Not to mention, that the fewer goods or possessions of this kind any people enjoy, the fewer quarrels are likely to arise amongst them, and the less necessity will there be for a settled police or regular authority to protect and defend them from foreign enemies, or from each other.

Of refinement in the arts[1]

LUXURY is a word of an uncertain signification, and may be taken in a good as well as in a bad sense. In general, it means great refinement in the gratification of the senses; and any degree of it may be innocent or blameable, according to the age, or country, or condition of the person. The bounds between the virtue and the vice cannot here be exactly fixed, more than in other moral subjects. To imagine, that the gratifying of any sense, or the indulging of any delicacy in meat, drink, or apparel, is of itself a vice, can never enter into a head, that is not disordered by the frenzies of enthusiasm. I have, indeed, heard of a monk abroad, who, because the windows of his cell opened upon a noble prospect, made a *covenant with his eyes* never to turn that way, or receive so sensual a gratification. And such is the crime of drinking CHAMPAGNE or BURGUNDY, preferably to small beer or porter. These indulgences are only vices, when they are pursued at the expence of some virtue, as liberality or charity; in like manner as they are follies, when for them a man ruins his fortune, and reduces himself to want and beggary. Where they entrench upon no virtue, but leave ample subject whence to provide for friends, family, and every proper object of generosity or compassion, they are entirely innocent, and have in every age been acknowledged such by almost all moralists. To be entirely occupied with the luxury of the table, for instance, without any relish for the pleasures of ambition, study, or conversation, is a mark of stupidity, and is incompatible with any vigour of temper or genius. To confine one's expence entirely to such a gratification, without regard to friends or family, is an indication of a heart destitute of humanity or benevolence. But if a man reserve time sufficient for all laudable pursuits, and money sufficient for all generous purposes, he is free from every shadow of blame or reproach.

Since luxury may be considered either as innocent or blameable, one may be surprized at those preposterous opinions, which have been entertained concerning it; while men of libertine principles bestow praises even on vicious luxury, and represent it as highly advantageous to society; and on the other hand, men of severe morals blame even the most innocent luxury, and represent it as the source of all the corruptions, disorders, and factions, incident to civil government. We shall here endeavour to correct both these extremes, by proving, *first*, that the ages of refinement are both the happiest and most virtuous; *secondly*, that wherever luxury ceases to be innocent, it also ceases to be beneficial; and when carried a degree too far, is a quality pernicious, though perhaps not the most pernicious, to political society.

To prove the first point, we need but consider the effects of refinement both on *private* and on *public* life. Human happiness, according to the most received notions, seems to consist in three ingredients; action, pleasure, and indolence: And though these ingredients ought to be mixed in different proportions, according to the particular disposition of the person; yet no one ingredient can be entirely wanting, without destroying, in some measure, the relish of the whole composition. Indolence or repose, indeed, seems not of itself to contribute much to our enjoyment; but, like sleep, is requisite as an indulgence to the weakness of human nature, which cannot support an uninterrupted course of business or pleasure. That quick march of the spirits, which takes a man from himself, and chiefly gives satisfaction, does in the end exhaust the mind, and requires some intervals of repose, which, though agreeable for a moment, yet, if prolonged, beget a languor and lethargy, that destroys all enjoyment. Education, custom, and example, have a mighty influence in turning the mind to any of these pursuits; and it must be owned, that, where they promote a relish for action and pleasure, they are so far favourable to human happiness. In times when industry and the arts flourish, men are kept in perpetual occupation, and enjoy, as their reward, the occupation itself, as well as those pleasures which are the fruit of their labour. The mind acquires new vigour; enlarges its powers and faculties; and by an assiduity in honest industry, both satisfies its natural appetites, and prevents the growth of unnatural ones, which commonly spring up, when nourished by ease and idleness. Banish those arts from society, you deprive men both of action and of pleasure; and leaving nothing but indolence in their place, you even destroy the relish of indolence, which never is agreeable, but when it succeeds to labour, and recruits the spirits, exhausted by too much application and fatigue.

Another advantage of industry and of refinements in the mechanical arts, is, that they commonly produce some refinements in the liberal; nor can one be carried to perfection, without being accompanied, in some degree, with the other. The same age, which produces great philosophers and politicians, renowned generals and poets, usually abounds with skilful weavers and ship-carpenters. We cannot reasonably expect, that a piece of woollen cloth will be wrought to perfection in a nation, which is ignorant of astronomy, or where ethics are neglected. The spirit of the age affects all the arts; and the minds of men, being once roused from their lethargy, and put into a fermentation, turn themselves on all sides, and carry improvements into every art and science. Profound ignorance is totally banished, and men enjoy the privilege of rational creatures, to think as well as to act, to cultivate the pleasures of the mind as well as those of the body.

The more these refined arts advance, the more sociable men become; nor is it possible, that, when enriched with science, and possessed of a fund of conversation, they should be contented to remain in solitude, or live with their fellow-citizens in that distant manner, which is peculiar to ignorant and barbarous nations. They flock into cities; love to receive and communicate knowledge; to show their wit or their breeding; their taste in conversation or living, in clothes or furniture. Curiosity allures the wise; vanity the foolish; and pleasure both. Particular clubs and societies are every where formed: Both sexes meet in an easy and sociable manner; and the tempers of men, as well as their behaviour, refine apace. So that, beside the improvements which they receive from knowledge and the liberal arts, it is impossible but they must feel an encrease of humanity, from the very habit of conversing together, and contributing to each other's pleasure and entertainment. Thus *industry*, *knowledge*, and *humanity*, are linked together by an indissoluble chain, and are found, from experience as well as reason, to be peculiar to the more polished, and, what are commonly denominated, the more luxurious ages.

Nor are these advantages attended with disadvantages, that bear any proportion to them. The more men refine upon pleasure, the less will they indulge in excesses of any kind; because nothing is more destructive to true pleasure than such excesses. One may safely affirm, that the TARTARS are oftener guilty of beastly gluttony, when they feast on their dead horses, than EUROPEAN courtiers with all their refinements of cookery.[2] And if libertine love, or even infidelity to the marriage-bed, be more frequent in polite ages, when it is often regarded only as a piece of gallantry; drunkenness, on the other hand, is much less common: A vice more odious, and more pernicious both to mind and body. And in this matter I would appeal, not only to an OVID or a PETRONIUS, but to a SENECA or a CATO. We know, that CAESAR, during CATILINE's conspiracy, being necessitated to put into CATO's hands a *billet-doux*, which discovered an intrigue with SERVI-LIA, CATO's own sister, that stern philosopher threw it back to him with indignation; and, in the bitterness of his wrath, gave him the appellation of drunkard, as a term more opprobrious than that with which he could more justly have reproached him.[3]

But industry, knowledge, and humanity, are not advantageous in private life alone: They diffuse their beneficial influence on the *public*, and render the government as great and flourishing as they make individuals happy and prosperous. The encrease and consumption of all the commodities, which serve to the ornament and pleasure of life, are advantageous to society; because, at the same time that they multiply those innocent gratifications to individuals, they are a kind of *storehouse* of labour, which, in the exigencies of state, may be turned to the public service. In a nation, where there is no demand for such superfluities, men sink into indolence, lose all enjoyment of life, and are useless to the public, which cannot maintain or support its fleets and armies, from the industry of such slothful members.

The bounds of all the EUROPEAN kingdoms are, at present, nearly the same they were two hundred years ago: But what a difference is there in the power and grandeur of those kingdoms? Which can be ascribed to nothing but the encrease of art and industry. When CHARLES VIII. of FRANCE invaded ITALY, he carried with him about 20,000 men: Yet this armament so exhausted the nation, as we learn from GUICCIARDIN, that for some years it was not able to make so great an effort.[4] The late king of FRANCE, in time of war, kept in pay above 400,000 men;[a] though from MAZARINE's death to his own, he was engaged in a course of wars that lasted near thirty years.[5]

This industry is much promoted by the knowledge inseparable from ages of art and refinement; as, on the other hand, this knowledge enables the public to make the best advantage of the industry of its subjects. Laws, order, police, discipline; these can never be carried to any degree of perfection, before human reason has refined itself by exercise, and by an application to the more vulgar arts, at least, of commerce and manufacture. Can we expect, that a government will be well modelled by a people, who know not how to make a spinning-wheel, or to employ a loom to advantage? Not to mention, that all ignorant ages are infested with superstition, which throws the government off its bias, and disturbs men in the pursuit of their interest and happiness.

Knowledge in the arts of government naturally begets mildness and moderation, by instructing men in the advantages of humane maxims above rigour and severity, which drive subjects into rebellion, and make the return to submission impracticable, by cutting off all hopes of pardon. When the tempers of men are softened as well as their knowledge improved, this humanity appears still more conspicuous, and is the chief characteristic which distinguishes a civilized age from times of barbarity and ignorance. Factions are then less inveterate, revolutions less tragical, authority less severe, and seditions less frequent. Even foreign wars abate of their cruelty; and after the field of battle, where honour and interest steel men against compassion as well as fear, the combatants divest themselves of the brute, and resume the man.

Nor need we fear, that men, by losing their ferocity, will lose their martial spirit, or become less undaunted and vigorous in defence of their country or their liberty. The arts have no such effect in enervating either the mind or body. On the contrary, industry, their inseparable attendant, adds new force to both. And if anger, which is said to be the whetstone of courage, loses somewhat of its asperity, by politeness and refinement; a sense of honour, which is a stronger, more constant, and more governable principle, acquires fresh vigour by that elevation of genius which arises from knowledge and a good

---

[a] The inscription on the PLACE-DE-VENDOME says 440,000.

education. Add to this, that courage can neither have any duration, nor be of any use, when not accompanied with discipline and martial skill, which are seldom found among a barbarous people. The ancients remarked, that DATAMES was the only barbarian that ever knew the art of war.[6] And PYRRHUS, seeing the ROMANS marshal their army with some art and skill, said with surprize, *These barbarians have nothing barbarous in their discipline!*[7] It is observable, that, as the old ROMANS, by applying themselves solely to war, were almost the only uncivilized people that ever possessed military discipline; so the modern ITALIANS are the only civilized people, among EUROPEANS, that ever wanted courage and a martial spirit. Those who would ascribe this effeminacy of the ITALIANS to their luxury, or politeness, or application to the arts, need but consider the FRENCH and ENGLISH, whose bravery is as uncontestable, as their love for the arts, and their assiduity in commerce. The ITALIAN historians give us a more satisfactory reason for this degeneracy of their countrymen.[8] They shew us how the sword was dropped at once by all the ITALIAN sovereigns; while the VENETIAN aristocracy was jealous of its subjects, the FLORENTINE democracy applied itself entirely to commerce; ROME was governed by priests, and NAPLES by women. War then became the business of soldiers of fortune, who spared one another, and to the astonishment of the world, could engage a whole day in what they called a battle, and return at night to their camp, without the least bloodshed.

What has chiefly induced severe moralists to declaim against refinement in the arts, is the example of ancient ROME, which, joining, to its poverty and rusticity, virtue and public spirit, rose to such a surprizing height of grandeur and liberty; but having learned from its conquered provinces the ASIATIC luxury, fell into every kind of corruption; whence arose sedition and civil wars, attended at last with the total loss of liberty. All the LATIN classics, whom we peruse in our infancy, are full of these sentiments, and universally ascribe the ruin of their state to the arts and riches imported from the East: Insomuch that SALLUST represents a taste for painting as a vice, no less than lewdness and drinking. And so popular were these sentiments, during the later ages of the republic, that this author abounds in praises of the old rigid ROMAN virtue, though himself the most egregious instance of modern luxury and corruption; speaks contemptuously of the GRECIAN eloquence, though the most elegant writer in the world; nay, employs preposterous digressions and declamations to this purpose, though a model of taste and correctness.[9]

But it would be easy to prove, that these writers mistook the cause of the disorders in the ROMAN state, and ascribed to luxury and the arts, what really proceeded from an ill-modelled government, and the unlimited extent of conquests. Refinement on the pleasures and conveniencies of life has no natural tendency to beget venality and corruption. The value, which all men put upon any particular pleasure, depends on comparison and experience; nor is a porter less greedy of money, which he spends on bacon and brandy, than a courtier, who purchases champagne and ortolans. Riches are valuable at all times, and to all men; because they always purchase pleasures, such as men are accustomed to, and desire: Nor can any thing restrain or regulate the love of money, but a sense of honour and virtue; which, if it be not nearly equal at all times, will naturally abound most in ages of knowledge and refinement.

Of all EUROPEAN kingdoms, POLAND seems the most defective in the arts of war as well as peace, mechanical as well as liberal; yet it is there that venality and corruption do most prevail. The nobles seem to have preserved their crown elective for no other purpose, than regularly to sell it to the highest bidder. This is almost the only species of commerce, with which that people are acquainted.

The liberties of ENGLAND, so far from decaying since the improvements in the arts, have never flourished so much as during that period. And though corruption may seem to encrease of late years; this is chiefly to be ascribed to our established liberty, when our princes have found the impossibility of governing without parliaments, or of terrifying parliaments by the phantom of prerogative. Not to mention, that this corruption or venality prevails much more among the electors than the elected; and therefore cannot justly be ascribed to any refinements in luxury.

If we consider the matter in a proper light, we shall find, that a progress in the arts is rather favourable to liberty, and has a natural tendency to preserve, if not produce a free government. In rude unpolished nations, where the arts are neglected, all labour is bestowed on the cultivation of the ground; and the whole society is divided into two classes, proprietors of land, and their vassals or tenants. The latter are necessarily dependent, and fitted for slavery and subjection; especially where they possess no riches, and are not valued for their knowledge in agriculture; as must always be the case where the arts are neglected. The former naturally erect themselves into petty tyrants; and must either submit to an absolute master, for the sake of peace and order; or if they will preserve their independency, like the ancient barons, they must fall into feuds and contests among themselves, and throw the whole society into such confusion, as is perhaps worse than the most despotic government. But where luxury nourishes commerce and industry, the peasants, by a proper cultivation of the land, become rich and independent; while the tradesmen and merchants acquire a share of the property, and draw authority and consideration to that middling rank of men, who are the best and firmest basis of public liberty. These submit not to slavery, like the peasants, from poverty and meanness of spirit; and having no hopes of tyrannizing over others, like the barons, they are not tempted, for the sake of that gratification, to submit to the tyranny of their sovereign. They covet equal laws, which may secure their property, and preserve them from monarchical, as well as aristocratical tyranny.[10]

The lower house is the support of our popular government; and all the world acknowledges, that it owed its chief influence and consideration to the encrease of commerce, which threw such a balance of property into the hands of the commons. How inconsistent then is it to blame so violently a refinement in the arts, and to represent it as the bane of liberty and public spirit!

To declaim against present times, and magnify the virtue of remote ancestors, is a propensity almost inherent in human nature: And as the sentiments and opinions of civilized ages alone are transmitted to posterity, hence it is that we meet with so many severe judgments pronounced against luxury, and even science; and hence it is that at present we give so ready an assent to them. But the fallacy is easily perceived, by comparing different nations that are contemporaries; where we both judge more impartially, and can better set in opposition those manners, with which we are sufficiently acquainted. Treachery and cruelty, the most pernicious and most odious of all vices, seem peculiar to uncivilized ages; and by the refined GREEKS and ROMANS were ascribed to all the barbarous nations, which surrounded them. They might justly, therefore, have presumed, that their own ancestors, so highly celebrated, possessed no greater virtue, and were as much inferior to their posterity in honour and humanity, as in taste and science. An ancient FRANK or SAXON may be highly extolled: But I believe every man would think his life or fortune much less secure in the hands of a MOOR or TARTAR, than in those of a FRENCH or ENGLISH gentleman, the rank of men the most civilized in the most civilized nations.

We come now to the *second* position which we proposed to illustrate, to wit, that, as innocent luxury, or a refinement in the arts and conveniencies of life, is advantageous to the public; so wherever luxury ceases to be innocent, it also ceases to be beneficial; and when carried a degree farther, begins to be a quality pernicious, though, perhaps, not the most pernicious, to political society.

Let us consider what we call vicious luxury. No gratification, however sensual, can of itself be esteemed vicious. A gratification is only vicious, when it engrosses all a man's expence, and leaves no ability for such acts of duty and generosity as are required by his situation and fortune. Suppose, that he correct the vice, and employ part of his expence in the education of his children, in the support of his friends, and in relieving the poor; would any prejudice result to society? On the contrary, the same consumption would arise; and that labour, which, at present, is employed only in producing a slender gratification to one man, would relieve the necessitous, and bestow satisfaction on hundreds. The same care and toil that raise a dish of peas at CHRISTMAS, would give bread to a whole family during six months. To say, that, without a vicious luxury, the labour would not have been employed at all, is only to say, that there is some other defect in human nature, such as indolence, selfishness, inattention to others, for which luxury, in some measure, provides a remedy; as one poison may be an antidote to another. But virtue, like wholesome food, is better than poisons, however corrected.

Suppose the same number of men, that are at present in BRITAIN, with the same soil and climate; I ask, is it not possible for them to be happier, by the most perfect way of life that can be imagined, and by the greatest reformation that Omnipotence itself could work in their temper and disposition? To assert, that they cannot, appears evidently ridiculous. As the land is able to maintain more than all its inhabitants, they could never, in such a UTOPIAN state, feel any other ills than those which arise from bodily sickness; and these are not the half of human miseries. All other ills spring from some vice, either in ourselves or others; and even many of our diseases proceed from the same origin. Remove the vices, and the ills follow. You must only take care to remove all the vices. If you remove part, you may render the matter worse. By banishing *vicious* luxury, without curing sloth and an indifference to others, you only diminish industry in the state, and add nothing to men's charity or their generosity. Let us, therefore, rest contented with asserting, that two opposite vices in a state may be more advantageous than either of them alone; but let us never pronounce vice in itself advantageous. Is it not very inconsistent for an author to assert in one page, that moral distinctions are inventions of politicians for public interest; and in the next page maintain, that vice is advantageous to the public?[b] And indeed it seems upon any system of morality, little less than a contradiction in terms, to talk of a vice, which is in general beneficial to society.

I thought this reasoning necessary, in order to give some light to a philosophical question, which has been much disputed in BRITAIN. I call it a *philosophical* question, not a *political* one. For whatever may be the consequence of such a miraculous transformation of mankind, as would endow them with every species of virtue, and free them from every species of vice; this concerns not the magistrate, who aims only at possibilities. He cannot cure every vice by substituting a virtue in its place. Very often he can only cure one vice by another; and in that case, he ought to prefer what is least pernicious to society. Luxury, when excessive, is the source of many ills; but is in general preferable to sloth and idleness, which would commonly succeed in its place, and are more hurtful both to private persons and to the public. When sloth reigns, a mean uncultivated way of life prevails amongst individuals, without society, without enjoyment. And if the sovereign, in such a situation, demands the service of his subjects, the labour of the state suffices only to furnish the necessaries of life to the labourers, and can afford nothing to those who are employed in the public service.

[b] Fable of the Bees.[11]

ESSAY FIFTEEN

Of money

MONEY is not, properly speaking, one of the subjects of commerce; but only the instrument which men have agreed upon to facilitate the exchange of one commodity for another. It is none of the wheels of trade: It is the oil which renders the motion of the wheels more smooth and easy. If we consider any one kingdom by itself, it is evident, that the greater or less plenty of money is of no consequence; since the prices of commodities are always proportioned to the plenty of money, and a crown in HARRY VII.'s time served the same purpose as a pound does at present.[1] It is only the *public* which draws any advantage from the greater plenty of money; and that only in its wars and negociations with foreign states. And this is the reason, why all rich and trading countries, from CARTHAGE to BRITAIN and HOL-LAND, have employed mercenary troops, which they hired from their poorer neighbours. Were they to make use of their native subjects, they would find less advantage from their superior riches, and from their great plenty of gold and silver; since the pay of all their servants must rise in proportion to the public opulence. Our small army in BRITAIN of 20,000 men is maintained at as great expence as a FRENCH army twice as numerous. The ENGLISH fleet, during the late war,[2] required as much money to support it as all the ROMAN legions, which kept the whole world in subjection, during the time of the emperors.[a]

---

[a] A Private soldier in the ROMAN infantry had a denarius a day, somewhat less than eight pence. The ROMAN emperors had commonly 25 legions in pay, which, allowing 5000 men to a legion, makes 125,000. TACIT. *Ann.* lib. iv. It is true, there were also auxiliaries to the legions; but their numbers are uncertain, as well as their pay. To

The greater number of people and their greater industry are serviceable in all cases; at home and abroad, in private, and in public. But the greater plenty of money, is very limited in its use, and may even sometimes be a loss to a nation in its commerce with foreigners.

There seems to be a happy concurrence of causes in human affairs, which checks the growth of trade and riches, and hinders them from being confined entirely to one people; as might naturally at first be dreaded from the advantages of an established commerce. Where one nation has got the start of another in trade, it is very difficult for the latter to regain the ground it has lost; because of the superior industry and skill of the former, and the greater stocks, of which its merchants are possessed, and which enable them to trade on so much smaller profits. But these advantages are compensated, in some measure, by the low price of labour in every nation which has not an extensive commerce, and does not much abound in gold and silver. Manufactures, therefore, gradually shift their places, leaving those countries and provinces which they have already enriched, and flying to others, whither they are allured by the cheapness of provisions and labour; till they have enriched these also, and are again banished by the same causes. And, in general, we may observe, that the dearness of every thing, from plenty of money, is a disadvantage, which attends an established commerce, and sets bounds to it in every country, by enabling the poorer states to undersel the richer in all foreign markets.

This has made me entertain a doubt concerning the benefit of *banks* and *paper-credit*, which are so generally esteemed advantageous to every nation. That provisions and labour should become dear by the encrease of trade and money, is, in many respects, an inconveni-

consider only the legionaries, the pay of the private men could not exceed 1,600,000 pounds. Now, the parliament in the last war commonly allowed for the fleet 2,500,000. We have therefore 900,000 over for the officers and other expences of the ROMAN legions. There seem to have been but few officers in the ROMAN armies, in comparison of what are employed in all our modern troops, except some SWISS corps. And these officers had very small pay: A centurion, for instance, only double a common soldier. And as the soldiers from their pay (TACIT. *Ann.* lib. i.) bought their own cloaths, arms, tents, and baggage; this must also diminish considerably the other charges of the army. So little expensive was that mighty government, and so easy was its yoke over the world. And, indeed, this is the more natural conclusion from the foregoing calculations. For money, after the conquest of ÆGYPT, seems to have been nearly in as great plenty at ROME, as it is at present in the richest of the EUROPEAN kingdoms.[3]

ence; but an inconvenience that is unavoidable, and the effect of that public wealth and prosperity which are the end of all our wishes. It is compensated by the advantages, which we reap from the possession of these precious metals, and the weight, which they give the nation in all foreign wars and negociations. But there appears no reason for encreasing that inconvenience by a counterfeit money, which foreigners will not accept of in any payment, and which any great disorder in the state will reduce to nothing. There are, it is true, many people in every rich state, who, having large sums of money, would prefer paper with good security; as being of more easy transport and more safe custody. If the public provide not a bank, private bankers will take advantage of this circumstance; as the goldsmiths formerly did in LONDON, or as the bankers do at present in DUBLIN: And therefore it is better, it may be thought, that a public company should enjoy the benefit of that paper-credit, which always will have place in every opulent kingdom. But to endeavour artificially to encrease such a credit, can never be the interest of any trading nation; but must lay them under disadvantages, by encreasing money beyond its natural proportion to labour and commodities, and thereby heightening their price to the merchant and manufacturer. And in this view, it must be allowed, that no bank could be more advantageous, than such a one as locked up all the money it received,[b] and never augmented the circulating coin, as is usual, by returning part of its treasure into commerce. A public bank, by this expedient, might cut off much of the dealings of private bankers and money-jobbers; and though the state bore the charge of salaries to the directors and tellers of this bank (for, according to the preceding supposition, it would have no profit from its dealings), the national advantage, resulting from the low price of labour and the destruction of paper-credit, would be a sufficient compensation. Not to mention, that so large a sum, lying ready at command, would be a convenience in times of great public danger and distress; and what part of it was used might be replaced at leisure, when peace and tranquillity was restored to the nation.

But of this subject of paper credit we shall treat more largely hereafter. And I shall finish this essay on money, by proposing and explaining two observations, which may, perhaps, serve to employ the thoughts of our speculative politicians.

[b] This is the case with the bank of AMSTERDAM.

It was a shrewd observation of ANACHARSIS[c] the SCYTHIAN, who had never seen money in his own country, that gold and silver seemed to him of no use to the GREEKS, but to assist them in numeration and arithmetic. It is indeed evident, that money is nothing but the representation of labour and commodities, and serves only as a method of rating or estimating them. Where coin is in greater plenty; as a greater quantity of it is required to represent the same quantity of goods; it can have no effect, either good or bad, taking a nation within itself; any more than it would make an alteration on a merchant's books, if, instead of the ARABIAN method of notation, which requires few characters, he should make use of the ROMAN, which requires a great many. Nay, the greater quantity of money, like the ROMAN characters, is rather inconvenient, and requires greater trouble both to keep and transport it. But notwithstanding this conclusion, which must be allowed just, it is certain, that, since the discovery of the mines in AMERICA, industry has encreased in all the nations of EUROPE, except in the possessors of those mines; and this may justly be ascribed, amongst other reasons, to the encrease of gold and silver. Accordingly we find, that, in every kingdom, into which money begins to flow in greater abundance than formerly, every thing takes a new face; labour and industry gain life; the merchant becomes more enterprising, the manufacturer more diligent and skilful, and even the farmer follows his plough with greater alacrity and attention. This is not easily to be accounted for, if we consider only the influence which a greater abundance of coin has in the kingdom itself, by heightening the price of commodities, and obliging every one to pay a greater number of these little yellow or white pieces for every thing he purchases. And as to foreign trade, it appears, that great plenty of money is rather disadvantageous, by raising the price of every kind of labour.

To account, then, for this phenomenon, we must consider, that, though the high price of commodities be a necessary consequence of the encrease of gold and silver, yet it follows not immediately upon that encrease; but some time is required before the money circulates through the whole state, and makes its effect be felt on all ranks of people. At first, no alteration is perceived; by degrees the price rises, first of one commodity, then of another; till the whole at last reaches

[c] PLUT. *Quomodo quis suos profectus in virtute sentire possit.*[4]

a just proportion with the new quantity of specie which is in the kingdom. In my opinion, it is only in this interval or intermediate situation, between the acquisition of money and rise of prices, that the encreasing quantity of gold and silver is favourable to industry. When any quantity of money is imported into a nation, it is not at first dispersed into many hands; but is confined to the coffers of a few persons, who immediately seek to employ it to advantages. Here are a set of manufacturers or merchants, we shall suppose, who have received returns of gold and silver for goods which they sent to CADIZ.[5] They are thereby enabled to employ more workmen than formerly, who never dream of demanding higher wages, but are glad of employment from such good paymasters. If workmen become scarce, the manufacturer gives higher wages, but at first requires an encrease of labour; and this is willingly submitted to by the artisan, who can now eat and drink better, to compensate his additional toil and fatigue. He carries his money to market, where he finds every thing at the same price as formerly, but returns with greater quantity and of better kinds, for the use of his family. The farmer and gardener, finding, that all their commodities are taken off, apply themselves with alacrity to the raising more; and at the same time can afford to take better and more cloths from their tradesmen, whose price is the same as formerly, and their industry only whetted by so much new gain. It is easy to trace the money in its progress through the whole commonwealth; where we shall find that it must first quicken the diligence of every individual, before it encrease the price of labour.

And that the specie may encrease to a considerable pitch, before it have this latter effect, appears, amongst other instances, from the frequent operations of the FRENCH king on the money; where it was always found, that the augmenting of the numerary value did not produce a proportional rise of the prices, at least for some time. In the last year of LOUIS XIV. money was raised three-sevenths, but prices augmented only one. Corn in FRANCE is now sold at the same price, or for the same number of livres, it was in 1683; though silver was then at 30 livres the mark, and is now at 50.[d] Not to mention

---

[d] THESE facts I give upon the authority of Mons. du TOT in his *Reflections politiques*, an author of reputation. Though I must confess, that the facts which he advances on other occasions, are often so suspicious, as to make his authority less in this matter. However, the general observation, that the augmenting of the money in FRANCE does

the great addition of gold and silver, which may have come into that kingdom since the former period.

From the whole of this reasoning we may conclude, that it is of no manner of consequence, with regard to the domestic happiness of a state, whether money be in a greater or less quantity. The good policy of the magistrate consists only in keeping it, if possible still encreasing; because, by that means, he keeps alive a spirit of industry in the nation, and encreases the stock of labour, in which consists all real power and riches. A nation, whose money decreases, is actually, at that time, weaker and more miserable than another nation, which possesses no more money, but is on the encreasing hand. This will be easily accounted for, if we consider, that the alterations in the quantity of money, either on one side or the other, are not immediately attended with proportionable alterations in the price of commodities. There is always an interval before matters be adjusted to their new situation; and this interval is as pernicious to industry, when gold and silver are diminishing, as it is advantageous when these metals are encreasing. The workman has not the same employment from the manufacturer and merchant; though he pays the same price for every thing in the market. The farmer cannot dispose of his corn and cattle; though he must pay the same rent to his landlord. The poverty, and beggary, and sloth, which must ensue, are easily foreseen.

II. The second observation which I proposed to make with regard to money, may be explained after the following manner. There are some kingdoms, and many provinces in EUROPE, (and all of them were once in the same condition) where money is so scarce, that the

not at first proportionably augment the prices, is certainly just.

By the by, this seems to be one of the best reasons which can be given, for a gradual and universal augmentation of the money, though it has been entirely overlooked in all those volumes which have been written on that question by MELON, du TOT, and PARIS de VERNEY. Were all our money, for instance, recoined, and a penny's worth of silver taken from every shilling, the new shilling would probably purchase every thing that could have been bought by the old; the prices of every thing would thereby be insensibly diminished; foreign trade enlivened; and domestic industry, by the circulation of a greater number of pounds and shillings, would receive some encrease and encouragement. In executing such a project, it would be better to make the new shilling pass for 24 half-pence, in order to preserve the illusion, and make it be taken for the same. And as a recoinage of our silver begins to be requisite, by the continual wearing of our shillings and sixpences, it maybe doubtful, whether we ought to imitate the example in King WILLIAM's reign, when the clipt money was raised to the old standard.[6]

landlord can get none at all from his tenants; but is obliged to take his rent in kind, and either to consume it himself, or transport it to places where he may find a market. In those countries, the prince can levy few or no taxes, but in the same manner: And as he will receive small benefit from impositions so paid, it is evident that such a kingdom has little force even at home; and cannot maintain fleets and armies to the same extent, as if every part of it abounded in gold and silver. There is surely a greater disproportion between the force of GERMANY, at present, and what it was three centuries ago,[e] than there is in its industry, people, and manufactures. The AUSTRIAN dominions in the empire are in general well peopled and well cultivated, and are of great extent; but have not a proportionable weight in the balance of EUROPE; proceeding, as is commonly supposed, from the scarcity of money. How do all these facts agree with that principle of reason, that the quantity of gold and silver is in itself altogether indifferent? According to that principle, wherever a sovereign has numbers of subjects, and these have plenty of commodities, he should of course be great and powerful, and they rich and happy, independent of the greater or lesser abundance of the precious metals. These admit of divisions and subdivisions to a great extent; and where the pieces might become so small as to be in danger of being lost, it is easy to mix the gold or silver with a baser metal, as is practised in some countries of EUROPE; and by that means raise the pieces to a bulk more sensible and convenient. They still serve the same purposes of exchange, whatever their number may be, or whatever colour they may be supposed to have.

To these difficulties I answer, that the effect, here supposed to flow from scarcity of money, really arises from the manners and customs of the people; and that we mistake, as is too usual, a collateral effect for a cause. The contradiction is only apparent; but it requires some thought and reflection to discover the principles, by which we can reconcile *reason* to *experience*.

It seems a maxim almost self-evident, that the prices of every thing depend on the proportion between commodities and money, and that any considerable alteration on either of these has the same effect, either of heightening or lowering the price. Encrease the commodit-

---

[e] The ITALIANS gave to the Emperor MAXIMILIAN, the nickname of POCCI-DANARI. None of the enterprises of that prince ever succeeded, for want of money.[7]

ies, they become cheaper; encrease the money, they rise in their value. As, on the other hand, a diminution of the former, and that of the latter, have contrary tendencies.

It is also evident, that the prices do not so much depend on the absolute quantity of commodities and that of money, which are in a nation, as on that of the commodities, which come or may come to market, and of the money which circulates. If the coin be locked up in chests, it is the same thing with regard to prices, as if it were annihilated; if the commodities be hoarded in magazines and granaries, a like effect follows. As the money and commodities, in these cases, never meet, they cannot affect each other. Were we, at any time, to form conjectures concerning the price of provisions, the corn, which the farmer must reserve for seed and for the maintenance of himself and family, ought never to enter into the estimation. It is only the overplus, compared to the demand, that determines the value.

To apply these principles, we must consider, that, in the first and more uncultivated ages of any state, ere fancy has confounded her wants with those of nature, men, content with the produce of their own fields, or with those rude improvements which they themselves can work upon them, have little occasion for exchange, at least for money, which, by agreement, is the common measure of exchange. The wool of the farmer's own flock, spun in his own family, and wrought by a neighbouring weaver, who receives his payment in corn or wool, suffices for furniture and cloathing. The carpenter, the smith, the mason, the tailor, are retained by wages of a like nature; and the landlord himself, dwelling in the neighbourhood, is content to receive his rent in the commodities raised by the farmer. The greatest part of these he consumes at home, in rustic hospitality: The rest, perhaps, he disposes of for money to the neighbouring town, whence he draws the few materials of his expence and luxury.

But after men begin to refine on all these enjoyments, and live not always at home, nor are content with what can be raised in their neighbourhood, there is more exchange and commerce of all kinds, and more money enters into that exchange. The tradesmen will not be paid in corn; because they want something more than barely to eat. The farmer goes beyond his own parish for the commodities he purchases, and cannot always carry his commodities to the merchant who supplies him. The landlord lives in the capital, or in a foreign country; and demands his rent in gold and silver, which can easily be transported to him. Great undertakers, and manufacturers, and merchants, arise in every commodity; and these can conveniently deal in nothing but in specie. And consequently, in this situation of society, the coin enters into many more contracts, and by that means is much more employed than in the former.

The necessary effect is, that, provided the money does not encrease in the nation, every thing must become much cheaper in times of industry and refinement, than in rude, uncultivated ages. It is the proportion between the circulating money, and the commodities in the market, which determines the prices. Goods, that are consumed at home, or exchanged with other goods in the neighbourhood, never come to market; they affect not in the least the current specie; with regard to it they are as if totally annihilated; and consequently this method of using them sinks the proportion on the side of the commodities, and encreases the prices. But after money enters into all contracts and sales, and is every where the measure of exchange, the same national cash has a much greater task to perform; all commodities are then in the market; the sphere of circulation is enlarged; it is the same case as if that individual sum were to serve a larger kingdom; and therefore, the proportion being here lessened on the side of the money, every thing must become cheaper, and the prices gradually fall.

By the most exact computations, that have been formed all over EUROPE, after making allowance for the alteration in the numerary value or the denomination, it is found, that the prices of all things have only risen three, or at most, four times, since the discovery of the WEST INDIES.[8] But will any one assert, that there is not much more than four times the coin in EUROPE, that was in the fifteenth century, and the centuries preceding it? The SPANIARDS and PORTUGUESE from their mines, the ENGLISH, FRENCH, and DUTCH, by their AFRICAN trade, and by their interlopers in the WEST INDIES, bring home about six millions a year, of which not above a third part goes to the EAST INDIES. This sum alone, in ten years, would probably double the ancient stock of money in EUROPE. And no other satisfactory reason can be given, why all prices have not risen to a much more exorbitant height, except that which is derived from a change of customs and manners. Besides that more commodities are produced by additional industry, the same commodities come more to market, after men depart from their ancient simplicity of manners.

And though this encrease has not been equal to that of money, it has, however, been considerable, and has preserved the proportion between coin and commodities nearer the ancient standard.

Were the question proposed, Which of these methods of living in the people, the simple or refined, is the most advantageous to the state or public? I should, without much scruple, prefer the latter, in a view to politics at least; and should produce this as an additional reason for the encouragement of trade and manufactures.

While men live in the ancient simple manner and supply all their necessaries from domestic industry or from the neighbourhood, the sovereign can levy no taxes in money from a considerable part of his subjects; and if he will impose on them any burdens, he must take payment in commodities, with which alone they abound; a method attended with such great and obvious inconveniencies, that they need not here be insisted on. All the money he can pretend to raise, must be from his principal cities, where alone it circulates; and these, it is evident, cannot afford him so much as the whole state could, did gold and silver circulate through the whole. But besides this obvious diminution of the revenue, there is another cause of the poverty of the public in such a situation. Not only the sovereign receives less money, but the same money goes not so far as in times of industry and general commerce. Every thing is dearer, where the gold and silver are supposed equal; and that because fewer commodities come to market, and the whole coin bears a higher proportion to what is to be purchased by it; whence alone the prices of every thing are fixed and determined.

Here then we may learn the fallacy of the remark, often to be met with in historians, and even in common conversation, that any particular state is weak, though fertile, populous, and well cultivated, merely because it wants money. It appears, that the want of money can never injure any state within itself: For men and commodities are the real strength of any community. It is the simple manner of living which here hurts the public, by confining the gold and silver to few hands, and preventing its universal diffusion and circulation. On the contrary, industry and refinements of all kinds incorporate it with the whole state, however small its quantity may be: They digest it into every vein, so to speak; and make it enter into every transaction and contract. No hand is entirely empty of it. And as the prices of every thing fall by that means, the sovereign has a double advantage:

He may draw money by his taxes from every part of the state; and what he receives, goes farther in every purchase and payment.

We may infer, from a comparison of prices, that money is not more plentiful in CHINA, than it was in EUROPE three centuries ago: But what immense power is that empire possessed of, if we may judge by the civil and military list maintained by it? POLYBIUS[f] tells us, that provisions were so cheap in ITALY during his time, that in some places the stated price for a meal at the inns was a *semis* a head, little more than a farthing! Yet the ROMAN power had even then subdued the whole known world. About a century before that period, the CARTHAGINIAN ambassador said, by way of raillery, that no people lived more sociably amongst themselves than the ROMANS; for that, in every entertainment, which as foreign ministers, they received, they still observed the same plate at every table.[g] The absolute quantity of the precious metals is a matter of great indifference. There are only two circumstances of any importance, namely, their gradual encrease, and their thorough concoction and circulation through the state; and the influence of both these circumstances has here been explained.

In the following Essay we shall see an instance of a like fallacy as that above mentioned; where a collateral effect is taken for a cause, and where a consequence is ascribed to the plenty of money; though it be really owing to a change in the manners and customs of the people.

---

[f] Lib. ii. cap. 15.
[g] PLIN. lib. xxxiii. cap. 11.[9]

ESSAY SIXTEEN

Of interest

NOTHING is esteemed a more certain sign of the flourishing condition of any nation than the lowness of interest: And with reason; though I believe the cause is somewhat different from what is commonly apprehended. Lowness of interest is generally ascribed to plenty of money. But money, however plentiful, has no other effect, *if fixed*, than to raise the price of labour. Silver is more common than gold; and therefore you receive a greater quantity of it for the same commodities. But do you pay less interest for it? Interest in BATAVIA and JAMAICA is at 10 *per cent.* in PORTUGAL at 6; though these places, as we may learn from the prices of every thing, abound more in gold and silver than either LONDON or AMSTERDAM.

Were all the gold in ENGLAND annihilated at once, and one and twenty shillings substituted in the place of every guinea, would money be more plentiful or interest lower?[1] No surely: We should only use silver instead of gold. Were gold rendered as common as silver, and silver as common as copper; would money be more plentiful or interest lower? We may assuredly give the same answer. Our shillings would then be yellow, and our halfpence white; and we should have no guineas. No other difference would ever be observed; no alteration on commerce, manufactures, navigation, or interest; unless we imagine, that the colour of the metal is of any consequence.

Now, what is so visible in these greater variations of scarcity or abundance in the precious metals, must hold in all inferior changes. If the multiplying of gold and silver fifteen times makes no difference, much less can the doubling or tripling them. All augmentation has no other effect than to heighten the price of labour and commodities;

126

and even this variation is little more than that of a name. In the progress towards these changes, the augmentation may have some influence, by exciting industry; but after the prices are settled, suitably to the new abundance of gold and silver, it has no manner of influence.

An effect always holds proportion with its cause. Prices have risen near four times since the discovery of the INDIES; and it is probable gold and silver have multiplied much more: But interest has not fallen much above half. The rate of interest, therefore, is not derived from the quantity of the precious metals.

Money having chiefly a fictitious value, the greater or less plenty of it is of no consequence, if we consider a nation within itself; and the quantity of specie, when once fixed, though ever so large, has no other effect, than to oblige every one to tell out a greater number of those shining bits of metal, for clothes, furniture or equipage, without encreasing any one convenience of life. If a man borrows money to build a house, he then carries home a greater load; because the stone, timber, lead, glass, &c. with the labour of the masons and carpenters, are represented by a greater quantity of gold and silver. But as these metals are considered chiefly as representations, there can no alteration arise, from their bulk or quantity, their weight or colour, either upon their real value or their interest. The same interest, in all cases, bears the same proportion to the sum. And if you lent me so much labour and so many commodities; by receiving five *per cent.* you always receive proportional labour and commodities, however represented, whether by yellow or white coin, whether by a pound or an ounce. It is in vain, therefore, to look for the cause of the fall or rise of interest in the greater or less quantity of gold and silver, which is fixed in any nation.

High interest arises from *three* circumstances: A great demand for borrowing; little riches to supply that demand; and great profits arising from commerce: And these circumstances are a clear proof of the small advance of commerce and industry, not of the scarcity of gold and silver. Low interest, on the other hand, proceeds from the three opposite circumstances: A small demand for borrowing; great riches to supply that demand; and small profits arising from commerce: And these circumstances are all connected together, and proceed from the encrease of industry and commerce, not of gold and silver. We shall endeavour to prove these points; and shall begin with the causes and the effects of a great or small demand for borrowing.

When a people have emerged ever so little from a savage state, and their numbers have encreased beyond the original multitude, there must immediately arise an inequality of property; and while some possess large tracts of land, others are confined within narrow limits, and some are entirely without any landed property. Those who possess more land than they can labour, employ those who possess none, and agree to receive a determinate part of the product. Thus the *landed* interest is immediately established; nor is there any settled government, however rude, in which affairs are not on this footing. Of these proprietors of land, some must presently discover themselves to be of different tempers from others; and while one would willingly store up the produce of his land for futurity, another desires to consume at present what should suffice for many years. But as the spending of a settled revenue is a way of life entirely without occupation; men have so much need of somewhat to fix and engage them, that pleasures, such as they are, will be the pursuit of the greatest part of the landholders, and the prodigals among them will always be more numerous than the misers. In a state, therefore, where there is nothing but a landed interest, as there is little frugality, the borrowers must be very numerous, and the rate of interest must hold proportion to it. The difference depends not on the quantity of money, but on the habits and manners which prevail. By this alone the demand for borrowing is encreased or diminished. Were money so plentiful as to make an egg be sold for sixpence; so long as there are only landed gentry and peasants in the state, the borrowers must be numerous, and interest high. The rent for the same farm would be heavier and more bulky: But the same idleness of the landlord, with the higher price of commodities, would dissipate it in the same time, and produce the same necessity and demand for borrowing.

Nor is the case different with regard to the *second* circumstance which we proposed to consider, namely, the great or little riches to supply the demand. This effect also depends on the habits and way of living of the people, not on the quantity of gold and silver. In order to have, in any state, a great number of lenders, it is not sufficient nor requisite, that there be great abundance of the precious metals. It is only requisite, that the property or command of that quantity, which is in the state, whether great or small, should be collected in particular hands, so as to form considerable sums, or compose a great monied interest. This begets a number of lenders, and sinks the rate of usury; and this, I shall venture to affirm, depends not on the quantity of specie, but on particular manners and customs, which make the specie gather into separate sums or masses of considerable value.

For suppose, that, by miracle, every man in BRITAIN should have five pounds slipt into his pocket in one night; this would much more than double the whole money that is at present in the kingdom; and yet there would not next day, nor for some time, be any more lenders, nor any variation in the interest. And were there nothing but land-lords and peasants in the state, this money, however abundant, could never gather into sums; and would only serve to encrease the prices of every thing, without any farther consequence. The prodigal landlord dissipates it, as fast as he receives it; and the beggarly peasant has no means, nor view, nor ambition of obtaining above a bare livelihood. The overplus of borrowers above that of lenders continuing still the same, there will follow no reduction of interest. That depends upon another principle; and must proceed from an encrease of industry and frugality, of arts and commerce.

Every thing useful to the life of man arises from the ground; but few things arise in that condition which is requisite to render them useful. There must, therefore, beside the peasants and the proprietors of land, be another rank of men, who, receiving from the former the rude materials, work them into their proper form, and retain part for their own use and subsistance. In the infancy of society, these contracts between the artisans and the peasants, and between one species of artisans and another, are commonly entered into immediately by the persons themselves, who, being neighbours, are easily acquainted with each other's necessities, and can lend their mutual assistance to supply them. But when men's industry encreases, and their views enlarge, it is found, that the most remote parts of the state can assist each other as well as the more contiguous, and that this intercourse of good offices may be carried on to the greatest extent and intricacy. Hence the origin of *merchants*, one of the most useful races of men, who serve as agents between those parts of the state, that are wholly unacquainted, and are ignorant of each other's necessities. Here are in a city fifty workmen in silk and linen, and a thousand customers; and these two ranks of men, so necessary to each other, can never rightly meet, till one man erects a shop, to which all the workmen and all the customers repair. In this province, grass rises in abundance: The inhabitants abound in cheese, and butter, and cattle; but want bread and corn, which, in a neighbouring province, are in too great abundance for the use of the inhabitants. One man discovers this. He brings corn from the one province and returns with cattle; and supplying the wants of both, he is, so far, a common benefactor. As the people encrease in numbers and industry, the difficulty of their intercourse encreases: The business of the agency or merchandize becomes more intricate; and divides, subdivides, compounds, and mixes to a greater variety. In all these transactions, it is necessary, and reasonable, that a considerable part of the commodities and labour should belong to the merchant, to whom, in a great measure, they are owing. And these commodities he will sometimes preserve in kind, or more commonly convert into money, which is their common representation. If gold and silver have encreased in the state together with the industry, it will require a great quantity of these metals to represent a great quantity of commodities and labour. If industry alone has encreased, the prices of every thing must sink, and a very small quantity of specie will serve as a representation.

There is no craving or demand of the human mind more constant and insatiable than that for exercise and employment; and this desire seems the foundation of most of our passions and pursuits. Deprive a man of all business and serious occupation, he runs restless from one amusement to another; and the weight and oppression, which he feels from idleness, is so great, that he forgets the ruin which must follow him from his immoderate expences. Give him a more harmless way of employing his mind or body, he is satisfied, and feels no longer that insatiable thirst after pleasure. But if the employment you give him be profitable, especially if the profit be attached to every particular exertion of industry, he has gain so often in his eye, that he acquires, by degrees, a passion for it, and knows no such pleasure as that of seeing the daily encrease of his fortune. And this is the reason why trade encreases frugality, and why, among merchants, there is the same overplus of misers above prodigals, as, among the possessors of land, there is the contrary.

Commerce encreases industry, by conveying it readily from one member of the state to another, and allowing none of it to perish or become useless. It encreases frugality, by giving occupation to men, and employing them in the arts of gain, which soon engage their affection, and remove all relish for pleasure and expence. It is an infallible consequence of all industrious professions, to beget frugality, and make the love of gain prevail over the love of pleasure. Among lawyers and physicians who have any practice, there are many more who live within their income, than who exceed it, or even live up to it. But lawyers and physicians beget no industry; and it is even at the expence of others they acquire their riches; so that they are sure to diminish the possessions of some of their fellow-citizens, as fast as they encrease their own. Merchants, on the contrary, beget industry, by serving as canals to convey it through every corner of the state: And at the same time, by their frugality, they acquire great power over that industry, and collect a large property in the labour and commodities, which they are the chief instruments in producing. There is no other profession, therefore, except merchandize, which can make the monied interest considerable, or, in other words, can encrease industry, and, by also encreasing frugality, give a great command of that industry to particular members of the society. Without commerce, the state must consist chiefly of landed gentry, whose prodigality and expence make a continual demand for borrowing; and of peasants, who have no sums to supply that demand. The money never gathers into large stocks or sums, which can be lent at interest. It is dispersed into numberless hands, who either squander it in idle show and magnificence, or employ it in the purchase of the common necessaries of life. Commerce alone assembles it into considerable sums; and this effect it has merely from the industry which it begets, and the frugality which it inspires, independent of that particular quantity of precious metal which may circulate in the state.

Thus an encrease of commerce, by a necessary consequence, raises a great number of lenders, and by that means produces a lowness of interest. We must now consider how far this encrease of commerce diminishes the profits arising from that profession, and gives rise to the *third* circumstance requisite to produce a lowness of interest.

It may be proper to observe on this head, that low interest and low profits of merchandize are two events, that mutually forward each other, and are both originally derived from that extensive commerce, which produces opulent merchants, and renders the monied interest considerable. Where merchants possess great stocks, whether represented by few or many pieces of metal, it must frequently happen, that, when they either become tired of business, or have heirs unwilling or unfit to engage in commerce, a great proportion of these riches naturally seeks an annual and secure revenue. The plenty diminishes the price, and makes the lenders accept of a low interest. This consideration obliges many to keep their stock employed in trade, and rather be content with low profits than dispose of their money at an undervalue. On the other hand, when commerce has become extensive, and employs large stocks, there must arise rivalships among the merchants, which diminish the profits of trade, at the same time that they encrease the trade itself. The low profits of merchandize induce the merchants to accept more willingly of a low interest, when they leave off business, and begin to indulge themselves in ease and indolence. It is needless, therefore, to enquire which of these circumstances, to wit, *low interest or low profits*, is the cause, and which the effect? They both arise from an extensive commerce, and mutually forward each other. No man will accept of low profits, where he can have high interest; and no man will accept of low interest, where he can have high profits. An extensive commerce, by producing large stocks, diminishes both interest and profits; and is always assisted, in its diminution of the one, by the proportional sinking of the other. I may add, that, as low profits arise from the encrease of commerce and industry, they serve in their turn to its farther encrease, by rendering the commodities cheaper, encouraging the consumption, and heightening the industry. And thus, if we consider the whole connexion of causes and effects, interest is the barometer of the state, and its lowness is a sign almost infallible of the flourishing condition of a people. It proves the encrease of industry, and its prompt circulation through the whole state, little inferior to a demonstration. And though, perhaps, it may not be impossible but a sudden and a great check to commerce may have a momentary effect of the same kind, by throwing so many stocks out of trade; it must be attended with such misery and want of employment in the poor, that, besides its short duration, it will not be possible to mistake the one case for the other.

Those who have asserted, that the plenty of money was the cause of low interest, seem to have taken a collateral effect for a cause; since the same industry, which sinks the interest, does commonly acquire great abundance of the precious metals. A variety of fine manufactures, with vigilant enterprising merchants, will soon draw money to a state, if it be any where to be found in the world. The same cause, by multiplying the conveniencies of life, and encreasing industry, collects great riches into the hands of persons, who are not proprietors of land, and produces, by that means, a lowness of interest. But though both these effects, plenty of money and low interest, naturally arise from commerce and industry, they are altogether independent of each other. For suppose a nation removed into the *Pacific* ocean, without any foreign commerce, or any knowledge of navigation: Suppose, that this nation possesses always the same stock of coin, but is continually encreasing in its numbers and industry: It is evident, that the price of every commodity must gradually diminish in that kingdom; since it is the proportion between money and any species of goods, which fixes their mutual value; and, upon the present supposition, the conveniencies of life become very day more abundant, without any alteration on the current specie. A less quantity of money, therefore, among this people, will make a rich man, during the times of industry, than would suffice to that purpose, in ignorant and slothful ages. Less money will build a house, portion a daughter, buy an estate, support a manufactory, or maintain a family and equipage. These are the uses for which men borrow money; and therefore, the greater or less quantity of it in a state has no influence on the interest. But it is evident, that the greater or less stock of labour and commodities must have a great influence; since we really and in effect borrow these, when we take money upon interest. It is true, when commerce is extended all over the globe, the most industrious nations always abound most with the precious metals: So that low interest and plenty of money are in fact almost inseparable. But still it is of consequence to know the principle whence any phenomenon arises, and to distinguish between a cause and a concomitant effect. Besides that the speculation is curious, it may frequently be of use in the conduct of public affairs. At least, it must be owned, that nothing can be of more use than to improve, by practice, the method of reasoning on these subjects, which of all others are the most important; though they are commonly treated in the loosest and most careless manner.

Another reason of this popular mistake with regard to the cause of low interest, seems to be the instance of some nations; where, after a sudden acquisition of money, or of the precious metals, by means of foreign conquest, the interest has fallen, not only among them, but in all the neighbouring states, as soon as that money was dispersed, and had insinuated itself into every corner. Thus, interest in SPAIN fell near a half immediately after the discovery of the WEST INDIES, as we are informed by GARCILASSO DE LA VEGA:[2] And it has been ever since gradually sinking in every kingdom of EUROPE. Interest in ROME, after the conquest of EGYPT, fell from 6 to 4 *per cent.* as we learn from DION.[a]

The causes of the sinking of interest, upon such an event, seem different in the conquering country and in the neighbouring states; but in neither of them can we justly ascribe that effect merely to the encrease of gold and silver.

In the conquering country, it is natural to imagine, that this new acquisition of money will fall into a few hands, and be gathered into large sums, which seek a secure revenue, either by the purchase of land or by interest; and consequently the same effect follows, for a little time, as if there had been a great accession of industry and commerce. The encrease of lenders above the borrowers sinks the interest; and so much the faster, if those, who have acquired those large sums, find no industry or commerce in the state, and no method of employing their money but by lending it at interest. But after this new mass of gold and silver has been digested, and has circulated through the whole state, affairs will soon return to their former situation; while the landlords and new money-holders, living idly, squander above their income; and the former daily contract debt, and the latter encroach on their stock till its final extinction. The whole money may still be in the state, and make itself felt by the encrease of prices: But not being now collected into any large masses or stocks, the disproportion between the borrowers and lenders is the same as formerly, and consequently the high interest returns.

Accordingly we find, in ROME, that, so early as TIBERIUS's time, interest had again mounted to 6 *per cent.*[b] though no accident had happened to drain the empire of money. In TRAJAN's time, money lent on mortgages in ITALY, bore 6 *per cent.*;[c] on common securities in BITHYNIA, 12.[d] And if interest in SPAIN has not risen to its old pitch; this can be ascribed to nothing but the continuance of the

[a] Lib. li.[3]
[b] COLUMELLA, lib. iii. cap. 3.[4]
[c] PLINII epist. lib. vii. ep. 18.
[d] Id. lib. ep. 62.[5]

same cause that sunk it, to wit, the large fortunes continually made in the INDIES, which come over to SPAIN from time to time, and supply the demand of the borrowers. By this accidental and extraneous cause, more money is to be lent in SPAIN, that is, more money is collected into large sums than would be otherwise found in a state, where there are so little commerce and industry.

As to the reduction of interest, which has followed in ENGLAND, FRANCE, and other kingdoms of EUROPE, that have no mines, it has been gradual; and has not proceeded from the encrease of money, considered merely in itself; but from that of industry, which is the natural effect of the former encrease, in that interval, before it raises the price of labour and provisions. For to return to the foregoing supposition; if the industry of ENGLAND had risen as much from other causes, (and that rise might easily have happened, though the stock of money had remained the same) must not all the same consequences have followed, which we observe at present? The same people would, in that case, be found in the kingdom, the same commodities, the same industry, manufactures, and commerce; and consequently the same merchants, with the same stocks, that is, with the same command over labour and commodities, only represented by a smaller number of white or yellow pieces; which being a circumstance of no moment, would only affect the waggoner, porter, and trunk-maker. Luxury, therefore, manufactures, arts, industry, frugality, flourishing equally as at present, it is evident, that interest must also have been as low; since that is the necessary result of all these circumstances; so far as they determine the profits of commerce, and the proportion between the borrowers and lenders in any state.

ESSAY SEVENTEEN

Of the balance of trade

It is very usual, in nations ignorant of the nature of commerce, to prohibit the exportation of commodities, and to preserve among themselves whatever they think valuable and useful. They do not consider, that, in this prohibition, they act directly contrary to their intention; and that the more is exported of any commodity, the more will be raised at home, of which they themselves will always have the first offer.

It is well known to the learned, that the ancient laws of ATHENS rendered the exportation of figs criminal; that being supposed a species of fruit so excellent in ATTICA, that the ATHENIANS deemed it too delicious for the palate of any foreigner. And in this ridiculous prohibition they were so much in earnest, that informers were thence called *sycophants* among them, from two GREEK words, which signify *figs* and *discoverer*.[a] There are proofs in many old acts of parliament of the same ignorance in the nature of commerce, particularly in the reign of EDWARD III.[2] And to this day, in FRANCE, the exportation of corn is almost always prohibited; in order, as they say, to prevent famines; though it is evident, that nothing contributes more to the frequent famines, which so much distress that fertile country.

The same jealous fear, with regard to money, has also prevailed among several nations; and it required both reason and experience to convince any people, that these prohibitions serve to no other

[a] PLUT. *De Curiositate.*[1]

136

purpose than to raise the exchange against them, and produce a still greater exportation.

These errors, one may say, are gross and palpable: But there still prevails, even in nations well acquainted with commerce, a strong jealousy with regard to the balance of trade, and a fear, that all their gold and silver may be leaving them. This seems to me, almost in every case, a groundless apprehension; and I should as soon dread, that all our springs and rivers should be exhausted, as that money should abandon a kingdom where there are people and industry. Let us carefully preserve these latter advantages; and we need never be apprehensive of losing the former.

It is easy to observe, that all calculations concerning the balance of trade are founded on very uncertain facts and suppositions. The custom-house books are allowed to be an insufficient ground of reasoning; nor is the rate of exchange much better; unless we consider it with all nations, and know also the proportions of the several sums remitted; which one may safely pronounce impossible. Every man, who has ever reasoned on this subject, has always proved his theory, whatever it was, by facts and calculations, and by an enumeration of all the commodities sent to all foreign kingdoms.

The writings of Mr. GEE struck the nation with an universal panic, when they saw it plainly demonstrated, by a detail of particulars, that the balance was against them for so considerable a sum as must leave them without a single shilling in five or six years. But luckily, twenty years have since elapsed, with an expensive foreign war; yet is it commonly supposed, that money is still more plentiful among us than in any former period.[3]

Nothing can be more entertaining on this head than Dr. SWIFT; an author so quick in discerning the mistakes and absurdities of others. He says, in his *short view of the state of* IRELAND, that the whole cash of that kingdom formerly amounted but to 500,000*l.*; that out of this the IRISH remitted every year a neat million to ENGLAND, and had scarcely any other source from which they could compensate themselves, and little other foreign trade than the importation of FRENCH wines, for which they paid ready money. The consequence of this situation which must be owned to be disadvantageous, was, that, in a course of three years, the current money of IRELAND, from 500,000*l.* was reduced to less than two. And at present, I suppose, in a course of 30 years, it is absolutely nothing. Yet I know not how, that opinion of the advance of riches in IRELAND, which gave the Doctor so much indignation, seems still to continue, and gain ground with every body.[4]

In short, this apprehension of the wrong balance of trade, appears of such a nature, that it discovers itself, wherever one is out of humour with the ministry, or is in low spirits; and as it can never be refuted by a particular detail of all the exports, which counterbalance the imports, it may here be proper to form a general argument, that may prove the impossibility of this event, as long as we preserve our people and our industry.

Suppose four-fifths of all the money in BRITAIN to be annihilated in one night, and the nation reduced to the same condition, with regard to specie, as in the reigns of the HARRYS and EDWARDS, what would be the consequence?[5] Must not the price of all labour and commodities sink in proportion, and every thing be sold as cheap as they were in those ages? What nation could then dispute with us in any foreign market, or pretend to navigate or to sell manufactures at the same price, which to us would afford sufficient profit? In how little time, therefore, must this bring back the money which we had lost, and raise us to the level of all the neighbouring nations? Where, after we have arrived, we immediately lose the advantage of the cheapness of labour and commodities; and the farther flowing in of money is stopped by our fulness and repletion.

Again, suppose, that all the money of BRITAIN were multiplied fivefold in a night, must not the contrary effect follow? Must not all labour and commodities rise to such an exorbitant height, that no neighbouring nations could afford to buy from us; while their commodities, on the other hand, became comparatively so cheap, that, in spite of all the laws which could be formed, they would be run in upon us, and our money flow out; till we fall to a level with foreigners, and lose that great superiority of riches, which had laid us under such disadvantages?

Now, it is evident, that the same causes, which would correct these exorbitant inequalities, were they to happen miraculously, must prevent their happening in the common course of nature, and must for ever, in all neighbouring nations, preserve money nearly proportionable to the art and industry of each nation. All water, wherever it communicates, remains always at a level. Ask naturalists the reason;

they tell you, that, were it to be raised in any one place, the superior gravity of that part not being balanced, must depress it, till it meet a counterpoise; and that the same cause, which redresses the inequality when it happens, must for ever prevent it, without some violent external operation.[b]

Can one imagine, that it had ever been possible, by any laws, or even by any art or industry, to have kept all the money in SPAIN, which the galleons have brought from the INDIES? Or that all commodities could be sold in FRANCE for a tenth of the price which they would yield on the other side of the PYRENEES, without finding their way thither, and draining from that immense treasure? What other reason, indeed, is there, why all nations, at present, gain in their trade with SPAIN and PORTUGAL; but because it is impossible to heap up money, or than any fluid, beyond its proper level? The sovereigns of these countries have shown, that they wanted not inclination to keep their gold and silver to themselves, had it been in any degree practicable.

But as any body of water may be raised above the level of the surrounding element, if the former has no communication with the latter; so in money, if the communication be cut off, by any material or physical impediment, (for all laws alone are ineffectual) there may, in such a case, be a very great inequality of money. Thus the immense distance of CHINA, together with the monopolies of our INDIA companies, obstructing the communication, preserve in EUROPE the gold and silver, especially the latter, in much greater plenty than they are found in that kingdom.[6] But, notwithstanding this great obstruction, the force of the causes above mentioned is still evident. The skill and ingenuity of EUROPE in general surpasses perhaps that of CHINA, with regard to manual arts and manufactures; yet are we never able to trade thither without great disadvantage. And were it not for the continual recruits, which we receive from AMERICA, money would soon sink in EUROPE, and rise in CHINA, till it came nearly to a level in both places. Nor can any reasonable man doubt, but that industri-

---

[b] There is another cause, though more limited in its operation, which checks the wrong balance of trade, to every particular nation to which the kingdom trades. When we import more goods than we export, the exchange turns against us, and this becomes a new encouragement to export; as much as the charge of carriage and insurance of the money which becomes due would amount to. For the exchange can never rise higher than that sum.

ous nation, were they as near us as POLAND or BARBARY, would drain us of the overplus of our specie and draw to themselves a larger share of the WEST INDIAN treasures. We need not have recourse to a physical attraction, in order to explain the necessity of this operation. There is a moral attraction, arising from the interests and passions of men, which is full as potent and infallible.

How is the balance kept in the provinces of every kingdom among themselves, but by the force of this principle, which makes it impossible for money to lose its level, and either to rise or sink beyond the proportion of the labour and commodities which are in each province? Did not long experience make people easy on this head, what a fund of gloomy reflections might calculations afford to a melancholy YORKSHIREMAN, while he computed and magnified the sums drawn to LONDON by taxes, absentees,[7] commodities, and found on comparison the opposite articles so much inferior? And no doubt, had the Heptarchy subsisted in ENGLAND, the legislature of each state had been continually alarmed by the fear of a wrong balance; and as it is probable that the mutual hatred of these states would have been extremely violent on account of their close neighbourhood, they would have loaded and oppressed all commerce, by a jealous and superfluous caution.[8] Since the union has removed the barriers between SCOTLAND and ENGLAND, which of these nations gains from the other by this free commerce? Or if the former kingdom has received any encrease of riches, can it reasonably be accounted for by any thing but the encrease of its art and industry? It was a common apprehension in ENGLAND, before the union, as we learn from L'ABBE DU BOS,[c] that SCOTLAND would soon drain them of their treasure, were an open trade allowed; and on the other side the TWEED a contrary apprehension prevailed: With what justice in both, time has shown.

What happens in small portions of mankind, must take place in greater. The provinces of the ROMAN empire, no doubt, kept their balance with each other, and with ITALY, independent of the legislature: as much as the several counties of BRITAIN, or the several parishes of each county. And any man who travels over EUROPE at this day, may see, by the prices of commodities, that money, in spite of the absurd jealousy of princes and states, has brought itself nearly to

---

[c] *Les intérêts d'*ANGLETERRE *mal-entendus.*[9]

a level; and that the difference between one kingdom and another is not greater in this respect, than it is often between different provinces of the same kingdom. Men naturally flock to capital cities, sea-ports, and navigable rivers. There we find more men, more industry, more commodities, and consequently more money; but still the latter difference holds proportion with the former, and the level is preserved.[d]

Our jealousy and our hatred of FRANCE are without bounds; and the former sentiment, at least, must be acknowledged reasonable and well-grounded. These passions have occasioned innumerable barriers and obstructions upon commerce, where we are accused of being commonly the aggressors. But what have we gained by the bargain? We lost the FRENCH market for our woollen manufactures, and transferred the commerce of wine to SPAIN and PORTUGAL, where we buy worse liquor at a higher price. There are few ENGLISH-MEN who would not think their country absolutely ruined, were FRENCH wines sold in ENGLAND so cheap and in such abundance as to supplant, in some measure, all ale, and home-brewed liquors: But would we lay aside prejudice, it would not be difficult to prove, that nothing could be more innocent, perhaps advantageous. Each new acre of vineyard planted in FRANCE, in order to supply ENGLAND with wine, would make it requisite for the FRENCH to take the produce of an ENGLISH acre, sown in wheat or barley, in order to subsist themselves; and it is evident, that we should thereby get command of the better commodity.

There are many edicts of the FRENCH king, prohibiting the planting of new vineyards, and ordering all those which are lately planted to be grubbed up: So sensible are they, in that country, of the superior value of corn, above every other product.

Mareschal VAUBAN complains often, and with reason, of the absurd duties which load the entry of those wines of LANGUEDOC, GUIENNE,

---

[d] IT must carefully be remarked, that throughout this discourse, wherever I speak of the level of money, I mean always its proportional level to the commodities, labour, industry, and skill, which is in the several states. And I assert, that where these advantages are double, triple, quadruple, to what they are in the neighbouring states, the money infallibly will also be double, triple, quadruple. The only circumstance that can obstruct the exactness of these proportions, is the expence of transporting the commodities from one place to another; and this expence is sometimes unequal. Thus the corn, cattle, cheese, butter, of DERBYSHIRE, cannot draw the money of LONDON, so much as the manufactures of LONDON draw the money of DERBYSHIRE. But this objection is only a seeming one: For so far as the transport of commodities is expensive, so far is the communication between the place obstructed and imperfect.

and other southern provinces, that are imported into BRITANY and NORMANDY. He entertained no doubt but these latter provinces could preserve their balance, notwithstanding the open commerce which he recommends.[10] And it is evident, that a few leagues more navigation to ENGLAND would make no difference; or if it did, that it must operate alike on the commodities of both kingdoms.

There is indeed one expedient by which it is possible to sink, and another by which we may raise, money beyond its natural level in any kingdom; but these cases, when examined, will be found to resolve into our general theory, and to bring additional authority to it.

I scarcely know any method of sinking money below its level, but those institutions of banks, funds, and paper-credit, which are so much practised in this kingdom. These render paper equivalent to money, circulate it through the whole state, make it supply the place of gold and silver, raise proportionably the price of labour and commodities, and by that means either banish a great part of those precious metals, or prevent their farther encrease. What can be more short-sighted than our reasonings on this head? We fancy, because an individual would be much richer, were his stock of money doubled, that the same good effect would follow were the money of every one encreased; not considering, that this would raise as much the price of every commodity, and reduce every man, in time, to the same condition as before. It is only in our public negociations and transactions with foreigners, that a greater stock of money is advantageous; and as our paper is there absolutely insignificant, we feel, by its means, all the ill effects arising from a great abundance of money, without reaping any of the advantages.[e]

Suppose that there are 12 millions of paper, which circulate in the kingdom as money, (for we are not to imagine, that all our enormous funds are employed in that shape) and suppose the real cash of the kingdom to be 18 millions: Here is a state which is found by experience to be able to hold a stock of 30 millions. I say, if it be able to hold it, it must of necessity have acquired it in gold and silver, had we not obstructed the entrance of these metals by this new invention

---

[e] We observed in Essay III. ['Of money'] that money, when encreasing, gives encouragement to industry, during the interval between the encrease of money and rise of the prices. A good effect of this nature may follow too from paper-credit; but it is dangerous to precipitate matters, at the risk of losing all by the failing of that credit, as must happen upon any violent shock in public affairs.

of paper. *Whence would it have acquired that sum?* From all the king-doms of the world. *But why?* Because, if you remove these 12 millions, money in this state is below its level, compared with our neighbours; and we must immediately draw from all of them, till we be full and saturate, so to speak, and can hold no more. By our present politics, we are as careful to stuff the nation with this fine commodity of bank-bills and chequer-notes, as if we were afraid of being over-burthened with the precious metals.

It is not to be doubted, but the great plenty of bullion in FRANCE is, in a great measure, owing to the want of paper-credit. The FRENCH have no banks: Merchants' bills do not there circulate as with us: Usury or lending on interest is not directly permitted; so that many have large sums in their coffers: Great quantities of plate are used in private houses; and all the churches are full of it. By this means, provisions and labour still remain cheaper among them, than in nations that are not half so rich in gold and silver. The advantages of this situation, in point of trade as well as in great public emergen-cies, are too evident to be disputed.

The same fashion a few years ago prevailed in GENOA, which still has place in ENGLAND and HOLLAND, of using services of CHINA-ware instead of plate; but the senate, foreseeing the consequence, prohibited the use of that brittle commodity beyond a certain extent; while the use of silver-plate was left unlimited. And I suppose, in their late distresses, they felt the good effect of this ordinance.[11] Our tax on plate is, perhaps, in this view, somewhat unpolitic.

Before the introduction of paper-money into our colonies, they had gold and silver sufficient for their circulation. Since the introduc-tion of that commodity, the least inconveniency that has followed is the total banishment of the precious metals.[12] And after the abolition of paper, can it be doubted but money will return, while these colon-ies possess manufactures and commodities, the only thing valuable in commerce, and for whose sake alone all men desire money.

What pity LYCURGUS did not think of paper-credit, when he wanted to banish gold and silver from SPARTA! It would have served his purpose better than the lumps of iron he made use of as money; and would also have prevented more effectually all commerce with strangers, as being of so much less real and intrinsic value.[13]

It must, however, be confessed, that, as all these questions of trade and money are extremely complicated, there are certain lights, in which this subject may be placed, so as to represent the advantages of paper-credit and banks to be superior to their disadvantages. That they banish specie and bullion from a state is undoubtedly true; and whoever looks no farther than this circumstance does well to condemn them; but specie and bullion are not of so great consequence as not to admit of a compensation, and even an overbalance from the encrease of industry and of credit, which may be promoted by the right use of paper-money. It is well known of what advantage it is to a merchant to be able to discount his bills upon occasion; and every thing that facilitates this species of traffic is favourable to the general commerce of a state. But private bankers are enabled to give such credit by the credit they receive from the depositing of money in their shops; and the bank of ENGLAND in the same manner, from the liberty it has to issue its notes in all payments. There was an invention of this kind, which was fallen upon some years ago by the banks of EDINBURGH; and which, as it is one of the most ingenious ideas that has been executed in commerce, has also been thought advantageous to SCOTLAND.[14] It is there called a BANK-CREDIT; and is of this nature. A man goes to the bank and finds surety to the amount, we shall suppose, of five thousand pounds. This money, or any part of it, he has the liberty of drawing out whenever he pleases, and he pays only the ordinary interest for it, while it is in his hands. He may, when he pleases, repay any sum so small as twenty pounds, and the interest is discounted from the very day of the repayment. The advantages, resulting from this contrivance, are manifold. As a man may find surety nearly to the amount of his substance, and his bank-credit is equivalent to ready money, a merchant does hereby in a manner coin his houses, his household furniture, the goods in his warehouse, the foreign debts due to him, his ships at sea; and can, upon occasion, employ them in all payments, as if they were the current money of the country. If a man borrow five thousand pounds from a private hand, besides that it is not always to be found when required, he pays interest for it, whether he be using it or not: His bank-credit costs him nothing except during the very moment, in which it is of service to him: And this circumstance is of equal advantage as if he had borrowed money at much lower interest. Merchants, likewise, from this invention, acquire a great facility in supporting each other's credit, which is a considerable security against bankruptcies. A man, when his own bank-credit is exhausted, goes to any of his neighbours who is not in the same condition; and he gets the money, which he replaces at his convenience.

After this practice had taken place during some years at EDIN-BURGH, several companies of merchants at GLASGOW carried the matter farther.[15] They associated themselves into different banks, and issued notes so low as ten shillings, which they used in all payments for goods, manufactures, tradesmen's labour of all kinds; and these notes, from the established credit of the companies, passed as money in all payments throughout the country. By this means, a stock of five thousand pounds was able to perform the same operations as if it were six or seven; and merchants were thereby enabled to trade to a greater extent, and to require less profit in all their transactions. But whatever other advantages result from these inventions, it must still be allowed that they banish the precious metals; and nothing can be a more evident proof of it, than a comparison of the past and present condition of SCOTLAND in that particular. It was found, upon the recoinage made after the union, that there was near a million of specie in that country:[16] But notwithstanding the great encrease of riches, commerce, and manufactures of all kinds, it is thought, that, even where there is no extraordinary drain made by ENGLAND, the current specie will not now amount to a third of that sum.

But as our projects of paper-credit are almost the only expedient, by which we can sink money below its level; so, in my opinion, the only expedient, by which we can raise money above it, is a practice which we should all exclaim against as destructive, namely, the gathering of large sums into a public treasure, locking them up, and absolutely preventing their circulation. The fluid, not communicating with the neighbouring element, may, by such an artifice, be raised to what height we please. To prove this, we need only return to our first supposition, of annihilating the half or any part of our cash; where we found, that the immediate consequence of such an event would be the attraction of an equal sum from all the neighbouring kingdoms. Nor does there seem to be any necessary bounds set, by the nature of things, to this practice of hoarding. A small city, like GENEVA, continuing this policy for ages, might ingross nine-tenths of the money of EUROPE. There seems, indeed, in the nature of man, an invincible obstacle to that immense growth of riches. A weak state, with an enormous treasure, will soon become a prey to some of its poorer, but more powerful neighbours. A great state would dissipate its wealth in dangerous and ill-concerted projects; and probably destroy, with it, what is much more valuable, the industry, morals, and numbers of its people. The fluid, in this case, raised to too great a height, bursts and destroys the vessel that contains it; and mixing itself with the surrounding element, soon falls to its proper level.

So little are we commonly acquainted with this principle, that, though all historians agree in relating uniformly so recent an event, as the immense treasure amassed by HARRY VII. (which they make amount to 2,700,000 pounds,) we rather reject their concurring testimony, than admit of a fact, which agrees so ill with our inveterate prejudices.[17] It is indeed probable, that this sum might be three-fourths of all the money in ENGLAND. But where is the difficulty in conceiving, that such a sum might be amassed in twenty years, by a cunning, rapacious, frugal, and almost absolute monarch? Nor is it probable, that the diminution of circulating money was ever sensibly felt by the people, or ever did them any prejudice. The sinking of the prices of all commodities would immediately replace it, by giving ENGLAND the advantage in its commerce with the neighbouring kingdoms.

Have we not an instance, in the small republic of ATHENS with its allies, who, in about fifty years, between the MEDIAN and PELOPONNESIAN wars, amassed a sum not much inferior to that of HARRY VII.?[f] For all the GREEK historians[g] and orators[h] agree, that the ATHENIANS collected in the citadel more than 10,000 talents, which they afterwards dissipated to their own ruin, in rash and imprudent enterprizes. But when this money was set a running, and began to communicate with the surrounding fluid; what was the consequence? Did it remain in the state? No. For we find, by the memorable *census* mentioned by DEMOSTHENES[i] and POLYBIUS,[j] that, in about fifty years afterwards, the whole value of the republic, comprehending lands, houses, commodities, slaves, and money, was less than 6000 talents.[18]

What an ambitious high-spirited people was this, to collect and keep in their treasury, with a view to conquests, a sum, which it was every day in the power of the citizens, by a single vote, to distribute

[f] There were about eight ounces of silver in a pound *Sterling* in HARRY VII.'s time.
[g] THUCYDIDES, lib. ii. and DIOD. SIC. lib. xii.
[h] *Vid.* ÆSCHINIS *et* DEMOSTHENIS *Epist.*
[i] Peri Symmorias.
[j] Lib. ii. cap. 62.

among themselves, and which would have gone near to triple the riches of every individual! For we must observe, that the numbers and private riches of the ATHENIANS are said, by ancient writers, to have been no greater at the beginning of the PELOPONNESIAN war, than at the beginning of the MACEDONIAN.[19]

Money was little more plentiful in GREECE during the age of PHILIP and PERSEUS, than in ENGLAND during that of HARRY VII.: Yet these two monarchs in thirty years[k] collected from the small kingdom of MACEDON, a larger treasure than that of the ENGLISH monarch. PAULUS AEMILIUS brought to ROME about 1,700,000 pounds *Sterling*.[l] PLINY says, 2,400,000.[m] And that was but a part of the MACEDONIAN treasure. The rest was dissipated by the resistance and flight of PERSEUS.[n20]

We may learn from STANIAN, that the canton of BERNE had 300,000 pounds lent at interest, and had above six times as much in their treasury. Here then is a sum hoarded of 1,800,000 pounds *Sterling*, which is at least quadruple what should naturally circulate in such a petty state; and yet no one, who travels in the PAIS DE VAUX, or any part of that canton, observes any want of money more than could be supposed in a country of that extent, soil, and situation. On the contrary, there are scarce any inland provinces in the continent of FRANCE or GERMANY, where the inhabitants are at this time so opulent, though that canton has vastly encreased its treasure since 1714, the time when STANIAN wrote his judicious account of SWITZERLAND.[o21]

The account given by APPIAN[p] of the treasure of the PTOLEMIES, is so prodigious, that one cannot admit of it; and so much the less, because the historian says, that the other successors of ALEXANDER were also frugal, and had many of them treasures not much inferior. For this saving humour of the neighbouring princes must necessarily have checked the frugality of the EGYPTIAN monarchs, according to

---

[k] TITI LIVII, lib. xlv. cap. 40.

[l] VEL. PATERC. lib. i. cap. 9.

[m] Lib. xxxiii. cap. 3.

[n] TITI LIVII, *ibid.*

[o] The poverty which STANIAN speaks of is only to be seen in the most mountainous cantons, where there is no commodity to bring money: And even there the people are not poorer than in the diocese of SALTSBURGH on the one hand, or SAVOY on the other.

[p] *Proem.*

the foregoing theory. The sum he mentions is 740,000 talents, or 191,166,666 pounds 13 shillings and 4 pence, according to Dr. ARBUTHNOT's computation. And yet APPIAN says, that he extracted his account from the public records; and he was himself a native of ALEXANDRIA.[22]

From these principles we may learn what judgment we ought to form of those numberless bars, obstructions and imposts, which all nations of EUROPE, and none more than ENGLAND, have put upon trade; from an exorbitant desire of amassing money, which never will heap up beyond its level, while it circulates; or from an ill-grounded apprehension of losing their specie, which never will sink below it. Could any thing scatter our riches, it would be such unpolitic contrivances. But this general ill effect, however, results from them, that they deprive neighbouring nations of that free communication and exchange which the Author of the world has intended, by giving them soils, climates, and geniuses, so different from each other.

Our modern politics embrace the only method of banishing money, the using of paper-credit; they reject the only method of amassing it, the practice of hoarding; and they adopt a hundred contrivances, which serve to no purpose but to check industry, and rob ourselves and our neighbours of the common benefits of art and nature.

All taxes, however, upon foreign commodities, are not to be regarded as prejudicial or useless, but those only which are founded on the jealousy above-mentioned. A tax on German linen encourages home manufactures, and thereby multiplies our people and industry. A tax on brandy encreases the sale of rum, and supports our southern colonies. And as it is necessary, that imposts should be levied, for the support of government, it may be thought more convenient to lay them on foreign commodities, which can easily be intercepted at the port, and subjected to the impost. We ought, however, always to remember the maxim of Dr. SWIFT, That, in the arithmetic of the customs, two and two make not four, but often make only one.[23] It can scarcely be doubted, but if the duties on wine were lowered to a third, they would yield much more to the government than at present: Our people might thereby afford to drink commonly a better and more wholesome liquor; and no prejudice would ensue to the balance of trade, of which we are so jealous. The manufacture of ale beyond the agriculture is but inconsiderable, and gives employment to few hands. The transport of wine and corn would not be much inferior.

But are there not frequent instances, you will say, of states and kingdoms, which were formerly rich and opulent, and are now poor and beggarly? Has not the money left them, with which they formerly abounded? I answer, If they lose their trade, industry, and people, they cannot expect to keep their gold and silver: For these precious metals will hold proportion to the former advantages. When LISBON and AMSTERDAM got the EAST-INDIA trade from VENICE and GENOA, they also got the profits and money which arose from it. Where the seat of government is transferred, where expensive armies are maintained at a distance, where great funds are possessed by foreigners; there naturally follows from these causes a diminution of the specie. But these, we may observe, are violent and forcible methods of carrying away money, and are in time commonly attended with the transport of people and industry. But where these remain, and the drain is not continued, the money always finds its way back again, by a hundred canals, of which we have no notion or suspicion. What immense treasures have been spent, by so many nations, in FLANDERS, since the revolution, in the course of three long wars?[24] More money perhaps than the half of what is at present in EUROPE. But what has now become of it? Is it in the narrow compass of the AUSTRIAN provinces? No, surely: It has most of it returned to the several countries whence it came, and has followed that art and industry, by which at first it was acquired. For above a thousand years, the money of EUROPE has been flowing to ROME, by an open and sensible current; but it has been emptied by many secret and insensible canals: And the want of industry and commerce renders at present the papal dominions the poorest territory in all ITALY.

IN short, a government has great reason to preserve with care its people and its manufactures. Its money, it may safely trust to the course of human affairs, without fear or jealousy. Or if it ever give attention to this latter circumstance, it ought only to be so far as it affects the former.

ESSAY EIGHTEEN

Of the jealousy of trade

HAVING endeavoured to remove one species of ill-founded jealousy, which is so prevalent among commercial nations, it may not be amiss to mention another, which seems equally groundless. Nothing is more usual, among states which have made some advances in commerce, than to look on the progress of their neighbours with a suspicious eye, to consider all trading states as their rivals, and to suppose that it is impossible for any of them to flourish, but at their expence. In opposition to this narrow and malignant opinion, I will venture to assert, that the encrease of riches and commerce in any one nation, instead of hurting, commonly promotes the riches and commerce of all its neighbours; and that a state can scarcely carry its trade and industry very far, where all the surrounding states are buried in ignorance, sloth, and barbarism.

It is obvious, that the domestic industry of a people cannot be hurt by the greatest prosperity of their neighbours; and as this branch of commerce is undoubtedly the most important in any extensive kingdom, we are so far removed from all reason of jealousy. But I go farther, and observe, that where an open communication is preserved among nations, it is impossible but the domestic industry of every one must receive an encrease from the improvements of the others. Compare the situation of GREAT BRITAIN at present, with what it was two centuries ago. All the arts both of agriculture and manufactures were then extremely rude and imperfect. Every improvement, which we have since made, has arisen from our imitation of foreigners; and we ought so far to esteem it happy, that they had previously made advances in arts and ingenuity. But this intercourse is still upheld to our great advantage: Notwithstanding the advanced state of our manufactures, we daily adopt, in every art, the inventions and improvements of our neighbours. The commodity is first important from abroad, to our great discontent, while we imagine that it drains us of our money: Afterwards, the art itself is gradually imported, to our visible advantage: Yet we continue still to repine, that our neighbours should possess any art, industry, and invention; forgetting that, had they not first instructed us, we should have been at present barbarians; and did they not still continue their instructions, the arts must fall into a state of languor, and lose that emulation and novelty, which contribute so much to their advancement.

The encrease of domestic industry lays the foundation of foreign commerce. Where a great number of commodities are raised and perfected for the home-market, there will always be found some which can be exported with advantage. But if our neighbours have no art or cultivation, they cannot take them; because they will have nothing to give in exchange. In this respect, states are in the same condition as individuals. A single man can scarcely be industrious, where all his fellow-citizens are idle. The riches of the several members of a community contribute to encrease my riches, whatever profession I may follow. They consume the produce of my industry, and afford me the produce of theirs in return.

Nor needs any state entertain apprehensions, that their neighbours will improve to such a degree in every art and manufacture, as to have no demand from them. Nature, by giving a diversity of geniuses, climates, and soils, to different nations, has secured their mutual intercourse and commerce, as long as they all remain industrious and civilized. Nay, the more the arts encrease in any state, the more will be its demands from its industrious neighbours. The inhabitants, having become opulent and skilful, desire to have every commodity in the utmost perfection; and as they have plenty of commodities to give in exchange, they make large importations from every foreign country. The industry of the nations, from whom they import, receives encouragement: Their own is also encreased, by the sale of the commodities which they give in exchange.

But what if a nation has any staple commodity, such as the woollen manufactory is in ENGLAND? Must not the interfering of their neighbours in that manufacture be a loss to them? I answer, that, when any commodity is denominated the staple of a kingdom, it is supposed that this kingdom has some peculiar and natural advantages for raising the commodity; and if, notwithstanding these advantages, they lose such a manufactory, they ought to blame their own idleness, or bad government, not the industry of their neighbours. It ought also to be considered, that, by the encrease of industry among the neighbouring nations, the consumption of every particular species of commodity is also encreased; and though foreign manufactures interfere with us in the market, the demand for our product may still continue, or even encrease. And should it diminish, ought the consequence to be esteemed so fatal? If the spirit of industry be preserved, it may easily be diverted from one branch to another; and the manufacturers of wool, for instance, be employed in linen, silk, iron, or any other commodities, for which there appears to be a demand. We need not apprehend, that all the objects of industry will be exhausted, or that our manufacturers, while they remain on an equal footing with those of our neighbours, will be in danger of wanting employment. The emulation among rival nations serves rather to keep industry alive in all of them: And any people is happier who possess a variety of manufactures, than if they enjoyed one single great manufacture, in which they are all employed. Their situation is less precarious; and they will feel less sensibly those revolutions and uncertainties, to which every particular branch of commerce will always be exposed.

The only commercial state, that ought to dread the improvements and industry of their neighbours, is such a one as the DUTCH, who, enjoying no extent of land, nor possessing any number of native commodities, flourish only by their being the brokers, and factors, and carriers of others. Such a people may naturally apprehend, that, as soon as the neighbouring states come to know and pursue their interest, they will take into their own hands the management of their affairs, and deprive their brokers of that profit, which they formerly reaped from it. But though this consequence may naturally be dreaded, it is very long before it takes place; and by art and industry it may be warded off for many generations, if not wholly eluded. The advantage of superior stocks and correspondence is so great, that it is not easily overcome; and as all the transactions encrease by the encrease of industry in the neighbouring states, even a people whose commerce stands on this precarious basis, may at first reap a considerable profit from the flourishing condition of their neighbours. The DUTCH, having mortgaged all their revenues, make not such a figure in political transactions as formerly; but their commerce is surely equal to what it was in the middle of the last century, when they were reckoned among the great powers of EUROPE.

Were our narrow and malignant politics to meet with success, we should reduce all our neighbouring nations to the same state of sloth and ignorance that prevails in MOROCCO and the coast of BARBARY. But what would be the consequence? They could send us no commodities: They could take none from us: Our domestic commerce itself would languish for want of emulation, example, and instruction: And we ourselves should soon fall into the same abject condition, to which we had reduced them. I shall therefore venture to acknowledge, that, not only as a man, but as a BRITISH subject, I pray for the flourishing commerce of GERMANY, SPAIN, ITALY, and even FRANCE itself. I am at least certain, that GREAT BRITAIN, and all those nations, would flourish more, did their sovereigns and ministers adopt such enlarged and benevolent sentiments towards each other.

ESSAY NINETEEN

Of the balance of power

It is a question, whether the *idea* of the balance of power be owing entirely to modern policy, or whether the *phrase* only has been invented in these later ages? It is certain, that Xenophon,[a] in his Institution of Cyrus, represents the combination of the Asiatic powers to have arisen from a jealousy of the encreasing force of the Medes and Persians; and though that elegant composition should be supposed altogether a romance, this sentiment, ascribed by the author to the eastern princes, is at least a proof of the prevailing notion of ancient times.[1]

In all the politics of Greece, the anxiety, with regard to the balance of power, is apparent, and is expressly pointed out to us, even by the ancient historians. Thucydides[b] represents the league, which was formed against Athens, and which produced the Peloponnesian war, as entirely owing to this principle. And after the decline of Athens, when the Thebans and Lacedemonians disputed for sovereignty, we find, that the Athenians (as well as many other republics) always threw themselves into the lighter scale, and endeavoured to preserve the balance. They supported Thebes against Sparta, till the great victory gained by Epaminondas at Leuctra; after which they immediately went over to the conquered, from generosity, as they pretended, but, in reality from their jealousy of the conquerors.[c2]

---

[a] Lib. i.
[b] Lib. i.
[c] Xenoph. Hist. Graec. lib. vi. & vii.

Whoever will read DEMOSTHENES's oration for the MEGALOPOLIT-
ANS, may see the utmost refinements on this principle, that ever
entered into the head of a VENETIAN or ENGLISH speculatist. And
upon the first rise of the MACEDONIAN power, this orator immediately
discovered the danger, sounded the alarm through all GREECE, and
at last assembled that confederacy under the banners of ATHENS,
which fought the great and decisive battle of CHAERONEA.[3]

It is true, the GRECIAN wars are regarded by historians as wars of
emulation rather than of politics; and each state seems to have had
more in view the honour of leading the rest, than any well-grounded
hopes of authority and dominion. If we consider, indeed, the small
number of inhabitants in any one republic, compared to the whole,
the great difficulty of forming sieges in those times, and the extraordinary bravery and discipline of every freeman among that noble
people; we shall conclude, that the balance of power was, of itself,
sufficiently secured in GREECE, and needed not to have been guarded
with that caution which may be requisite in other ages. But whether
we ascribe the shifting of sides in all the GRECIAN republics to *jealous
emulation* or *cautious politics*, the effects were alike, and every prevailing power was sure to meet with a confederacy against it, and that
often composed of its former friends and allies.

The same principle, call it envy or prudence, which produced the
Ostracism of ATHENS, and *Petalism* of SYRACUSE, and expelled every
citizen whose fame or power overtopped the rest;[4] the same principle,
I say, naturally discovered itself in foreign politics, and soon raised
enemies to the leading state, however moderate in the exercise of its
authority.

The PERSIAN monarch was really, in his force, a petty prince,
compared to the GRECIAN republics; and therefore it behoved him,
from views of safety more than from emulation, to interest himself
in their quarrels, and to support the weaker side in every contest.
This was the advice given by ALCIBIADES to TISSAPHERNES,[d] and
it prolonged near a century the date of the PERSIAN empire; till
the neglect of it for a moment, after the first appearance of the
aspiring genius of PHILIP, brought that lofty and frail edifice to
the ground, with a rapidity of which there are few instances in
the history of mankind.[5]

---

[d] THUCYD. lib. viii.

The successors of ALEXANDER showed great jealousy of the balance of power; a jealousy founded on true politics and prudence, and which preserved distinct for several ages the partitions made after the death of that famous conqueror. The fortune and ambition of ANTIGONUS[e] threatened them anew with a universal monarchy; but their combination, and their victory at IPSUS saved them. And in after times, we find, that, as the Eastern princes considered the GREEKS and MACEDONIANS as the only real military force, with whom they had any intercourse, they kept always a watchful eye over that part of the world. The PTOLEMIES, in particular, supported first ARATUS and the ACHAEANS, and then CLEOMENES king of SPARTA, from no other view than as a counterbalance to the MACEDONIAN monarchs. For this is the account which POLYBIUS gives of the EGYPTIAN politics.[f6]

The reason, why it is supposed, that the ancients were entirely ignorant of the *balance of power*, seems to be drawn from the ROMAN history more than the GRECIAN; and as the transactions of the former are generally the most familiar to us, we have thence formed all our conclusions. It must be owned, that the ROMANS never met with any such general combination or confederacy against them, as might naturally have been expected from their rapid conquests and declared ambition; but were allowed peaceably to subdue their neighbours, one after another, till they extended their dominion over the whole known world. Not to mention the fabulous history of their[7] ITALIC wars; there was, upon HANNIBAL's invasion of the ROMAN state, a remarkable crisis, which ought to have called up the attention of all civilized nations. It appeared afterwards (nor was it difficult to be observed at the time)[g] that this was a contest for universal empire; and yet no prince or state seems to have been in the least alarmed about the event or issue of the quarrel. PHILIP of MACEDON remained neuter, till he saw the victories of HANNIBAL; and then most imprudently formed an alliance with the conqueror, upon terms still more imprudent. He stipulated, that he was to assist the CARTHAGINIAN state in their conquest of ITALY; after which they engaged to send

[e] DIOD. SIC. lib. xx.
[f] Lib. ii. cap. 51.
[g] It was observed by some, as appears by the speech of AGELAUS of NAUPACTUM, in the general congress of GREECE. See POLYB. lib. v. cap. 104.

over forces into GREECE, to assist him in subduing the GRECIAN commonwealths.[h8]

The RHODIAN and ACHAEAN republics are much celebrated by ancient historians for their wisdom and sound policy; yet both of them assisted the ROMANS in their wars against PHILIP and ANTIOCHUS. And what may be esteemed still a stronger proof, that this maxim was not generally known in those ages; no ancient author has remarked the imprudence of these measures, nor has even blamed that absurd treaty above mentioned, made by PHILIP with the CARTHAGINIANS. Princes and statesmen, in all ages, may, before-hand, be blinded in their reasonings with regard to events: But it is somewhat extraordinary, that historians, afterwards, should not form a sounder judgment of them.

MASSINISSA, ATTALUS, PRUSIAS, in gratifying their private passions, were, all of them, the instruments of the ROMAN greatness; and never seem to have suspected, that they were forging their own chains, while they advanced the conquests of their ally. A simple treaty and agreement between MASSINISSA and the CARTHAGINIANS, so much required by mutual interest, barred the ROMANS from all entrance into AFRICA, and preserved liberty to mankind.[9]

The only prince we meet with in the ROMAN history, who seems to have understood the balance of power, is HIERO king of SYRACUSE. Though the ally of ROME, he sent assistance to the CARTHAGINIANS, during the war of the auxiliaries; 'Esteeming it requisite,' says POLYBIUS,[i] 'both in order to retain his dominions in SICILY, and to preserve the ROMAN friendship, that CARTHAGE should be safe; lest by its fall the remaining power should be able, without contrast or opposition, to execute every purpose and undertaking. And here he acted with great wisdom and prudence. For that is never, on any account, to be overlooked; nor ought such a force ever to be thrown into one hand, as to incapacitate the neighbouring states from defending their rights against it.' Here is the aim of modern politics pointed out in express terms.[10]

In short, the maxim of preserving the balance of power is founded so much on common sense and obvious reasoning, that it is imposs-

---

[h] TITI LIVII, lib. xxiii. cap. 33.
[i] Lib. i. cap. 83.

ible it could altogether have escaped antiquity, where we find, in other particulars, so many marks of deep penetration and discernment. If it was not so generally known and acknowledged as at present, it had, at least, an influence on all the wiser and more experienced princes and politicians. And indeed, even at present, however generally known and acknowledged among speculative reasoners, it has not, in practice, an authority much more extensive among those who govern the world.

After the fall of the ROMAN empire, the form of government, established by the northern conquerors, incapacitated them, in a great measure, for farther conquests, and long maintained each state in its proper boundaries. But when vassalage and the feudal militia were abolished, mankind were anew alarmed by the danger of universal monarchy, from the union of so many kingdoms and principalities in the person of the emperor CHARLES. But the power of the house of AUSTRIA, founded on extensive but divided dominions, and their riches, derived chiefly from mines of gold and silver, were more likely to decay, of themselves, from internal defects, than to overthrow all the bulwarks raised against them. In less than a century, the force of that violent and haughty race was shattered, their opulence dissipated, their splendor eclipsed.[11] A new power succeeded, more formidable to the liberties of EUROPE, possessing all the advantage of the former, and labouring under none of its defects; except a share of that spirit of bigotry and persecution, with which the house of AUSTRIA was so long, and still is so much infatuated.[12]

In the general wars, maintained against this ambitious power, BRITAIN has stood foremost; and she still maintains her station. Beside her advantages of riches and situation, her people are animated with such a national spirit and are so fully sensible of the blessings of their government, that we may hope their vigour never will languish in so necessary and so just a cause. On the contrary, if we may judge by the past, their passionate ardour seems rather to require some moderation; and they have oftener erred from a laudable excess than from a blameable deficiency.

In the first place, we seem to have been more possessed with the ancient GREEK spirit of jealous emulation, than actuated by the prudent views of modern politics. Our wars with FRANCE have been begun with justice, and even, perhaps, from necessity; but have always been too far pushed from obstinacy and passion. The same peace, which was afterwards made at Ryswick in 1697, was offered so early as the year ninety-two; that concluded at Utrecht in 1712 might have been finished on as good conditions at Ger-truytenberg in the year eight; and we might have given at Frankfort, in 1743, the same terms, which we were glad to accept of at Aix-la-Chapelle in the year forty-eight.[13] Here then we see, that above half of our wars with France, and all our public debts, are owing more to our own imprudent vehemence, than to the ambition of our neighbours.

In the second place, we are so declared in our opposition to French power, and so alert in defence of our allies, that they always reckon upon our force as upon their own; and expecting to carry on war at our expence, refuse all reasonable terms of accommodation. *Habet subjectos, tanquam suos; viles, ut alienos.*[14] All the world knows, that the factious vote of the House of Commons, in the beginning of the last parliament, with the professed humour of the nation, made the queen of Hungary inflexible in her terms, and prevented that agreement with Prussia, which would immediately have restored the general tranquillity of Europe.[15]

In the third place, we are such true combatants, that, when once engaged, we lose all concern for ourselves and our posterity, and consider only how we may best annoy the enemy. To mortgage our revenues at so deep a rate, in wars, where we were only accessories, was surely the most fatal delusion, that a nation, which had any pretension to politics and prudence, has ever yet been guilty of. That remedy of funding, if it be a remedy, and not rather a poison, ought, in all reason, to be reserved to the last extremity; and no evil, but the greatest and most urgent, should ever induce us to embrace so dangerous an expedient.

These excesses, to which we have been carried, are prejudicial; and may, perhaps, in time, become still more prejudicial another way, by begetting, as is usual, the opposite extreme, and rendering us totally careless and supine with regard to the fate of Europe. The Athenians, from the most bustling, intriguing, warlike people of Greece, finding their error in thrusting themselves into every quarrel, abandoned all attention to foreign affairs; and in no contest, ever took part on either side, except by their flatteries and complaisance to the victor.

Enormous monarchies are, probably, destructive to human nature; in their progress, in their continuance,[j] and even in their downfal, which never can be very distant from their establishment. The military genius, which aggrandized the monarchy, soon leaves the court, the capital, and the center of such a government; while the wars are carried on at a great distance, and interest so small a part of the state. The ancient nobility, whose affections attach them to their sovereign, live all at court; and never will accept of military employments, which would carry them to remote and barbarous frontiers, where they are distant both from their pleasures and their fortune. The arms of the state, must, therefore, be entrusted to mercenary strangers, without zeal, without attachment, without honour; ready on every occasion to turn them against the prince, and join each desperate malcontent, who offers pay and plunder. This is the necessary progress of human affairs: Thus human nature checks itself in its airy elevations: Thus ambition blindly labours for the destruction of the conqueror, of his family, and of every thing near and dear to him. The BOURBONS, trusting to the support of their brave, faithful, and affectionate nobility, would push their advantage, without reserve or limitation.[16] These, while fired with glory and emulation, can bear the fatigues and dangers of war; but never would submit to languish in the garrisons of HUNGARY or LITHUANIA, forgot at court, and sacrificed to the intrigues of every minion or mistress, who approaches the prince. The troops are filled with CRAVATES and TARTARS, HUSSARS and COSSACS; intermingled, perhaps, with a few soldiers of fortune from the better provinces: And the melancholy fate of the ROMAN emperors, from the same cause, is renewed over and over again, till the final dissolution of the monarchy.

---

[j] If the ROMAN empire was of advantage, it could only proceed from this, that mankind were generally in a very disorderly, uncivilized condition, before its establishment.

ESSAY TWENTY

Of taxes

THERE is a prevailing maxim, among some reasoners, *that every new tax creates a new ability in the subject to bear it, and that each encrease of public burdens encreases proportionably the industry of the people.* This maxim is of such a nature as is most likely to be abused; and is so much the more dangerous, as its truth cannot be altogether denied: but it must be owned, when kept within certain bounds, to have some foundation in reason and experience.

When a tax is laid upon commodities, which are consumed by the common people, the necessary consequence may seem to be, either that the poor must retrench something from their way of living, or raise their wages, so as to make the burden of the tax fall entirely upon the rich. But there is a third consequence, which often follows upon taxes, namely, that the poor encrease their industry, perform more work, and live as well as before, without demanding more for their labour. Where taxes are moderate, are laid on gradually, and affect not the necessaries of life, this consequence naturally follows; and it is certain, that such difficulties often serve to excite the industry of a people, and render them more opulent and laborious, than others, who enjoy the greatest advantages. For we may observe, as a parallel instance, that the most commercial nations have not always possessed the greatest extent of fertile land; but, on the contrary, that they have laboured under many natural disadvantages. TYRE, ATHENS, CARTHAGE, RHODES, GENOA, VENICE, HOLLAND, are strong examples to this purpose. And in all history, we find only three instances of large and fertile countries, which have possessed much trade; the NETHERLANDS, ENGLAND, and FRANCE. The two former

161

seem to have been allured by the advantages of their maritime situation and the necessity they lay under of frequenting foreign ports, in order to procure what their own climate refused them. And as to FRANCE, trade has come late into that kingdom, and seems to have been the effect of reflection and observation in an ingenious and enterprizing people, who remarked the riches acquired by such of the neighbouring nations as cultivated navigation and commerce.

The places mentioned by CICERO,[a] as possessed of the greatest commerce in his time, are ALEXANDRIA, COLCHUS, TYRE, SIDON, ANDROS, CYPRUS, PAMPHYLIA, LYCIA, RHODES, CHIOS, BYZANTIUM, LESBOS, SMYRNA, MILETUM, COOS.[1] All these, except ALEXANDRIA, were either small islands, or narrow territories. And that city owed its trade entirely to the happiness of its situation.

Since therefore some natural necessities or disadvantages may be thought favourable to industry, why may not artificial burdens have the same effect? Sir WILLIAM TEMPLE,[b] we may observe, ascribes the industry of the DUTCH entirely to necessity, proceeding from their natural disadvantages; and illustrates his doctrine by a striking comparison with IRELAND; 'where,' says he, 'by the largeness and plenty of the soil, and scarcity of people, all things necessary to life are so cheap, that an industrious man, by two days labour, may gain enough to feed him the rest of the week. Which I take to be a very plain ground of the laziness attributed to the people. For men naturally prefer ease before labour, and will not take pains if they can live idle; though when, by necessity, they have been inured to it, they cannot leave it, being grown a custom necessary to their health, and to their very entertainment. Nor perhaps is the change harder, from constant ease to labour, than from constant labour to ease.'[2] After which the author proceeds to confirm his doctrine, by enumerating, as above, the places where trade has most flourished, in ancient and modern times; and which are commonly observed to be such narrow confined territories, as beget a necessity for industry.

The best taxes are such as are levied upon consumptions, especially those of luxury; because such taxes are least felt by the people. They seem, in some measure, voluntary; since a man may chuse how far he will use the commodity which is taxed: They are paid gradually

---

[a] Epist. ad ATT. lib. ix. ep. II.
[b] Account of the NETHERLANDS, chap. 6.

and insensibly: They naturally produce sobriety and frugality, if judiciously imposed: And being confounded with the natural price of the commodity, they are scarcely perceived by the consumers. Their only disadvantage is, that they are expensive in the levying.

Taxes upon possessions are levied without expence; but have every other disadvantage. Most states, however, are obliged to have recourse to them, in order to supply the deficiencies of the other.

But the most pernicious of all taxes are the arbitrary. They are commonly converted, by their management, into punishments on industry; and also, by their unavoidable inequality, are more grievous than by the real burden which they impose. It is surprising, therefore, to see them have place among any civilized people.

In general, all poll-taxes, even when not arbitrary, which they commonly are, may be esteemed dangerous:[3] Because it is so easy for the sovereign to add a little more, and a little more, to the sum demanded, that these taxes are apt to become altogether oppressive and intolerable. On the other hand, a duty upon commodities checks itself; and a prince will soon find, that an encrease of the impost is no encrease of his revenue. It is not easy, therefore, for a people to be altogether ruined by such taxes.

Historians inform us, that one of the chief causes of the destruction of the ROMAN state, was the alteration, which CONSTANTINE introduced into the finances, by substituting an universal poll-tax, in lieu of almost all the tithes, customs, and excises, which formerly composed the revenue of the *empire*. The people, in all the provinces, were so grinded and oppressed by the *publicans*, that they were glad to take refuge under the conquering arms of the barbarians; whose dominion, as they had fewer necessities and less art, was found preferable to the refined tyranny of the ROMANS.[4]

It is an opinion, zealously promoted by some political writers, that since all taxes, as they pretend, fall ultimately upon land, it were better to lay them originally there, and abolish every duty upon consumptions. But it is denied, that all taxes fall ultimately upon land. If a duty be laid upon any commodity, consumed by an artisan, he has two obvious expedients for paying it; he may retrench somewhat of his expence, or he may encrease his labour. Both these resources are more easy and natural, than that of heightening his wages. We see, that, in years of scarcity, the weaver either consumes less or labours more, or employs both these expedients of frugality and industry, by which he is enabled to reach the end of the year. It is but just, that he should subject himself to the same hardships, if they deserve the name, for the sake of the publick, which gives him protection. By what contrivance can he raise the price of his labour? The manufacturer who employs him, will not give him more: Neither can he, because the merchant, who exports the cloth, cannot raise its price, being limited by the price which it yields in foreign markets.[5] Every man, to be sure, is desirous of pushing off from himself the burden of any tax, which is imposed, and of laying it upon others: But as every man has the same inclination, and is upon the defensive; no set of men can be supposed to prevail altogether in this contest. And why the landed gentleman should be the victim of the whole, and should not be able to defend himself, as well as others are, I cannot readily imagine. All tradesmen, indeed, would willingly prey upon him, and divide him among them, if they could: But this inclination they always have, though no taxes were levied; and the same methods, by which he guards against the imposition of tradesmen before taxes, will serve him afterwards, and make them share the burden with him. They must be very heavy taxes, indeed, and very injudiciously levied, which the artizan will not, of himself, be enabled to pay, by superior industry and frugality, without raising the price of his labour.

I shall conclude this subject with observing, that we have, with regard to taxes, an instance of what frequently happens in political institutions, that the consequences of things are diametrically opposite to what we should expect on the first appearance. It is regarded as a fundamental maxim of the TURKISH government, that the *Grand Signior*, though absolute master of the lives and fortunes of each individual, has no authority to impose a new tax; and every OTTOMAN prince, who has made such an attempt, either has been obliged to retract, or has found the fatal effects of his perseverance. One would imagine, that this prejudice or established opinion were the firmest barrier in the world against oppression; yet it is certain, that its effect is quite contrary. The emperor, having no regular method of encreasing his revenue, must allow all the bashaws and governors to oppress and abuse the subjects: And these he squeezes after their return from their government. Whereas, if he could impose a new tax, like our EUROPEAN princes, his interest would so far be united with that of his people, that he would immediately feel the bad effects of these disorderly levies of money, and would find, that a pound, raised by general imposition, would have less pernicious effects, than a shilling taken in so unequal and arbitrary a manner.

ESSAY TWENTY-ONE

Of public credit

It appears to have been the common practice of antiquity, to make provision, during peace, for the necessities of war, and to hoard up treasures before-hand, as the instruments either of conquest or defence; without trusting to extraordinary impositions, much less to borrowing, in times of disorder and confusion. Besides the immense sums above mentioned,[a] which were amassed by ATHENS, and by the PTOLEMIES, and other successors of ALEXANDER; we learn from PLATO,[b] that the frugal LACEDEMONIANS had also collected a great treasure; and ARRIAN[c] and PLUTARCH[d] take notice of the riches which ALEXANDER got possession of on the conquest of SUSA and ECBATANA, and which were reserved, some of them, from the time of CYRUS.[1] If I remember right the scripture also mentions the treasure of HEZEKIAH and the JEWISH princes; as profane history does that of PHILIP and PERSEUS, kings of MACEDON.[2] The ancient republics of GAUL had commonly large sums in reserve.[e] Every one knows the treasure seized in ROME by JULIUS CAESAR, during the civil wars;[4] and we find afterwards, that the wiser emperors, AUGUSTUS, TIBERIUS, VESPASIAN, SEVERUS, &c. always discovered the prudent foresight, of saving great sums against any public exigency.

---

[a] Essay V ['Of the balance of trade'].
[b] ALCIB. I.
[c] Lib. iii.
[d] PLUT. *in vita* ALEX. He makes these treasures amount to 80,000 talents, or about 15 millions sterl. QUINTUS CURTIUS (lib. v. cap. 2.) says, that ALEXANDER found in SUSA above 50,000 talents.
[e] STRABO, lib. iv.[3]

On the contrary, our modern expedient, which has become very general, is to mortgage the public revenues, and to trust that posterity will pay off the incumbrances contracted by their ancestors: And they, having before their eyes, so good an example of their wise fathers, have the same prudent reliance on *their* posterity; who, at last, from necessity more than choice, are obliged to place the same confidence in a new posterity. But not to waste time in declaiming against a practice which appears ruinous, beyond all controversy; it seems pretty apparent, that the ancient maxims are, in this respect, more prudent than the modern; even though the latter had been confined within some reasonable bounds, and had ever, in any instance, been attended with such frugality, in time of peace, as to discharge the debts incurred by an expensive war. For why should the case be so different between the public and an individual, as to make us establish different maxims of conduct for each? If the funds of the former be greater, its necessary expences are proportionably larger; if its resources be more numerous, they are not infinite; and as its frame should be calculated for a much longer duration than the date of a single life, or even of a family, it should embrace maxims, large, durable, and generous, agreeably to the supposed extent of its existence. To trust to chances and temporary expedients, is, indeed, what the necessity of human affairs frequently renders unavoidable; but whoever voluntarily depend on such resources, have not necessity, but their own folly, to accuse for their misfortunes, when any such befal them.

If the abuses of treasures be dangerous, either by engaging the state in rash enterprizes, or making it neglect military discipline, in confidence of its riches; the abuses of mortgaging are more certain and inevitable; poverty, impotence, and subjection to foreign powers.

According to modern policy war is attended with every destructive circumstance; loss of men, encrease of taxes, decay of commerce, dissipation of money, devastation by sea and land. According to ancient maxims, the opening of the public treasure, as it produced an uncommon affluence of gold and silver, served as a temporary encouragement to industry, and atoned, in some degree, for the inevitable calamities of war.

It is very tempting to a minister to employ such an expedient, as enables him to make a great figure during his administration, without overburthening the people with taxes, or exciting any immediate clamours against himself. The practice, therefore, of contracting debt will almost infallibly be abused, in every government. It would scarcely be more imprudent to give a prodigal son a credit in every banker's shop in London, than to impower a statesman to draw bills, in this manner, upon posterity.

What then shall we say to the new paradox, that public incumbrances, are, of themselves, advantageous, independent of the necessity of contracting them; and that any state, even though it were not pressed by a foreign enemy, could not possibly have embraced a wiser expedient for promoting commerce and riches than to create funds, and debts, and taxes, without limitation? Reasonings, such as these, might naturally have passed for trials of wit among rhetoricians, like the panegyrics on folly and a fever, on BUSIRIS[5] and NERO, had we not seen such absurd maxims patronized by great ministers, and by a whole party among us.[6]

Let us examine the consequences of public debts, both in our domestic management, by their influence on commerce and industry; and in our foreign transactions, by their effect on wars and negociations.[7]

Public securities are with us become a kind of money, and pass as readily at the current price as gold or silver. Wherever any profitable undertaking offers itself, how expensive soever, there are never wanting hands enow to embrace it; nor need a trader, who has sums in the public stocks, fear to launch out into the most extensive trade; since he is possessed of funds which will answer the most sudden demand that can be made upon him. No merchant thinks it necessary to keep by him any considerable cash. Bank-stock, or India-bonds, especially the latter, serve all the same purposes;[8] because he can dispose of them, or pledge them to a banker, in a quarter of an hour; and at the same time they are not idle, even when in his scritoire, but bring him in a constant revenue. In short, our national debts furnish merchants with a specie of money, that is continually multiplying in their hands, and produces sure gain, besides the profits of their commerce. This must enable them to trade upon less profit. The small profit of the merchant renders the commodity cheaper, causes a great consumption, quickens the labour of the common people, and helps to spread arts and industry throughout the whole society.

There are also, we may observe, in ENGLAND, and in all states, which have both commerce and public debts, a set of men, who are half merchants, half stock-holders, and may be supposed willing to trade for small profits; because commerce is not their principal or sole support, and their revenues in the funds are a sure resource for themselves and their families. Were there no funds, great merchants would have no expedient for realizing or securing any part of their profit, but by making purchases of land; and land has many disadvantages in comparison of funds. Requiring more care and inspection, it divides the time and attention of the merchant; upon any tempting offer or extraordinary accident in trade, it is not so easily converted into money; and as it attracts too much, both by the many natural pleasures it affords, and the authority it gives, it soon converts the citizen into the country gentleman. More men, therefore, with large stocks and incomes, may naturally be supposed to continue in trade, where there are public debts; and this, it must be owned, is of some advantage to commerce, by diminishing its profits, promoting circulation, and encouraging industry.

But, in opposition to these two favourable circumstances, perhaps of no very great importance, weigh the many disadvantages which attend our public debts, in the whole *interior* oeconomy of the state: You will find no comparison between the ill and the good which result from them.

First, It is certain, that national debts cause a mighty confluence of people and riches to the capital, by the great sums, levied in the provinces to pay the interest; and perhaps, too, by the advantages in trade above mentioned, which they give the merchants in the capital above the rest of the kingdom. The question is, whether, in our case, it be for the public interest, that so many privileges should be conferred on LONDON, which has already arrived at such an enormous size, and seems still encreasing? Some men are apprehensive of the consequences. For my own part, I cannot forbear thinking, that, though the head is undoubtedly too large for the body, yet that great city is so happily situated, that its excessive bulk causes less inconvenience than even a smaller capital to a greater kingdom. There is more difference between the prices of all provisions in PARIS and LANGUEDOC, than between those in LONDON and YORKSHIRE. The immense greatness, indeed, of LONDON, under a government which admits not of discretionary power, renders the people factious, mutinous, seditious, and even perhaps rebellious. But to this evil the national debts themselves tend to provide a remedy. The first visible eruption, or even immediate danger, of public disorders must alarm all the stock-holders, whose property is the most precarious of any; and will make them fly to the support of government, whether menaced by Jacobitish violence or democratical frenzy.

Secondly, Public stocks, being a kind of paper-credit, have all the disadvantages attending that species of money. They banish gold and silver from the most considerable commerce of the state, reduce them to common circulation, and by that means render all provisions and labour dearer than otherwise they would be.

Thirdly, The taxes, which are levied to pay the interests of these debts, are apt either to heighten the price of labour, or be an oppression on the poorer sort.

Fourthly, As foreigners possess a great share of our national funds, they render the public, in a manner, tributary to them, and may in time occasion the transport of our people and our industry.

Fifthly, The greatest part of public stock being always in the hands of idle people, who live on their revenue, our funds give great encouragement to an useless and unactive life.

But though the injury, that arises to commerce and industry from our public funds, will appear, upon balancing the whole, not inconsiderable, it is trivial, in comparison of the prejudice that results to the state considered as a body politic, which must support itself in the society of nations, and have various transactions with other states in wars and negociations. The ill, there, is pure and unmixed, without any favourable circumstance to atone for it; and it is an ill too of a nature the highest and most important.

We have, indeed, been told, that the public is no weaker upon account of its debts; since they are mostly due among ourselves, and bring as much property to one as they take from another. It is like transferring money from the right hand to the left; which leaves the person neither richer nor poorer than before.[9] Such loose reasonings and specious comparisons will always pass, where we judge not upon principles. I ask, Is it possible, in the nature of things, to overburthen a nation with taxes, even where the sovereign resides among them? The very doubt seems extravagant; since it is requisite, in every community, that there be a certain proportion observed between the laborious and the idle part of it. But if all our present taxes be mort-gaged, must we not invent new ones? And may not this matter be carried to a length that is ruinous and destructive?

In every nation, there are always some methods of levying money more easy than others, agreeably to the way of living of the people, and the commodities they make use of. In BRITAIN, the excises upon malt and beer afford a large revenue; because the operations of malt-ing and brewing are tedious, and are impossible to be concealed; and at the same time, these commodities are not so absolutely necessary to life, as that the raising their price would very much affect the poorer sort. These taxes being all mortgaged, what difficulty to find new ones! what vexation and ruin of the poor!

Duties upon consumptions are more equal and easy than those upon possessions. What a loss to the public, that the former are all exhausted, and that we must have recourse to the more grievous method of levying taxes!

Were all the proprietors of land only stewards to the public, must not necessity force them to practise all the arts of oppression used by stewards; where the absence or negligence of the proprietor render them secure against enquiry?

It will scarcely be asserted, that no bounds ought ever to be set to national debts; and that the public would be no weaker, were twelve or fifteen shillings in the pound, land-tax, mortgaged, with all the present customs and excises. There is something, therefore, in the case, beside the mere transferring of property from one hand to another. In 500 years, the posterity of those now in the coaches, and of those upon the boxes, will probably have changed places, without affecting the public by these revolutions.

Suppose the public once fairly brought to that condition, to which it is hastening with such amazing rapidity; suppose the land to be taxed eighteen or nineteen shillings in the pound; for it can never bear the whole twenty; suppose all the excises and customs to be screwed up to the utmost which the nation can bear, without entirely losing its commerce and industry; and suppose that all those funds are mortgaged to perpetuity, and that the invention and wit of all our projectors can find no new imposition, which may serve as the foundation of a new loan; and let us consider the necessary con-sequences of this situation. Though the imperfect state of our polit-ical knowledge, and the narrow capacities of men, make it difficult to foretel the effects which will result from any untried measure, the seeds of ruin are here scattered with such profusion as not to escape the eye of the most careless observer.

In this unnatural state of society, the only persons, who possess any revenue beyond the immediate effects of their industry, are the stock-holders, who draw almost all the rent of the land and houses, besides the produce of all the customs and excises. These are men, who have no connexions in the state, who can enjoy their revenue in any part of the globe in which they chuse to reside, who will naturally bury themselves in the capital or in great cities, and who will sink into the lethargy of a stupid and pampered luxury, without spirit, ambition, or enjoyment. Adieu to all ideas of nobility, gentry, and family. The stocks can be transferred in an instant, and being in such a fluctuating state, will seldom be transmitted during three generations from father to son. Or were they to remain ever so long in one family, they convey no hereditary authority or credit to the possessor; and by this means, the several ranks of men, which form a kind of independent magistracy in a state, instituted by the hand of nature, are entirely lost; and every man in authority derives his influence from the commission alone of the sovereign. No expedient remains for preventing or suppressing insurrections, but mercenary armies: No expedient at all remains for resisting tyranny: Elections are swayed by bribery and corruption alone: And the middle power between king and people being totally removed, a grievous despotism must infallibly prevail. The landholders, despised for their poverty, and hated for their oppressions, will be utterly unable to make any opposition to it.

Though a resolution should be formed by the legislature never to impose any tax which hurts commerce and discourages industry, it will be impossible for men, in subjects of such extreme delicacy, to reason so justly as never to be mistaken, or amidst difficulties so urgent, never to be seduced from their resolution. The continual fluctuations in commerce require continual alterations in the nature of the taxes; which exposes the legislature every moment to the danger both of wilful and involuntary error. And any great blow given to trade, whether by injudicious taxes or by other accidents, throws the whole system of government into confusion.

But what expedient can the public now employ, even supposing trade to continue in the most flourishing condition, in order to support its foreign wars and enterprizes, and to defend its own honour and interests or those of its allies? I do not ask how the public is to exert such a prodigious power as it has maintained during our late wars; where we have so much exceeded, not only our own natural strength, but even that of the greatest empires. This extravagance is the abuse complained of, as the source of all the dangers, to which we are at present exposed. But since we must still suppose great commerce and opulence to remain, even after every fund is mortgaged; those riches must be defended by proportional power; and whence is the public to derive the revenue which supports it? It must plainly be from a continual taxation of the annuitants, or, which is the same thing, from mortgaging anew, on every exigency, a certain part of their annuity; and thus making them contribute to their own defence, and to that of the nation. But the difficulties, attending this system of policy, will easily appear, whether we suppose the king to have become absolute master, or to be still controuled by national councils, in which the annuitants themselves must necessarily bear the principal sway.

If the prince has become absolute, as may naturally be expected from this situation of affairs, it is so easy for him to encrease his exactions upon the annuitants, which amount only to the retaining money in his own hands, that this species of property would soon lose all its credit, and the whole income of every individual in the state must lie entirely at the mercy of the sovereign: A degree of despotism, which no oriental monarchy has ever yet attained. If, on the contrary, the consent of the annuitants be requisite for every taxation, they will never be persuaded to contribute sufficiently even to the support of government; as the diminution of their revenue must in that case be very sensible, would not be disguised under the appearance of a branch of excise or customs, and would not be shared by any other order of the state, who are already supposed to be taxed to the utmost. There are instances, in some republics, of a hundredth penny, and sometimes of the fiftieth, being given to the support of the state; but this is always an extraordinary exertion of power, and can never become the foundation of a constant national defence. We have always found, where a government has mortgaged all its revenues, that it necessarily sinks into a state of languor, inactivity and impotence.

Such are the inconveniencies, which may reasonably be foreseen, of this situation, to which GREAT BRITAIN is visibly tending. Not to mention, the numberless inconveniencies, which cannot be foreseen, and which must result from so monstrous a situation as that of making the public the chief or sole proprietor of land, besides investing it with every branch of customs and excise, which the fertile imagination of ministers and projectors have been able to invent.

I must confess, that there is a strange supineness, from long custom, creeped into all ranks of men, with regard to public debts, not unlike what divines so vehemently complain of with regard to their religious doctrines. We all own, that the most sanguine imagination cannot hope, either that this or any future ministry will be possessed of such rigid and steady frugality, as to make a considerable progress in the payment of our debts; or that the situation of foreign affairs will, for any long time, allow them leisure and tranquillity for such an undertaking. *What then is to become of us?* Were we ever so good Christians, and ever so resigned to Providence; this, methinks, were a curious question, even considered as a speculative one, and what it might not be altogether impossible to form some conjectural solution of. The events here will depend little upon the contingencies of battles, negociations, intrigues, and factions. There seems to be a natural progress of things, which may guide our reasoning. As it would have required but a moderate share of prudence, when we first began this practice of mortgaging, to have foretold, from the nature of men and ministers, that things would necessarily be carried to the length we see; so now, that they have at last happily reached it, it may not be difficult to guess at the consequences. It must, indeed, be one of these two events; either the nation must destroy public credit, or public credit will destroy the nation. It is impossible that they can both subsist, after the manner they have been hitherto managed, in this, as well as in some other countries.

There was, indeed, a scheme for the payment of our debts, which was proposed by an excellent citizen, Mr. HUTCHINSON, above thirty years ago, and which was much approved of by some men of sense, but never was likely to take effect. He asserted, that there was a fallacy in imagining that the public owed this debt; for that really every individual owed a proportional share of it, and paid, in his taxes, a proportional share of the interest, beside the expence of levying these taxes. Had we not better, then, says he, make a distribution of the debt among ourselves, and each of us contribute a sum suitable to his property, and by that means discharge at once all our funds and public mortgages?[10] He seems not to have considered, that the laborious poor pay a considerable part of the taxes by their annual consumptions, though they could not advance, at once, a proportional part of the sum required. Not to mention, that property in money and stock in trade might easily be concealed or disguised; and that visible property in lands and houses would really at last answer for the whole: An inequality and oppression, which never would be submitted to. But though this project is never likely to take place; it is not altogether improbable, that, when the nation becomes heartily sick of their debts, and is cruelly oppressed by them, some daring projector may arise with visionary schemes for their discharge. And as public credit will begin, by that time, to be a little frail, the least touch will destroy it, as happened in FRANCE during the regency;[11] and in this manner it will *die of the doctor.*

But it is more probable, that the breach of national faith will be the necessary effect of wars, defeats, misfortunes, and public calamities, or even perhaps of victories and conquests. I must confess, when I see princes and states fighting and quarrelling, amidst their debts, funds, and public mortgages, it always brings to my mind a match of cudgel-playing fought in a *China* shop.[12] How can it be expected, that sovereigns will spare a species of property, which is pernicious to themselves and to the public, when they have so little compassion on lives and properties, that are useful to both? Let the time come (and surely it will come) when the new funds, created for the exigencies of the year, are not subscribed to, and raise not the money projected. Suppose, either that the cash of the nation is exhausted; or that our faith, which has been hitherto so ample, begins to fail us. Suppose, that, in this distress, the nation is threatened with an invasion; a rebellion is suspected or broken out at home; a squadron cannot be equipped for want of pay, victuals, or repairs; or even a foreign subsidy cannot be advanced. What must a prince or minister do in such an emergence? The right of self-preservation is unalienable in every individual, much more in every community. And the folly of our statesmen must then be greater than the folly of those who first contracted debt, or, what is more, than that of those who trusted, or continue to trust this security, if these statesmen have the means of safety in their hands, and do not employ them. The funds, created and mortgaged, will, by that time, bring in a large yearly revenue, sufficient for the defence and security of the nation: Money is perhaps lying in the exchequer, ready for the discharge of the quarterly interest: Necessity calls, fear urges, reason exhorts, compassion alone exclaims: The money will immediately be seized for the current service, under the most solemn protestations, perhaps, of being immediately replaced. But no more is requisite. The whole fabric, already tottering, falls to the ground, and buries thousands in its ruins. And this, I think, may be called the *natural death* of public credit: For to this period it tends as naturally as an animal body to its dissolution and destruction.

So great dupes are the generality of mankind, that, notwithstanding such a violent shock to public credit, as a voluntary bankruptcy in ENGLAND would occasion, it would not probably be long, ere credit would again revive in as flourishing a condition as before. The present king of FRANCE, during the late war, borrowed money at lower interest than ever his grandfather did;[13] and as low as the BRITISH parliament, comparing the natural rate of interest in both kingdoms. And though men are commonly more governed by what they have seen, than by what they foresee, with whatever certainty; yet promises, protestations, fair appearances, with the allurements of present interest, have such powerful influence as few are able to resist. Mankind are in all ages, caught by the same baits: The same tricks, played over and over again, still trepan them. The heights of popularity and patriotism are still the beaten road to power and tyranny; flattery to treachery; standing armies to arbitrary government; and the glory of God to the temporal interest of the clergy. The fear of an everlasting destruction of credit, allowing it to be an evil, is a needless bugbear. A prudent man, in reality, would rather lend to the public immediately after they had taken a spunge to their debts, than at present; as much as an opulent knave, even though one could not force him to pay, is a preferable debtor to an honest bankrupt: For the former, in order to carry on business, may find it his interest to discharge his debts, where they are not exorbitant: The latter has it not in his power. The reasoning of TACITUS,[f] as it is eternally true, is very applicable to our present case. *Sed vulgus ad magnitudinem beneficiorum aderat: Stultissimus quisque pecuniis mercabatur: Apud sapientes cassa habebantur, quae neque dari neque accipi, salva republica, poterant.*[14] The public is a debtor, whom no man can oblige to pay. The only check which the creditors have upon her, is the interest of preserving credit;

---

[f] *Hist. lib.* iii.

an interest, which may easily be overbalanced by a great debt, and by a difficult and extraordinary emergence, even supposing that credit irrecoverable. Not to mention, that a present necessity often forces states into measures, which are, strictly speaking, against their interest.

These two events, supposed above, are calamitous, but not the most calamitous. Thousands are thereby sacrificed to the safety of millions. But we are not without danger that the contrary event may take place, and that millions may be sacrificed for ever to the temporary safety of thousands.[g] Our popular government, perhaps, will render it difficult or dangerous for a minister to venture on so desperate an expedient as that of a voluntary bankruptcy. And though the house of Lords be altogether composed of proprietors of land, and the house of Commons chiefly; and consequently neither of them can be supposed to have great property in the funds: Yet the connections of the members may be so great with the proprietors, as to render them more tenacious of public faith, than prudence, policy, or even justice, strictly speaking, requires. And perhaps too, our foreign enemies may be so politic as to discover, that our safety lies in despair, and may not, therefore, show the danger, open and barefaced, till it be inevitable. The balance of power in EUROPE, our grandfathers, our fathers, and we, have all esteemed too unequal to be preserved without our attention and assistance. But our children, weary of the struggle, and fettered with incumbrances, may sit down secure, and see their neighbours oppressed and conquered; till, at last, they themselves and their creditors lie both at the mercy of the conqueror. And this may properly enough be denominated the *violent death* of our public credit.

These seem to be the events, which are not very remote, and which reason foresees as clearly almost as she can do any thing that lies in

---

[g] I have heard it has been computed, that all the creditors of the public, natives and foreigners, amount only to 17,000. These make a figure at present on their income; but in case of a public bankruptcy, would, in an instant, become the lowest, as well as the most wretched of the people. The dignity and authority of the landed gentry and nobility is much better rooted; and would render the contention very unequal, if ever we come to that extremity. One would incline to assign to this event a very near period, such as half a century, had not our fathers' prophecies of this kind been already found fallacious, by the duration of our public credit, so much beyond all reasonable expectation. When the astrologers in FRANCE were every year foretelling the death of HENRY IV. *These fellows*, says he, *must be right at last*. We shall, therefore,

the womb of time. And though the ancient maintained, that in order to reach the gift of prophecy, a certain divine fury or madness was requisite, one may safely affirm, that, in order to deliver such prophecies as these, no more is necessary, than merely to be in one's senses, free from the influence of popular madness and delusion.

be more cautious than to assign any precise date; and shall content ourselves with pointing out the event in general.

Of some remarkable customs

I SHALL observe three remarkable customs in three celebrated governments; and shall conclude from the whole, that all general maxims in politics ought to be established with great caution; and that irregular and extraordinary appearances are frequently discovered in the moral, as well as in the physical world. The former, perhaps, we can better account for, after they happen, from springs and principles, of which every one has, within himself, or from observation, the strongest assurance and conviction: But it is often fully as impossible for human prudence, before-hand, to foresee and foretel them.

I. One would think it essential to every supreme council or assembly, which debates, that entire liberty of speech should be granted to every member, and that all motions or reasonings should be received, which can any wise tend to illustrate the point under deliberation. One would conclude, with still greater assurance, that, after a motion was made, which was voted and approved by that assembly in which the legislative power is lodged, the member who made the motion must for ever be exempted from future trial or enquiry. But no political maxim can, at first sight, appear more undisputable, than that he must, at least, be secured from all inferior jurisdiction; and that nothing less than the same supreme legislative assembly, in their subsequent meetings, could render him accountable for those motions and harangues, to which they had before given their approbation. But these axioms, however irrefragable they may appear, have all failed in the ATHENIAN government, from causes and principles too, which appear almost inevitable.

By the *graphe paranomon*, or *indictment of illegality*, (though it has not been remarked by antiquaries or commentators) any man was tried and punished in a common court of judicature, for any law which had passed upon his motion, in the assembly of the people, if that law appeared to the court unjust, or prejudicial to the public. Thus DEMOSTHENES, finding that ship-money was levied irregularly, and that the poor bore the same burden as the rich in equipping the gallies, corrected this inequality by a very useful law, which proportioned the expence to the revenue and income of each individual. He moved for this law in the assembly; he proved its advantages;[a] he convinced the people, the only legislature in ATHENS; the law passed, and was carried into execution: Yet was he tried in a criminal court for that law, upon the complaint of the rich, who resented the alteration that he had introduced into the finances.[b] He was indeed acquitted, upon proving anew the usefulness of his law.[1]

CTESIPHON moved in the assembly of the people, that particular honours should be conferred on DEMOSTHENES, as on a citizen affectionate and useful to the commonwealth: The people, convinced of this truth, voted those honours: Yet was CTESIPHON tried by the *graphe paranomon*. It was asserted, among other topics, that DEMOSTHENES was not a good citizen, nor affectionate to the commonwealth: And the orator was called upon to defend his friend, and consequently himself; which he executed by that sublime piece of eloquence, that has ever since been the admiration of mankind.

After the battle of CHAERONEA, a law was passed upon the motion of HYPERIDES, giving liberty to slaves, and inrolling them in the troops.[c] On account of this law, the orator was afterwards tried by the indictment above-mentioned, and defended himself, among other topics, by that stroke celebrated by PLUTARCH and LONGINUS. *It was not I*, said he, *that moved for this law: It was the necessities of war; it was the battle of* CHAERONEA. The orations of DEMOSTHENES abound with many instances of trials of this nature, and prove clearly, that nothing was more commonly practised.[2]

---

[a] His harangue for it is still extant; *Peri Symmorias*.
[b] Pro CTESIPHONTE.
[c] PLUTARCHUS *in vita decem oratorum*. DEMOSTHENES gives a different account of this law. *Contra* ARISTOGITON. *orat.* II. He says, that its purport was, to render the *atimoi epitimoi*, or to restore the privilege of bearing offices to those who had been declared incapable. Perhaps these were both clauses of the same law.

The ATHENIAN Democracy was such a tumultuous government as
we can scarcely form a notion of in the present age of the world.
The whole collective body of the people voted in every law, without
any limitation of property, without any distinction of rank, without
controul from any magistracy or senate;[d] and consequently without
regard to order, justice, or prudence. The ATHENIANS soon became
sensible of the mischiefs attending this constitution: But being averse
to checking themselves by any rule or restriction, they resolved, at
least, to check their demagogues or counsellors, by the fear of future
punishment and enquiry. They accordingly instituted this remarkable
law; a law esteemed so essential to their form of government, that
ÆSCHINES insists on it as a known truth, that, were it abolished or
neglected, it were impossible for the Democracy to subsist.[e]

The people feared not any ill consequence to liberty from the
authority of the criminal courts; because these were nothing but very
numerous juries, chosen by lot from among the people. And they
justly considered themselves as in a state of perpetual pupillage;
where they had an authority, after they came to the use of reason,
not only to retract and controul whatever had been determined, but
to punish any guardian for measures which they had embraced by
his persuasion. The same law had place in THEBES;[f] and for the same
reason.

It appears to have been a usual practice in ATHENS, on the establishment of any law esteemed very useful or popular, to prohibit for
ever its abrogation and repeal. Thus the demagogue, who diverted
all the public revenues to the support of shows and spectacles, made
it criminal so much as to move for a repeal of this law.[g] Thus LEP-
TINES moved for a law, not only to recal all the immunities formerly
granted, but to deprive the people for the future of the power of
granting any more.[h] Thus all bills of attainder[i] were forbid, or laws

---

[d] The senate of the Bean was only a less numerous mob, chosen by lot from among
the people; and their authority was not great.[3]

[e] *In* CTESIPHONTEM. It is remarkable, that the first step after the dissolution of the
Democracy by CRITIAS and the Thirty, was to annul the *graphe paranomon*, as we
learn from *Demosthenes kata Timok.* The orator in this oration gives us the words of
the law, establishing the *graphe paranomon*, pag. 297. *ex edit.* ALDI. And he accounts
for it, from the same principles we here reason upon.[4]

[f] PLUT. *in vita* PELOP.[5]

[g] DEMOST. *Olynth.* I. 2.

[h] DEMOST. *contra* LEPT.

[i] DEMOST. *contra* ARISTOCRATEM.

that affected one ATHENIAN, without extending to the whole commonwealth. These absurd clauses, by which the legislature vainly attempted to bind itself for ever, proceeded from an universal sense in the people of their own levity and inconstancy.[6]

II. A wheel within a wheel, such as we observe in the GERMAN empire, is considered by Lord SHAFTESBURY[j] as an absurdity in politics: But what must we say to two equal wheels, which govern the same political machine, without any mutual check, controul, or subordination; and yet preserve the greatest harmony and concord? To establish two distinct legislatures, each of which possesses full and absolute authority within itself, and stands in no need of the other's assistance, in order to give validity to its acts; this may appear, beforehand, altogether impracticable, as long as men are actuated by the passions of ambition, emulation, and avarice, which have hitherto been their chief governing principles. And should I assert, that the state I have in my eye was divided into two distinct factions, each of which predominated in a distinct legislature, and yet produced no clashing in these independent powers; the supposition may appear incredible. And if, to augment the paradox, I should affirm, that this disjointed, irregular government, was the most active, triumphant, and illustrious commonwealth, that ever yet appeared; I should certainly be told, that such a political chimera was as absurd as any vision of priests or poets. But there is no need for searching long, in order to prove the reality of the foregoing suppositions: For this was actually the case with the ROMAN republic.

The legislative power was there lodged in the *comitia centuriata* and *comitia tributa*. In the former, it is well known, the people voted according to their *census*; so that when the first class was unanimous, though it contained not, perhaps, the hundredth part of the commonwealth, it determined the whole; and, with the authority of the senate, established a law. In the latter, every vote was equal; and as the authority of the senate was not there requisite, the lower people entirely prevailed, and gave law to the whole state.[8] In all party-divisions, at first between the PATRICIANS and PLEBEIANS, afterwards between the nobles and the people, the interest of the Aristocracy was predominant in the first legislature; that of the Democracy in the second: The one could always destroy what the other had estab-

---

[j] Essay on the freedom of wit and humour, part 3. sec. 2.[7]

lished: Nay, the one by a sudden and unforeseen motion, might take the start of the other, and totally annihilate its rival, by a vote, which, from the nature of the constitution, had the full authority of a law. But no such contest is observed in the history of ROME: No instance of a quarrel between these two legislatures; though many between the parties that governed in each. Whence arose this concord, which may seem so extraordinary?

The legislature established in ROME, by the authority of SERVIUS TULLIUS, was the *comitia centuriata*, which, after the expulsion of the kings, rendered the government, for some time, very aristocratical. But the people, having numbers and force on their side, and being elated with frequent conquests and victories in their foreign wars, always prevailed when pushed to extremity, and first extorted from the senate the magistracy of the tribunes, and next the legislative power of the *comitia tributa*. It then behoved the nobles to be more careful than ever not to provoke the people. For beside the force which the latter were always possessed of, they had now got possession of legal authority, and could instantly break in pieces any order or institution which directly opposed them. By intrigue, by influence, by money, by combination, and by the respect paid to their character, the nobles might often prevail, and direct the whole machine of government: But had they openly set their *comitia centuriata* in opposition to the *tributa*, they had soon lost the advantage of that institution, together with their consuls, praetors, ediles, and all the magistrates elected by it.[9] But the *comitia tributa*, not having the same reason for respecting the *centuriata*, frequently repealed laws favourable to the Aristocracy: They limited the authority of the nobles, protected the people from oppression, and controuled the actions of the senate and magistracy. The *centuriata* found it convenient always to submit; and though equal in authority, yet being inferior in power, durst never directly give any shock to the other legislature, either by repealing its laws, or establishing laws, which, it foresaw, would soon be repealed by it.

No instance is found of any opposition or struggle between these *comitia*; except one slight attempt of this kind, mentioned by APPIAN in the third book of his civil wars.[10] MARK ANTHONY, resolving to deprive DECIMUS BRUTUS of the government of CISALPINE GAUL, railed in the *Forum*, and called one of the *comitia*, in order to prevent the meeting of the other, which had been ordered by the senate.

But affairs were then fallen into such confusion, and the ROMAN constitution was so near its final dissolution, that no inference can be drawn from such an expedient. This contest, besides, was founded more on form than party. It was the senate who ordered the *comitia tributa*, that they might obstruct the meeting of the *centuriata*, which, by the constitution, or at least forms of the government, could alone dispose of provinces.

CICERO was recalled by the *comitia centuriata*, though banished by the *tributa*, that is, by a *plebiscitum*. But his banishment, we may observe, never was considered as a legal deed, arising from the free choice and inclination of the people. It was always ascribed to the violence alone of CLODIUS, and to the disorders introduced by him into the government.

III. The *third* custom, which we propose to remark, regards ENG-LAND; and though it be not so important as those which we have pointed out in ATHENS and ROME, is no less singular and unexpected. It is a maxim in politics, which we readily admit as undisputed and universal, that a power, however great, when granted by law to an eminent magistrate, is not so dangerous to liberty, as an authority, however inconsiderable, which he acquires from violence and usurpation. For, besides that the law always limits every power which it bestows, the very receiving it as a concession establishes the author-ity whence it is derived, and preserves the harmony of the constitu-tion. By the same right that one prerogative is assumed without law, another may also be claimed, and another, with still greater facility; while the first usurpations both serve as precedents to the following, and give force to maintain them. Hence the heroism of HAMPDEN's conduct, who sustained the whole violence of royal prosecution, rather than pay a tax of twenty shillings, not imposed by parliament; hence the care of all ENGLISH patriots to guard against the first encroachments of the crown; and hence alone the existence, at this day, of ENGLISH liberty.[11]

There is, however, one occasion, where the parliament has depar-ted from this maxim; and that is, in the *pressing of seamen*.[12] The exercise of an irregular power is here tacitly permitted in the crown; and though it has frequently been under deliberation, how that power might be rendered legal, and granted, under proper restrictions to the sovereign, no safe expedient could ever be proposed for that purpose; and the danger to liberty always appeared greater from law than from usurpation. While this power is exercised to no other end than to man the navy, men willingly submit to it, from a sense of its use and necessity; and the sailors, who are alone affected by it, find no body to support them, in claiming the rights and privileges, which the law grants, without distinction, to all ENGLISH subjects. But were this power, on any occasion, made an instrument of faction or ministerial tyranny, the opposite faction, and indeed all lovers of their country, would immediately take the alarm, and support the injured party; the liberty of ENGLISHMEN would be asserted; juries would be implacable; and the tools of tyranny, acting both against law and equity, would meet with the severest vengeance. On the other hand, were the parliament to grant such an authority, they would probably fall into one of these two inconveniencies: They would either bestow it under so many restrictions as would make it lose its effect, by cramping the authority of the crown; or they would render it so large and comprehensive, as might give occasion to great abuses, for which we could, in that case, have no remedy. The very irregularity of the practice, at present, prevents its abuses, by affording so easy a remedy against them.

I pretend not, by this reasoning, to exclude all possibility of contriving a register for seamen, which might man the navy without being dangerous to liberty. I only observe, that no satisfactory scheme of that nature has yet been proposed. Rather than adopt any project hitherto invented, we continue a practice seemingly the most absurd and unaccountable. Authority, in times of full internal peace and concord, is armed against law. A continued violence is permitted in the crown, amidst the greatest jealousy and watchfulness in the people; nay proceeding from those very principles: Liberty, in a country of the highest liberty, is left entirely to its own defence, without any countenance or protection: The wild state of nature is renewed, in one of the most civilized societies of mankind: And great violence and disorder are committed with impunity; while the one party pleads obedience to the supreme magistrate, the other the sanction of fundamental laws.

Of the original contract

As no party, in the present age, can well support itself, without a philosophical or speculative system of principles, annexed to its political or practical one; we accordingly find, that each of the factions, into which this nation is divided, has reared up a fabric of the former kind, in order to protect and cover that scheme of actions, which it pursues. The people being commonly very rude builders, especially in this speculative way, and more especially still, when actuated by party-zeal; it is natural to imagine, that their workmanship must be a little unshapely, and discover evident marks of that violence and hurry, in which it was raised. The one party, by tracing up government to the DEITY, endeavour to render it so sacred and inviolate, that it must be little less than sacrilege, however tyrannical it may become, to touch or invade it, in the smallest article. The other party, by founding government altogether on the consent of the PEOPLE, suppose that there is a kind of *original contract*, by which the subjects have reserved the power of resisting their sovereign, whenever they find themselves aggrieved by that authority, with which they have, for certain purposes, voluntarily entrusted him. These are the speculative principles of the two parties; and these too are the practical consequences deduced from them.

I shall venture to affirm, *That both these* systems *of speculative principles are just; though not in the sense, intended by the parties*: And, *That both the* schemes *of practical consequences are prudent; though not in the extremes, to which each party, in opposition to the other, has commonly endeavoured to carry them.*

That the DEITY is the ultimate author of all government, will never be denied by any, who admit a general providence, and allow, that all events in the universe are conducted by an uniform plan, and directed to wise purposes. As it is impossible for the human race to subsist, at least in any comfortable or secure state, without the protection of government; this institution must certainly have been intended by that beneficent Being, who means the good of all his creatures: And as it has universally, in fact, taken place, in all countries, and all ages; we may conclude, with still greater certainty, that it was intended by that omniscient Being, who can never be deceived by any event or operation. But since he gave rise to it, not by any particular or miraculous interposition, but by his concealed and universal efficacy; a sovereign cannot, properly speaking, be called his viceregent, in any other sense than every power or force, being derived from him, may be said to act by his commission. Whatever actually happens is comprehended in the general plan or intention of providence; nor has the greatest and most lawful prince any more reason, upon that account, to plead a peculiar sacredness or inviolable authority, than an inferior magistrate, or even an usurper, or even a robber and a pyrate. The same divine superintendant, who, for wise purposes, invested a TITUS or a TRAJAN with authority, did also, for purposes, no doubt, equally wise, though unknown, bestow power on a BORGIA or an ANGRIA.[1] The same causes, which gave rise to the sovereign power in every state, established likewise every petty jurisdiction in it, and every limited authority. A constable, therefore, no less than a king, acts by a divine commission, and possesses an indefeasible right.

When we consider how nearly equal all men are in their bodily force, and even in their mental powers and faculties, till cultivated by education; we must necessarily allow, that nothing but their own consent could, at first, associate them together, and subject them to any authority. The people, if we trace government to its first origin in the woods and desarts, are the source of all power and jurisdiction, and voluntarily, for the sake of peace and order, abandoned their native liberty, and received laws from their equal and companion. The conditions, upon which they were willing to submit, were either expressed, or were so clear and obvious, that it might well be esteemed superfluous to express them. If this, then, be meant by the *original contract*, it cannot be denied, that all government is, at first, founded on a contract, and that the most ancient rude combinations of mankind were formed entirely by that principle. In vain, are we asked in what records this charter of our liberties is registered. It was not writ on parchment, nor yet on leaves or barks of trees. It preceded the use of writing and all the other civilized arts of life. But we trace it plainly in the nature of man, and in the equality, or something approaching equality, which we find in all the individuals of that species. The force, which now prevails, and which is founded on fleets and armies, is plainly political, and derived from authority, the effect of established government. A man's natural force consists only in the vigour of his limbs, and the firmness of his courage; which could never subject multitudes to the command of one. Nothing but their own consent, and their sense of the advantages resulting from peace and order, could have had that influence.[2]

But philosophers, who have embraced a party (if that be not a contradiction in terms) are not contented with these concessions. They assert, not only that government in its earliest infancy arose from consent, or the voluntary combination of the people; but also, that, even at present, when it has attained its full maturity, it rests on no other foundation. They affirm, that all men are still born equal, and owe allegiance to no prince or government, unless bound by the obligation and sanction of a *promise*. And as no man, without some equivalent, would forego the advantages of his native liberty, and subject himself to the will of another; this promise is always understood to be conditional, and imposes on him no obligation, unless he met with justice and protection from his sovereign. These advantages the sovereign promises him in return; and if he fail in the execution, he has broken, on his part, the articles of engagement, and has thereby freed his subject from all obligations to allegiance. Such, according to these philosophers, is the foundation of authority in every government; and such the right of resistance, possessed by every subject.

But would these reasoners look abroad into the world, they would meet with nothing that, in the least, corresponds to their ideas, or can warrant so refined and philosophical a system. On the contrary, we find, every where, princes, who claim their subjects as their property, and assert their independent right of sovereignty, from conquest or succession. We find also, every where, subjects, who acknowledge this right in their prince, and suppose themselves born under obligations of obedience to a certain sovereign, as much as under the ties of reverence and duty to certain parents. These connexions are always conceived to be equally independent of our consent, in PERSIA and CHINA; in FRANCE and SPAIN; and even in HOLLAND and ENGLAND, whereever the doctrines above-mentioned have not been carefully inculcated. Obedience or subjection becomes so familiar, that most men never make any enquiry about its origin or cause, more than about the principle of gravity, resistance, or the most universal laws of nature. Or if curiosity ever move them; as soon as they learn, that they themselves and their ancestors have, for several ages, or from time immemorial, been subject to such a government or such a family; they immediately acquiesce, and acknowledge their obligation to allegiance. Were you to preach, in most parts of the world, that political connexions are founded altogether on voluntary consent or a mutual promise, the magistrate would soon imprison you, as seditious, for loosening the ties of obedience; if your friends did not before shut you up as delirious, for advancing such absurdities. It is strange, that an act of the mind, which every individual is supposed to have formed, and after he came to the use of reason too, otherwise it could have no authority; that this act, I say, should be so unknown to all of them, that, over the face of the whole earth, there scarcely remain any traces or memory of it.

But the contract, on which government is founded, is said to be the *original contract*; and consequently may be supposed too old to fall under the knowledge of the present generation. If the agreement, by which savage men first associated and conjoined their force, be here meant, this is acknowledged to be real; but being so ancient, and being obliterated by a thousand changes of government and princes, it cannot now be supposed to retain any authority. If we would say any thing to the purpose, we must assert, that every particular government, which is lawful, and which imposes any duty of allegiance on the subject, was, at first, founded on consent and a voluntary compact. But besides that this supposes the consent of the fathers to bind the children, even to the most remote generations (which republican writers will never allow) besides this, I say, it is not justified by history or experience, in any age or country of the world.

Almost all the governments, which exist at present, or of which there remains any record in story, have been founded originally, either on usurpation or conquest, or both, without any pretence of a fair consent, or voluntary subjection of the people. When an artful and bold man is placed at the head of an army or faction, it is often easy for him, by employing sometimes violence, sometimes false pretences, to establish his dominion over a people a hundred times more numerous than his partizans. He allows no such open communication, that his enemies can know, with certainty, their number or force. He gives them no leisure to assemble together in a body to oppose him. Even all those, who are the instruments of his usurpation, may wish his fall; but their ignorance of each other's intention keeps them in awe, and is the sole cause of his security. By such arts as these, many governments have been established; and this is all the *original contract*, which they have to boast of.

The face of the earth is continually changing, by the encrease of small kingdoms into great empires, by the dissolution of great empires into smaller kingdoms, by the planting of colonies, by the migration of tribes. Is there any thing discoverable in all these events, but force and violence? Where is the mutual agreement or voluntary association so much talked of?

Even the smoothest way, by which a nation may receive a foreign master, by marriage or a will, is not extremely honourable for the people; but supposes them to be disposed of, like a dowry or a legacy, according to the pleasure or interest of their rulers.

But where no force interposes, and election takes place; what is this election so highly vaunted? It is either the combination of a few great men, who decide for the whole, and will allow of no opposition: Or it is the fury of a multitude, that follow a seditious ringleader, who is not known, perhaps, to a dozen among them, and who owes his advancement merely to his own impudence, or to the momentary caprice of his fellows.

Are these disorderly elections, which are rare too, of such mighty authority, as to be the only lawful foundation of all government and allegiance?

In reality, there is not a more terrible event, than a total dissolution of government, which gives liberty to the multitude, and makes the determination or choice of a new establishment depend upon a number, which nearly approaches the body of the people: For it never comes entirely to the whole body of them. Every wise man, then, wishes to see, at the head of a powerful and obedient army, a general, who may speedily seize the prize, and give to the people a master,

which they are so unfit to chuse for themselves. So little correspondent is fact and reality to those philosophical notions. Let not the
establishment at the *revolution* deceive us, or make us so much in
love with a philosophical origin to government, as to imagine all
others monstrous and irregular. Even that event was far from corresponding to these refined ideas. It was only the succession, and that
only in the regal part of the government, which was then changed:
And it was only the majority of seven hundred, who determined that
change for near ten millions. I doubt not, indeed, but the bulk of
those ten millions acquiesced willingly in the determination: But was
the matter left, in the least, to their choice? Was it not justly supposed
to be, from that moment, decided, and every man punished, who
refused to submit to the new sovereign? How otherwise could the
matter have ever been brought to any issue or conclusion?[3]

The republic of ATHENS was, I believe, the most extensive democracy, that we read of in history: Yet if we make the requisite allow-
ances for the women, the slaves, and the strangers, we shall find, that
that establishment was not, at first, made, nor any law ever voted, by
a tenth part of those who were bound to pay obedience to it. Not to
mention the islands and foreign dominions, which the ATHENIANS
claimed as theirs by right of conquest. And as it is well known, that
popular assemblies in that city were always full of licence and disorder, notwithstanding the institutions and laws by which they were
checked: How much more disorderly must they prove, where they
form not the established constitution, but meet tumultuously on the
dissolution of the ancient government, in order to give rise to a new
one? How chimerical must it be to talk of a choice in any such
circumstances?

The ACHAEANS enjoyed the freest and most perfect democracy of
all antiquity; yet they employed force to oblige some cities to enter
into their league, as we learn from POLYBIUS.[a]

HARRY the IVth and HARRY the VIIth of ENGLAND, had really no
other title to the throne but a parliamentary election; yet they never
would acknowledge it, for fear of weakening their authority. Strange,
if the only real foundation of all authority be consent and promise![4]

It is in vain to say, that all governments are or should be, at first,
founded on popular consent, as much as the necessity of human

[a] Lib. ii. cap. 38.

affairs will admit. This favours entirely my pretension. I maintain, that human affairs will never admit of this consent; seldom of the appearance of it. But that conquest or usurpation, that is, in plain terms, force, by dissolving the ancient governments, is the origin of almost all the new ones, which were ever established in the world. And that in the few cases, where consent may seem to have taken place, it was commonly so irregular, so confined, or so much intermixed either with fraud or violence, that it cannot have any great authority.

My intention here is not to exclude the consent of the people from being one just foundation of government where it has place. It is surely the best and most sacred of any. I only pretend that it has very seldom had place in any degree, and never almost in its full extent. And that therefore some other foundation of government must also be admitted.

Were all men possessed of so inflexible a regard to justice, that, of themselves, they would totally abstain from the properties of others; they had for ever remained in a state of absolute liberty, without subjection to any magistrate or political society: But this is a state of perfection, of which human nature is justly deemed incapable. Again; were all men possessed of so perfect an understanding, as always to know their own interest, no form of government had ever been submitted to, but what was established on consent, and was fully canvassed by every member of the society: But this state of perfection is likewise much superior to human nature. Reason, history, and experience shew us, that all political societies have had an origin much less accurate and regular; and were one to choose a period of time, when the people's consent was the least regarded in public transactions, it would be precisely on the establishment of a new government. In a settled constitution, their inclinations are often studied; but during the fury of revolutions, conquests, and public convulsions, military force or political craft usually decides the controversy.

When a new government is established, by whatever means, the people are commonly dissatisfied with it, and pay obedience more from fear and necessity, than from any idea of allegiance or of moral obligation. The prince is watchful and jealous, and must carefully guard against every beginning or appearance of insurrection. Time, by degrees, removes all these difficulties, and accustoms the nation to regard, as their lawful or native princes, that family, which, at first, they considered as usurpers or foreign conquerors. In order to found this opinion, they have no recourse to any notion of voluntary consent or promise, which, they know, never was, in this case, either expected or demanded. The original establishment was formed by violence, and submitted to from necessity. The subsequent administration is also supported by power, and acquiesced in by the people, not as a matter of choice, but of obligation. They imagine not, that their consent gives their prince a title: But they willingly consent, because they think, that, from long possession, he has acquired a title, independent of their choice or inclination.

Should it be said, that, by living under the dominion of a prince, which one might leave, every individual has given a *tacit* consent to his authority, and promised him obedience; it may be answered, that such an implied consent can only have place, where a man imagines, that the matter depends on his choice. But where he thinks (as all mankind do who are born under established governments) that by his birth he owes allegiance to a certain prince or certain government; it would be absurd to infer a consent or choice, which he expressly, in this case, renounces and disclaims.

Can we seriously say, that a poor peasant or artizan has a free choice to leave his country, when he knows no foreign language or manners, and lives from day to day, by the small wages which he acquires? We may as well assert, that a man, by remaining in a vessel, freely consents to the dominion of the master; though he was carried on board while asleep, and must leap into the ocean, and perish, the moment he leaves her.

What if the prince forbid his subjects to quit his dominions; as in TIBERIUS's time, it was regarded as a crime in a ROMAN knight that he had attempted to fly to the PARTHIANS, in order to escape the tyranny of that emperor?[b] Or as the ancient MUSCOVITES prohibited all travelling under pain of death? And did a prince observe, that many of his subjects were seized with the frenzy of transporting themselves into foreign countries, he would doubtless, with great reason and justice, restrain them, in order to prevent the depopulation of his own kingdom. Would he forfeit the allegiance of all his subjects, by so wise and reasonable a law? Yet the freedom of their choice is surely, in that case, ravished from them.

[b] TACIT. Ann. vi. cap. 14.[5]

A company of men, who should leave their native country, in order to people some uninhabited region, might dream of recovering their native freedom; but they would soon find, that their prince still laid claim to them, and called them his subjects, even in their new settlement. And in this he would but act conformably to the common ideas of mankind.

The truest *tacit* consent of this kind, that is ever observed, is when a foreigner settles in any country, and is beforehand acquainted with the prince, and government and laws, to which he must submit: Yet is his allegiance, though more voluntary, much less expected or depended on, than that of a natural born subject. On the contrary, his native prince still asserts a claim to him. And if he punish not the renegade, when he seizes him in war with his new prince's commission; this clemency is not founded on the municipal law, which in all countries condemns the prisoner; but on the consent of princes, who have agreed to this indulgence, in order to prevent reprisals.[6]

Suppose, that an usurper, after having banished his lawful prince and royal family, should establish his dominion for ten or a dozen years in any country, and should preserve so exact a discipline in his troops, and so regular a disposition in his garrisons, that no insurrection had ever been raised, or even murmur heard, against his administration: Can it be asserted, that the people, who in their hearts abhor his treason, have tacitly consented to his authority, and promised him allegiance, merely because, from necessity, they live under his dominion? Suppose again their native prince restored, by means of an army, which he levies in foreign countries: They receive him with joy and exultation, and shew plainly with what reluctance they had submitted to any other yoke. I may now ask, upon what foundation the prince's title stands? Not on popular consent surely: For though the people willingly acquiesce in his authority, they never imagine, that their consent made him sovereign. They consent; because they apprehend him to be already, by birth, their lawful sovereign. And as to that tacit consent, which may now be inferred from their living under his dominion, this is no more than what they formerly gave to the tyrant and usurper.

When we assert, that all lawful government arises from the consent of the people, we certainly do them a great deal more honour than they deserve, or even expect and desire from us. After the ROMAN dominions became too unwieldy for the republic to govern them, the people, over the whole known world, were extremely grateful to AUGUSTUS for that authority, which, by violence, he had established over them; and they shewed an equal disposition to submit to the successor, whom he left them, by his last will and testament.[7] It was afterwards their misfortune, that there never was, in one family, any long regular succession; but that their line of princes was continually broken, either by private assassinations or public rebellions. The *praetorian* bands, on the failure of every family, set up one emperor; the legions in the East a second; those in GERMANY, perhaps, a third: And the sword alone could decide the controversy. The condition of the people, in that mighty monarchy, was to be lamented, not because the choice of the emperor was never left to them; for that was impracticable: But because they never fell under any succession of masters, who might regularly follow each other. As to the violence and wars and bloodshed, occasioned by every new settlement; these were not blameable, because they were inevitable.

The house of LANCASTER ruled in this island about sixty years; yet the partizans of the white rose seemed daily to multiply in ENGLAND.[8] The present establishment has taken place during a still longer period. Have all views of right in another family been utterly extinguished; even though scarce any man now alive had arrived at years of discretion, when it was expelled, or could have consented to its dominion, or have promised it allegiance? A sufficient indication surely of the general sentiment of mankind on this head. For we blame not the partizans of the abdicated family, merely on account of the long time, during which they have preserved their imaginary fidelity. We blame them for adhering to a family, which, we affirm, has been justly expelled, and which, from the moment the new settlement took place, had forfeited all title to authority.

But would we have a more regular, at least, a more philosophical refutation of this principle of an original contract or popular consent; perhaps, the following observations may suffice.

All *moral* duties may be divided into two kinds. The *first* are those, to which men are impelled by a natural instinct or immediate propensity, which operates on them, independent of all ideas of obligation, and of all views, either to public or private utility. Of this nature are, love of children, gratitude to benefactors, pity to the unfortunate. When we reflect on the advantage, which results to society from such humane instincts, we pay them the just tribute of moral approbation and esteem: But the person, actuated by them, feels their power and influence, antecedent to any such reflection.

The *second* kind of moral duties are such as are not supported by any original instinct of nature, but are performed entirely from a sense of obligation, when we consider the necessities of human society, and the impossibility of supporting it, if these duties were neglected. It is thus *justice* or a regard to the property of others, *fidelity* or the observance of promises, become obligatory, and acquire an authority over mankind. For as it is evident, that every man loves himself better than any other person, he is naturally impelled to extend his acquisitions as much as possible; and nothing can restrain him in this propensity, but reflection and experience, by which he learns the pernicious effects of that licence, and the total dissolution of society, which must ensue from it. His original inclination, therefore, or instinct, is here checked and restrained by a subsequent judgment or observation.

The case is precisely the same with the political or civil duty of *allegiance*, as with the natural duties of justice and fidelity. Our primary instincts lead us, either to indulge ourselves in unlimited liberty, or to seek dominion over others: And it is reflection only, which engages us to sacrifice such strong passions to the interests of peace and public order. A small degree of experience and observation suffices to teach us, that society cannot possibly be maintained without the authority of magistrates, and that this authority must soon fall into contempt, where exact obedience is not payed to it. The observation of these general and obvious interests is the source of all allegiance, and of that moral obligation, which we attribute to it.

What necessity, therefore, is there to found the duty of *allegiance* or obedience to magistrates on that of *fidelity* or a regard to promises, and to suppose, that it is the consent of each individual, which subjects him to government; when it appears, that both allegiance and fidelity stand precisely on the same foundation, and are both submitted to by mankind, on account of the apparent interests and necessities of human society? We are bound to obey our sovereign, it is said; because we have given a tacit promise to that purpose. But why are we bound to observe our promise? It must here be asserted, that the commerce and intercourse of mankind, which are of such mighty advantage, can have no security where men pay no regard to their engagements. In like manner, may it be said, that men could not live

at all in society, at least in a civilized society, without laws and magistrates and judges, to prevent the encroachments of the strong upon
the weak, of the violent upon the just and equitable. The obligation
to allegiance being of like force and authority with the obligation to
fidelity, we gain nothing by resolving the one into the other. The
general interests or necessities of society are sufficient to establish
both.

If the reason be asked of that obedience, which we are bound to
pay to government, I readily answer, *because society could not otherwise
subsist*: And this answer is clear and intelligible to all mankind. Your
answer is, *because we should keep our word*. But besides, that no body,
till trained in a philosophical system, can either comprehend or relish
this answer: Besides this, I say, you find yourself embarrassed, when
it is asked, *why we are bound to keep our word?* Nor can you give
any answer, but what would, immediately, without any circuit, have
accounted for our obligation to allegiance.

But *to whom is allegiance due? And who are our lawful sovereigns?*
This question is often the most difficult of any, and liable to infinite
discussions. When people are so happy, that they can answer, *Our
present sovereign, who inherits, in a direct line, from ancestors, that have
governed us for many ages*; this answer admits of no reply; even though
historians, in tracing up to the remotest antiquity the origin of that
royal family, may find, as commonly happens, that its first authority
was derived from usurpation and violence. It is confessed, that private
justice, or the abstinence from the properties of others, is a most
cardinal virtue: Yet reason tells us, that there is no property in durable
objects, such as lands or houses, when carefully examined in passing
from hand to hand, but must, in some period, have been founded on
fraud and injustice. The necessities of human society, neither in
private nor public life, will allow of such an accurate enquiry: And
there is no virtue or moral duty, but what may, with facility, be refined
away, if we indulge a false philosophy, in sifting and scrutinizing it,
by every captious rule of logic, in every light or position, in which it
may be placed.

The questions with regard to private property have filled infinite
volumes of law and philosophy, if in both we add the commentators
to the original text; and in the end, we may safely pronounce, that
many of the rules, there established, are uncertain, ambiguous, and
arbitrary. The like opinion may be formed with regard to the succes-

sion and rights of princes and forms of government. Several cases, no doubt, occur, especially in the infancy of any constitution, which admit of no determination from the laws of justice and equity: And our historian RAPIN pretends, that the controversy between EDWARD the Third and PHILIP DE VALOIS was of this nature, and could be decided only by an appeal to heaven, that is, by war and violence.[9]

Who shall tell me, whether GERMANICUS or DRUSUS ought to have succeeded to TIBERIUS, had he died, while they were both alive, without naming any of them for his successor? Ought the right of adoption to be received as equivalent to that of blood, in a nation, where it had the same effect in private families, and had already, in two instances, taken place in the public? Ought GERMANICUS to be esteemed the eldest son because he was born before DRUSUS;[10] or the younger, because he was adopted after the birth of his brother? Ought the right of the elder to be regarded in a nation, where he had no advantage in the succession of private families? Ought the ROMAN empire at that time to be deemed hereditary, because of two examples; or ought it, even so early, to be regarded as belonging to the stronger or to the present possessor, as being founded on so recent an usurpation?

COMMODUS mounted the throne after a pretty long succession of excellent emperors, who had acquired their title, not by birth, or public election, but by the fictitious rite of adoption. That bloody debauchee being murdered by a conspiracy suddenly formed between his wench and her gallant, who happened at that time to be *Praetorian Praefect*; these immediately deliberated about choosing a master to human kind, to speak in the style of those ages; and they cast their eyes on PERTINAX. Before the tyrant's death was known, the *Praefect* went secretly to that senator, who, on the appearance of the soldiers, imagined that his execution had been ordered by COMMODUS. He was immediately saluted emperor by the officer and his attendants; chearfully proclaimed by the populace; unwillingly submitted to by the guards; formally recognized by the senate; and passively received by the provinces and armies of the empire.

The discontent of the *Praetorian* bands broke out in a sudden sedition, which occasioned the murder of that excellent prince: And the world being now without a master and without government, the guards thought proper to set the empire formally to sale. JULIAN, the purchaser, was proclaimed by the soldiers, recognized by the senate, and submitted to by the people; and must also have been submitted to by the provinces, had not the envy of the legions begot opposition and resistance. PESCENNIUS NIGER in SYRIA elected himself emperor, gained the tumultuary consent of his army, and was attended with the secret good-will of the senate and people of ROME. ALBINUS in BRITAIN found an equal right to set up his claim; but SEVERUS, who governed PANNONIA, prevailed in the end above both of them. That able politician and warrior, finding his own birth and dignity too much inferior to the imperial crown, professed, at first, an intention only of revenging the death of PERTINAX. He marched as general into ITALY; defeated JULIAN; and without our being able to fix any precise commencement even of the soldiers' consent, he was from necessity acknowledged emperor by the senate and people; and fully established in his violent authority by subduing NIGER and ALBINUS.[c]

Inter haec Gordianus CAESAR (says CAPITOLINUS, speaking of another period) *sublatus a militibus*, Imperator *est appellatus, quia non erat alius in praesenti*.[12] It is to be remarked that GORDIAN was a boy of fourteen years of age.

Frequent instances of a like nature occur in the history of the emperors; in that of ALEXANDER's successors; and of many other countries: Nor can any thing be more unhappy than a despotic government of that kind; where the succession is disjointed and irregular, and must be determined, on every vacancy, by force or election. In a free government, the matter is often unavoidable, and is also much less dangerous. The interests of liberty may there frequently lead the people, in their own defence, to alter the succession of the crown. And the constitution, being compounded of parts, may still maintain a sufficient stability, by resting on the aristocratical or democratical members, though the monarchical be altered, from time to time, in order to accommodate it to the former.

In an absolute government, when there is no legal prince, who has a title to the throne, it may safely be determined to belong to the first occupier. Instances of this kind are but too frequent, especially in the eastern monarchies. When any race of princes expires, the will or destination of the last sovereign will be regarded as a title. Thus the edict of LEWIS the XIVth, who called the bastard princes to the succession in case of the failure of all the legitimate princes, would,

[c] HERODIAN, lib. ii.[11]

in such an event have some authority.[d] Thus the will of CHARLES the Second disposed of the whole SPANISH monarchy.[14] The cession of the ancient proprietor, especially when joined to conquest, is likewise deemed a good title. The general bond or obligation, which binds us to government, is the interest and necessities of society; and this obligation is very strong. The determination of it to this or that particular prince or form of government is frequently more uncertain and dubious. Present possession has considerable authority in these cases, and greater than in private property; because of the disorders which attend all revolutions and changes of government.

We shall only observe, before we conclude, that, though an appeal to general opinion may justly, in the speculative sciences of metaphysics, natural philosophy, or astronomy, be esteemed unfair and inconclusive, yet in all questions with regard to morals, as well as criticism, there is really no other standard, by which any controversy can ever be decided. And nothing is a clearer proof, that a theory of this kind is erroneous, than to find, that it leads to paradoxes, repugnant to the common sentiments of mankind, and to the practice and opinion of all nations and all ages. The doctrine, which founds all lawful government on an *original contract*, or consent of the people, is plainly of this kind; nor has the most noted of its partizans, in prosecution of it, scrupled to affirm, *that absolute monarchy is inconsistent with civil society, and so can be no form of civil government at all;*[e] and *that the supreme power in a state cannot take from any man, by taxes and impositions, any part of his property, without his own consent or that*

---

[d] IT is remarkable, that, in the remonstrance of the duke of BOURBON and the legitimate princes, against this destination of LOUIS the XIVth, the doctrine of the *original contract* is insisted on, even in that absolute government. The FRENCH nation, say they, choosing HUGH CAPET and his posterity to rule over them and their posterity, where the former line fails, there is a tacit right reserved to choose a new royal family; and this right is invaded by calling the bastard princes to the throne, without the consent of the nation. But the Comte de BOULAINVILLIERS, who wrote in defence of the bastard princes, ridicules this notion of an original contract, especially when applied to HUGH CAPET; who mounted the throne, says he, by the same arts, which have ever been employed by all conquerors and usurpers. He got his title, indeed, recognized by the states after he had put himself in possession: But is this a choice or contract? The Comte de BOULAINVILLIERS, we may observe, was a noted republican; but being a man of learning, and very conversant in history, he knew that the people were never almost consulted in these revolutions and new establishments, and that time alone bestowed right and authority on what was commonly at first founded on force and violence. See *Etat de la France*, Vol. III.[13]

[e] See LOCKE on government, chap. vii. sec. 90.

of his representatives.[f15] What authority any moral reasoning can have, which leads into opinions so wide of the general practice of mankind, in every place but this single kingdom, it is easy to determine.

The only passage I meet with in antiquity, where the obligation of obedience to government is ascribed to a promise, is in PLATO's *Crito*; where SOCRATES refuses to escape from prison, because he had tacitly promised to obey the laws.[16] Thus he builds a *tory* consequence of passive obedience, on a *whig* foundation of the original contract.

New discoveries are not to be expected in these matters. If scarce any man, till very lately, ever imagined that government was founded on contract, it is certain, that it cannot, in general, have any such foundation.

The crime of rebellion among the ancients was commonly expressed by the terms *neoterizein, novas res moliri.*[17]

---

[f] Id. chap. xi. sec. 138, 139, 140.

ESSAY TWENTY-FOUR

Of passive obedience

In the former essay, we endeavoured to refute the *speculative* systems of politics advanced in this nation; as well the religious system of the one party, as the philosophical of the other. We come now to examine the *practical* consequences, deduced by each party, with regard to the measures of submission due to sovereigns.

As the obligation to justice is founded entirely on the interests of society, which require mutual abstinence from property, in order to preserve peace among mankind; it is evident, that, when the execution of justice would be attended with very pernicious consequences, that virtue must be suspended, and give place to public utility, in such extraordinary and such pressing emergencies. The maxim, *fiat Justitia & ruat Coelum*, let justice be performed, though the universe be destroyed, is apparently false, and by sacrificing the end to the means, shews a preposterous idea of the subordination of duties. What governor of a town makes any scruple of burning the suburbs, when they facilitate the approaches of the enemy? Or what general abstains from plundering a neutral country, when the necessities of war require it, and he cannot otherwise maintain his army?[1] The case is the same with the duty of allegiance; and common sense teaches us, that, as government binds us to obedience only on account of its tendency to public utility, that duty must always, in extraordinary cases, when public ruin would evidently attend obedience, yield to the primary and original obligation. *Salus populi suprema Lex*, the safety of the people is the supreme law.[2] This maxim is agreeable to the sentiments of mankind in all ages: Nor is any one, when he reads of the insurrections against Nero or Philip the Second, so infatuated with party-systems, as not to wish success to the enterprize, and praise the undertakers.[3] Even our high monarchical party, in spite of their sublime theory, are forced, in such cases, to judge, and feel, and approve, in conformity to the rest of mankind.

Resistance, therefore, being admitted in extraordinary emergencies, the question can only be among good reasoners, with regard to the degree of necessity, which can justify resistance, and render it lawful or commendable. And here I must confess, that I shall always incline to their side, who draw the bond of allegiance very close, and consider an infringement of it, as the last refuge in desperate cases, when the public is in the highest danger, from violence and tyranny. For besides the mischiefs of a civil war, which commonly attends insurrection; it is certain, that, where a disposition to rebellion appears among any people, it is one chief cause of tyranny in the rulers, and forces them into many violent measures which they never would have embraced, had every one been inclined to submission and obedience. Thus the *tyrannicide* or assassination, approved of by ancient maxims, instead of keeping tyrants and usurpers in awe, made them ten times more fierce and unrelenting; and is now justly, upon that account, abolished by the laws of nations, and universally condemned as a base and treacherous method of bringing to justice these disturbers of society.

Besides; we must consider, that, as obedience is our duty in the common course of things, it ought chiefly to be inculcated; nor can any thing be more preposterous than an anxious care and sollicitude in stating all the cases, in which resistance may be allowed. In like manner, though a philosopher reasonably acknowledges, in the course of an argument, that the rules of justice may be dispensed with in cases of urgent necessity; what should we think of a preacher or casuist, who should make it his chief study to find out such cases, and enforce them with all the vehemence of argument and eloquence? Would he not be better employed in inculcating the general doctrine, than in displaying the particular exceptions, which we are, perhaps, but too much inclined, of ourselves, to embrace and to extend?

There are, however, two reasons, which may be pleaded in defence of that party among us, who have, with so much industry, propagated the maxims of resistance; maxims, which, it must be confessed, are, in general, so pernicious, and so destructive of civil society. The *first* is, that their antagonists carrying the doctrine of obedience to such an extravagant height, as not only never to mention the exceptions in extraordinary cases (which might, perhaps, be excusable) but even positively to exclude them; it became necessary to insist on these exceptions, and defend the rights of injured truth and liberty. The *second*, and, perhaps, better reason, is founded on the nature of the BRITISH constitution and form of government.

It is almost peculiar to our constitution to establish a first magistrate with such high pre-eminence and dignity, that, though limited by the laws, he is, in a manner, so far as regards his own person, above the laws, and can neither be questioned nor punished for any injury or wrong, which may be committed by him. His ministers alone, or those who act by his commission, are obnoxious to justice; and while the prince is thus allured, by the prospect of personal safety, to give the laws their free course, an equal security is, in effect, obtained by the punishment of lesser offenders, and at the same time a civil war is avoided, which would be the infallible consequence, were an attack, at every turn, made directly upon the sovereign. But though the constitution pays this salutary compliment to the prince, it can never reasonably be understood, by that maxim, to have determined its own destruction, or to have established a tame submission, where he protects his ministers, perseveres in injustice, and usurps the whole power of the commonwealth. This case, indeed, is never expressly put by the laws; because it is impossible for them, in their ordinary course, to provide a remedy for it, or establish any magistrate, with superior authority, to chastise the exorbitancies of the prince. But as a right without a remedy would be an absurdity; the remedy in this case, is the extraordinary one of resistance, when affairs come to that extremity, that the constitution can be defended by it alone. Resistance therefore must, of course, become more frequent in the BRITISH government, than in others, which are simpler, and consist of fewer parts and movements. Where the king is an absolute sovereign, he has little temptation to commit such enormous tyranny as may justly provoke rebellion: But where he is limited, his imprudent ambition, without any great vices, may run him into that perilous situation. This is frequently supposed to have been the case with CHARLES the First; and if we may now speak truth, after animosities are ceased, this was also the case with JAMES the Second. These were harmless, if not, in their private character, good men; but mistaking the nature of our constitution, and engrossing the whole legislative power, it became necessary to oppose them with some vehemence; and even to deprive the latter formally of that authority, which he had used with such imprudence and indiscretion.[4]

ESSAY TWENTY-FIVE

Of the coalition of parties

To abolish all distinctions of party may not be practicable, perhaps not desirable, in a free government. The only dangerous parties are such as entertain opposite views with regard to the essentials of government, the succession of the crown, or the more considerable privileges belonging to the several members of the constitution; where there is no room for any compromize or accommodation, and where the controversy may appear so momentous as to justify even an opposition by arms to the pretensions of antagonists. Of this nature was the animosity, continued for above a century past, between the parties in ENGLAND; an animosity which broke out sometimes into civil war, which occasioned violent revolutions, and which continually endangered the peace and tranquillity of the nation. But as there have appeared of late the strongest symptoms of an universal desire to abolish these party distinctions; this tendency to a coalition affords the most agreeable prospect of future happiness, and ought to be carefully cherished and promoted by every lover of his country.

There is not a more effectual method of promoting so good an end, than to prevent all unreasonable insult and triumph of the one party over the other, to encourage moderate opinions, to find the proper medium in all disputes, to persuade each that its antagonist may possibly be sometimes in the right, and to keep a balance in the praise and blame, which we bestow on either side. The two former Essays, concerning the *original contract* and *passive obedience*, are calculated for this purpose with regard to the *philosophical* and *practical* controversies between the parties, and tend to show that neither side are in these respects so fully supported by reason as they endeavour

to flatter themselves. We shall proceed to exercise the same moderation with regard to the historical disputes between the parties, by
proving that each of them was justified by plausible topics; that there
were on both sides wise men, who meant well to their country; and
that the past animosity between the factions had no better foundation
than narrow prejudice or interested passion.

The popular party, who afterwards acquired the name of whigs,
might justify, by very specious arguments, that opposition to the
crown, from which our present free constitution is derived. Though
obliged to acknowledge, that precedents in favour of prerogative had
uniformly taken place during many reigns before CHARLES the First,
they thought, that there was no reason for submitting any longer to
so dangerous an authority. Such might have been their reasoning: As
the rights of mankind are for ever to be deemed sacred, no prescription of tyranny or arbitrary power can have authority sufficient to
abolish them. Liberty is a blessing so inestimable, that, wherever
there appears any probability of recovering it, a nation may willingly
run many hazards, and ought not even to repine at the greatest effu-
sion of blood or dissipation of treasure. All human institutions, and
none more than government, are in continual fluctuation. Kings are
sure to embrace every opportunity of extending their prerogatives:
And if favourable incidents be not also laid hold of for extending and
securing the privileges of the people, an universal despotism must for
ever prevail amongst mankind. The example of all the neighbouring
nations proves, that it is no longer safe to entrust with the crown the
same high prerogatives, which had formerly been exercised during
rude and simple ages. And though the example of many late reigns
may be pleaded in favour of a power in the prince somewhat arbitrary,
more remote reigns afford instances of stricter limitations imposed
on the crown; and those pretensions of the parliament, now branded
with the title of innovations, are only a recovery of the just rights of
the people.

These views, far from being odious, are surely large, and generous,
and noble: To their prevalence and success the kingdom owes its
liberty; perhaps its learning, its industry, commerce, and naval power:
By them chiefly the ENGLISH name is distinguished among the society
of nations, and aspires to a rivalship with that of the freest and most
illustrious commonwealths of antiquity. But as all these mighty consequences could not reasonably be foreseen at the time when the

contest began, the royalists of that age wanted not specious arguments on their side, by which they could justify their defence of the then established prerogatives of the prince. We shall state the question, as it might have appeared to them at the assembling of that parliament, which, by its violent encroachments on the crown, began the civil wars.[1]

The only rule of government, they might have said, known and acknowledged among men, is use and practice: Reason is so uncertain a guide that it will always be exposed to doubt and controversy: Could it ever render itself prevalent over the people, men had always retained it as their sole rule of conduct: They had still continued in the primitive, unconnected state of nature, without submitting to political government, whose sole basis is, not pure reason, but authority and precedent. Dissolve these ties, you break all the bonds of civil society, and leave every man at liberty to consult his private interest, by those expedients, which his appetite, disguised under the appearance of reason, shall dictate to him. The spirit of innovation is in itself pernicious, however favourable its particular object may sometimes appear: A truth so obvious, that the popular party themselves are sensible of it; and therefore cover their encroachments on the crown by the plausible pretence of their recovering the ancient liberties of the people.

But the present prerogatives of the crown, allowing all the suppositions of that party, have been incontestably established ever since the accession of the House of TUDOR; a period, which, as it now comprehends an hundred and sixty years, may be allowed sufficient to give stability to any constitution. Would it not have appeared ridiculous, in the reign of the Emperor ADRIAN, to have talked of the republican constitution as the rule of government; or to have supposed, that the former rights of the senate, and consuls, and tribunes were still subsisting?[2]

But the present claims of the ENGLISH monarchs are much more favourable than those of the ROMAN emperors during that age. The authority of AUGUSTUS was a plain usurpation, grounded only on military violence, and forms such an epoch in the ROMAN history, as is obvious to every reader. But if HENRY VII. really, as some pretend, enlarged the power of the crown, it was only by insensible acquisitions, which escaped the apprehension of the people, and have scarcely been remarked even by historians and politicians.[3] The new government, if it deserve the epithet, is an imperceptible transition from the former; is entirely engrafted on it; derives its title fully from that root; and is to be considered only as one of those gradual revolutions, to which human affairs, in every nation, will be for ever subject.

The House of TUDOR, and after them that of STUART, exercised no prerogatives, but what had been claimed and exercised by the PLANTAGENETS.[4] Not a single branch of their authority can be said to be an innovation. The only difference is, that, perhaps, former kings exerted these powers only by intervals, and were not able, by reason of the opposition of their barons, to render them so steady a rule of administration.[5] But the sole inference from this fact is, that those ancient times were more turbulent and seditious; and that royal authority, the constitution, and the laws have happily of late gained the ascendant.

Under what pretence can the popular party now speak of recovering the ancient constitution? The former controul over the kings was not placed in the commons, but in the barons: The people had no authority, and even little or no liberty; till the crown, by suppressing these factious tyrants, enforced the execution of the laws, and obliged all the subjects equally to respect each others rights, privileges, and properties. If we must return to the ancient barbarous and feudal constitution; let those gentlemen, who now behave themselves with so much insolence to their sovereign, set the first example. Let them make court to be admitted as retainers to a neighbouring baron; and by submitting to slavery under him, acquire some protection to themselves; together with the power of exercising rapine and oppression over their inferior slaves and villains. This was the condition of the commons among their remote ancestors.

But how far back must we go, in having recourse to ancient constitutions and governments? There was a constitution still more ancient than that to which these innovators affect so much to appeal. During that period there was no *magna charta*:[6] The barons themselves possessed few regular, stated privileges: And the house of commons probably had not an existence.

It is ridiculous to hear the commons, while they are assuming, by usurpation, the whole power of government, talk of reviving ancient institutions. Is it not known, that, though representatives received wages from their constituents; to be a member of the lower house was always considered as a burthen, and a freedom from it as a privilege? Will they persuade us, that power, which, of all human acquisitions, is the most coveted, and in comparison of which even reputation and pleasure and riches are slighted, could ever be regarded as a burthen by any man?

The property, acquired of late by the commons, it is said, entitles them to more power than their ancestors enjoyed. But to what is this encrease of their property owing, but to an encrease of their liberty and their security? Let them therefore acknowledge, that their ancestors, while the crown was restrained by the seditious barons, really enjoyed less liberty than they themselves have attained, after the sovereign acquired the superiority: And let them enjoy that liberty with moderation; and not forfeit it by new exorbitant claims, and by rendering it a pretence for endless innovations.

The true rule of government is the present established practice of the age. That has most authority, because it is recent: It is also better known, for the same reason. Who has assured those tribunes, that the PLANTAGENETS did not exercise as high acts of authority as the TUDORS? Historians, they say, do not mention them. But historians are also silent with regard to the chief exertions of prerogative by the TUDORS. Where any power or prerogative is fully and undoubtedly established, the exercise of it passes for a thing of course, and readily escapes the notice of history and annals. Had we no other monuments of ELIZABETH's reign, than what are preserved even by CAMDEN, the most copious, judicious, and exact of our historians, we should be entirely ignorant of the most important maxims of her government.[7]

Was not the present monarchical government, in its full extent, authorized by lawyers, recommended by divines, acknowledged by politicians, acquiesced in, nay passionately cherished, by the people in general; and all this during a period of at least a hundred and sixty years, and till of late, without the smallest murmur or controversy? This general consent surely, during so long a time, must be sufficient to render a constitution legal and valid. If the origin of all power be derived, as is pretended, from the people; here is their consent in the fullest and most ample terms that can be desired or imagined.

But the people must not pretend, because they can, by their consent, lay the foundations of government, that therefore they are to be permitted, at their pleasure, to overthrow and subvert them. There is no end of these seditious and arrogant claims. The power of the crown is now openly struck at: The nobility are also in visible peril: The gentry will soon follow: The popular leaders, who will then assume the name of gentry, will next be exposed to danger: And the people themselves, having become incapable of civil government, and lying under the restraint of no authority, must, for the sake of peace, admit, instead of their legal and mild monarchs, a succession of military and despotic tyrants.

These consequences are the more to be dreaded, as the present fury of the people, though glossed over by pretensions to civil liberty, is in reality incited by the fanaticism of religion; a principle the most blind, headstrong, and ungovernable, by which human nature can possibly be actuated. Popular rage is dreadful, from whatever motive derived: But must be attended with the most pernicious consequences, when it arises from a principle, which disclaims all controul by human law, reason, or authority.

These are the arguments, which each party may make use of to justify the conduct of their predecessors, during that great crisis. The event, if that can be admitted as a reason, has shown, that the arguments of the popular party were better founded; but perhaps, according to the established maxims of lawyers and politicians the views of the royalists ought, before-hand, to have appeared more solid, more safe, and more legal. But this is certain, that the greater moderation we now employ in representing past events; the nearer shall we be to produce a full coalition of the parties, and an entire acquiescence in our present establishment. Moderation is of advantage to every establishment: Nothing but zeal can overturn a settled power: And an over-active zeal in friends is apt to beget a like spirit in antagonists. The transition from a moderate opposition against an establishment, to an entire acquiescence in it, is easy and insensible.

There are many invincible arguments, which should induce the malcontent party to acquiesce entirely in the present settlement of the constitution. They now find, that the spirit of civil liberty, though at first connected with religious fanaticism, could purge itself from that pollution, and appear under a more genuine and engaging aspect; a friend to toleration, and an encourager of all the enlarged and generous sentiments that do honour to human nature. They may observe, that the popular claims could stop at a proper period; and after retrenching the high claims of prerogative, could still maintain a due respect to monarchy, to nobility, and to all ancient institutions.

Above all, they must be sensible, that the very principle, which made the strength of their party, and from which it derived its chief authority, has now deserted them, and gone over to their antagonists. The plan of liberty is settled; its happy effects are proved by experience; a long tract of time has given it stability; and whoever would attempt to overturn it, and to recall the past government or abdicated family, would, besides other more criminal imputations, be exposed, in their turn, to the reproach of faction and innovation. While they peruse the history of past events, they ought to reflect, both that these rights of the crown are long since annihilated, and that the tyranny, and violence, and oppression, to which they often give rise, are ills, from which the established liberty of the constitution has now at last happily protected the people. These reflections will prove a better security to our freedom and privileges, than to deny, contrary to the clearest evidence of facts, that such regal powers ever had any existence. There is not a more effectual method of betraying a cause, than to lay the stress of the argument on a wrong place, and by disputing an untenable post, enure the adversaries to success and victory.

Of the Protestant succession

I suppose, that a member of parliament, in the reign of King WIL-
LIAM or Queen ANNE, while the establishment of the *Protestant Succession* was yet uncertain, were deliberating concerning the party he
would chuse in that important question, and weighing, with impartiality, the advantages and disadvantages on each side. I believe the
following particulars would have entered into his consideration.

He would easily perceive the great advantage resulting from the
restoration of the STUART family; by which we should preserve the
succession clear and undisputed, free from a pretender, with such a
specious title as that of blood, which, with the multitude, is always
the claim, the strongest and most easily comprehended. It is in vain
to say, as many have done, that the question with regard to *governors*,
independent of *government*, is frivolous, and little worth disputing,
much less fighting about. The generality of mankind never will enter
into these sentiments; and it is much happier, I believe, for society,
that they do not, but rather continue in their natural prepossessions.
How could stability be preserved in any monarchical government,
(which, though, perhaps, not the best, is, and always has been, the
most common of any) unless men had so passionate a regard for
the true heir of their royal family; and even though he be weak in
understanding, or infirm in years, gave him so sensible a preference
above persons the most accomplished in shining talents, or celebrated
for great atchievements? Would not every popular leader put in his
claim at every vacancy, or even without any vacancy; and the kingdom
become the theatre of perpetual wars and convulsions? The condition
of the ROMAN empire, surely, was not, in this respect, much to be

envied; nor is that of the *Eastern* nations, who pay little regard to the titles of their sovereign, but sacrifice them, every day, to the caprice or momentary humour of the populace or soldiery. It is but a foolish wisdom, which is so carefully displayed, in undervaluing princes, and placing them on a level with the meanest of mankind. To be sure, an anatomist finds no more in the greatest monarch than in the lowest peasant or day-labourer; and a moralist may, perhaps, frequently find less. But what do all these reflections tend to? We, all of us, still retain these prejudices in favour of birth and family; and neither in our serious occupations, nor most careless amusements, can we ever get entirely rid of them. A tragedy, that should represent the adventures of sailors, or porters, or even of private gentlemen, would presently disgust us; but one that introduces kings and princes, acquires in our eyes an air of importance and dignity. Or should a man be able, by his superior wisdom, to get entirely above such prepossessions, he would soon, by means of the same wisdom, again bring himself down to them, for the sake of society, whose welfare he would perceive to be intimately connected with them. Far from endeavouring to undeceive the people in this particular, he would cherish such sentiments of reverence to their princes; as requisite to preserve a due subordination in society. And though the lives of twenty thousand men be often sacrificed to maintain a king in possession of his throne, or preserve the right of succession undisturbed, he entertains no indignation at the loss, on pretence that every individual of these was, perhaps, in himself, as valuable as the prince he served. He considers the consequences of violating the hereditary right of kings: Consequences, which may be felt for many centuries; while the loss of several thousand men brings so little prejudice to a large kingdom, that it may not be perceived a few years after.

The advantages of the HANOVER succession are of an opposite nature, and arise from this very circumstance, that it violates hereditary right; and places on the throne a prince, to whom birth gave no title to that dignity. It is evident, from the history of this island, that the privileges of the people have, during the two last centuries, been continually upon the encrease, by the division of the church-lands, by the alienations of the barons' estates, by the progress of trade, and above all, by the happiness of our situation, which, for a long time, gave us sufficient security, without any standing army or military establishment. On the contrary, public liberty has, almost in every other nation of Europe, been, during the same period, extremely upon the decline; while the people were disgusted at the hardships of the old feudal militia, and rather chose to entrust their prince with mercenary armies, which he easily turned against themselves. It was nothing extraordinary, therefore, that some of our British sovereigns mistook the nature of the constitution, at least, the genius of the people; and as they embraced all the favourable precedents left them by their ancestors, they overlooked all those which were contrary, and which supposed a limitation in our government. They were encouraged in this mistake, by the example of all the neighbouring princes, who bearing the same title or appellation, and being adorned with the same ensigns of authority, naturally led them to claim the same powers and prerogatives. It appears from the speeches, and proclamations of James I. and the whole train of that prince's actions, as well as his son's, that he regarded the English government as a simple monarchy, and never imagined that any considerable part of his subjects entertained a contrary idea. This opinion made those monarchs discover their pretensions, without preparing any force to support them; and even without reserve or disguise, which are always employed by those, who enter upon any new project, or endeavour to innovate in any government.[1] The flattery of courtiers farther confirmed their prejudices; and above all, that of the clergy, who from several passages of *scripture*, and these wrested too, had erected a regular and avowed system of arbitrary power. The only method of destroying, at once, all these high claims and pretensions, was to depart from the true hereditary line, and choose a prince, who, being plainly a creature of the public, and receiving the crown on conditions, expressed and avowed, found his authority established on the same bottom with the privileges of the people. By electing him in the royal line, we cut off all hopes of ambitious subjects, who might, in future emergencies, disturb the government by their cabals and pretensions: By rendering the crown hereditary in his family, we avoided all the inconveniencies of elective monarchy: And by excluding the lineal heir, we secured all our constitutional limitations and rendered our government uniform and of a piece. The people cherish monarchy, because protected by it: The monarch favours liberty, because created by it. And thus every advantage is obtained by the new establishment, as far as human skill and wisdom can extend itself.

These are the separate advantages of fixing the succession, either in the house of STUART, or in that of HANOVER. There are also disadvantages in each establishment, which an impartial patriot would ponder and examine, in order to form a just judgment on the whole.

The disadvantages of the protestant succession consist in the foreign dominions, which are possessed by the princes of the HANOVER line, and which, it might be supposed, would engage us in the intrigues and wars of the continent, and lose us, in some measure, the inestimable advantage we possess, of being surrounded and guarded by the sea, which we command. The disadvantages of recalling the abdicated family consist chiefly in their religion, which is more prejudicial to society than that established amongst us, is contrary to it, and affords no toleration, or peace, or security to any other communion.

It appears to me, that these advantages and disadvantages are allowed on both sides; at least, by every one who is at all susceptible of argument or reasoning. No subject, however loyal, pretends to deny, that the disputed title and foreign dominions of the present royal family are a loss. Nor is there any partizan of the STUARTS, but will confess, that the claim of hereditary, indefeasible right, and the Roman Catholic religion, are also disadvantages in that family. It belongs, therefore, to a philosopher alone, who is of neither party, to put all these circumstances in the scale, and assign to each of them its proper poise and influence. Such a one will readily, at first, acknowledge, that all political questions are infinitely complicated, and that there scarcely ever occurs, in any deliberation, a choice, which is either purely good, or purely ill. Consequences, mixed and varied, may be foreseen to flow from every measure: And many consequences, unforeseen, do always, in fact, result from every one. Hesitation, and reserve, and suspence, are, therefore, the only sentiments he brings to this essay or trial. Or if he indulges any passion, it is that of derision against the ignorant multitude, who are always clamorous and dogmatical, even in the nicest questions, of which, from want of temper, perhaps still more than of understanding, they are altogether unfit judges.

But to say something more determinate on this head, the following reflections will, I hope, show the temper, if not the understanding of a philosopher.

Were we to judge merely by first appearances, and by past experience, we must allow that the advantages of a parliamentary title in
the house of HANOVER are greater than those of an undisputed hereditary title in the house of STUART; and that our fathers acted wisely
in preferring the former to the latter. So long as the house of STUART
ruled in BRITAIN, which, with some interruption, was above 80 years,
the government was kept in a continual fever, by the contention
between the privileges of the people and the prerogatives of the
crown. If arms were dropped, the noise of disputes continued: Or if
these were silenced, jealousy still corroded the heart, and threw the
nation into an unnatural ferment and disorder. And while we were
thus occupied in domestic disputes, a foreign power, dangerous, if
not fatal, to public liberty, erected itself in EUROPE, without any
opposition from us, and even sometimes with our assistance.

But during these last sixty years, when a parliamentary establishment has taken place; whatever factions may have prevailed either
among the people or in public assemblies, the whole force of our
constitution has always fallen to one side, and an uninterrupted harmony has been preserved between our princes and our parliaments.
Public liberty, with internal peace and order, has flourished almost
without interruption: Trade and manufactures, and agriculture, have
encreased: The arts, and sciences, and philosophy, have been cultivated. Even religious parties have been necessitated to lay aside their
mutual rancour: And the glory of the nation has spread itself all over
EUROPE; derived equally from our progress in the arts of peace, and
from valour and success in war. So long and so glorious a period no
nation almost can boast of: Nor is there another instance in the whole
history of mankind, that so many millions of people have, during such
a space of time, been held together, in a manner so free, so rational,
and so suitable to the dignity of human nature.

But though this recent instance seems clearly to decide in favour
of the present establishment, there are some circumstances to be
thrown into the other scale; and it is dangerous to regulate our judgment by one event or example.

We have had two rebellions during the flourishing period above
mentioned, besides plots and conspiracies without number.[2] And if
none of these have produced any very fatal event, we may ascribe
our escape chiefly to the narrow genius of those princes who disputed

our establishment; and we may esteem ourselves so far fortunate. But the claims of the banished family, I fear, are not yet antiquated; and who can foretel, that their future attempts will produce no greater disorder?

The disputes between privilege and prerogative may easily be composed by laws, and votes, and conferences, and concessions; where there is tolerable temper or prudence on both sides, or on either side. Among contending titles, the question can only be determined by the sword, and by devastation, and by civil war.

A prince, who fills the throne with a disputed title, dares not arm his subjects; the only method of securing a people fully, both against domestic oppression and foreign conquest.

Notwithstanding our riches and renown, what a critical escape did we make, by the late peace, from dangers, which were owing not so much to bad conduct and ill success in war, as to the pernicious practice of mortgaging our finances, and the still more pernicious maxim of never paying off our incumbrances? Such fatal measures would not probably have been embraced, had it not been to secure a precarious establishment.

But to convince us, that an hereditary title is to be embraced rather than a parliamentary one, which is not supported by any other views or motives; a man needs only transport himself back to the æra of the restoration, and suppose, that he had had a seat in that parliament which recalled the royal family, and put a period to the greatest disorders that ever arose from the opposite pretensions of prince and people. What would have been thought of one, that had proposed, at that time, to set aside CHARLES II. and settle the crown on the Duke of YORK or GLOUCESTER, merely in order to exclude all high claims, like those of their father and grandfather?[3] Would not such a one have been regarded as an extravagant projector, who loved dangerous remedies, and could tamper and play with a government and national constitution, like a quack with a sickly patient?[4]

In reality, the reason assigned by the nation for excluding the race of STUART, and so many other branches of the royal family, is not on account of their hereditary title (a reason, which would, to vulgar apprehensions, have appeared altogether absurd) but on account of their religion. Which leads us to compare the disadvantage above mentioned in each establishment.

I confess, that, considering the matter in general, it were much to be wished, that our prince had no foreign dominions, and could confine all his attention to the government of this island. For not to mention some real inconveniencies that may result from territories on the continent, they afford such a handle for calumny and defamation, as is greedily seized by the people, always disposed to think ill of their superiors. It must, however, be acknowledged, that HANOVER, is, perhaps, the spot of ground in EUROPE the least inconvenient for a King of BRITAIN. It lies in the heart of GERMANY, at a distance from the great powers, which are our natural rivals: It is protected by the laws of the empire, as well as by the arms of its own sovereign: And it serves only to connect us more closely with the house of AUSTRIA, our natural ally.[5]

The religious persuasion of the house of STUART is an inconvenience of a much deeper dye, and would threaten us with much more dismal consequences. The Roman Catholic religion, with its train of priests and friers, is more expensive than ours: Even though unaccompanied with its natural attendants of inquisitors, and stakes, and gibbets, it is less tolerating: And not content with dividing the sacerdotal from the regal office (which must be prejudicial to any state) it bestows the former on a foreigner, who has always a separate interest from that of the public, and may often have an opposite one.

But were this religion ever so advantageous to society, it is contrary to that which is established among us, and which is likely to keep possession, for a long time, of the minds of the people. And though it is much to be hoped, that the progress of reason will, by degrees, abate the acrimony of opposite religions all over EUROPE; yet the spirit of moderation has, as yet, made too slow advances to be entirely trusted.[6]

Thus, upon the whole, the advantages of the settlement in the family of STUART, which frees us from a disputed title, seem to bear some proportion with those of the settlement in the family of HANOVER, which frees us from the claims of prerogative: But at the same time, its disadvantages, by placing on the throne a Roman Catholic, are greater than those of the other establishment, in settling the crown on a foreign prince. What party an impartial patriot, in the reign of K. WILLIAM or Q. ANNE, would have chosen amidst these opposite views, may, perhaps, to some appear hard to determine.[7]

But the settlement in the house of HANOVER has actually taken place. The princes of that family, without intrigue, without cabal, without solicitation on their part, have been called to mount our throne, by the united voice of the whole legislative body. They have, since their accession, displayed, in all their actions, the utmost mildness, equity, and regard to the laws and constitution. Our own ministers, our own parliaments, ourselves have governed us; and if aught ill has befallen us, we can only blame fortune or ourselves. What a reproach must we become among nations, if, disgusted with a settlement so deliberately made, and whose conditions have been so religiously observed, we should throw every thing again into confusion; and by our levity and rebellious disposition, prove ourselves totally unfit for any state but that of absolute slavery and subjection?

The greatest inconvenience, attending a disputed title, is, that it brings us in danger of civil wars and rebellions. What wise man, to avoid this inconvenience, would run directly upon a civil war and rebellion? Not to mention, that so long possession, secured by so many laws, must, ere this time, in the apprehension of a great part of the nation, have begot a title in the house of HANOVER, independent of their present possession: So that now we should not, even by a revolution, obtain the end of avoiding a disputed title.

No revolution made by national forces, will ever be able, without some other great necessity, to abolish our debts and incumbrances, in which the interest of so many persons is concerned. And a revolution made by foreign forces, is a conquest: A calamity, with which the precarious balance of power threatens us, and which our civil dissentions are likely, above all other circumstances, to bring upon us.

Idea of a perfect commonwealth

IT is not with forms of government, as with other artificial contrivances; where an old engine may be rejected, if we can discover another more accurate and commodious, or where trials may safely be made, even though the success be doubtful. An established government has an infinite advantage, by that very circumstance of its being established; the bulk of mankind being governed by authority, not reason, and never attributing authority to any thing that has not the recommendation of antiquity. To tamper, therefore, in this affair, or try experiments merely upon the credit of supposed argument and philosophy, can never be the part of a wise magistrate, who will bear a reverence to what carries the marks of age; and though he may attempt some improvements for the public good, yet will he adjust his innovations, as much as possible, to the ancient fabric, and preserve entire the chief pillars and supports of the constitution.

The mathematicians in EUROPE have been much divided concerning that figure of a ship, which is the most commodious for sailing; and HUYGENS, who at last determined this controversy, is justly thought to have obliged the learned, as well as commercial world; though COLUMBUS had sailed to AMERICA, and Sir FRANCIS DRAKE made the tour of the world, without any such discovery.[1] As one form of government must be allowed more perfect than another, independent of the manners and humours of particular men; why may we not enquire what is the most perfect of all, though the common botched and inaccurate governments seem to serve the purposes of society, and though it be not so easy to establish a new system of government, as to build a vessel upon a new plan? The subject is surely the most worthy curiosity of any the wit of man can possibly devise. And who knows, if this controversy were fixed by the universal consent of the wise and learned, but, in some future age, an opportunity might be afforded of reducing the theory to practice, either by a dissolution of some old government, or by the combination of men to form a new one, in some distant part of the world? In all cases, it must be advantageous to know what is most perfect in the kind, that we may be able to bring any real constitution or form of government as near it as possible, by such gentle alterations and innovations as may not give too great disturbance to society.

All I pretend to in the present essay is to revive this subject of speculation; and therefore I shall deliver my sentiments in as few words as possible. A long dissertation on that head would not, I apprehend, be very acceptable to the public, who will be apt to regard such disquisitions both as useless and chimerical.

All plans of government, which suppose great reformation in the manners of mankind, are plainly imaginary. Of this nature, are the *Republic* of PLATO, and the *Utopia* of Sir THOMAS MORE. The OCEANA is the only valuable model of a commonwealth, that has as yet been offered to the public.

The chief defects of the OCEANA seem to be these. *First*, Its rotation is inconvenient, by throwing men, of whatever ability, by intervals, out of public employments. *Secondly*, Its *Agrarian* is impracticable. Men will soon learn the art, which was practised in ancient ROME, of concealing their possessions under other people's name; till at last, the abuse will become so common, that they will throw off even the appearance of restraint. *Thirdly*, The OCEANA provides not a sufficient security for liberty, or the redress of grievances. The senate must propose, and the people consent; by which means, the senate have not only a negative upon the people, but, what is of much greater consequence, their negative goes before the votes of the people. Were the King's negative of the same nature in the ENGLISH constitution, and could he prevent any bill from coming into parliament, he would be an absolute monarch. As his negative follows the votes of the houses, it is of little consequence: Such a difference is there in the manner of placing the same thing. When a popular bill has been debated in parliament, is brought to maturity, all its conveniencies and inconveniencies weighed and balanced; if afterwards it be presented for the royal assent, few princes will venture to reject the unanimous desire of the people. But could the King crush a disagreeable bill in embrio (as was the case, for some time, in the SCOTCH parliament, by means of the lords of the articles) the BRITISH government would have no balance, nor would grievances ever be redressed: And it is certain, that exorbitant power proceeds not, in any government, from new laws, so much as from neglecting to remedy the abuses, which frequently rise from the old ones. A government, says MACHIAVEL, must often be brought back to its original principles. It appears then, that, in the OCEANA, the whole legislature may be said to rest in the senate; which HARRINGTON would own to be an inconvenient form of government, especially after the *Agrarian* is abolished.[2]

Here is a form of government, to which I cannot, in theory, discover any considerable objection.

Let GREAT BRITAIN and IRELAND, or any territory of equal extent, be divided into 100 counties, and each county into 100 parishes, making in all 10,000. If the country, proposed to be erected into a commonwealth be of more narrow extent, we may diminish the number of counties; but never bring them below thirty. If it be of greater extent, it were better to enlarge the parishes, or throw more parishes into a county, than increase the number of counties.

Let all the freeholders of twenty pounds a-year in the country, and all the householders worth 500 pounds in the town parishes, meet annually in the parish church, and chuse, by ballot, some freeholder of the county for their member, whom we shall call the county *representative.*

Let the 100 county representatives, two days after their election, meet in the county-town, and chuse by ballot, from their own body, ten county *magistrates*, and one *senator*. There are, therefore, in the whole commonwealth, 100 senators, 1100 county magistrates, and 10,000 county representatives. For we shall bestow on all senators the authority of county magistrates, and on all county magistrates the authority of county representatives.

Let the senators meet in the capital, and be endowed with the whole executive power of the commonwealth; the power of peace and war, of giving orders to generals, admirals, and ambassadors, and, in short, all the prerogatives of a BRITISH King, except his negative.

Let the county representatives meet in their particular counties, and possess the whole legislative power of the commonwealth; the greatest number of counties deciding the question; and where these are equal, let the senate have the casting vote.

Every new law must first be debated in the senate; and though rejected by it, if ten senators insist and protest, it must be sent down to the counties. The senate, if they please, may join to the copy of the law their reasons for receiving or rejecting it.

Because it would be troublesome to assemble all the country representatives for every trivial law, that may be requisite, the senate have their choice of sending down the law either to the county magistrates or county representatives.

The magistrates, though the law be referred to them, may, if they please, call the representatives, and submit the affair to their determination.

Whether the law be referred by the senate to the county magistrates or representatives, a copy of it, and of the senate's reasons, must be sent to every representative eight days before the day appointed for the assembling, in order to deliberate concerning it. And though the determination be, by the senate, referred to the magistrates, if five representatives of the county order the magistrates to assemble the whole court of representatives, and submit the affair to their determination, they must obey.

Either the county magistrates or representatives may give, to the senator of the county, the copy of a law to be proposed to the senate; and if five counties concur in the same order, the law, though refused by the senate, must come either to the county magistrates or representatives, as is contained in the order of the five counties.

Any twenty counties, by a vote either of their magistrates or representatives, may throw any man out of all public offices for a year. Thirty counties for three years.

The senate has a power of throwing out any member or number of members of its own body, not to be re-elected for that year. The senate cannot throw out twice in a year the senator of the same county.

The power of the old senate continues for three weeks after the annual election of the county representatives. Then all the new senators are shut up in a conclave, like the cardinals; and by an intricate ballot, such as that of VENICE or MALTA,[3] they chuse the following magistrates; a protector, who represents the dignity of the commonwealth, and presides in the senate; two secretaries of state; these six councils, a council of state, a council of religion and learning, a council of trade, a council of laws, a council of war, a council of the admiralty, each council consisting of five persons; together with six commissioners of the treasury and a first commissioner. All these must be senators. The senate also names all the ambassadors to foreign courts, who may either be senators or not.

The senate may continue any or all of these, but must re-elect them every year.

The protector and two secretaries have session and suffrage in the council of state. The business of that council is all foreign politics. The council of state has session and suffrage in all the other councils.

The council of religion and learning inspects the universities and clergy. That of trade inspects every thing that may affect commerce. That of laws inspects all the abuses of laws by the inferior magistrates, and examines what improvements may be made of the municipal law. That of war inspects the militia and its discipline, magazines, stores, &c. and when the republic is in war, examines into the proper orders for generals. The council of admiralty has the same power with regard to the navy, together with the nomination of the captains and all inferior officers.

None of these councils can give orders themselves, except where they receive such powers from the senate. In other cases, they must communicate every thing to the senate.

When the senate is under adjournment, any of the councils may assemble it before the day appointed for its meeting.

Besides these councils or courts, there is another called the court of *competitors*; which is thus constituted. If any candidates for the office of senator have more votes than a third of the representatives, that candidate, who has most votes, next to the senator elected, becomes incapable for one year of all public offices, even of being a magistrate or representative: But he takes his seat in the court of competitors. Here then is a court which may sometimes consist of a hundred members, sometimes have no members at all; and by that means, be for a year abolished.

The court of competitors has no power in the commonwealth. It has only the inspection of public accounts and the accusing of any man before the senate. If the senate acquit him, the court of competitors may, if they please, appeal to the people, either magistrates or representatives. Upon that appeal, the magistrates or representatives meet on the day appointed by the court of competitors, and chuse in each county three persons; from which number every senator is excluded. These, to the number of 300, meet in the capital, and bring the person accused to a new trial.

The court of competitors may propose any law to the senate; and if refused, may appeal to the people, that is, to the magistrates or representatives, who examine it in their counties. Every senator, who is thrown out of the senate by a vote of the court, takes his seat in the court of competitors.

The senate possesses all the judicative authority of the house of Lords, that is, all the appeals from the inferior courts. It likewise appoints the Lord Chancellor, and all the officers of the law.

Every county is a kind of republic within itself, and the representatives may make county-laws; which have no authority 'till three months after they are voted. A copy of the law is sent to the senate, and to every other county. The senate, or any single county, may, at any time, annul any law of another county.

The representatives have all the authority of the BRITISH justices of peace in trials, commitments, &c.

The magistrates have the appointment of all the officers of the revenue in each county. All causes with regard to the revenue are carried ultimately by appeal before the magistrates. They pass the accompts of all the officers; but must have all their own accompts examined and passed at the end of the year by the representatives.

The magistrates name rectors or ministers to all the parishes.

The Presbyterian government is established; and the highest ecclesiastical court is an assembly or synod of all the presbyters of the county. The magistrates may take any cause from this court, and determine it themselves.

The magistrates may try, and depose or suspend any presbyter.

The militia is established in imitation of that of SWISSERLAND, which being well known, we shall not insist upon it.[4] It will only be proper to make this addition, that an army of 20,000 men be annually drawn out by rotation, paid and encamped during six weeks in summer; that the duty of a camp may not be altogether unknown.

The magistrates appoint all the colonels and downwards. The senate all upwards. During war, the general appoints the colonel and downwards, and his commission is good for a twelvemonth. But after that, it must be confirmed by the magistrates of the county, to which the regiment belongs. The magistrates may break any officer in the county regiment. And the senate may do the same to any officer in the service. If the magistrates do not think proper to confirm the general's choice, they may appoint another officer in the place of him they reject.

All crimes are tried within the county by the magistrates and a jury. But the senate can stop any trial, and bring it before themselves.

Any county may indict any man before the senate for any crime.

The protector, the two secretaries, the council of state, with any five more that the senate appoints, are possessed, on extraordinary emergencies, of *dictatorial* power for six months.

The protector may pardon any person condemned by the inferior courts.

In time of war, no officer of the army that is in the field can have any civil office in the commonwealth.

The capital, which we shall call LONDON, may be allowed four members in the senate. It may therefore be divided into four counties. The representatives of each of these chuse one senator, and ten magistrates. There are therefore in the city four senators, forty-four magistrates, and four hundred representatives. The magistrates have the same authority as in the counties. The representatives also have the same authority; but they never meet in one general court: They give their votes in their particular county, or division of hundreds.

When they enact any bye-law, the greatest number of counties or divisions determines the matter. And where these are equal, the magistrates have the casting vote.

The magistrates chuse the mayor, sheriff, recorder, and other officers of the city.

In the commonwealth, no representative, magistrate, or senator, as such has any salary. The protector, secretaries, councils, and ambassadors, have salaries.

The first year in every century is set apart for correcting all inequalities, which time may have produced in the representative. This must be done by the legislature.

The following political aphorisms may explain the reason of these orders.

The lower sort of people and small proprietors are good judges enough of one not very distant from them in rank or habitation; and therefore, in their parochial meetings, will probably chuse the best, or nearly the best representative: But they are wholly unfit for county-meetings, and for electing into the higher offices of the republic. Their ignorance gives the grandees an opportunity of deceiving them.

Ten thousand, even though they were not annually elected, are a basis large enough for any free government. It is true, the nobles in POLAND are more than 10,000, and yet these oppress the people. But as power always continues there in the same persons and families, this makes them, in a manner, a different nation from the people. Besides the nobles are there united under a few heads of families.

All free governments must consist of two councils, a less and greater; or, in other words, of a senate and people. The people, as HARRINGTON[5] observes, would want wisdom, without the senate: The senate, without the people, would want honesty.

A large assembly of 1000, for instance, to represent the people, if allowed to debate, would fall into disorder. If not allowed to debate, the senate has a negative upon them, and the worst kind of negative, that before resolution.

Here therefore is an inconvenience, which no government has yet fully remedied, but which is the easiest to be remedied in the world. If the people debate, all is confusion: If they do not debate, they can only resolve; and then the senate carves for them. Divide the people into many separate bodies; and then they may debate with safety, and every inconvenience seems to be prevented.

Cardinal de RETZ says, that all numerous assemblies, however composed, are mere mob, and swayed in their debates by the least motive.[6] This we find confirmed by daily experience. When an absurdity strikes a member, he conveys it to his neighbour, and so on, till the whole be infected. Separate this great body; and though every member be only of middling sense, it is not probable, that anything but reason can prevail over the whole. Influence and example being removed, good sense will always get the better of bad among a number of people.

There are two things to be guarded against in every *senate*: Its combination, and its division. Its combination is most dangerous. And against this inconvenience we have provided the following remedies. 1. The great dependence of the senators on the people by annual election; and that not by an undistinguishing rabble, like the ENGLISH electors, but by men of fortune and education. 2. The small power they are allowed. They have few offices to dispose of. Almost all are given by the magistrates in the counties. 3. The court of competitors, which being composed of men that are their rivals, next to them in interest, and uneasy in their present situation, will be sure to take all advantages against them.

The division of the senate is prevented, 1. By the smallness of their number. 2. As faction supposes a combination in a separate interest, it is prevented by their dependence on the people. 3. They have a power of expelling any factious member. It is true, when another member of the same spirit comes from the county, they have no power of expelling him: Nor is it fit they should; for that shows the humour to be in the people, and may possibly arise from some ill conduct in public affairs. 4. Almost any man, in a senate so regularly chosen by the people, may be supposed fit for any civil office. It would be proper, therefore, for the senate to form some *general* resolutions with regard to the disposing of offices among the members: Which resolutions would not confine them in critical times, when extraordinary parts on the one hand, or extraordinary stupidity on the other, appears in any senator; but they would be sufficient to prevent intrigue and faction, by making the disposal of the offices a thing of course. For instance, let it be a resolution, That no man shall enjoy any office, till he has sat four years in the senate: That, except ambassadors, no man shall be in office two years following: That no man shall attain the higher offices but through the lower: That no man shall be protector twice, &c. The senate of VENICE govern themselves by such resolutions.

In foreign politics the interest of the senate can scarcely ever be divided from that of the people; and therefore it is fit to make the senate absolute with regard to them; otherwise there could be no secrecy or refined policy. Besides, without money no alliance can be executed; and the senate is still sufficiently dependant. Not to mention, that the legislative power being always superior to the executive, the magistrates or representatives may interpose whenever they think proper.

The chief support of the BRITISH government is the opposition of interests; but that, though in the main serviceable, breeds endless factions. In the foregoing plan, it does all the good without any of the harm. The *competitors* have no power of controlling the senate:

They have only the power of accusing, and appealing to the people.

It is necessary, likewise, to prevent both combination and division in the thousand magistrates. This is done sufficiently by the separation of places and interests.

But lest that should not be sufficient, their dependence on the 10,000 for their elections, serves to the same purpose.

Nor is that all: For the 10,000 may resume the power whenever they please; and not only when they all please, but when any five of a hundred please, which will happen upon the very first suspicion of a separate interest.

The 10,000 are too large a body either to unite or divide, except when they meet in one place, and fall under the guidance of ambitious leaders. Not to mention their annual election, by the whole body of the people, that are of any consideration.

A small commonwealth is the happiest government in the world within itself, because every thing lies under the eye of the rulers: But it may be subdued by great force from without. This scheme seems to have all the advantages both of a great and a little commonwealth.

Every county-law may be annulled either by the senate or another county; because that shows an opposition of interest: In which case no part ought to decide for itself. The matter must be referred to the whole, which will best determine what agrees with general interest.

As to the clergy and militia, the reasons of these orders are obvious. Without the dependence of the clergy on the civil magistrates, and without a militia, it is vain to think that any free government will ever have security or stability.

In many governments, the inferior magistrates have no rewards but what arise from their ambition, vanity, or public spirit. The salaries of the FRENCH judges amount not to the interest of the sums they pay for their offices. The DUTCH burgo-masters have little more immediate profit than the ENGLISH justices of peace, or the members of the house of commons formerly.[7] But lest any should suspect, that this would beget negligence in the administration, (which is little to be feared, considering the natural ambition of mankind) let the magistrates have competent salaries. The senators have access to so many honourable and lucrative offices, that their attendance needs not be bought. There is little attendance required of the representatives.

That the foregoing plan of government is practicable, no one can doubt, who considers the resemblance that it bears to the commonwealth of the United Provinces, a wise and renowned government. The alterations in the present scheme seem all evidently for the better. 1. The representation is more equal. 2. The unlimited power of the burgo-masters in the towns, which forms a perfect aristocracy in the DUTCH commonwealth, is corrected by a well-tempered democracy, in giving to the people the annual election of the county representatives. 3. The negative, which every province and town has upon the whole body of the DUTCH republic, with regard to alliances, peace and war, and the imposition of taxes, is here removed. 4. The counties, in the present plan, are not so independent of each other, nor do they form separate bodies so much as the seven provinces; where the jealousy and envy of the smaller provinces and towns against the greater, particularly HOLLAND and AMSTERDAM, have frequently disturbed the government. 5. Larger powers, though of the safest kind, are intrusted to the senate than the States-General possess; by which means, the former may become more expeditious, and secret in their resolutions, than it is possible for the latter.

The chief alterations that could be made on the BRITISH government, in order to bring it to the most perfect model of limited monarchy, seem to be the following. *First*, The plan of CROMWELL's parliament ought to be restored, by making the representation equal, and by allowing none to vote in the county elections who possess not a property of 200 pounds value.[8] *Secondly*, As such a house of Commons would be too weighty for a frail house of Lords, like the present, the Bishops and SCOTCH Peers ought to be removed:[9] The number of the upper house ought to be raised to three or four hundred: Their seats not hereditary, but during life: They ought to have the election of their own members; and no commoner should be allowed to refuse a seat that was offered him. By this means the house of Lords would consist entirely of the men of chief credit, ability, and interest in the nation; and every turbulent leader in the house of Commons might be taken off, and connected in interest with the house of Peers. Such an aristocracy would be an excellent barrier both to the monarchy and against it. At present, the balance of our government depends in some measure on the ability and behaviour of the sovereign; which are variable and uncertain circumstances.

This plan of limited monarchy, however corrected, seems still liable to three great inconveniences. *First*, It removes not entirely, though it may soften the parties of *court* and *country*. *Secondly*, The king's personal character must still have a great influence on the government. *Thirdly*, The sword is in the hands of a single person, who will always neglect to discipline the militia, in order to have a pretence for keeping up a standing army.[10]

We shall conclude this subject, with observing the falsehood of the common opinion, that no large state, such as FRANCE or BRITAIN, could ever be modelled into a commonwealth, but that such a form of government can only take place in a city or small territory. The contrary seems probable. Though it is more difficult to form a republican government in an extensive country than in a city; there is more facility, when once it is formed, of preserving it steady and uniform, without tumult and faction. It is not easy, for the distant parts of a large state to combine in any plan of free government; but they easily conspire in the esteem and reverence for a single person, who, by means of this popular favour, may seize the power, and forcing the more obstinate to submit, may establish a monarchical government. On the other hand, a city readily concurs in the same notions of government, the natural equality of property favours liberty, and the nearness of habitation enables the citizens mutually to assist each other. Even under absolute princes, the subordinate government of cities is commonly republican; while that of counties and provinces is monarchical. But these same circumstances, which facilitate the erection of commonwealths in cities, render their constitution more frail and uncertain. Democracies are turbulent. For however the people may be separated or divided into small parties, either in their votes or elections; their near habitation in a city will always make the force of popular tides and currents very sensible. Aristocracies are better adapted for peace and order, and accordingly were most admired by ancient writers; but they are jealous and oppressive. In a large government, which is modelled with masterly skill, there is compass and room enough to refine the democracy from the lower people, who may be admitted into the first elections or first concoction of the commonwealth, to the higher magistrates, who direct all the movements. At the same time, the parts are so distant and remote, that it is very difficult, either by intrigue, prejudice, or passion, to hurry them into any measures against the public interest.

It is needless to enquire, whether such a government would be immortal. I allow the justness of the poet's exclamation on the endless projects of human race, *Man and for ever!*[11] The world itself probably is not immortal. Such consuming plagues may arise as would leave even a perfect government a weak prey to its neighbours. We know not to what length enthusiasm, or other extraordinary movements of the human mind, may transport men, to the neglect of all order and public good. Where difference of interest is removed, whimsical and unaccountable factions often arise, from personal favour or enmity. Perhaps, rust may grow to the springs of the most accurate political machine, and disorder its motions. Lastly, extensive conquests, when pursued, must be the ruin of every free government; and of the more perfect governments sooner than of the imperfect; because of the very advantages which the former possess above the latter. And though such a state ought to establish a fundamental law against conquest; yet republics have ambition as well as individuals, and present interest makes men forgetful of their posterity. It is a sufficient incitement to human endeavours, that such a government would flourish for many ages; without pretending to bestow, on any work of man, that immortality, which the Almighty seems to have refused to his own productions.

Appendix: Excerpts from Hume's *History of England*

I Parties and the Revolution settlement

The Petition of Right (History of England, *ch. 41* (v: *192–5*))[1]

The . . . commons . . . knew, that their own vote . . . had not, of itself, sufficient authority to secure the constitution against future invasion. Some act to that purpose must receive the sanction of the whole legislature; and they appointed a committee to prepare the model of so important a law. By collecting into one effort all the dangerous and oppressive claims of his prerogative, Charles had exposed them to the hazard of one assault; and had farther, by presenting a nearer view of the consequences attending them, rouzed the independent genius of the commons. Forced loans, benevolences, taxes without consent of parliament, arbitrary imprisonments, the billeting of soldiers, martial law; these were the grievances complained of, and against these an eternal remedy was to be provided. The commons pretended not, as they affirmed, to any unusual powers or privileges: They aimed only at securing those which had been transmitted them from their ancestors: And their law they resolved to call a PETITION OF RIGHT; as implying that it contained a corroboration or explanation of the ancient constitution, not any infringement of royal prerogative, or acquisition of new liberties.

While the committee was employed in framing the petition of right, the favourers of each party, both in parliament and throughout the nation, were engaged in disputes about this bill, which, in all likelihood, was to form a memorable aera in the English government.

That the statutes, said the partizans of the commons, which secure English liberty, are not become obsolete, appears hence, that the English have ever been free, and have ever been governed by law and a limited constitution. Privileges in particular, which are founded on the GREAT CHARTER, must always remain in force, because derived from a source of never-failing authority; regarded in all ages, as the most sacred contract between king and people. Such attention was paid to this charter by our generous ancestors, that they got the confirmation of it re-iterated thirty several times; and even secured it by a rule, which, though vulgarly received, seems in the execution impracticable. They have established it as a maxim, *That even a statute, which should be enacted in contradiction to any article of that charter, cannot have force or validity.* But with regard to that important article, which secures personal liberty; so far from attempting, at any time, any legal infringement of it, they have corroborated it by six statutes, and put it out of all doubt and controversy. If in practice it has often been violated, abuses can never come in the place of rules; nor can any rights or legal powers be derived from injury and injustice. But the title of the subject to personal liberty not only is founded on ancient and therefore the more sacred laws: It is confirmed by the whole ANALOGY of the government and constitution. A free monarchy in which every individual is a slave, is a glaring contradiction; and it is requisite, where the laws assign privileges to the different orders of the state, that it likewise secure the independence of the members. If any difference could be made in this particular, it were better to abandon even life or property to the arbitrary will of the prince; nor would such immediate danger ensue, from that concession, to the laws and to the privileges of the people. To bereave of his life a man not condemned by any legal trial, is so egregious an exercise of tyranny, that it must at once shock the natural humanity of princes, and convey an alarm throughout the whole commonwealth. To confiscate a man's fortune, besides its being a most atrocious act of violence, exposes the monarch so much to the imputation of avarice and rapacity, that it will seldom be attempted in any civilized government. But confinement, though a less striking, is no less severe a punishment; nor is there any spirit, so erect and independent, as not to be broken by the long continuance of the silent and inglorious sufferings of a jail. The power of imprisonment, therefore, being the most natural and potent engine of arbitrary government, it is absolutely necessary to remove it from a government which is free and legal.

The partizans of the court reasoned after a different manner. The true rule of government, said they, during any period, is that to which the people, from time immemorial, have been accustomed and to which they naturally pay a prompt obedience. A practice which has ever struck their senses, and of which they have seen and heard innumerable precedents, has an authority with them much superior to that which attends maxims, derived from antiquated statutes and mouldy records. In vain do the lawyers establish it as a principle, that a statute can never be abrogated by opposite custom; but requires to be expressly repealed by a contrary statute: While they pretend to inculcate an axiom, peculiar to English jurisprudence, they violate the most established principles of human nature; and even, by necessary consequence, reason in contradiction to law itself, which they would represent as so sacred and inviolable. A law, to have any authority, must be derived from a legislature, which has right. And whence do all legislatures derive their right but from long custom and established practice? If a statute, contrary to public good, has, at any time, been rashly voted and assented to, either from the violence of faction, or the inexperience of senates and princes; it cannot be more effectually abrogated, than by a train of contrary precedents, which prove, that, by common consent, it has been tacitly set aside, as inconvenient and impracticable. Such has been the case with all those statutes enacted during turbulent times, in order to limit royal prerogative, and cramp the sovereign in his protection of the public, and his execution of the laws. But above all branches of prerogative, that which is most necessary to be preserved, is the power of imprisonment. Faction and discontent, like diseases, frequently arise in every political body; and during these disorders, it is by the salutary exercise alone of this discretionary power, that rebellious and civil wars can be prevented. To circumscribe this power, is to destroy its nature: Entirely to abrogate it, is impracticable; and the attempt itself must prove dangerous, if not pernicious to the public. The supreme magistrate, in critical and turbulent times, will never, agreeably either to prudence or duty, allow the state to perish, while there remains a remedy, which, how irregular soever, it is still in his power to apply. And if, moved by a regard to public good, he employs any exercise of power condemned by recent and express statute, how greedily, in such dangerous times, will factious leaders seize this pretence of throwing on his government the imputation of tyranny and despotism? Were the alternative quite necessary, it were surely much better for human society to be deprived of liberty than to be destitute of government.

Impartial reasoners will confess, that the subject is not, on both sides, without its difficulties. Where a general and rigid law is enacted against arbitrary imprisonment, it would appear, that government cannot, in times of sedition and faction, be conducted but by temporary suspensions of the law; and such an expedient was never thought of during the age of Charles. The meetings of parliament were too precarious, and their determinations might be too dilatory, to serve in cases of urgent necessity. Nor was it then conceived, that the king did not possess of himself sufficient power for the security and protection of his people, or that the authority of these popular assemblies was ever to become so absolute, that the prince must always conform himself to it, and could never have any occasion to guard against *their* practices, as well as against those of his other subjects.

The Convention Parliament (History of England, *ch. 71* (VI: *523–34*))[2]

The English convention was assembled; and it immediately appeared, that the house of commons, both from the prevailing humour of the people, and from the influence of present authority, were mostly chosen from among the whig party. After thanks were unanimously given by both houses to the prince of Orange for the deliverance, which he had brought them, a less decisive vote, than that of the Scottish convention, was in a few days passed by a great majority of the commons, and sent up to the peers for their concurrence. It was contained in these words: "That king James II. having endeavoured to subvert the constitution of the kingdom, by breaking the original contract between king and people; and having, by the advice of jesuits and other wicked persons, violated the fundamental laws, and withdrawn himself out of the kingdom, has abdicated the government, and that the throne is thereby vacant." This vote, when carried to the upper house, met with great opposition; of which it is here necessary for us to explain the causes.

The tories and the high-church party, finding themselves at once menaced with a subversion of the laws and of their religion, had zealously promoted the national revolt, and had on this occasion departed from those principles of non-resistance, of which, while the king favoured them, they had formerly made such loud professions.

Their present apprehensions had prevailed over their political tenets; and the unfortunate James, who had too much trusted to those general declarations, which never will be reduced to practice, found in the issue, that both parties were secretly united against him. But no sooner was the danger past, and the general fears somewhat allayed, than party prejudices resumed, in some degree, their former authority; and the tories were abashed at that victory, which their antagonists, during the late transactions, had obtained over them. They were inclined, therefore, to steer a middle course; and, though generally determined to oppose the king's return, they resolved not to consent to dethroning him, or altering the line of succession. A regent with kingly power was the expedient, which they proposed; and a late instance in Portugal seemed to give some authority and precedent to that plan of government.

In favour of this scheme the tories urged, that, by the uniform tenor of the English laws, the title to the crown was ever regarded as sacred, and could, on no account, and by no mal-administration, be forfeited by the sovereign: That to dethrone a king and to elect his successor, was a practice quite unknown to the constitution, and had a tendency to render kingly power entirely dependent and precarious: That where the sovereign, from his tender years, from lunacy, or from other natural infirmity, was incapacitated to hold the reins of government, both the laws and former practice agreed in appointing a regent, who, during the interval, was invested with the whole power of the administration: That the inveterate and dangerous prejudices of king James had rendered him as unfit to sway the English scepter, as if he had fallen into lunacy; and it was therefore natural for the people to have recourse to the same remedy: That the election of one king was a precedent for the election of another; and the government, by that means, would either degenerate into a republic, or, what was worse, into a turbulent and seditious monarchy: That the case was still more dangerous, if there remained a prince, who claimed the crown by right of succession, and disputed, on so plausible a ground, the title of the present sovereign: That though the doctrine of non-resistance might not, in every possible circumstance, be absolutely true, yet was the belief of it very expedient; and to establish a government, which should have the contrary principle for its basis, was to lay a foundation for perpetual revolutions and convulsions: That the appointment of a regent was indeed exposed to many inconveniences; but so long as the line of succession was preserved entire, there was still a prospect of putting an end, some time or other, to the public disorders: And that scarcely an instance occurred in history, especially in the English history, where a disputed title had not, in the issue, been attended with much greater ills, than all those, which the people had sought to shun, by departing from the lineal successor.

The leaders of the whig party, on the other hand, asserted, that, if there were any ill in the precedent, that ill would result as much from establishing a regent, as from dethroning one king, and appointing his successor; nor would the one expedient, if wantonly and rashly embraced by the people, be less the source of public convulsions than the other: That if the laws gave no express permission to depose the sovereign, neither did they authorize resisting his authority or separating the power from the title: That a regent was unknown, except where the king, by reason of his tender age or his infirmities, was incapable of a will; and in that case, his will was supposed to be involved in that of the regent: That it would be the height of absurdity to try a man for acting upon a commission, received from a prince, whom we ourselves acknowledge to be the lawful sovereign; and no jury would decide so contrary both to law and common sense, as to condemn such a pretended criminal: That even the prospect of being delivered from this monstrous inconvenience was, in the present situation of affairs, more distant than that of putting an end to a disputed succession: That allowing the young prince to be the legitimate heir, he had been carried abroad; he would be educated in principles destructive of the constitution and established religion; and he would probably leave a son, liable to the same insuperable objection: That if the whole line were cut off by law, the people would in time forget or neglect their claim; an advantage, which could not be hoped for, while the administration was conducted in their name, and while they were still acknowledged to possess the legal title: And that a nation, thus perpetually governed by regents or protectors, approached much nearer to a republic than one subject to monarchs, whose hereditary regular succession, as well as present authority, was fixed and appointed by the people.

This question was agitated with great zeal by the opposite parties in the house of peers. The chief speakers among the tories were Clarendon, Rochester, and Nottingham; among the whigs, Halifax and Danby. The question was carried for a king by two voices only, fifty-one against forty-nine. All the prelates, except two, the bishops of London and Bristol, voted for a regent. The primate, a disinterested but pusillanimous man, kept at a distance, both from the prince's court and from parliament.

The house of peers proceeded next to examine piece-meal the vote, sent up to them by the commons. They debated, "Whether there were an original contract between king and people?" and the affirmative was carried by fifty-three against forty-six; a proof that the tories were already losing ground. The next question was, "Whether king James had broken that original contract?" and after a slight opposition, the affirmative prevailed. The lords proceeded to take into consideration the word *abdicated*; and it was carried, that *deserted* was more proper. The concluding question was, "Whether king James having broken the original contract, and *deserted* the government, the throne was thereby vacant?" This question was debated with more heat and contention than any of the former; and upon a division, the tories prevailed by eleven voices, and it was carried to omit the last article, with regard to the vacancy of the throne. The vote was sent back to the commons with these amendments.

The earl of Danby had entertained the project of bestowing the crown solely upon the princess of Orange, and of admitting her as hereditary legal successor to king James: Passing by the infant prince as illegitimate or suppositious. His change of party in the last question gave the tories so considerable a majority in the number of voices.

The commons still insisted on their own vote, and sent up reasons, why the lords should depart from their amendments. The lords were not convinced; and it was necessary to have a free conference, in order to settle this controversy. Never surely was national debate more important, or managed by more able speakers; yet is one surprised to find the topics, insisted on by both sides, so frivolous; more resembling the verbal disputes of the schools than the solid reasonings of statesmen and legislators. In public transactions of such consequence, the true motives, which produce any measure, are seldom avowed. The whigs, now the ruling party, having united with the tories, in order to bring about the revolution, had so much deference for their new allies, as not to insist, that the crown should be declared *forfeited*, on account of the king's mal-administration: Such a declaration, they thought, would imply too express a censure of the old tory principles, and too open a preference of their own. They agreed, therefore, to confound together the king's abusing his power, and his withdrawing from the kingdom; and they called the whole an *abdication*; as if he had given a virtual, though not a verbal, consent to dethroning himself. The tories took advantage of this obvious impropriety, which had been occasioned merely by the complaisance or prudence of the whigs; and they insisted upon the word *desertion*, as more significant and intelligible. It was retorted on them, that, however that expression might be justly applied to the king's withdrawing himself, it could not, with any propriety, be extended to his violation of the fundamental laws. And thus both parties, while they warped their principles from regard to their antagonists, and from prudential considerations, lost the praise of consistence and uniformity.

The managers for the lords next insisted, that, even allowing the king's abuse of power to be equivalent to an abdication, or in other words, to a civil death, it could operate no otherwise than his voluntary resignation or his natural death; and could only make way for the next successor. It was a maxim of English law, *that the throne was never vacant*; but instantly, upon the demise of one king, was filled with his legal heir, who was entitled to all the authority of his predecessor. And however young or unfit for government the successor, however unfortunate in his situation, though he were even a captive in the hands of public enemies; yet no just reason, they thought, could be assigned, why, without any default of his own, he should lose a crown, to which, by birth, he was fully intitled. The managers for the commons might have opposed this reasoning by many specious and even solid arguments. They might have said, that the great security for allegiance being merely opinion, any scheme of settlement should be adopted, in which, it was most probable, the people would acquiesce and persevere. That though, upon the natural death of a king, whose administration had been agreeable to the laws, many and great inconveniences would be endured rather than exclude his lineal successor; yet the case was not the same, when the people had been obliged, by their revolt, to dethrone a prince, whose illegal measures had, in every circumstance, violated the constitution. That in these extraordinary revolutions, the government reverted, in some degree, to its first principles, and the community acquired a right of providing for the public interest by expedients, which, on other occasions, might be deemed violent and irregular. That the recent use of one extraordinary remedy reconciled the people to the practice of another, and more familiarized their minds to such licences, than if the government had run on in its usual tenor. And that king James, having carried abroad his son, as well as withdrawn himself, had given such just provocation to the kingdom, had voluntarily involved it in such difficulties, that the interests of his family were justly sacrificed to the public settlement and tranquillity. Though these topics seem reasonable, they were entirely forborne by the whig managers; both because they implied an acknowledgement of the infant prince's legitimacy, which it was agreed to keep in obscurity, and because they contained too express a condemnation of tory principles. They were content to maintain the vote of the commons by shifts and evasions; and both sides parted at last without coming to any agreement.

But it was impossible for the public to remain long in the present situation. The perseverance, therefore, of the lower house obliged the lords to comply; and by the desertion of some peers to the whig party, the vote of the commons, without any alteration, passed by a majority of fifteen in the upper house, and received the sanction of every part of the legislature, which then subsisted.

It happens unluckily for those, who maintain an original contract between the magistrate and people, that great revolutions of government, and new settlements of civil constitutions, are commonly conducted with such violence, tumult, and disorder, that the public voice can scarcely ever be heard; and the opinions of the citizens are at that time less attended to than even in the common course of administration. The present transactions in England, it must be confessed, are a singular exception to this observation. The new elections had been carried on with great tranquillity and freedom: The prince had ordered the troops to depart from all the towns, where the voters assembled: A tumultuary petition to the two houses having been promoted, he took care, though the petition was calculated for his advantage, effectually to suppress it: He entered into no intrigues, either with the electors or the members: He kept himself in a total silence, as if he had been no wise concerned in these transactions: And so far from forming cabals with the leaders of parties, he disdained even to bestow caresses on those, whose assistance might be useful to him. This conduct was highly meritorious, and discovered great moderation and magnanimity; even though the prince unfortunately, through the whole course of his life, and on every occasion, was noted for an address so cold, dry, and distant, that it was very difficult for him, on account of any interest, to soften or familiarize it.

At length, the prince, deigned to break silence, and to express, though in a private manner, his sentiments on the present situation of affairs. He called together Halifax, Shrewsbury, Danby, and a few more; and he told them, that, having been invited over to restore their liberty, he had engaged in this enterprize, and had at last happily effected his purpose. That it belonged to the parliament, now chosen and assembled with freedom, to concert measures for the public settlement; and he pretended not to interpose in their determinations. That he heard of several schemes proposed for establishing the government: Some insisted on a regent; others were desirous of bestowing the crown on the princess: It was their concern alone to chuse the plan of administration most agreeable or advantageous to them. That if they judged it proper to settle a regent, he had no objection: He only thought it incumbent on him to inform them, that he was determined not to be the regent, nor ever to engage in a scheme, which, he knew, would be exposed to such insuperable difficulties. That no man could have a juster or deeper sense of the princess's merit than he was impressed with; but he would rather remain a private person than enjoy a crown, which must depend on the will or life of another. And that they must therefore make account, if they were inclined to either of these two plans of settlement, that it would be totally out of his power to assist them in carrying it into execution: His affairs abroad were too important to be abandoned for so precarious a dignity, or even to allow him so much leisure as would be requisite to introduce order into their disjointed government.

These views of the prince were seconded by the princess herself, who, as she possessed many virtues, was a most obsequious wife to a husband, who, in the judgment of the generality of her sex, would have appeared so little attractive and amiable. All considerations were neglected, when they came in competition with that she deemed her duty to the prince. When Danby and others of her partizans wrote her an account of their schemes and proceedings, she expressed great displeasure; and even transmitted their letters to her husband, as a sacrifice to conjugal fidelity. The princess Anne also concurred in the same plan for the public settlement; and being promised an ample revenue, was content to be postponed in the succession to the crown. And as the title of her infant brother was, in the present establishment, entirely neglected, she might, on the whole, deem herself, in point of interest, a gainer by this revolution.

The chief parties, therefore, being agreed, the convention passed a bill, in which they settled the crown on the prince and princess of Orange, the sole administration to remain in the prince: The princess of Denmark to succeed after the death of the prince and princess of Orange; her posterity after those of the princess, but before those of the prince by any other wise. The convention annexed to this settlement of the crown a declaration of rights, where all the points, which had, of late years, been disputed between the king and people, were finally determined; and the powers of royal prerogative were more narrowly circumscribed and more exactly defined, than in any former period of the English government.

Thus have we seen, through the course of four reigns, a continual struggle maintained between the crown and the people: Privilege and prerogative were ever at variance: And both parties, beside the present object of dispute, had many latent claims, which, on a favourable occasion, they produced against their adversaries. Governments too steady and uniform, as they are seldom free, so are they, in the judgment of some, attended with another sensible inconvenience: They abate the active powers of men; depress courage, invention, and genius; and produce an universal lethargy in the people. Though this opinion may be just, the fluctuation and contest, it must be allowed, of the English government were, during these reigns, much too violent both for the repose and safety of the people. Foreign affairs, at that time, were either entirely neglected, or managed to pernicious purposes: And in the domestic administration there was felt a continued fever, either secret or manifest; sometimes the most furious convulsions and disorders. The revolution forms a new epoch in the constitution; and was probably attended with consequences more advantageous to the people, than barely freeing them from an exceptionable administration. By deciding many important questions in favour of liberty, and still more, by that great precedent of deposing one king, and establishing a new family, it gave such an ascendant to popular principles, as has put the nature of the English constitution beyond all controversy. And it may justly be affirmed, without any danger of exaggeration, that we, in this island, have ever since enjoyed, if not the best system of government, at least the most entire system of liberty, that ever was known amongst mankind.

To decry with such violence, as is affected by some, the whole line of Stuart; to maintain, that their administration was one continued encroachment on the *incontestible* rights of the people; is not giving due honour to that great event, which not only put a period to their hereditary succession, but made a new settlement of the whole constitution. The inconveniences, suffered by the people under the two first reigns of that family (for in the main they were fortunate) proceeded in a great measure from the unavoidable situation of affairs; and scarcely any thing could have prevented those events, but such vigour of genius in the sovereign, attended with such good fortune, as might have enabled him entirely to overpower the liberties of his people. While the parliaments, in those reigns, were taking advantage of the necessities of the prince, and attempting every session to abolish, or circumscribe, or define, some prerogative of the crown, and innovate in the usual tenor of government: What could be expected, but that the prince would exert himself, in defending, against such inveterate enemies, an authority, which, during the most regular course of the former English government, had been exercised without dispute or controversy? And though Charles II. in 1672, may with reason be deemed the aggressor, nor is it possible to justify his conduct; yet were there some motives surely, which could engage a prince, so soft and indolent, and at the same time so judicious, to attempt such hazardous enterprizes. He felt, that public affairs had reached a situation, at which they could not possibly remain without some farther innovation. Frequent parliaments were become almost absolutely necessary to the conducting of public business; yet these assemblies were still, in the judgment of the royalists, much inferior in dignity to the sovereign, whom they seemed better calculated to counsel than controul. The crown still possessed considerable power of opposing parliaments; and had not as yet acquired the means of influencing them. Hence a continual jealousy between these parts of the legislature: Hence the inclination mutually to take advantage of each other's necessities: Hence the impossibility, under which the king lay, of finding ministers, who could at once be serviceable and faithful to him. If he followed his own choice in appointing his servants, without regard to their parliamentary interest, a refractory session was instantly to be expected: If he chose them from among the leaders of popular assemblies, they either lost their influence with the people, by adhering to the crown, or they betrayed the crown, in order to preserve their influence. Neither Hambden, whom Charles I. was willing to gain at any price; nor Shaftesbury, whom Charles II. after the popish plot, attempted to engage in his counsels, would renounce their popularity for the precarious, and, as they esteemed it, deceitful favour of the prince. The root of their authority they still thought to lie in the parliament; and as the power of that assembly was not yet uncontroulable, they still resolved to augment it, though at the expence of the royal prerogatives.

It is no wonder, that these events have long, by the representations of faction, been extremely clouded and obscured. No man has yet arisen, who has payed an entire regard to truth, and has dared to expose her, without covering or disguise, to the eyes of the prejudiced public. Even that party amongst us, which boasts of the highest regard to liberty, has not possessed sufficient liberty of thought in this particular; nor has been able to decide impartially of their own merit, compared with that of their antagonists. More noble perhaps in their ends, and highly beneficial to mankind; they must also be allowed to have often been less justifiable in the means, and in many of their enterprizes to have payed more regard to political than to moral considerations. Obliged to court the favour of the populace, they found it necessary to comply with their rage and folly; and have even, on many occasions, by propagating calumnies, and by promoting violence, served to infatuate, as well as corrupt that people, to whom they made a tender of liberty and justice. Charles I. was a tyrant, a papist, and a contriver of the Irish massacre: The church of England was relapsing fast into idolatry: Puritanism was the only true religion, and the covenant the favourite object of heavenly regard. Through these delusions the party proceeded, and, what may seem wonderful, still to the encrease of law and liberty; till they reached the imposture of the popish plot, a fiction which exceeds the ordinary bounds of vulgar credulity. But however singular these events may appear, there is really nothing altogether new in any period of modern history: And it is remarkable, that tribunitian arts, though sometimes useful in a free constitution, have usually been such as men of probity and honour could not bring themselves either to practice or approve. The other faction, which, since the revolution, has been obliged to cultivate popularity, sometimes found it necessary to employ like artifices.

The Whig party, for a course of near seventy years, has, almost without interruption, enjoyed the whole authority of government; and no honours or offices could be obtained but by their countenance and protection. But this event, which, in some particulars, has been advantageous to the state, has proved destructive to the truth of history, and has established many gross falsehoods, which it is unaccountable how any civilized nation could have embraced with regard to its domestic occurrences. Compositions the most despicable, both for style and matter, have been extolled, and propagated, and read; as if they had equalled the most celebrated remains of antiquity. And forgetting that a regard to liberty, though a laudable passion, ought commonly to be subordinate to a reverence for established government, the prevailing faction has celebrated only the partizans of the former, who pursued as their object the perfection of civil society, and has extolled them at the expence of their antagonists, who maintained those maxims, that are essential to its very existence. But extremes of all kinds are to be avoided; and though no one will ever please either faction by moderate opinions, it is there we are most likely to meet with truth and certainty.

II Prerogative and Parliament

History of England, *note W to ch. 53* (v: *568–70*)[3]

It must be confessed, that the king in this declaration touched upon that circumstance in the English constitution, which it is most difficult, or rather altogether impossible, to regulate by laws, and which must be governed by certain delicate ideas of propriety and decency, rather than by any exact rule or prescription. To deny the parliament all right of remonstrating against what they esteem grievances, were to reduce that assembly to a total insignificancy, and to deprive the people of every advantage, which they could reap from popular councils. To complain of the parliament's employing the power of taxation, as the means of extorting concessions from their sovereign, were to expect, that they would entirely disarm themselves, and renounce the sole expedient, provided by the constitution, for ensuring to the kingdom a just and legal administration. In different periods of

English story, there occur instances of their remonstrating with their princes in the freest manner, and sometimes of their refusing supply when disgusted with any circumstance of public conduct. 'Tis, however, certain, that this power, though essential to parliaments, may easily be abused, as well by the frequency and minuteness of their remonstrances, as by their intrusion into every part of the king's counsels and determinations. Under colour of advice, they may give disguised orders; and in complaining of grievances, they may draw to themselves every power of government. Whatever measure is embraced, without consulting them, may be pronounced an oppression of the people; and till corrected, they may refuse the most necessary supplies to their indigent sovereign. From the very nature of this parliamentary liberty, it is evident, that it must be left unbounded by law: For who can foretell, how frequently grievances may occur, or what part of administration may be affected by them? From the nature too of the human frame, it may be expected, that this liberty would be exerted in its full extent, and no branch of authority be allowed to remain unmolested in the hands of the prince: For will the weak limitations of respect and decorum be sufficient to restrain human ambition, which so frequently breaks through all the prescriptions of law and justice?

But, here it is observable, that the wisdom of the English constitution, or rather the concurrence of accidents, has provided, in different periods, certain irregular checks to this privilege of parliament, and thereby maintained, in some tolerable measure, the dignity and authority of the crown.

In the ancient constitution, before the beginning of the seventeenth century, the meetings of parliament were precarious and were not frequent. The sessions were short; and the members had no leisure, either to get acquainted with each other, or with public business. The ignorance of the age made men more submissive to that authority which governed them. And above all, the large demesnes of the crown, with the small expence of government during that period, rendered the prince almost independent, and taught the parliament to preserve great submission and duty towards him.

In our present constitution, many accidents, which have rendered governments, every where, as well as in Great Britain, much more burthensome than formerly, have thrown into the hands of the crown the disposal of a large revenue, and have enabled the king, by the private interest and ambition of the members, to restrain the public interest and ambition of the body. While the opposition (for we must still have an opposition, open or disguised) endeavours to draw every branch of administration under the cognizance of parliament, the courtiers reserve a part to the disposal of the crown; and the royal prerogative, though deprived of its ancient powers, still maintains a due weight in the balance of the constitution.

It was the fate of the house of Stuart to govern England at a period, when the former source of authority was already much diminished, and before the latter began to show in any tolerable abundance. Without a regular and fixed foundation, the throne perpetually tottered; and the prince sat upon it anxiously and precariously. Every expedient, used by James and Charles, in order to support their dignity, we have seen, attended with sensible inconveniences. The majesty of the crown, derived from ancient powers and prerogatives, procured respect; and checked the approaches of insolent intruders: But it begat in the king so high an idea of his own rank and station, as made him incapable of stooping to popular courses, or submitting, in any degree, to the controul of parliament. The alliance with the hierarchy strengthened law by the sanction of religion: But it enraged the puritanical party, and exposed the prince to the attacks of enemies, numerous, violent and implacable. The memory too of these two kings, from like causes, has been attended, in some degree, with the same infelicity, which pursued them during the whole course of their lives. Though it must be confessed, that their skill in government was not proportioned to the extreme delicacy of their situation; a sufficient indulgence has not been given them, and all the blame, by several historians, has been unjustly thrown on *their* side. Their violations of law, particularly those of Charles, are, in some few instances, transgressions of a plain limit, which was marked out to royal authority. But the encroachments of the commons, though, in the beginning, less positive and determinate, are no less discernible by good judges, and were equally capable of destroying the just balance of the constitution. While they exercised the powers, transmitted to them, in a manner more independent, and less compliant, than had ever before been practised; the kings were, perhaps imprudently, but, as they imagined, from necessity, tempted to assume powers, which had scarcely ever been exercised, or had been exercised in a different manner, by the crown. And from the shock of these opposite pretensions, together with religious controversy, arose all the factions, convulsions, and disorders, which attended that period.

History of England, *ch. 49* (v: *544–6*)[4]

The tragical death of Charles begat a question, whether the people, in any case, were intitled to judge and to punish their sovereign; and most men, regarding chiefly the atrocious usurpation of the pretended judges, and the merit of the virtuous prince who suffered, were inclined to condemn the republican principle, as highly seditious and extravagant: But there still were a few, who, abstracting from the particular circumstances of this case, were able to consider the question in general, and were inclined to moderate, not contradict, the prevailing sentiment. Such might have been their reasoning. If ever, on any occasion, it were laudable to conceal truth from the populace; it must be confessed, that the doctrine of resistance affords such an example; and that all speculative reasoners ought to observe, with regard to this principle, the same cautious silence, which the laws, in every species of government, have ever prescribed to themselves. Government is instituted, in order to restrain the fury and injustice of the people; and being always founded on opinion, not on force, it is dangerous to weaken, by these speculations, the reverence, which the multitude owe to authority, and to instruct them beforehand, that the case can ever happen, when they may be freed from their duty of allegiance. Or should it be found impossible to restrain the licence of human disquisitions, it must be acknowledged, that the doctrine of obedience ought alone to be *inculcated*, and that the exceptions, which are rare, ought seldom or never to be mentioned in popular reasonings and discourses. Nor is there any danger, that mankind, by this prudent reserve, should universally degenerate into a state of abject servitude. When the exception really occurs, even though it be not previously expected and descanted on, it must, from its very nature, be so obvious and undisputed, as to remove all doubt, and overpower the restraint, however great, imposed by teaching the general doctrine of obedience. But between resisting a prince and dethroning him, there is a wide interval; and the abuses of power, which can warrant the latter violence, are greater and more enormous, than those which will justify the former. History, however, supplies us with examples even of this kind; and the reality of the supposition, though, for the future, it ought ever to be little looked for, must, by all candid enquirers, be acknowledged in the past. But between dethroning a prince and punishing him, there is another very wide interval; and it were not strange, if even men of the most enlarged thought should question, whether human nature could ever, in any monarch, reach that height of depravity, as to warrant, in revolted subjects, this last act of extraordinary jurisdiction. That illusion, if it be an illusion, which teaches us to pay a sacred regard to the persons of princes, is so salutary, that to dissipate it by the formal trial and punishment of a sovereign, will have more pernicious effects upon the people, than the example of justice can be supposed to have a beneficial influence upon princes, by checking their career of tyranny. It is dangerous also, by these examples, to reduce princes to despair, or bring matters to such extremities against persons endowed with great power, as to leave them no resource, but in the most violent and most sanguinary counsels. This general position being established, it must, however, be observed, that no reader, almost of any party or principle, was ever shocked, when he read, in ancient history, that the Roman senate voted Nero, their absolute sovereign, to be a public enemy, and, even without trial, condemned him to the severest and most ignominious punishment; a punishment, from which the meanest Roman citizen, was, by the laws, exempted. The crimes of that bloody tyrant are so enormous, that they break through all rules; and extort a confession, that such a dethroned prince is no longer superior to his people, and can no longer plead, in his own defence, laws, which were established for conducting the ordinary course of administration. But when we pass from the case of Nero to that of Charles, the great disproportion, or rather total contrariety, of character immediately strikes us; and we stand astonished, that, among a civilized people, so much virtue could ever meet with so fatal a catastrophe. History, the great mistress of wisdom, furnishes examples of all kinds; and every prudential, as well as moral precept, may be authorized by those events, which her enlarged mirror is able to present to us. From the memorable revolutions, which passed in England during this period, we may naturally deduce the same useful lesson, which Charles himself, in his later years, inferred; that it is dangerous for princes, even from the appearance of necessity, to assume more authority, than the laws have allowed them. But, it must be confessed, that these events furnish us with another instruction, no less natural, and no less useful, concerning the madness of the people, the furies of fanaticism, and the danger of mercenary armies.

III Clergy and religion

History of England, *ch. 45* (v: *10–13*)[5]

The next occupation of the king was entirely according to his heart's content. He was employed, in dictating magisterially to an assembly of divines concerning points of faith and discipline, and in receiving the applauses of these holy men for his superior zeal and learning. The religious disputes between the church and the puritans had induced him to call a conference at Hampton-court, on pretence of finding expedients, which might reconcile both parties.

Though the severities of Elizabeth towards the catholics had much weakened that party, whose genius was opposite to the prevailing spirit of the nation; like severities had had so little influence on the puritans, who were encouraged by that spirit, that no less than seven hundred and fifty clergymen of that party signed a petition to the king on his accession; and many more seemed willing to adhere to it. They all hoped, that James, having received his education in Scotland, and having sometimes professed an attachment to the church, established there, would at least abate the rigour of the laws enacted in support of the ceremonies and against puritans; if he did not show more particular grace and encouragement to that sect. But the king's disposition had taken strongly a contrary biass. The more he knew the puritanical clergy, the less favour he bore to them. He had remarked in their Scottish brethren a violent turn towards republicanism, and a zealous attachment to civil liberty; principles nearly allied to that religious enthusiasm, with which they were actuated. He had found, that being mostly persons of low birth and mean education, the same lofty pretensions, which attended them in their familiar addresses to their Maker, of whom they believed themselves the peculiar favourites, induced them to use the utmost freedoms with their earthly sovereign. In both capacities, of monarch and of theologian, he had experienced the little complaisance, which they were disposed to show him; whilst they controuled his commands, disputed his tenets, and to his face, before the whole people, censured his conduct and behaviour. If he had submitted to the indignity of courting their favour, he treasured up, on that account, the stronger resentment against them, and was determined to make them feel, in their turn, the weight of his authority. Though he had often met with resistance and faction and obstinacy in the Scottish nobility, he retained no ill will to that order, or rather showed them favour and kindness in England, beyond what reason and sound policy could well justify: But the ascendant, which the presbyterian clergy had assumed over him, was what his monarchical pride could never thoroughly digest.[a]

He dreaded likewise the popularity, which attended this order of men in both kingdoms. As useless austerities and self-denial are imagined, in many religions, to render us acceptable to a benevolent Being, who created us solely for happiness, James remarked, that the rustic severity of these clergymen and of their whole sect had given them, in the eyes of the multitude, the appearance of sanctity and virtue. Strongly inclined himself to mirth and wine and sports of all kinds, he apprehended their censure for his manner of life, free and disengaged. And, being thus averse, from temper as well as policy, to the sect of puritans, he was resolved, if possible, to prevent its farther growth in England. But it was the character of James's councils, throughout his whole reign, that they were more wise and equitable, in their end, than prudent and political, in the means. Though justly sensible, that no part of civil administration required greater care or a nicer judgment than the conduct of religious parties; he had not perceived, that, in the same proportion as this practical knowledge of theology is requisite, the speculative refinements in it are mean, and even dangerous in a monarch. By entering zealously into frivolous disputes, James gave them an air of importance and dignity, which they could not otherwise have acquired; and being himself inlisted in the quarrel, he could no longer have recourse to contempt and ridicule, the only proper method of appeasing it. The church of England had not yet abandoned the rigid doctrines of grace and predestination: the puritans had not yet separated themselves from

---

[a] James ventured to say in his Basilicon Doron, published while he was in Scotland: 'I protest before the great God, and since I am here as upon my Testament, it is no place for me to lie in, that ye shall never find with any Highland or Borderer Thieves, greater ingratitude and more lies and vile perjuries, than with these fanatic spirits: And suffer not the principal of them to brook your land' *K. James's Works*, p. 161.

the church, nor openly renounced episcopacy. Though the spirit of the parties was considerably different, the only appearing subjects of dispute were concerning the cross in baptism, the ring in marriage, the use of the surplice, and the bowing at the name of Jesus. These were the mighty questions, which were solemnly agitated in the conference at Hampton-court between some bishops and dignified clergymen on the one hand, and some leaders of the puritanical party on the other; the king and his ministers being present.

The puritans were here so unreasonable as to complain of a partial and unfair management of the dispute; as if the search after truth were in any degree the object of such conferences, and a candid indifference, so rare even among private enquirers in *philosophical* questions, could ever be expected among princes and prelates, in a *theological* controversy. The king, it must be confessed, from the beginning of the conference, showed the strongest propensity to the established church, and frequently inculcated a maxim, which, though it has some foundation, is to be received with great limitations. NO BISHOP, NO KING. The bishops, in their turn, were very liberal of their praises towards the royal disputant; and the archbishop of Canterbury said, that *undoubtedly his majesty spake by the special assistance of God's spirit.* A few alterations in the liturgy were agreed to, and both parties separated with mutual dissatisfaction.

It had frequently been the practice of the puritans to form certain assemblies, which they called *prophesyings*; where alternately, as moved by the spirit, they displayed their zeal in prayers and exhortations, and raised their own enthusiasm, as well as that of their audience, to the highest pitch, from that social contagion, which has so mighty an influence on holy fervours, and from the mutual emulation, which arose in those trials of religious eloquence. Such dangerous societies had been suppressed by Elizabeth; and the ministers in this conference moved the king for their revival. But James sharply replied, *If you aim at a* Scottish *presbytery it agrees as well with monarchy as God and the devil. There* Jack *and* Tom *and* Will *and* Dick *shall meet and censure me and my council. Therefore I reiterate my former speech:* Le Roi s'avisera. *Stay, I pray, for one seven years before you demand; and then, if you find me grow pursie and fat, I may perchance hearken unto you. For that government will keep me in breath, and give me work enough.* Such were the political considerations, which determined the king in his choice among religious parties.

History of England, *ch. 51* (v: *211–13*)[6]

It was not possible, that this century, so fertile in religious sects and disputes, could escape the controversy concerning fatalism and free-will, which, being strongly interwoven both with philosophy and theology, had, in all ages, thrown every school and every church into such inextricable doubt and perplexity. The first reformers in England, as in other European countries, had embraced the most rigid tenets of predestination and absolute decrees, and had composed, upon that system, all the articles of their religious creed. But these principles having met with opposition from Arminius and his sectaries, the controversy was soon brought into this island, and began here to diffuse itself. The Arminians, finding more encouragement from the superstitious spirit of the church than from the fanaticism of the puritans, gradually incorporated themselves with the former; and some of that sect, by the indulgence of James and Charles, had attained the highest preferments in the hierarchy. But their success with the public had not been altogether answerable to that which they met with in the church and the court. Throughout the nation, they still lay under the reproach of innovation and heresy. The commons now levelled against them their formidable censures, and made them the objects of daily invective and declamation. Their protectors were stigmatized; their tenets canvassed; their views represented as dangerous and pernicious. To impartial spectators surely, if any such had been at that time in England, it must have given great entertainment, to see a popular assembly, enflamed with faction and enthusiasm, pretend to discuss questions, to which the greatest philosophers, in the tranquillity of retreat, had never hitherto been able to find any satisfactory solution.

Amidst that complication of disputes, in which men were then involved, we may observe, that the appellation *puritan* stood for three parties, which, though commonly united, were yet actuated by very different views and motives. There were the political puritans, who maintained the highest principles of civil liberty; the puritans in discipline, who were averse to the ceremonies and episcopal government of the church; and the doctrinal puritans, who rigidly defended the speculative system of the first reformers. In opposition to all these stood the court party, the hierarchy, and the Arminians; only with this distinction, that the latter sect, being introduced a few years before, did not as yet comprehend all those who were favourable to the church and to monarchy. But, as the controversies on every subject grew daily warmer, men united themselves wider from their antagonists; and the distinction gradually became quite uniform and regular.

This house of commons, which, like all the preceding, during the reigns of James and Charles, and even of Elizabeth, was much governed by the puritanical party, thought that they could not better serve their cause, than by branding and punishing the Arminian sect, which, introducing an innovation in the church, were the least favoured and least powerful of all their antagonists. From this measure, it was easily foreseen, that, besides gratifying the animosity of the doctrinal puritans, both the puritans in discipline and those in politics would reap considerable advantages. Laud, Neile, Montague, and other bishops, who were the chief supporters of episcopal government, and the most zealous partizans of the discipline and ceremonies of the church, were all supposed to be tainted with Arminianism. The same men and their disciples were the strenuous preachers of passive obedience, and of entire submission to princes; and if these could once be censured, and be expelled the church and court, it was concluded, that the hierarchy would receive a mortal blow, the ceremonies be less rigidly insisted on, and the king, deprived of his most faithful friends, be obliged to abate those high claims of prerogative, on which at present he insisted.

But Charles, besides a view of the political consequences, which must result from a compliance with such pretensions, was strongly determined, from principles of piety and conscience, to oppose them. Neither the dissipation incident to youth, nor the pleasures attending a high fortune, had been able to prevent this virtuous prince from embracing the most sincere sentiments of religion; and that character, which, in that religious age, should have been of infinite advantage to him, proved in the end the chief cause of his ruin: Merely because the religion, adopted by him, was not of that precise mode and sect, which *began* to prevail among his subjects. His piety, though remote from popery, had a tincture of superstition in it; and, being averse to the gloomy spirit of the puritans, was represented by them as tending towards the abominations of antichrist. Laud also had unfortunately acquired a great ascendant over him: And as all those prelates, obnoxious to the commons, were regarded as his chief friends and most favoured courtiers; he was resolved not to disarm and dishonour himself, by abandoning them to the resentment of his enemies. Being totally unprovided with military force, and finding a refractory independent spirit to prevail among the people; the most solid basis of his authority, he thought, consisted in the support, which he received from the hierarchy.

History of England, *ch. 52* (v: *223–4 and 227–8*)

The humour of the nation ran at that time into the extreme opposite to superstition; and it was with difficulty that the ancient ceremonies, to which men had been accustomed, and which had been sanctified by the practice of the first reformers, could be retained in divine service: Yet was this the time which Laud chose for the introduction of new ceremonies and observances. Besides that these were sure to displease as innovations, there lay, in the opinion of the public, another very forcible objection against them. Laud, and the other prelates who embraced his measures, were generally well-instructed in sacred antiquity, and had adopted many of those religious sentiments, which prevailed during the fourth and fifth centuries; when the Christian church, as is well known, was already sunk into those superstitions, which were afterwards continued and augmented by the policy of Rome. The revival, therefore, of the ideas and practices of that age, could not fail of giving the English faith and liturgy some resemblance to the catholic superstition, which the kingdom in general, and the puritans in particular, held in the greatest horror and detestation. Men also were apt to think, that without some secret purpose, such insignificant observances would not be imposed with such unrelenting zeal on the refractory nation; and that Laud's scheme was to lead back the English, by gradual steps, to the religion of their ancestors. They considered not, that the very insignificancy of these ceremonies recommended them to the superstitious prelate, and made them appear the more peculiarly sacred and religious, as they could serve to no other purpose. Nor was the resemblance to the Romish ritual any objection, but rather a merit, with Laud and his brethren; who bore a much greater kindness to the mother-church, as they called her, than to the sectaries and presbyterians, and frequently recommended her as a true

257

Christian church; an appellation which they refused, or at least scrupled to give to the others. So openly were these tenets espoused, that not only the discontented puritans believed the church of England to be relapsing fast into Romish superstition: The court of Rome itself entertained hopes of regaining its authority in this island; and, in order to forward Laud's supposed good intentions, an offer was twice made him, in private, of a cardinal's hat, which he declined accepting . . .

It must be confessed, that though Laud deserved not the appellation of papist, the genius of his religion was, though in a less degree, the same with that of the Romish: The same profound respect was exacted to the sacerdotal character, the same submission required to the creeds and decrees of synods and councils, the same pomp and ceremony was affected in worship, and the same superstitious regard to days, postures, meats, and vestments. No wonder, therefore, that this prelate was, every-where, among the puritans, regarded with horror, as the forerunner of antichrist . . .

In return for Charles's indulgence towards the church, Laud and his followers took care to magnify, on every occasion, the regal authority, and to treat, with the utmost disdain or detestation, all puritanical pretensions to a free and independent constitution. But while these prelates were so liberal in raising the crown at the expence of public liberty, they made no scruple of encroaching themselves, on the royal rights the most incontestible; in order to exalt the hierarchy, and procure to their own order dominion and independence. All the doctrines which the Romish church had borrowed from some of the fathers, and which freed the spiritual from subordination to the civil power, were now adopted by the church of England, and interwoven with her political and religious tenets. A divine and apostolical charter was insisted on, preferably to a legal and parliamentary one. The sacerdotal character was magnified as sacred and indefeizable: All right to spiritual authority, or even to private judgment in spiritual subjects, was refused to profane laymen: Ecclesiastical courts were held by the bishops in their own name, without any notice taken of the king's authority: And Charles, though extremely jealous of every claim in popular assemblies, seemed rather to encourage than repress those encroachments of his clergy. Having felt many sensible inconveniences from the independent spirit of parliaments, he attached himself entirely to those who professed a devoted obedience to his crown and person; nor did he foresee, that the ecclesiastical power, which he exalted, not admitting of any precise boundary, might in time become more dangerous to public peace, and no less fatal to royal prerogative than the other.

Notes

1. Of the liberty of the press (1741)

1 In the *History of England*, ch. 71 (VI: 540), Hume gives a brief description of the old system whereby all publications had to receive a licence and of its abolition when Parliament in 1695 did not renew the Licensing Act. Thereafter the only means of controlling publication was through the libel laws, which were often toughly administered in the eighteenth century. The free press became a central part of British politics, especially when the life of a Parliament was extended from three to seven years (Septennial Act, 1716). When opposition could not be expressed in frequent electioneering, it took to the press, and the government responded in kind (cf. 'Of the first principles of government', note 4). The 1730s, at the end of which Hume wrote this essay, had been turbulent in the politics of the press and this is reflected in his reference to 'rumour and popular clamour' (note 4 below). The attacks on the long-serving prime minister, Robert Walpole, in opposition papers such as Bolingbroke's *The Craftsman* and the government's reply in papers such as the *Free Briton* and the *London Journal* were often accompanied by rumours of Jacobite infiltration and the like. In later years Hume became critical of some of the excesses of liberty, and he dropped the last three paragraphs of the present essay in the edition of 1770 (reproduced below in note 4). In a letter to Turgot in 1768 he explained his reasoning (*Letters*, II: 180–1).

2 Tacitus, *The Histories* 1:16.28. In the striking English edition of Tacitus' *Works* by Thomas Gordon – co-author of *Cato's Letters* –

the passage is rendered: '[But you are about to govern the Romans; a people of too little virtue] to support compleat liberty, of too much spirit to bear absolute bondage' (*Works of Tacitus*, II: 15).

3 Voltaire, *La Henriade*, Canto I. First published in 1723 as *La Ligue*, Voltaire's celebration of the protector of French Protestants, Henri IV, rapidly gained fame also in Britain. The translation of 1732 (p. 19) renders the passage:

[*Elizabeth*, whose Wisdom holds the Scale
of *Europe*, and her Choice the Balance turns.]
The resty *English* bear her Yoke with Joy,
[A Nation fond of changing,] ne're alike
In Servitude or Liberty at Ease.

4 This last sentence was added in the edition of 1777. In editions from 1741 to 1768 the essay ended with the following three paragraphs:

Since therefore that liberty is so essential to the support of our mixed government; this sufficiently decides the second question, *Whether such a liberty be advantageous or prejudicial*; there being nothing of greater importance in every state than the preservation of the ancient government, especially if it be a free one. But I would fain go a step farther, and assert, that this liberty is attended with so few inconveniencies, that it may be claimed as the common right of mankind, and ought to be indulged them almost in every government: except the ecclesiastical, to which indeed it would prove fatal. We need not dread from this liberty any such ill consequences as followed from the harangues of the popular demagogues at ATHENS and tribunes of ROME. A man reads a book or pamphlet alone and coolly. There is none present from whom he can catch the passion by contagion. He is not hurried away by the force and energy of action. And should he be wrought up to ever so seditious a humour, there is no violent resolution presented to him, by which he can immediately vent his passion. The liberty of the press, therefore, however abused, can scarce ever excite popular tumults or rebellion. And as to those murmurs or secret discontents it may occasion, 'tis better they should get vent in words, that they may come to the knowledge of the magistrate before it be too late, in order to his providing a remedy against them. Mankind, it is true, have always a greater propension to believe what is said to the disadvantage of their governors, than the contrary; but this inclination is inseparable from them, whether they have liberty or not. A whisper may fly as quick, and be as pernicious as a pamphlet. Nay, it will be more pernicious, where men are not accustomed to think freely, or distinguish between truth and falsehood.

It has also been found, as the experience of mankind increases, that the *people* are no such dangerous monster as they have been represented, and that it is in every respect better to guide them, like rational creatures, than to lead or drive them, like brute beasts. Before the United Provinces set the example, toleration was deemed incompatible with good government; and it was thought impossible, that a number of religious sects could live together in harmony and peace, and have all of them an equal affection to their common country, and to each other. ENGLAND has set a like example of civil liberty; and though this liberty seems to occasion some small ferment at present, it has not as yet produced any pernicious effects; and it is to be hoped, that men, being every day more accustomed to the free discussion of public affairs, will improve in the judgment of them, and be with great difficulty seduced by every idle rumour and popular clamour.

It is a very comfortable reflection to the lovers of liberty, that this peculiar privilege of BRITAIN is of a kind that cannot easily be wrested from us, but must last as long as our government remains, in any degree, free and independent. It is seldom, that liberty of any kind is lost all at once. Slavery has so frightful an aspect to men accustomed to freedom, that it must steal upon them by degrees, and must disguise itself in a thousand shapes, in order to be received. But, if the liberty of the press ever be lost, it must be lost at once. The general laws against sedition and libelling are at present as strong as they possibly can be made. Nothing can impose a farther restraint, but either the clapping an IMPRIMATUR upon the press, or the giving to the court very large discretionary powers to punish whatever displeases them. But these concessions would be such a bare-faced violation of liberty, that they will probably be the last efforts of a despotic government. We may conclude, that the liberty of *Britain* is gone for ever when these attempts shall succeed.

2. That politics may be reduced to a science (1741)

1 Alexander Pope, *Essay on Man*, Epistle III, lines 303–4.

2 Hume discusses the two French kings in the *History*, chs. 40 and 43 (esp. v: 167–9; 278–82; 289–91).

3 The flood plain of the river Tiber, originally outside the city of Rome proper, was the meeting place for the assemblies – *comitia* – of the Roman people when electing magistrates. It was also the site of a horse-race dedicated to Mars.

4 Cicero, *In G. Verrem actio prima*, 1.14.41. This was the first plea in the private prosecution of Gaius Verres by Cicero on behalf of the inhabitants of Sicily. Verres was charged with illicit enrichment as governor (*praetor*) of that province from 73 to 70 BC, his crowning achievement in a lifetime of such activities.

5 Hume is referring to the tumultuous events which led to the dissolution of the republican form of government and the introduction of imperial rule. After the murder of Caesar in 44 BC, Marcus Antonius (Mark Antony), together with Lepidus and Octavian, gained control of Rome through special legislation which made them triumvirs for five years. In an attempt to shore up the new regime a number of rivals were proscribed, that is outlawed, and could be executed and have their property confiscated. Hume's references in the following four footnotes are: Tacitus, *Annals* 1.8; Suetonius, *Lives of the Caesars*, ch. 8 ('Life of Domitian'); Tacitus, *Annals* 3.40, i.e. vol. I, p. 134 of the translation used here ('[The Gauls] had now a glorious opportunity to recover their liberty ... they need only consider their own strength and numbers; while Italy was poor and exhausted; the Roman populace weak and unwarlike, the Roman armies destitute of all vigour, but that deriv'd from foreigners'); and Polybius, *Histories* 1.72.

6 Conquered lands.

7 Corsica was subject to the republic of Genoa but was in constant rebellion from the 1730s. France assumed sovereignty of the island in 1768. Cf. James Boswell, *An Account of Corsica, the Journal of a Tour of that Island; and Memoirs of Pascal Paoli* (1768) and Hume's reference in *Letters*, II: 11. Cf. also Rousseau, *Social Contract*, Book II, ch. 10 (p. 203). The general theme of the correlation between constitutional form and methods of colonial administration can be further pursued in Montesquieu's famous discussion in *Spirit of the Laws*, Part II, Book 10.

8 This paragraph is a précis of Machiavelli, *The Prince*, ch. 4, 'Why the kingdom of Darius conquered by Alexander did not rebel against his successors after his death'.

9 Hume's sources in the footnote are: Xenophon, *Education of Cyrus* (Cyropaedia) 2.1.9 (the Greek word means 'peers of the realm'); Arrian, *Expedition of Alexander*, III; Herodotus, *History*, VII.62 and 117, III.160; Thucydides, *History of the Peloponnesian War*, 1.109; Diodorus Siculus, *Library of History*, 16.47; Xenophon, *Hellenica*, IV.1; Xenophon, *Expedition of Cyrus*, Book II; Polybius, *The Histories*, V.43. The Greek quotation from Arrian, *Expedition of Alexander*, III.43, means 'among the first of the Persians'.

10 Machiavelli, *The Florentine History* p. 411: 'A rare order surely, and not found by the Philosophers among their imagined or visible Commonweales, to see within one circle, and among one number of Citizens, libertie and tirannie, civill life, and corruption, justice and licentiousnes: which order only mainteineth that towne full of auncient and venerable customes. And if it should happen (which in time will assuredly come to passe) that S. George shall be owner of all the Citie, that State will be more notable, then the Venetian Commonweale.'

11 Using Livy, *Roman History*, 40.43, Hume is referring to the period from the 260s to the 140s BC when the full development of republican Rome was secured by two kinds of struggle. *Externally* a number of successful wars made the city into a world power. The three wars with Carthage (264–241; 218–201; 149–146) gave control over the western Mediterranean, including Spain and parts of North Africa (Carthage stood roughly on the site of modern Tunis and had been colonised by the Phoenicians or *poeni*, hence 'Punic' wars). *Internally* the republican form of government was worked out in ways which particularly interested

political theorists from the Renaissance onwards. Like so many in the eighteenth century, Hume emphasised the achievement of what was taken to be a balance of the nobility and its representatives (the Senate) with the people and its representatives (the ten tribunes), the latter – through the tribunes – having a 'veto' on the policy and legislation of the former. (See 'The idea of a perfect commonwealth'.) Finally the eighteenth century commonly saw this period as the time when the administration of justice in Rome was becoming well established, with the institution of the praetor as a magistrate 'not unlike our lord chief justices, or lord chancellor, or both in one' (*Encyc. Brit.*, 509).

12 Livy is giving an account of the year 331 BC when a number of Roman matrons were reportedly involved in large-scale poisoning.

13 'Triumvirate, an absolute government, administered by three persons with equal authority' (*Encyc. Brit.*, 913). The first triumvirate was formed in 60 BC by Pompey, Caesar and Crassus. For the second, see note 5 above. In the footnote Hume has changed the lines from Corneille's tragedy *Cinna* to suit his purpose. Their sense is, 'Eagle against eagle, Romans against Romans/fighting only for the choice of tyrants' I. 3, 11; 179 and 187–8.

14 The reference is to Bolingbroke.

15 Hume describes the events of the Revolution of 1688–9 by which James II lost the crown and his daughter Mary and her husband, the Dutch prince William of Orange, were proclaimed in his stead, in the *History*, vol. VI, ch. 71.

16 Cato Uticensis (the younger Cato) and Marcus Junius Brutus were the undisputed heroes of the classical republican tradition, the former as martyr, the latter as tyrannicide.

17 Literally, 'for altars and fires'. As the altars in question were for the family gods, while the fires were the hearth with offerings for the household gods, the proper rendering is 'for hearth and home'. With this meaning the phrase is common in classical Latin literature and is often part of the litany of republican concerns – typically Sallust: 'pro patria, pro liberis, pro aris atque focis suis cernere' (to contend for one's fatherland, liberties, and hearth and home) (*The Wars of Catiline* 59.5). As Duncan Forbes points out (*Hume's Philosophical Politics*, 223) the tag was a favourite of Bolingbroke's. Hume is therefore suggesting that this traditional

republican link be broken in order to achieve a public moderation
suitable for a mixed constitution.

18 In editions from 1748 to 1768 Hume added as a footnote a sketch
of Sir Robert Walpole that had first appeared as a separate essay
in 1742, on the eve of Walpole's resignation as prime minister.
Cf. also Hume's letter to his friend William Mure of Caldwell
(14 November 1742; *Letters*, I, 43–5). The footnote version of
the 'Character' is added here:

What our author's opinion was of the famous minister pointed
at here, may be learned from that essay, printed in the former
editions, under the title of A character of Sir ROBERT WAL-
POLE: It was as follows.

THERE never was a Man, whose Actions and Character
have been more earnestly and openly canvassed, than those
of the present Minister, who, having govern'd a learn'd and
free Nation for so long a Time, amidst such mighty Opposition, may make a large Library of what has been wrote for
and against him, and is the Subject of above Half the Paper
that has been blotted in this Nation within these Twenty
Years. I wish, for the Honour of our Country, that any one
Character of him had been drawn with such *judgment* and
impartiality, as to have some Credit with Posterity, and to
show, that our Liberty has, once at least, been imploy'd to
good Purpose. I am only afraid of failing in the former Quality
of Judgment: But if it shou'd be so, 'tis but one Page more
thrown away, after an hundred Thousand, upon the same
Subject, that have perish'd, and become useless. In the mean
Time, I shall flatter myself with the pleasing Imagination, that
the following Character will be adopted by future Historians.

SIR *ROBERT WALPOLE*, Prime Minister of GREAT BRI-
TAIN, is a Man of Ability, not a Genius; good natur'd, not
virtuous; constant, not magnanimous; moderate, not equitable. [footnote: *Moderate in the exercise of power, not equitable
in engrossing it.*] His Virtues, in some Instances, are free from
the Allay of those Vices, which usually accompany such Virtues: He is a generous Friend, without being a bitter Enemy.
His Vices, in other Instances, are not compensated by those
Virtues which are nearly ally'd to them: His Want of Enter-

prise is not attended with Frugality. The private Character of the Man is better than the public: His Virtues more than his Vices: His Fortune greater than his Fame. With many good Qualities he has incurr'd the public Hatred: With good Capacity he has not escap'd Ridicule. He would have been esteem'd more worthy of his high Station, had he never possest it; and is better qualify'd for the second than for the first Place in any Government. His Ministry has been more advantageous to his Family than to the Public, better for this Age than for Posterity, and more pernicious by bad Precedents than by real Grievances. During his Time Trade has flourish'd, Liberty declin'd, and Learning has gone to Ruin. As I am a Man, I love him; as I am a Scholar, I hate him; as I am a Briton, I calmly wish his Fall. And were I a Member of either House, I wou'd give my Vote for removing him from St. James's; but shou'd be glad to see him retire to Houghton Hall, to pass the Remainder of his Days in Ease and Pleasure.

Walpole, now Earl of Orford, had three years at his country estate. He died in March 1745.

3. Of the first principles of government (1741)

1 Hume is invoking standard topoi in the republican demonology of military despotism. According to Harrington, 'the Mamelukes, which were at first foreign guards [slave-soldiers], extinguishing the royal line of the kings of Egypt, came to possess and hold that realm without opposition' – first with Egyptian sultans (or soldans) and after 1517 with Ottoman viceroys as their leader (*The Prerogative of Popular Government* I. 9; p. 446 in *Works*). Again in imperial Rome, to the regular military 'a matter of eight thousand, by the example of Augustus, were added, which departed not from his sides, but were his perpetual guard, called praetorian bands' (*The Commonwealth of Oceana*, Preliminaries 2; p. 189 in *Works*). Cf. also Machiavelli, *The Prince*, ch. 19.

2 For a more concentrated discussion of James Harrington's thesis, see the essay on 'Whether the British government inclines more to absolute monarchy, or to a republic'.

3 Hume is referring to the conflicts between William III and the Tory majority in the House of Commons at the turn of the cen-

tury. At issue were the king's involvement of Britain in European power politics and the question of the eventual succession of the Hanoverian line to the throne. The Whigs rallied various forces in the king's interest, including popular petitions to the Commons.

4 The duration of each Parliament had been extended from three to seven years in 1716. Cf. 'Of the liberty of the press', note 1.

5 Editions from 1741 to 1760 add:

I shall conclude this subject with observing, that the present political controversy, with regard to instructions, is a very frivolous one, and can never be brought to any decision, as it is managed by both parties. The country-party pretend not, that a member is absolutely bound to follow instructions, as an ambassador or general is confined by his orders, and that his vote is not to be received in the house, but so far as it is conformable to them. The court-party again, pretend not, that the sentiments of the people ought to have no weight with every member; much less that he ought to despise the sentiments of those he represents, and with whom he is more particularly connected. And if their sentiments be of weight, why ought they not to express these sentiments? The question, then, is only concerning the degrees of weight, which ought to be plac'd on instructions. But such is the nature of language, that it is impossible for it to express distinctly these different degrees; and if men will carry on a controversy on this head, it may well happen, that they differ in their language, and yet agree in their sentiments; or differ in their sentiments, and yet agree in their language. Besides, how is it possible to find these degrees, considering the variety of affairs which come before the house, and the variety of places which members represent? Ought the instructions of TOT-NESS to have the same weight as those of LONDON? or instructions, with regard to the *Convention*, which respected foreign politics, to have the same weight as those with regard to the *excise*, which respected only our domestic affairs?

Hume is referring to the frequent debates on the relationship between the electorate and their parliamentary representatives. It played a role in shaping the political profile of the Country interest in the first years of the eighteenth century, Defoe being an articulate spokesman, but it returned with particular vigour in 1733, 1738 and 1741–2, as well as later. On these occasions the Country opposition organised petitions with 'instructions' to their MPs. In 1733 it was over Walpole's important excise bill (cf. Adam Smith, *Wealth of Nations*, v.ii.k.40), which triggered a large number of instructions and petitions, including one from the Tory pocket borough of Totnes in Devon. In 1738 it was over the convention with the king of Spain to regulate maritime trade and to solve a host of other disputes. In both cases the trading interests of the City of London played a significant role.

4. Of the origin of government (1777)

1 Hume explains the point about the Turkish sultan towards the end of the essay 'Of taxes' and the point about France in the essay 'Of civil liberty'.

5. Of the independency of Parliament (1741)

1 In editions from 1741 to 1760 this essay begins with the following paragraphs:

I have frequently observed, in comparing the conduct of the *court* and *country* parties, that the former are commonly less assuming and dogmatical in conversation, more apt to make concessions; and tho' not, perhaps, more susceptible of conviction, yet more able to bear contradiction than the latter; who are apt to fly out upon any opposition, and to regard one as a mercenary designing fellow, if he argues with any coolness and impartiality, or makes any concessions to their adversaries. This is a fact, which, I believe, every one may have observed, who has been much in companies where political questions have been discussed; tho', were one to ask the reason of this difference, every party would be apt to assign a different reason. Gentlemen in the *Opposition* will ascribe it to the very nature of their party, which, being founded on public spirit, and a zeal for the constitution, cannot easily endure such doctrines, as are of pernicious consequence to liberty. The courtiers, on the other hand, will be apt to put us in mind of the clown mentioned by lord SHAFTESBURY. 'A clown,' says that excellent author, (Footnote: Miscellaneous

Reflections 107 [i.e. Shaftesbury, *Characteristics*, II: 222.])
'once took a fancy to hear the *Latin* disputes of doctors at an
university. He was asked what pleasure he could take in viewing such combatants, when he could never know so much, as
which of the parties had the better. *For that matter*, replied
the clown, *I a'n't such a fool neither, but I can see who's the first
that puts t'other into a passion.* Nature herself dictated this
lesson to the clown, that he who had the better of the argument would be easy and well-humoured: But he who was
unable to support his cause by reason would naturally lose
his temper and grow violent.'

To which of these reasons shall we adhere? To neither of
them, in my opinion; unless we have a mind to enlist ourselves
and become zealots in either party. I believe I can assign the
reason of this different conduct in the two parties, without
offending either. The country party are plainly most popular
at present, and perhaps have been so in most administrations:
So that, being accustomed to prevail in company, they cannot
endure to hear their opinions controverted, but are as confident on the public favour, as if they were supported in all
their sentiments by the most infallible demonstration. The
courtiers, on the other hand, are commonly so run down by
popular talkers, that if you speak with any moderation, or
make them the smallest concessions, they think themselves
extremely beholden to you, and are apt to return the favour
by a like moderation and facility on their part. To be furious
and passionate, they know, would only gain them the character of *shameless mercenaries*; not that of *zealous patriots*, which
is the character that such a warm behaviour is apt to acquire
to the other party.

In all the controversies, we find, without regarding the truth
or falsehood on either side, that those who defend the established and popular opinions, are always the most dogmatical
and imperious in their stile: while their adversaries affect
almost extraordinary gentleness and moderation, in order to
soften as much as possible, any prejudices that may lye against
them. Consider the behaviour of our *free-thinkers* of all
denominations, whether they be such as decry all revelation,
or only oppose the exorbitant power of the clergy; *Collins,
Tindal, Foster, Hoadley.* Compare their moderation and good

manners with the furious zeal and scurrility of their adversaries, and you will be convinced of the truth of my observation. A like difference may be observed in the conduct of those French writers, who maintained the controversy with regard to ancient and modern learning. *Boileau*, Monsieur and Madame *Dacier*, l'Abbé de *Bos*, who defended the party of the ancients, mixed their reasonings with satire and invective; while Fontenelle, la Motte, Charpentier, and even Perrault, never transgressed the bounds of moderation and good breeding; though provoked by the most injurious treatment of their adversaries.

I must, however, observe, that this Remark with regard to the seeming Moderation of the *Court* Party, is entirely confin'd to Conversation, and to Gentlemen, who have been engag'd by Interest or Inclination in that Party. For as to the Court-Writers, being commonly hir'd Scriblers, they are altogether as scurrilous as the Mercenaries of the other Party; nor has the *Gazeteer* any Advantage, in this Respect, above *Common Sense*. A man of Education will, in any Party, discover himself to be such, by his Good-breeding and Decency; as a Scoundrel will always betray the opposite Qualities. *The false Accusers accus'd*, &c. is very scurrilous, tho' that Side of the Question, being least popular, shou'd be defended with most Moderation. When L-d *B-e*, L-d *M-t*, *Mr. L-n* take the Pen in Hand, tho' they write with Warmth, they presume not upon their Popularity so far as to transgress the Bounds of Decency.

I am led into this train of reflection, by considering some papers wrote upon that grand topic of *court influence and parliamentary dependence*, where, in my humble opinion, the country party, besides vehemence and satyre, shew too rigid an inflexibility, and too great a jealousy of making concessions to their adversaries. Their reasonings lose their force by being carried too far; and the popularity of their oppinions has seduced them to neglect in some measure their justness and solidity. The following reason will, I hope, serve to justify me in this opinion.

'The quarrel between the ancients and the moderns', i.e. the protracted discussion in France in the second half of the seventeenth century on the relative merits of ancient and modern literature and art, was a high point in the attempt to understand the modernity of the modern world. It continued well into the eighteenth century and had its parallels in Britain. It is constantly present in Hume's writings, linking his thoughts on politics and culture (see 'Of refinement in the arts'; also 'The standard of taste', in *Essays*, pp. 226–49). On the whole his standpoint is more evenly balanced between the claims of the ancients and the moderns than his remarks here would suggest, not least because of the influence of the Abbé Dubos.

The fourth paragraph was only in the editions of 1741 and 1742. The references in it are to the government journal the *Daily Gazetteer*, the opposition *Common Sense or the Englishman's Journal* and an anonymous pamphlet *The False Accusers Accus'd, or the Undeceived Englishman: Being an Impartial Enquiry into the General Conduct of the Administration; and compared with that of their Enemies, whereby it will appear who Merits Impeachments, &c. &c. &c. In a Letter to the Pretended Patriots. Very Necessary to be perused by the Electors and Freeholders of Great Britain, on their Choice of Proper Persons to Represent them in a New Parliament*. By a Member of the House of Commons. The three gentlemen are Lord Bolingbroke, Lord Marchmont and George Lyttleton, all prominent anti-Walpole polemicists.

2 Hume's reference is to Bolingbroke, *Dissertation upon Parties*.

3 Hume's reference is Polybius, *Histories*, 6.15.

6. Whether the British government inclines more to absolute monarchy, or to a republic (1741)

1 See Harrington, *Oceana*, Preliminaries II (*Works*, 201). Harrington published his republican model for England during the Commonwealth in 1656, and the monarchy was restored four years later. For further discussion of the Harringtonian scheme, see the beginning of the essay on the 'Idea of a perfect commonwealth'.

2 Cf. Harrington, *The Prerogative of Popular Government*, 1.11 (*Works*, p. 459; cf. *ibid.*, 1.10, pp. 452–4; and *Oceana*, Preliminaries II, *Works*, p. 198). For Crassus' wealth, see Sallust, *The War of Catiline*, xlviii.4–9, and Plutarch, 'Life of Crassus', esp. ii and vi, in *Lives*, vol. III.

3 In the *History*, vol. VI, ch. 61 (pp. 64–5) Hume describes the 'Instrument of Government', drawn up by Oliver Cromwell's officers in 1653 as the foundation for the Commonwealth and for Cromwell's Protectorate; and *ibid.* (p. 255) he gives an account of the supposedly constitutional replacement for it, the 'Humble Petition and Advice', presented to Cromwell by the Parliament in 1657. Hume thought both a 'crude and undigested model of government'.

7. Of parties in general (1741)

1 *The Advancement of Learning*, I.v.12 and I.vii.1. (pp. 36 and 42–3).
2 Hume's main sources for the history of the Italian renaissance, Machiavelli's *Prince* and *Florentine Histories* and Guicciardini's *History of Italy*, are permeated by discussions of these factions in the fourteenth, fifteenth and early sixteenth centuries. These works were high points in the discussion of the first modern experience of republicanism and as such they remained on the agenda for political thinking right through the modern period. From the middle of the thirteenth century the Italian cities had achieved a large measure of independence from the Holy Roman Empire. Internally their elective municipal forms of government thus took on more significance and gave rise to the problem of the nature and role of parties and factions of the sort mentioned here. Externally the *de facto* sovereignty of many cities gave a new twist to the older debates about the relationship between the authority of the pope and the emperor. Sovereign republics did not fit easily into either. Accordingly there were within many cities both pro-papal and pro-imperial parties, known respectively as Guelphs and Ghibellines. As we see later in this essay, these 'real' factions were crossed and hence transformed by the 'personal' factions mentioned here. See note 6 below.
3 Early in the Roman Republic horse races were two-way contests and the contestants were distinguished by wearing red and white. With the emergence of four-chariot races, green (*prasinus*) and blue (*venetus*) were added. The colours soon became the identifying factor for the contending 'camps' or 'staples', *factiones*, which, like so many sports organisations since, became the centres of social networks and interest groups. Only the greens and blues survived over time and took on political overtones in the Empire,

the latter attracting aristocratic support, the former the support of the plebeians and the more demagogic emperors and would-be emperors. The system became a kind of replacement-politics for the volatile masses of the Eastern Empire and especially its capital, Constantinople. In a complex sequence of events, violent rivalry between the two factions and a momentary alliance between them led to a breakdown of law and order and very nearly to the downfall of the Eastern Emperor Justinian in AD 532. The best known source for these events is – and was in Hume's time – Procopius in his *History of the Wars of Justinian* (I.xxiv).

4 '[The same year, the inhabitants of Tusculum were tried before the Roman people, upon a bill preferred by M. Flavius the tribune, who proposed to punish them for advising and assisting the people of Velitrae and Privernum to make war upon the Romans. Upon this] the inhabitants of that city came to Rome with their wives and children, and having changed their dress, went round the several tribes in the habit of suppliants, and fell prostrate at their feet. And by this means pity suggested a more effectual motive to procure their pardon, than their plea afforded arguments for ruining the credit of the impeachment. All the tribes, except the Pollian, rejected the bill. The sentence of that tribe was, that all those who had attained to the age of fourteen should be scourged and beheaded, and their wives and children should be publickly exposed to sale by martial law. And it is certain that Tusculans retained to the time of our fathers a lively sense of resentment against the authors of this severe sentence. And hardly a person of the Pollian tribe, who stood candidate for any office, ever used to get the votes of the Papirian tribe' Livy, *The Roman History*, II: 365–6. As for the Venetian Castelani and Nicolloti, mentioned in the footnote, they were broad, territorial (parish-based) divisions of the lower orders, who on certain public holidays fought arranged battles with fists and sticks for possession of a bridge. See Limojon de Saint Didier, *The City and Republic of Venice*, Pt III, pp. 110–12.

5 As Rome expanded across Italy, it granted citizenship to the conquered peoples and divided them into 'country' tribes that were added to the original four 'city' tribes. The Pollia and Papiria were two of these – eventually thirty-one – country tribes, and

when the Tusculans became citizens, they were included in the Papirian tribe. Livy, who began his *History* around 29 BC, is referring to events in 324–323 BC.

6 In the *History*, ch. IV (I: 215–16) Hume describes the origins of the two factions in his account of the conflict between Pope Gregory VII and Emperor Henry IV in 1076. Hume had been reading Guicciardini's *History of Italy* in 1739 (see *Letters*, I: 33–4), and this is clearly his source in this essay. The intricate story of the alliance of the supposedly Guelph duke of Milan, Lodovico Sforza, with the emperor, Maximilian I, to rescue that city from the king of France, Louis XII, and his supposedly Ghibelline allies led by a traitor to the Sforza interest, Gian Giacomo Trivulzio, is told in detail in Book IV (vol. II: 324–32 and 361–79). Cf. Hume, *History*, ch. 26 (III: 64) and ch. 27 (III: 88ff.).

7 Eugene Miller's note on this passage suggests John Braithwaite, *The History of the Revolutions in the Empire of Morocco upon the Death of the Late Emperor Muley Ishmael*, London, 1729, as a possible source for Hume's reference to the violence in Morocco in 1727–8, which was in any case widely reported in the press.

8 'An universal medicine . . . called by way of excellence, the grand elixir' Chambers, *Cyclopedia*, Suppl. (quoted after OED 'Elixir').

9 The Twelve Tables were the first foundation of Roman law, drawn up by the decemvirs in 451–450 . The Tenth Table regulates religious practices, especially in connection with burial. Like other parts of the Twelve Tables, it is only preserved in fragments, which Hume knew from Cicero's discussion in *De legibus*, II.xxiii–xxiv (58ff.); cf. Hume, *History*, Appendix IV (V: 130). Hume describes the ferocious Druids in the *History*, ch. 1 (I: 6, 8–9), where he also mentions Claudius' unusual ban on their 'idolatrous worship'. He is probably drawing on Suetonius, 'Claudius', 25, (*Lives*, p. 202), and Pliny the Elder, *Natural History*, XXX.iv.

8. Of the parties of Great Britain (1741)

1 Hume's reference is Tacitus, *Histories*, 5.8 (vol. II, p. 307): 'The Jews [during the Maccabean revolt in the 160s BC] . . . assumed Kings of their own. These were afterwards expulsed through the inconstancy of the populace, but having again seized the Sovereignty by arms, let themselves loose to all the cruelties and

excesses usual to Kings, banished their citizens, destroyed cities, murdered their brethren, murdered their wives, murdered their parents, and with all this their tyranny, carefully supported and nourished the established superstition; for to the functions of Royalty they annex'd that of the Priesthood.'

2 From the end of the fifteenth century Sweden had been united with Denmark and Norway under the Danish monarchs. In 1523 Gustav Eriksson of the old Swedish royal family Vasa managed to regain Sweden's independence and set about establishing himself as absolute monarch and evicting the (Danish) Catholic bishops, thus paving the way for Lutheranism. A likely source for Hume is Pufendorf, *Compleat History of Sweden*, pp. 170–223. The topic had also been given currency by Henry Brooke, whose play *Gustavus Vasa* (1739) was one of the first to be prohibited under the new censorship laws, cf. note 13 to Essay 11.

3 In the late sixteenth and early seventeenth century the Dutch reformed church became deeply split when a faction led by the professor of theology, Jacobus Arminius, challenged Calvinist orthodoxy on central issues such as predestination, the incompatibility of divine sovereignty and human free will, the death of Christ for the elect only. This was as much a political as a theological division, for in rejecting these Calvinist dogmas, the Arminians emphasised the role of free personal faith for election and this they saw as requiring a certain degree of toleration of individual freedom that could only be securely provided by a strong aristocratic or oligarchic government. For this they looked to the leadership of Johan van Oldenbarneveldt, States' Advocate in the province of Holland and thus the most influential minister in the United Provinces. For the supporting theory, they looked to Hugo Grotius. The Calvinists, with their Presbyterian ideals of church-government and thus of community-government, saw Arminianism as heresy and little short of popery, which again suggested treasonous affiliations between the Arminians and the Spanish colonial masters who had only just been thrown out. The Calvinists looked for leadership to the princes of the house of Orange, who as stadtholders, or constitutional heads of state, controlled the militia. At the synod of Dort in 1618–19 Maurice of Orange managed to replace enough Arminian office-holders to make the meeting a trial of Oldenbarneveldt, who was executed, and of his

followers, who were banished or, like Grotius, imprisoned in the castle of Loevestein and elsewhere. Hume's likely sources are Janiçon's *Etat présent de la République des Provinces-Unies* and Le Clerc's *Histoire des Provinces-Unies des Pays Bas*. For the English version of the conflict, Arminians versus Puritans, see Hume, *History*, ch. 46 (V: 46), appendix to the Reign of James I (V: 129–32) and ch. 51 (V: 211ff.).

4 Hume's reference is Tacitus, *Annals*, 6.42 (vol. I, p. 242): 'the sovereignty of the People is an establishment of Liberty; but the domination of a few comes nearer to the uncheck'd lust of simple Monarchy'.

5 Hume's comments here and in the rest of the essay should be compared and, as he himself stresses in his note at the end, to some extent contrasted with the lengthy and detailed analyses in his *History*. The account of the great rebellion of the Parliament and its adherents against Charles I from 1642 until the King's execution in 1649 is in chapters 56 to 59. This has to be seen against the background of chapters 50 to 55 which explain the dispute between the king and Parliament over the proper balance of authority between them in matters of supply, church government, foreign policy and much else. Cf. section I (first extract) and section II of the appendix (pp. 234–52). The labels of roundheads and cavaliers for the Parliamentary and Royalist supporters, respectively, are explained in the *History*, ch. 55 (V: 362–3).

6 Cf. section III of the appendix.

7 Hume describes the restoration of the Stuart line with the return of Charles II in 1660 in the *History*, ch. 62 (esp. VI: 138–40), while the reign itself is dealt with in chs. 63 to 69. The new party labels are accounted for in ch. 68 (VI: 381).

8 The rest of the essay should be read alongside the extracts from the *History* in Section I of the appendix.

9 Editions from 1741 to 1768 add, with minor variations, the following note:

The author above cited has asserted, that the REAL distinction betwixt WHIG and TORY was lost at the *revolution*, and that ever since they have continued to be mere *personal* parties, like the GUELFS and GIBBELINES, after the emperors had lost all authority in ITALY. Such an opinion, were it received, would turn our whole history into an ænigma.

I shall first mention, as a proof of a real distinction between these parties, what every one may have observed or heard concerning the conduct and conversation of all his friends and acquaintance on both sides. Have not the TORIES always borne an avowed affection to the family of STUART, and have not their adversaries always opposed with vigour the succession of that family?

The TORY principles are confessedly the most favourable to monarchy. Yet the Tories have almost always opposed the court these fifty years; nor were they cordial friends to King WILLIAM, even when employed by him. Their quarrel, therefore, cannot be supposed to have lain with the throne, but with the person who sat on it.

They concurred heartily with the court during the four last years of Queen ANNE. But is any one at a loss to find the reason?

The succession of the crown in the BRITISH government is a point of too great consequence to be absolutely indifferent to persons who concern themselves, in any degree, about the fortune of the public; much less can it be supposed that the TORY party, who never valued themselves upon moderation, could maintain a *stoical* indifference in a point of such importance. Were they, therefore, zealous for the house of HANOVER? Or was there any thing that kept an opposite zeal from openly appearing, if it did not openly appear, but prudence, and a sense of decency?

'Tis monstrous to see an established episcopal clergy in declared opposition to the court, and a non-conformist presbyterian clergy in conjunction with it. What could have produced such an unnatural conduct in both? Nothing, but that the former espoused monarchical principles too high for the present settlement, which is founded on principles of liberty: And the latter, being afraid of the prevalence of those high principles, adhered to that party from whom they had reason to expect liberty and toleration.

The different conduct of the two parties, with regard to foreign politics, is also a proof to the same purpose, HOLLAND has always been most favoured by one, and FRANCE by the other. In short, the proofs of this kind seem so palpable and evident, that 'tis almost needless to collect them.

The first paragraph echoes a constant refrain in Bolingbroke; see, for example, *Dissertation on Parties*, Letters VII–IX (*Works* II: esp. pp. 97 and 108–117; cf. 85) and Letter XIX (II: 251).

In 1710 Queen Anne dismissed a Whig ministry in trouble at home and abroad. As Hume hints, the pickings were rich for the Tories – all but one of the ministerial positions, twelve new peers to secure them the Upper House and a general election to secure the Lower.

An established episcopal church was integral to the traditional Tory theory of an orderly hierarchical society with a divinely ordained hereditary monarch who enjoyed the non-resistance and passive obedience inculcated by the clergy as part of the moral order. All this had been set aside by the settlement of the crown on William of Orange and Mary, which also ensured that Whig ideas of religious toleration were to some extent made law, thus providing some protection to non-conformity with the church of England and securing the basic support of dissenters for the house of Hanover.

10 The final paragraph was introduced in 1770 to replace the following much longer passage.

'Tis however remarkable, that tho' the principles of WHIG and TORY were both of them of a compound nature; yet the ingredients, which predominated in both, were not correspondent to each other. A TORY loved monarchy, and bore an affection to the family of STUART; but the latter affection was the predominant inclination of the party. A WHIG loved liberty, and was a friend to the settlement in the PROTESTANT line; but the love of liberty was professedly his predominant inclination. The TORIES have frequently acted as republicans, where either policy or revenge has engaged them to that conduct; and there was no one of that party, who, upon the supposition, that he was to be disappointed in his views with regard to the succession, would not have desired to impose the strictest limitations on the crown, and to bring our form of government as near republican as possible, in order to depress the family, which, according to his apprehension, succeeded without any just title. The WHIGS, 'tis true, have also taken steps dangerous to liberty, under colour of securing the succession and settlement of the crown, according to their views: But as the body of the party had no passion for that succession, otherwise than as the means of securing liberty, they have been betrayed into these steps by ignorance, or frailty, or the interests of their leaders. The succession of the crown was, therefore, the chief point with the TORIES; the security of our liberties with the WHIGS. Nor is this seeming irregularity at all difficult to be accounted for, by our present theory. *Court* and *country* parties are the true parents of TORY and WHIG. But 'tis almost impossible, that the attachment of the *court* party to monarchy should not degenerate into an attachment to the monarch; there being so close a connexion between them, and the latter being so much the more natural object. How easily does the worship of the divinity degenerate into a worship of the idol? The connexion is not so great between liberty, the divinity of the old *country* party or WHIGS, and any monarch or royal family; nor is it so reasonable to suppose, that in that party, the worship can be so easily transferred from the one to the other. Tho' even that would be no great miracle.

'Tis difficult to penetrate into the thoughts and sentiments of any particular man; but 'tis almost impossible to distinguish those of a whole party, where it often happens, that no two persons agree precisely in the same maxims of conduct. Yet I will venture to affirm, that it was not so much PRINCIPLE, or an opinion of indefeasible right, which attached the TORIES to the ancient royal family, as AFFECTION, or a certain love and esteem for their persons. The same cause divided ENGLAND formerly between the houses of YORK and LANCASTER, and SCOTLAND between the families of BRUCE and BALIOL; in an age, when political disputes were but little in fashion, and when political *principles* must of course have had but little influence on mankind. The doctrine of passive obedience is so absurd in itself, and so opposite to our liberties, that it seems to have been chiefly left to pulpit-declaimers, and to their deluded followers among the vulgar. Men of better sense were guided by *affection*; and as to the leaders of this party, 'tis probable, that *interest* was their chief motive, and that they acted more contrary to their private sentiments, than the leaders of the opposite party. Tho' 'tis almost impossible to maintain with zeal the right of any person or family, without acquiring a good-will to them, and changing the *principle* into *affection*; yet this is less natural to people of an elevated station and liberal education, who have had full opportunity of observing the weakness, folly, and arrogance of monarchs, and have found them to be nothing superior, if not rather inferior to the rest of mankind. The *interest*, therefore, of being heads of a party does often, with such people, supply the place both of *principle* and *affection*.

Some, who will not venture to assert, that the *real* difference between WHIG and TORY was lost at the *revolution*, seem inclined to think, that the difference is now abolished, and that affairs are so far returned to their natural state, that there are at present no other parties amongst us but *court* and *country*; that is, men, who by interest or principle, are attached either to monarchy or to liberty. It must, indeed, be confest, that the TORY party seem, of late, to have decayed much in their numbers; still more in their zeal; and I may venture to say, still more in their credit and authority. There are few men of knowledge or learning, at least, few philosophers, since Mr. LOCKE has wrote, who would not be ashamed to be thought of that party; and in almost all companies the name of OLD WHIG is mentioned as an uncontestable appellation of honour and dignity. Accordingly, the enemies of the ministry, as a reproach, call the courtiers the true TORIES; and as an honour, denominate the gentlemen in the *opposition* the true WHIGS. The TORIES have been so long obliged to talk in the republican stile, that they seem to have made converts of themselves by their hypocrisy, and to have embraced the sentiments, as well as language of their adversaries. There are, however, very considerable remains of that party in ENGLAND, with all their prejudices; and a proof that *court* and *country* are not our only parties, is, that almost all the dissenters side with the court, and the lower clergy, at least, of the church of ENGLAND, with the opposition. This may convince us, that some biass still hangs upon our constitution, some intrinsic weight, which turns it from its natural course, and causes a confusion in our parties.

I shall conclude this subject with observing that we never had any TORIES in SCOTLAND, according to the proper signification of the word, and that the division of parties in this country was really into WHIGS and JACOBITES. A JACOBITE seems to be a TORY, who has no regard to the constitution, but is either a zealous partizan of absolute monarchy, or at least willing to sacrifice our liberties to the obtaining the succession in that family to which he is attached. The reason of the difference between ENGLAND and SCOTLAND, I take to be this: Political and religious divisions in the latter country, have been, since the *revolution*, regularly correspondent to each other. The PRESBYTERIANS were all WHIGS without exception: Those who favoured *episcopacy*, of the opposite party. And as the clergy of the latter sect were turned out of the churches at the *revolution*, they had no motive for making any compliances with the government in their oaths, or their forms of prayers, but openly avowed the highest principles of their party; which is the cause why their followers have been more violent than their brethren of the TORY party in ENGLAND.

As violent Things have not commonly so long a Duration as moderate, we actually find, that the *Jacobite* Party is almost entirely vanish'd from among us, and that the Distinction of *Court* and *Country*, which is but creeping in at LONDON, is the only one that is ever mention'd in this *kingdom*. Beside the Violence and Openness of the JACOBITE party, another Reason has, perhaps, contributed to produce so sudden and so visible an Alteration in this part of BRITAIN. There are only two Ranks of Men among us; Gentlemen, who have some Fortune and Education, and the meanest slaving Poor; without any considerable Number of that middling Rank of Men, which abounds more in ENGLAND, both in Cities and in the Country, than in any other part of the World. The slaving Poor are incapable of any Principles: Gentlemen may be converted to true Principles, by Time and Experience. The middling Rank of Men have Curiosity and Knowledge enough to form Principles, but not enough to form true ones, or correct any Prejudices that they may have imbib'd: And 'tis among the middling Rank, that TORY Principles do at present prevail most in ENGLAND.

Hume accounts for the wars of the Roses (1455 to 1485) between the houses of York (badge, a white rose) and Lancaster (badge, a red rose) in the *History*, ch. 22 (II: 456ff.); and for the contending Scottish dynasties Baliol and Bruce (in the 1280s and 1290s) *ibid.*, ch. 13 (II: 86, 91ff., and 190ff.).

The Jacobite rebellions of 1715 and 1719 lent credence to the belief in a Jacobite threat to the Hanoverian succession (George I had succeeded to the throne in 1714), and this made it easy for the government Whigs to tar all Tories with the Jacobite brush. Toryism, to be respectable, had to be absorbed into the Country opposition to the Whig Court establishment. Hume's remarks reflect the result.

With the emergence of a Whig establishment in the early years of the eighteenth century, more radical Whigs began to distance themselves from this merely 'nominal' and 'modern' Whiggism, seeing themselves as the 'real', 'true' and 'old' Whigs; see, for example, Robert Molesworth, *The Principles of a Real Whig* (1711).

9. Of superstition and enthusiasm (1741)

1 In the *History*, ch. 62 (VI: 142–6) Hume gives an inimitable account of how George Fox in the late 1640s and 1650s founded the sect known as the Quakers or, from the late eighteenth century, as the Religious Society of Friends. He stresses how belief in the presence of the spirit in each and every person led to an extreme egalitarianism in defiance of social mores and authorities – plainness of speech, dress and mode of living; complete pacifism; denial of all authority, including any priestly authority, and rejection of all signs of authority ('ceremonies, forms, orders, rites, and positive institutions. Even baptism and the Lord's supper ... [and the] holiness of churches'); assertion of the equality of all, including women, in divine worship. Satirising fanatical excesses, he also describes cruel persecution. For the eighteenth century the doctrines of the Quakers were those set out in the Scotsman Robert Barclay's *An Apology for the True*

Christian Divinity (Latin edn 1676; first English edn 1678 followed by many more), while the standard history of Quakerism was by the Dutchman William Sewel, *History of the Rise, Increase and Progress of the Christian People call'd Quakers* (1717). One of the most popular presentations was that of Voltaire in the first four of the *Letters on England.*

Taking literally Luther's idea of the priesthood of all believers, groups of people emerged in the middle of the sixteenth century claiming independence from all church establishments and insisting that the only true church was the local assembly or congregation of believers. The doctrines of the Independents – later known as Congregationalists – were formulated in the 1580s by R. Browne, H. Barrow and J. Greenwood. To the eighteenth century, the history of the Independents was first of all the history of a leading party in the resistance to Charles I and Archbishop Laud and of the dominant factor in Cromwell's army. It is in this connection that Hume gives his own analysis of the Independents and of their differences from the Presbyterians; see the *History*, ch. 57 (V: 441–3; see also section III of the appendix of this volume).

While Presbyterians agreed with the Independents in rejecting Anglican, let alone Catholic, ideas of church government (especially episcopacy), they subscribed to Calvin's strictly organised church run by the minister and elders of the congregation and eventually, particularly in Scotland, arranged into a hierarchy of church courts, ranging from the local Kirk session through regional presbyteries and synods to the national General Assembly. Hume gives brief accounts of early Scots Presbyterianism in the *History*, ch. 38 (IV: esp. 32 and 44–5).

2 Anabaptists comprised a variety of sects, especially Thomas Münzer's followers; the Swiss Brethren; Melchiorites (or Hoffmanites); the Hutterite Brethren; and Mennonites. They emerged in the 1520s and 1530s in Germany, Switzerland and the Netherlands. Their common ground was the rejection of infant baptism. Many early anabaptists held a doctrine of inspiration or inner light and rejected any authority of civil magistrates in religious matters; some went in for communal ownership, others for polygamy. As a consequence of such beliefs and practices they were persecuted by Protestant and Catholic authorities

alike. By the eighteenth century the remaining anabaptist sects were inoffensive pacifist groups, and the Mennonites harboured a liberal theology, but in historical perspective anabaptism was one of many synonyms for enthusiasm; cf. for example Henry More's analysis of enthusiasm, *Enthusiasmus Triumphatus*, pp. 15–29.

After Louis XIV's revocation of the Edict of Nantes in 1685 large numbers of French Protestants, mainly Calvinists, were driven abroad (see Hume, *History*, ch. 70 (VI: 470–1)), but the Calvinist camisards in the region of the Cévennes in southern France put up fierce armed resistance, especially in the years 1702–5, guided, as they believed, by divine inspiration. Apart from the presence in Britain of fugitives from these upheavals – known also as 'French Prophets' – the camisards were again a live issue during Hume's time in France from 1734 to 1737.

Among the most radical parliamentarians in the English Civil War (especially from 1645 to 1649), a group led by John Lilburne wanted to *level* all social inequalities, including inequalities of property. Although subdued by Cromwell, whom they did not consider egalitarian enough, they continued to influence radical political thought in England and by the eighteenth century their ideas, especially of natural rights and of the ancient constitution, were synonymous with radicalism.

Hume in the *History*, ch. 56 (V: 422–3) describes how the English Parliament in September 1643 negotiated the 'Solemn League and Covenant' with the reigning Presbyterians in Scotland, whereby the Parliament secured Scots support in the struggle against Charles I in return – as the Scots vainly believed – for the introduction of Presbyterianism in England and Ireland and securities for their own free Parliament. In ch. 63, as part of his account of the Restoration settlement for Scotland in 1661 (V: 167–70), Hume describes the re-introduction of episcopacy in Charles II's northern realm and, in ch. 64 (V: 223–8), the armed rebellion of the more fanatical Covenanters and their violent repression after the 'Conventicle Act' (1664) proscribed private heterodox worship of more than five people. The rebellion against the Conventicle Act was briefly resumed in 1679 by the extreme covenanting sect, the Cameronians, who were slaughtered by the duke of Monmouth at the battle of Bothwell Bridge,

22 June 1679, as described by Hume in the *History* ch. 67 (v: 371–4); cf. also Sir Walter Scott's portrait of the Cameronians in *Old Mortality*. The covenanting tradition in Scottish Presbyterianism goes back to the middle of the sixteenth century.

3 'DEISTS, in the modern sense of the word, are those persons in Christian countries, who, acknowledging all the obligations and duties of natural religion, disbelieve the Christian scheme, or revealed religion' *Encyc. Brit.*, 2: 413. 'LITERATI, in general, denotes men of learning; but is more particularly used by the Chinese for such persons as are able to read and write their language' *Encyc. Brit.*, 2: 976. The term was introduced, in the latter sense, by Robert Burton in *The Anatomy of Melancholy* (1621), see for example pp. 87 and 503. To the Enlightenment, the teachings of the ancient Chinese sage Confucius (551–479 BC) represented a truly rational and natural religion, well able to be the foundation of moral and civil life. This view had been prepared by the Jesuit missionaries' ill-fated attempt to present Confucianism as if it were proto-Catholic (cf. their presentation of Confucius' teaching in Latin [Anon.], *Confucius Sinarum philosophus, sive scientia Sinensis*, 1687), but it was Leibniz's correspondence with the missionaries (*Novissima Sinica*, 1697) and Christian Wolff's lecture on Chinese Philosophy, in which he likened Confucius to Jesus Christ (*Oratio de Sinarum philosophia practica*, 1721), and Voltaire's *Essai sur les moeurs*, ch. 2 (as well as several other works) that secured continued currency for the idea. Cf. also Malebranche's *Entretien d'un philosophe chrétien et d'un philosophe chinois*, 1708. A common source was the Jesuit Jean Baptiste Du Halde's *The General History of China* (1735), volume III of which contains repeated panegyrics on Confucianism, see especially pp. 293–303.

4 Molinism derived from the doctrine of the Spanish Jesuit Luis de Molina (1535–1600), according to whom God's grace is efficacious because God has a peculiar foreknowledge of man's free-willed compliance with this grace. The Dutch-born Otto Cornelius Jansen (1585–1638) introduced a strict Augustinian line into French theological debate in particular opposition to the largely Molinist Jesuits. The central point in Jansenism is that grace is irresistible, so that man is subject to a strict determinism

(which was variously interpreted). This led to frequent comparisons of Jansenism with Calvinism. Jansenism was repeatedly condemned and its adherents persecuted by the established church
in France during the seventeenth and eighteenth centuries.

10. Of civil liberty (1741)

1 In editions from 1741 to 1753–4 this essay was entitled 'Of liberty
 and despotism'.
2 This is not a quotation but gives the gist of ch. 23 of *The Prince*,
 though Machiavelli is concerned with the weakness called lack of
 prudence.
3 As prefect of the praetorians, the Roman emperor's personal
 guard, Aelius Sejanus (d. AD 31) was second only to the Emperor
 Tiberius himself, and he apparently tried to unseat him. The
 main sources are Tacitus, *Annals*, Book 4; Dio Cassius, *Roman
 History*, Book 57. 19ff. and Book 58. 4ff.; Suetonius, 'Life of
 Tiberius', *Lives*, esp. paras. 61–5. Cf. Ben Jonson's play *Sejanus
 His Fall* (1603). Cardinal André-Hercule de Fleury (1653–1743)
 had been tutor to the young Louis XV and from 1726 to his
 death he was the undisputed first minister of France in domestic
 as well as foreign affairs. But he was clearly the absolute monarch's first servant, much in the mould of earlier prelate-ministers
 like Richelieu and Mazarin.
4 Hume is referring to Xenophon, *Hiero*, 9.9: 'If commerce also
 brings gain to a city, [the award of honours for diligence in business would attract a larger number to a commercial career]'. For
 Plato's *Laws*, see for example Book VIII: 842d; 849a–50a and
 Book XI: 918a–21d.
5 See 'Longinus', *On the Sublime*, sect. 4.1–4. Longinus in fact puts
 the point in the mouth of a philosophical man of straw. Joseph
 Addison in *The Tatler*, No. 161, 20 April 1710, and *The Spectator*,
 No. 287, 29 January 1712; and Shaftesbury, *Characteristics*, 'Soli-
 loquy', part 2, sect. 2 (I: 154–5).
6 Antwerp was the capital of the marquisate of Antwerp which, in
 the early seventeenth century, was held by the absolute monarchs
 of Spain, while Amsterdam was the capital of Holland, one of
 the seven republics fighting to maintain their independence from
 Spain. Dresden was the capital of Upper Saxony and residence

of the elector of Saxony, while Hamburg was a free city-state. Concerning Ariosto, Tasso, Galileo, Raphael, Michelangelo and Rubens, see the biographical notes.

7 Horace, *Epistles*, 2.1.160 (in the Loeb edn). In context, the passage (underlined) means:

> 214   Greece conquer'd did the Conqu'ror o'ercome;
> Polish'd the Rude, and sent her Arts to Rome:
> The former Roughness flow'd in smoother Rhimes,
> And good facetious Humour pleas'd the Times:
> 218   Yet they continu'd long, and still we find
> 219   Some little Marks of the old Rustick Mind
> Some of the scurrilous Humour left behind.
>
> *Odes, Satyrs, and Epistles*, p. 317

Alexander Pope had just used these lines to make the parallel between Rome and Britain (and Greece and France) which Hume points to. In Pope's version, the two lines quoted by Hume sound like this:

> Tho' still some traces of our rustic vein,
> And splay-foot verse, remain'd, and will remain.
>
> [Pope], *The First Epistle of the Second Book of Horace, Imitated*, p. 20

8 Hume gives sharp characterisations of Temple, Bacon, Harrington and Milton in the *History*: ch. 71 (VI: 544); Appendix IV (ch. 49) (V: 153–4); ch. 62 (VI: 150–2), respectively. As a prose writer Thomas Sprat was mainly known for his history of the Royal Society and for a life of Abraham Cowley.

9 'POLICE. The regulation and government of a city or country, so far as regards the inhabitants' Johnson, *Dictionary*, art. 'Police'.

10 Sallust, *The Wars of Catiline*, 28.4.

11 Hume's reference in the text is to Cicero's 'Pro T. Annio Milone oratio' (Speech on behalf of Titus Annius Milo), sect. XIX, while the reference in the footnote is to Quintus Asconius Pedianus' commentary on the 'Oratio', sect. 2. Asconius' fragmentary *Commentarii* to Cicero's speeches were often printed as an appendix to the latter.

12 The idea of government by law, not by men, goes back at least to Aristotle's famous discussion in the *Politics*, esp. 1287a. But Hume undoubtedly has in mind Harrington: 'government (to

define it *de jure* or according to ancient prudence) is an art whereby a civil society of men is instituted and preserved upon the foundation of common right or interest, or (to follow Aristotle and Livy) it is the empire of laws and not of men' *Oceana*, 161. This is an explicit rejection of Hobbes's criticism of Aristotle on the point; *Leviathan*, 471.

13 Hume gives a character of Philip II of Spain in the *History*, ch. 39 (IV: 52–3) and ch. 45 (V: 6–7).

14 'FINANCER [sic]. One who collects or farms the publick revenue' Johnson, *Dictionary*, art. 'Financer'.

15 See Xenophon, *Ways and Means*, 3.9–10: 'But no investment can yield them so fine a return as the money advanced by them to form the capital fund ... But most of the Athenians will get over a hundred per cent. in a year, for those who advance one *mina* will draw an income of nearly two *minae* [guaranteed by the state], which is to all appearances the safest and most durable of human institutions.' Hume's ellipsis towards the end is peculiar.

11. Of the rise and progress of the arts and sciences (1742)

1 By statutes of alienation, Hume means the various measures to ensure that real estate could be alienated like other property and, presumably, especially Henry VII's (1457–1509) statute (4. Henry 7th, ch. 24) allowing entails to be broken. Cf. *History*, ch. 26 (III: 77).

2 Hume's account of the struggle for the title of Holy Roman Emperor and for dominance in continental Europe between Francis I of France and Charles I of Spain and of the latter's success in becoming Emperor Charles V (1519–56) is woven into the history of Henry VIII and Mary, i.e. the *History*, vol. III. The two monarchs are contrasted in ch. 28 (III: 126–7). The story of France's subsequent growth to preeminence from the late sixteenth to the late seventeenth century during the reigns of Henri IV, Louis XIII and his first minister Cardinal Richelieu, and Louis XIV, and Spain's decline from the glorious days of Philip II in the latter half of the sixteenth century through a succession of disasters under the subsequent Habsburg monarchs mentioned is a leading European theme in the rest of Hume's *History*.

3 The reference in the Loeb edition of Ovid's *Fasti* is 6.5–6.

4 Horace, *Epistles*, 2.2.187–9 (Loeb edn). The sense is:

That Genius only knows, that's wont to wait
On Birth-day Stars, the Guider of our Fate,
Our Nature's God, that doth his Influence shed,
Easy to any Shape, or good or bad.
Odes, Satyrs, and Epistles, p. 328, ll. 238–41

5 'BASHAW. A title of honour and command among the Turks; the viceroy of a province; the general of an army' Johnson, *Dictionary*, art. 'Bashaw'. 'CADI. A Magistrate among the Turks, whose office seems nearly to answer to that of a justice of peace' Johnson, *Dictionary* art. 'Cadi'.

6 While it is impossible to say with certainty who told Hume this, it seems likely that he is referring to Voltaire's account of Tsar Peter the Great towards the end of Book I of the *Histoire de Charles XII*, esp. pp. 55–8.

7 Tacitus, *Histories*, I. 37 (*Works*, II: 32): 'On his present situation he hath at once treated us, as if we were his Subjects, with oppression; and, as if we were miserable Strangers, with scorn.'

8 See note 9 to Essay 7.

9 This saying has not been located in Louis II de Bourbon, prince of Condé, his correspondence being the most likely source, nor in memoirs of his conversation.

10 See Plutarch, 'Life of Alexander', xxii.6 (*Lives*, VII, p. 287).

11 'Peripatetic philosophy, that system taught and established by Aristotle, and maintained by his followers the peripatetics, called also Aristotelians.' *Encyc. Brit.*, III: 468. 'Peripatetici ... derived this name from the place where they were taught, called *Peripaton*, in the Lyceum, or because they received the philosopher's lectures as they *walked* [Gr. *peripateo*]' Lemprière, *Classical Dictionary*, 463.

12 'Cartesians, a sect of philosophers, who adhere to the system of Des Cartes' *Encyc. Brit.*, II: 39.

13 After years of increasing 'licentiousness' on the London stage – not least of the political sort – the so-called Licensing Act of 1737 subjected all plays to censorship by the Lord Chamberlain.

14 While Hume's points about China are too general to identify a particular source, it is difficult to avoid the impression that he had read Jean Baptiste du Halde's recent extensive account in

Description géographique, historique, chronologique et physique de l'Empire de la Chine et de la Tartarie Chinoise.

15 'Eclectics, ancient philosophers, who, without attaching themselves to any particular sect, selected whatever appeared to them the best and most rational from each. Potamon of Alexandria [31 BC–AD 14] was the first of the eclectics: he lived in the reigns of Augustus and Tiberius; and being tired with the scepticism of the Pyrrhonians, he resolved upon a scheme that would allow him to believe something, but without being so implicit as to swallow any entire hypothesis' *Encyc. Brit.*, II: 466.

16 In the seventeenth and early eighteenth centuries the history of philosophy was generally written as the history of philosophical 'sects' or schools, often modelled on the ancient history of Diogenes Laertius. Along with the Peripatetics, the four sects mentioned here were the main ones used to organise the history of philosophy between the days of Plato and Aristotle and the predominance of Christian philosophy. Hume himself wrote essays characterising 'The Epicurean', 'The Stoic', 'The Platonist' and 'The Sceptic'.

17 See Jean-Baptiste Rousseau, *Poésies diverses*, 'Sonnet', ll. 13–14, in *Oeuvres*, II, p. 366.

18 See Arrian, *Anabasis of Alexander*, 1.12.4.

19 Sallust, *Bellum Catilinarium et Jugurthinum . . . I.E. The History of the Wars of Catiline and Jugurtha*, pp. 16–17 (14.2 in Loeb edn): 'all your catamites, cuckold-makers, rakes, that had spent their estates, in all the ways of luxury and lewdness . . .'.

20 Horace, *Odes, Satyrs, and Epistles*, p. 194, ll. 152–3 (*Satires*, 1.3.107 in Loeb edn):

For long ere Helen's time, the false, the fair,
A Woman was the stinking cause of War.

The reference is to Helen of Troy.

21 Lucretius, *De rerum natura*, 4.1165 (Loeb edn). In *Lucretius, His Six Books of Epicurean Philosophy*, p. 136, the passage in question was translated thus:

. . . grant the sweetest Face,
Grant each part lovely, grant each part a Grace,
Yet others equal Beauties do enjoy,

Yet we have liv'd before without this Toy:
Yes she is base, yet she perfumes, to hide
Her natural smell, her Maids on every side
Stand off, and smile, and waggishly deride.

As Hume plausibly hints, this was among the inspirations for some of the more scatological parts of Jonathan Swift's poetry; see, for example, *The Lady's Dressing-Room* and *A Beautiful Young Nymph Going to Bed*. The Earl of Rochester, one of the Restoration court wits, received a sharp characterisation in Hume's summary of the state of literature at the close of Charles II's reign; *History*, ch. 71 (VI: 543–4).

22 Cicero, *Tusculan Disputations*, 5.5.12: '*S.* [sophister] I *do not think* Vertue to be sufficient to Happiness. *M.* [magister, i.e. Cicero] But, truly, my Friend *Brutus* thinks it is so; whose judgment, without offence to you be it spoken, I far prefer before yours.' For Philalethes' friend, see Thomas Morgan, *The Moral Philosopher. In a Dialogue between Philalethes a Christian Deist, and Theophanes a Christian Jew*.

23 Books III and IV of Cicero's *De finibus bonorum et malorum* consist of dialogues between Cicero and the Stoic Cato (the Younger). Cicero's attitude is 'cavalier' in as much as he deals with the older man on equal terms and uses rather plain speech to gainsay him and to criticise his Stoic jargon; for example, *De finibus*, III. iii. 10–11.

24 See Polybius, *The Histories*, 18.4–7; Plutarch, *Lives*, 'Titus Flamininus', sect. 2 and 17.

25 Cardinal Wolsey figures prominently in Hume's *History*, chs. 28–30, and his character is summed up at III: 194. The accusation that he, in writing 'ego et rex meus', put himself above the king, was the fourth of the forty-four charges laid against him by Parliament; see Richard Fiddes, *Life of Cardinal Wolsey*, ('Collections'), pp. 216 and 234. Its fame is not least due to its repetition by Shakespeare in *Henry VIII*, III.ii.314.

26 See Plutarch, *Lives*, 'Life of Titus Flamininus', sect. 9.

27 See Shaftesbury, 'The Moralists: A Philosophical Rhapsody', II.ii, in *Characteristics*, II, p. 12.

28 See Pliny the Elder, *Natural History*, 14.14.91; Pliny the Younger, *Letters*, II.vi; Lucian, *On Salaried Posts in Great Houses*, 26, and *Saturnalia*, 17–18, 22, 32.

29 See Johann-Georg Korb, *Diarium itineris in Moscoviam perillustris ac magnifici domini Ignatii Christophori . . . anno MDCXCVIII . . .* (1700); hereafter the English translation, *Diary of the Journey into Muscovy*, II: 212–14.

30 [Guy Miège], *A Relation of Three Embassies from His Sacred Majestie Charles II to the Great Duke of Muscovie, the King of Sweden, and the King of Denmark. Performed by the Right Honble. the Earle of Carlisle in the Years 1663 & 1664*, p. 48.

31 Editions from 1742 to 1764 add the following paragraph:

> I must confess, That my own particular choice rather leads me to prefer the company of a few select companions, with whom I can, calmly and peaceably, enjoy the feast of reason, and try the justness of every reflection, whether gay or serious, that may occur to me. But as such a delightful society is not every day to be met with, I must think, that mixt companies, without the fair-sex, are the most insipid entertainment in the world, and destitute of gaiety and politeness, as much as of sense and reason. Nothing can keep them from excessive dulness but hard drinking; a remedy worse than the disease.

32 Xenophon, *Symposium*, II. 9–12. Presumably Hume has in mind Lucian's *Dialogues of the Courtesans*.

33 Horace, *Ars Poetica*, ll. 270–4, and *Epistles*, II.1.170–6.

34 In editions from 1742 to 1768 the text continues as follows:

> The point of *honour*, or duelling, is a modern invention, as well as *gallantry*; and by some esteemed equally useful for the refining of manners: But how it has contributed to that effect, I am at a loss to determine. Conversation, among the greatest rustics, is not commonly invested with such rudeness as can give occasion to duels, even according to the most refined laws of this fantastic honour; and as to the other small indecencies, which are the most offensive, because the most frequent, they can never be cured by the practice of duelling. But these notions are not only *useless*: They are also *pernicious*. By separating the man of honour from the man of virtue, the greatest profligates have got something to value themselves upon, and have been able to keep themselves in countenance, tho' guilty of the most shameful and most dangerous vices.

They are debauchees, spendthrifts, and never pay a farthing they owe: But they are men of honour; and therefore are to be received as gentlemen in all companies.

There are some of the parts of modern honour, which are the most essential parts of morality; such as fidelity, the observing promises, and telling truth. These points of honour Mr. ADDISON had in his eye when he made JUBA say,

Honour's a sacred tye, the law of kings,
The noble mind's distinguishing perfection,
That aids and strengthens virtue when it meets her,
And imitates her actions where she is not:
It ought not to be sported with.

These lines are very beautiful: But I am afraid, that Mr. ADDISON has here been guilty of that impropriety of sentiment, with which, on other occasions, he has so justly reproached our poets. The ancients certainly never had any notion of *honour* as distinct from *virtue*.

Hume is quoting, with near accuracy, from Addison's *Cato: A Tragedy*, Act II, sc. v.

35 See Shakespeare, *Pericles, Prince of Tyre* and *Othello, The Moor of Venice*; Ben Jonson, *Every Man in His Humour* and *Volpone*.

36 Hume was evidently fascinated by the poet–politician Edmund Waller, whose opposition to the course taken by Parliament in 1643 during the Civil War is outlined in the *History*, ch. 56 (v: 412–13), and whose character is given in ch. 62 (VI: 152). See also 'Of eloquence', *Essays*, pp. 106–7, and 'Of the middle station of life', *Essays*, p. 549.

12. Of national characters (1748)

1 The passage from Menander is fragment No. 554 in *Menandri quae supersunt*.

2 Dionysius of Halicarnassus, *Roman Antiquities*, 2.21.

3 Caesar, *The Gallic War*, 4.2 and 7.65; Strabo, *Geography*, 2.3.7.

4 Lucius Junius Brutus founded the Roman republic when in 509 BC he expelled the tyrant Tarquinius Superbus and, as consul, made the people swear never to allow a monarch in Rome again. But his own sons broke the oaths, conspiring to restore the Tar-

quins, and he is supposed to have condemned them to death and supervised their execution.

5 Hume probably remembered Plutarch's account of Themistocles' building of a fortified link between Athens and its port-city, Piraeus: 'And so it was that [Themistocles] increased the privileges of the common people as against the nobles, and filled them with boldness, since the controlling power came now into the hands of skippers and boatswains and pilots. Therefore it was, too, that the bema in Pnyx, which had stood so as to look off towards the sea, was afterwards turned by the thirty tyrants so as to look inland, because they thought that maritime empire was the mother of democracy, and that oligarchy was less distasteful to tillers of the soil' Plutarch, 'Themistocles', xix, in *Lives*, vol. II, p. 55. In other words, Hume was attempting a joke on the climatic theory of manners by drawing the parallel between Athens and Piraeus and the royal court at St James and the dockland area of Wapping: Piraeus and Wapping were equally notorious for radical politics (and loose women).

6 'ARMENIANS, in church-history, a sect among the eastern Christians; thus called from Armenia, the country anciently inhabited by them. There are two kinds of Armenians, the one catholic and subject to the pope, having a patriarch in Persia, and another in Poland; the other makes a peculiar sect, having two patriarchs in Natolia. They are generally accused of being monophysites, only allowing of one nature in Jesus Christ. As to the eucharist, they for the most part agree with the Greeks; they abstain rigorously from eating of blood and meats strangled, and are much addicted to fasting' *Encyc. Brit.*, I: 425.

The Society of Jesus was founded by St Ignatius Loyola in Paris in 1534 and recognised by Pope Paul III in a bull of 1540. See the *History*, ch. 41 (IV: 188). In Hume's time the Jesuits became increasingly controversial, and the order was suppressed in 1773 due to its resistance to centralised absolutism in France, Portugal, Spain and several Italian states.

The point made in Hume's footnote (d) is vividly illustrated by the case of the Jews under Richard I, *History*, ch. 10 (I: 378–9).

7 Livy, *History*, 34.17.

8 For Caesar's description of the character of the Gauls, see *The Gallic War*, esp. I.I and VI.11–20.

9 Berkeley, *Alciphron, or the Minute Philosopher*, 5.26.
10 Tacitus, *Dialogue on Oratory*, especially Aper's speech at xiv–xxiii.
11 Juvenal, *Satires*, 15.108–10 (Loeb edn). In the very free 1741 translation: 'but how could a poor Vascon become a Stoic? especially in the unlearned time of old Metellus? Now indeed the whole World receives the Benefit of the Grecian and Roman Literature; the Eloquence of the Gauls taught the British Lawyers how to plead, and the barbarous Island of Thule now talks of hiring a masterly Orator to instruct their Youth' *The Satires of Juvenal*, 15: 108–112. The Cantabrians, or Vascones were particularly uncivilised people in the Pyrenees.
12 Neither Guido Bentivoglio's *Relazioni in tempo delle sue nunziature* (1629) (trans. in part as *Historicall Relations of the United Provinces and of Flanders* (1652)), nor his *Della guerra di Fiandra* (1632–9) (trans. *The Compleat History of the Warrs of Flanders* (1654)) seems to make exactly the point mentioned by Hume.
13 William Temple, *Observations upon the United Provinces of the Netherlands*, p. 53.
14 See Caesar, *The Gallic War*, 1.40–2.
15 Diodorus Siculus, *Library of History*, 5.26. Hume's reference to Aristotle should be *Politics*, II.9.
16 See Quintus Curtius Rufus, *Historiæ Alexandri Magni Macedonis*, 5.1.37–8: 'the Babylonians in particular are lavishly devoted to wine and the concomitants of drunkenness'.
17 See Plutarch, *Symposiaca Problemata* [Table-Talk], I, quest. 4.2: '[A proper symposiarch] is neither easily overcome by drunkenness nor reluctant to drink, but like Cyrus, who said in a letter to the Lacedaemonians that he was in general more kingly than his brother [Artaxerxes] and besides found no difficulty in carrying a great deal of undiluted wine'.
18 See Athenaeus, *The Deipnosophists*, x.9 (434d): 'Darius . . . had an inscription written on his tomb: "I could drink much wine and yet carry it well." '

13. Of commerce (1752)

1 Hume's reference is Jean-François Melon, *Essai politique sur le commerce*, ch. 22, p. 289.
2 See Livy, *History of Rome*, 3.41 (7–10); 8.25. Dionysius of Halicarnassus, *Roman Antiquities*, 11.23 (1–2).

3 Thucydides, vii. 75.

4 See Diodorus Siculus, 2.5.

5 'Illyricum . . . a country bordering on the Adriatic sea, opposite Italy, whose boundaries have been different at different times' Lemprière, *Classical Dictionary*, p. 295.

6 'so strictly has our growth been limited to the only things for which we strive, – wealth and luxury.' Livy, *History of Rome*, 7.25.

7 The reference to Cicero, *De officiis*, should be 1.12 (37). In Polybius' *Histories* Hume is referring to iii.22–5, which present treatises of 509–8, 306 and 279 BC in which the two emerging superpowers of the Mediterranean attempt to regulate their competing interests, including that of 'marauding'. The problem was not under control until Pompey cleaned up the Mediterranean Sea in 67 BC. Piracy was also a serious problem for the maritime powers of early modern Europe and yet another point on which the modern world could be understood through parallels with the ancient. Indeed, the modern 'rovers' preferred some of the same bases as their ancient ancestors, including Algiers in Algeria and Salee in Morocco.

8 See Bacon, *Essayes*, 29, 'Of the true greatness of Kingdoms and Estates', pp. 92–3.

9 Virgil, *Georgics*, 1.123: 'sharpening men's wits by care'.

14. Of refinement in the arts (1752)

1 The title of this essay was 'Of luxury' in editions from 1752 to 1758.

2 'Tartary, a vast country in the northern parts of Asia, bounded by Siberia on the north and west' *Encyc. Brit.*, III: 887.

3 See Plutarch, *Lives*, 'Life of Cato the Younger', 24.

4 Hume is referring to events in 1494–5, when Charles VIII of France invaded Italy. Italian politics was dominated by a constantly shifting balance of power between the five main states (Venice, Milan, Florence, the Papal States and the Kingdom of Naples). A conspiracy of Florence and Naples in 1492 to conquer Milan led the Milanese ruler Ludovico Sforza to call for help from France, and Charles VIII was quite willing, as he thought he had a claim on the throne of Naples. The French were forced out fairly quickly, but the appetite of the large European monarchies for a slice of Italy had been roused. Hume is giving the

general drift of Guicciardini's account; for the size of the French army, see *the History of Italy*, I: 137 and 393. One of Charles's ministers stated exhaustion as the case against the war, pp. 389–94; and see p. 403.

5 Cardinal Jules Mazarin was first minister of France from the accession of Louis XIV at the age of five in 1643 until Mazarin's death in 1661. Thereafter no minister was allowed the kind of power wielded by Richelieu and Mazarin. Louis fought a succession of wars, all but the last of which figure in vol. VI of Hume's *History*: the first Dutch War, the 'War of Devolution', 1667–8 (ch. 64, pp. 201ff.); the second Dutch War, 1672–8 (ch. 65, pp. 256ff.); the War of the Grand Alliance, 1688–97 (ch. 71, pp. 498–9); the War of the Spanish Succession, 1702–13. Hume sketches Louis' character in the *History*, ch. 64 (VI: 216–7). The king purchased the Parisian house of one of his leading generals, Louis-Joseph, duc de Vendôme, and levelled it to create the Place de Vendôme referred to in Hume's note.

6 The source for Datames, a Persian general and governor in the 370s and 360s BC, is Cornelius Nepos, 'Datames'. See 6.6 (8).

7 See Plutarch, *Lives*, 'Life of Pyrrhus', sect. 16.5. Pyrrhus made his remark before defeating the Romans in the battle of Heraclea in Lucania, 280 BC. The following year he won again, at Asculum in Apulia, but this time it was his famous 'Pyrrhic victory' (*ibid.* 21.9).

8 See Machiavelli, *Florentine History*, I, ch. 39.

9 See Sallust, *The Wars of Catiline*, sects. 7–13. Hume is using some of Sallust's key terms. An aesthete, adulterer, upstart politician, disgraced senator, corrupt and tyrannical provincial governor, Sallust was also a notable historian who, in often celebrated and influential Latin prose, moralised about the traditional virtues of republican Rome and their increasing corruption in his own time.

10 This paragraph summarises some of the leading themes in Hume's account of the emergence of modern Europe. For his understanding of feudalism, see the *History*, ch. 43 (I: 203–4), ch. 11 (I: 437–8), and especially Appendix II (I: 455–88). For some of his analyses of the role of arts and commerce, see the *History*, ch. 26 (III: 76ff.); Appendix IV (V: 142 ff.); ch. 62 (VI: 148ff.); ch. 71 (VI: 537ff.).

11 See Bernard Mandeville, *The Fable of the Bees*, 'An Inquiry into the Origin of Moral Virtue' (I: 41–57); Remarks (F) and (G) (I: 85ff.); Sixth Dialogue (II: 341ff.), etc.

15. Of money (1752)

1 For Hume's analysis of English currency and wealth in the time of Henry VII, see the *History*, ch. 26 (III: 68).

2 The late war was that of the Austrian Succession, 1740–8. Hume's acknowledgment that the British army was small is politically significant, since to clamour for a further reduction and even abolition of the army was a constant part of the opposition campaigns against standing armies and for a militia.

3 The references in the footnote are: Tacitus, *Annals*, iv.5 and i.17.

4 See Plutarch, *Moralia*, vol. I, 'How a Man may become aware of his Progress in Virtue', sect. 7 (78).

5 Some twenty years later Adam Smith in a 'Digression concerning the Variations in the Value of Silver during the Course of the Four last Centuries', in the *Wealth of Nations*, I.xi.e–g, discussed the evidence for the role of Cadiz and Lisbon as the main places of import of bullion from the Americas (I.xi.g, 31–5).

6 Hume's references are Dutot, *Réflexions politiques sur les finances et le commerce* (1738); trans. *Political Reflexions upon the Finances and Commerce of France,* (1739); Melon, *Essai politique* (see note 1, Essay 13); Joseph Paris Duverney, *Examen du livre intitulé Réflexions politiques sur les finances et le commerce, par de Tott* (1740). While Dutot discusses the issues mentioned by Hume, it does not seem possible to pin down the exact points made in the footnote; cf. pp. 76–7, 94ff., 102ff., 116–7, 124ff., 136ff., 168ff., 188ff., in the English translation. Concerning the English recoinage and conversion of the old silver coins, on account of their being worn and clipped, to coins of full weight, the cost being covered by the government, see Martin Folkes, *A Table of English Silver Coins from the Norman Conquest to the Present Time*, London, 1745, pp. 116–26. The debate harks back to the great controversy about recoinage in England in the 1690s and, not least, to John Locke's strong plea for recoinage at full silver-weight, *Some Considerations of the Consequences of the Lowering of Interest and Raising the Value of Money*. It is difficult not to read Hume's cautious suggestion, at the end of the footnote, of a modest, stimulatory inflation of the coin as a rebuttal of Locke as well as of the three French theorists mentioned.

7 Maximilian, archduke of Austria, was elected king of the Romans in 1486 and Holy Roman Emperor in 1493. The French, trying to gain dominance over the Venetians in the Italian states, made

up the League of Cambrai with the Pope, Spain, France, England (Henry VIII), and the Emperor, and the ensuing war, 1508–13, prevented the Emperor from having the traditional coronation in Rome. His involvement in this war was, for Hume, as futile as many of his other initiatives. See Hume, *History*, chs. 27 (III: 88ff) and 28 (III: 121). Among the spectacular attempts by Maximilian to lay hands on money, Hume mentions his enlistment as an officer in the English army; *History*, ch. 27 (III: 102–3). Poccidanari, i.e. pochi denari, means very few funds.

8 As opposed to the East Indies. In the *History*, ch. 46 (V: 39) Hume explains the impact on early seventeenth-century England of the flow of bullion from the Americas since their rediscovery by Columbus in 1492. For a general view of the impact of the discovery of the new world, see also ch. 26 (III: 80).

9 See Pliny the Elder, *Natural History*, 33.50 (143). The point is that the same dinner set was circulating.

16. Of interest (1752)

1 'Guinea . . . A gold coin valued at one and twenty shillings' Johnson, *Dictionary*, art. 'Guinea'.

2 See Garcilaso de la Vega, *Commentarios Reales que tratan del origen de los Yncas* (1608 or 1609) and *Historia general de Peru* (1617); trans. *The Royal Commentaries of Peru, in Two Parts* (1688), Part II, Book 1, ch. 6.

3 See Dio Cassius, *Roman History*, 51.21.5: 'So vast an amount of money, in fact, circulated through all parts of the city alike, that the price of goods rose and loans for which the borrower had been glad to pay twelve per cent. could now be had for one third that rate.' Dio is talking of 29 BC.

4 See Columella, *De re rustica*, 3.3.9. The exact dates of Columella and his work are unknown, but Hume is probably not far out.

5 See Pliny the Younger, *Letters*, 7.18 (2) and 10.54 (1).

17. Of the balance of trade (1752)

1 See Plutarch, *Moralia*, vol. VI, 'On Curiosity', sect. 16 (523).

2 Hume gives details of this in the *History*, ch. 16 (II: 279–82), and Edward is characterised *ibid.*, pp. 271–2.

3 Joshua Gee was among the many who strongly criticised the free-trade clauses in the Anglo-French peace treaty at Utrecht in

1713. In the journal *The British Merchant* (1713) he and several others protested that the expected deterioration of the balance of trade would drain Britain of money and thus 'ruin' the country. He subsequently gave a detailed overview in a brief work which Hume presumably has in mind, *The Trade and Navigation of Great Britain Considered* (1729). The war Hume is referring to was that of the Austrian Succession, 1740–8.

4 Jonathan Swift, *A Short View of the State of Ireland* (1727–8), in *Prose Works*, vol. XII: *Irish Tracts 1728–1733*, ed. H. Davis, Oxford, 1955, pp. 3–12. Hume's paragraph is partly composed of phrases from pp. 9, 11 and 12 of the tract. This may account for the apparent paradox that 'out of [£500,000] the Irish remitted every year a neat million to ENGLAND' – reducing the former sum to less than £200,000 in three years! Swift's point is two-fold, that bankers had sent gold and silver to England to the tune of £300,000 in three years, and that the over-all trade balance between the two countries benefited England by about a million a year.

5 I.e. from the enthronement of Henry I in 1100 to the death of Edward VI in 1553.

6 Most European trading nations had created companies with more or less of a monopoly on their respective countries' trade with distant markets. Hume describes the general situation with the English monopoly companies in the *History*, ch. 45 (V: 20).

7 'ABSENTEE. He that is absent from his station, or employment, or country. . . . "A great part of estates in Ireland are owned by *absentees*; and such, as draw over the profits raised out of Ireland, refunding nothing" *Child's Discourse on Trade*': Johnson, *Dictionary*, art. 'Absentee'.

8 In the *History*, ch. 1 (I: 15ff.) Hume gives an account of the Heptarchy or seven kingdoms (Kent, Northumbria, East Anglia, Mercia, Essex, Sussex and Wessex) which the Saxons established in England between the departure of the Romans in the mid-fifth century and the attempts at English unification in the ninth century.

9 Jean Baptiste Dubos, *Les intérêts de l'Angleterre mal-entendus dans la présente guerre*, pp. 44–6, esp. p. 46.

10 Sébastien Le Prestre, seigneur de Vauban, *Projet d'une dixme royale*, pp. 26–7 and 31.

11 Hume is presumably referring to the severe financial difficulties in Genoa that arose after the Austrians pressed the republic to pay a huge war contribution in cash in 1746. The sum was largely paid out of the Bank of St George's deposits.

12 After an abortive attempt in Boston in 1681, paper bills were issued in Massachusetts in 1690 and soon after in other colonies, mainly in order to raise money for the colonial contribution to the wars of the Grand Alliance (1688–97) and of the Spanish Succession (1702–13). In contrast to Hume, modern historians think that coin was in very short supply in the colonies and that this led to the introduction of paper money, coining being forbidden outside London. Hard currency was favoured by the bigger merchants, while the landowners – as debtors – pushed for increase of the inflation-prone paper money. See R. C. Simmons, *The American Colonies. From Settlement to Independence*, pp. 171–3, 203–4 and 261–2.

13 See Plutarch, *Lives*, 'Life of Lycurgus', sect. 9 (1–2).

14 Hume is describing the Royal Bank of Scotland's revolutionary new cash credit system introduced in 1728 and soon imitated by the older Bank of Scotland and other banks.

15 Hume is writing of recent developments. The first bank in Glasgow was established in 1750.

16 One of the provisions of the Act of Union (1707) was the introduction of common currency – namely, the English – in the new Great Britain. For the two rounds of recoinage of Scottish silver coins to English in 1707 and 1708, see Folkes, *Table of English Silver Coins*, pp. 153–5. Hume's figure of 'near a million' is borne out by Folkes.

17 In the *History*, ch. 26 (III:66–8) Hume gives details of Henry's avarice and explains how the sum is arrived at. He also indicates his sources.

18 Hume is referring to the interval between the Persian wars of 490–479 BC and the second Peloponnesian war of 431–404 BC. Hume's references in the footnotes are as follows; Thucydides, ii.13; Diodorus Siculus, xii. 40; Aeschines, *The Speech on the Embassy*, sect. 175; Demosthenes, *Third Olynthiac Oration*, sect. 24; Demosthenes, *On the Navy-Boards*, sect. 19; Polybius, ii.62. For Henry VII, see note 20 below. In the *History* Hume gives a

helpful explanation of his method for comparing ancient and modern riches, Appendix I (I: 184–5).

19 Hume discusses the population and riches of Athens at some length and with copious ancient references in 'Of the populousness of ancient nations', *Essays*, pp. 427–37.

20 Hume's references in the footnotes are Livy, 40:45; Pliny the Elder, *Natural History*, 33.17 (56); and Velleius Paterculus, *Historiae Romanae*, 1.9.6. Hume is referring to the interval between the second and the third Macedonian wars (200–197 BC and 172–168/7 BC). In the former, Rome contained Philip V's ambitions and, in the latter, the Roman consul Aemilius Paulus demolished Philip's son's power and carried him and his enormous wealth, gained in part by plunder and piracy, in triumph to Rome. As for Henry VII, Hume discusses his avarice in the *History*, ch. 26 (III: 66–8); Henry was 'said to have possessed in ready money the sum of 1.800.000 pounds', which Hume estimates to equal 'near three millions in our present money'.

21 The details about Berne's finances are given by Abraham Stanyan, *An Account of Switzerland Written in the Year 1714*, p. 187, while the reference in the footnote is to pp. 5–6 of that work.

22 Appian, *Roman History*, Preface sect. 10. John Arbuthnot, *Tables of Ancient Coins, Weights and Measures . . .* , tables 23–4 and p. 34. In order to get the sterling sum mentioned, it must be noted that Appian is speaking of Egyptian talents.

23 See Jonathan Swift, *An Answer to a Paper called A Memorial of the Poor Inhabitants, Tradesmen and Labourers of the Kingdom of Ireland* (1728), in *Works*, vol. XII, p. 21.

24 During the wars of the League of Augsburg (1689–97), the Spanish Succession (1702–13) and the Austrian Succession (1740–8) some of the heaviest fighting took place in Flanders, which was left as a Spanish province on the formation of the United Provinces and was ceded to Austria in 1714. See also Hume's references to these conflicts in 'Of the balance of power'.

18. Of the jealousy of trade (1758)

No notes to this essay.

19. Of the balance of power (1752)

1 Xenophon, *Cyropaedia*, 1.5.2–3. Xenophon is obscuring the sequence and timing of events in Cyrus' reign over Persia 559–529 BC.

2 Book I of Thucydides' *History of the Peloponnesian War*, as indicated by Hume, is concerned with the shifting balance of power among the Greek city-states. The central overview at 1.89–117 explains how the predominance of Athens in the mid-fifth century BC caused the Peloponnesian League, formed by Sparta in the sixth century, to fight Athens from 431 until she was defeated and broken in 404 BC. The resulting domination by Sparta was resisted by Thebes, Argos and Corinth, and by 395 BC Athens was sufficiently recovered to join this alliance. In the battle of Leuctra in Boeotia in 371 the Thebans won a decisive victory over the Spartans. The Theban general Epaminondas went on to lead Thebes to supremacy until he was killed in the battle of Mantinea in 362 BC, in which Athens and Sparta were allied against the Thebans. Books VI and VII of Xenophon's *Hellenica*, or Greek history, deal with the changing balance of power and the battles from 374 BC to the close of this era in 362 BC – the battle of Leuctra at VI.4.4–15, that of Mantinea at VII.5.7–25. For Xenophon's analysis of the mixed motives of the Athenians after the battle of Leuctra, as reflected in Hume's remarks, see VI.4.19–20 and VI.5.33–52.

3 Following their indecisive defeat at Mantinea (see above), the Spartans remained restless and in 353 BC seemed to threaten Megalopolis, capital of Arcadia which was an ally of Thebes. The Megalopolitans sent ambassadors to Athens and in the Assembly's debate Demosthenes made one of his most intricate speeches: 'For the people of Megalopolis', in *Demosthenes*, I, pp. 440–59. Years later when the real danger against which he had warned became a reality with Philip II of Macedon's invasion of Attica, Demosthenes put together the alliance of Athens and Thebes that was finally defeated at Chaeronea, 338 BC.

4 In *The Constitution of Athens*, sect. 22, Aristotle describes the political role of banishment in Athens. Used against citizens considered dangerous to the public interest, it was normally for ten years and did not entail loss of property or citizenship. It was originally introduced, it seems, by Cleisthenes in 508/7 BC against

a relative of the would-be tyrant Pisistratus. During the fifth century BC, from being a security against tyranny it became a factional
political weapon. The name of a proposed exile was written on
an *ostrakon*, i.e. a broken piece of pottery, by the members of the
ecclesia or popular assembly. In Syracuse the transaction was done
by *petala*, i.e. olive leaves.

5   The politician and military commander Alcibiades was a leading
figure in Athens' empire-building in the late fifth century BC. In
415 BC he led an expedition to Sicily to achieve naval superiority
by reducing Syracuse, but was recalled to answer accusations of
sacrilege and profanation of the Eleusinian mysteries. When in
exile, he offered advice to Sparta – in the middle of the Peloponnesian War – and, while apparently conspiring with Sparta's ally,
Tissaphernes, the satrap (governor) of the Persian provinces in
Asia Minor, he offered the ambiguous advice mentioned by
Hume. See Thucydides, 8.46. Nearly a century later, when Alexander the Great died in 323, the Persian empire was in ruins
because, in Hume's view, the Persians had neglected to intervene
in time when Philip II of Macedon, had subdued the whole of
Greece, making it a unified force.

6   Hume is referring to the chaotic political situation in the huge
Macedonian empire on the death of Alexander the Great. His
generals fought and manoeuvred for predominance, and for long
Antigonus was the leading figure until defeated by a coalition of
his rivals in 301 BC at Ipsus in Phrygia. Another, Ptolemy, made
himself ruler over Egypt as Ptolemy I Soter, thus founding the
Ptolemaic dynasty that ruled until Rome conquered Egypt in 30
BC. The Achaean League was a proto-federal state founded by
the Achaean city-states of the Peloponnese in 280 BC to maintain
their independence from Macedonia. From 245 to 213 BC its
leading figure and general was Aratus of Sicyon. The reference
in Polybius is to Ptolemy III Euergetes, who in 225 BC switched
alliance as indicated; Sparta was then threatening to split the
League.

7   Editions from 1752 and 1757 have the following note:

There have strong suspicions, of late, arisen among critics,
and, in my opinion, not without reason, concerning the first
ages of the ROMAN history; as if they were almost entirely

fabulous, 'till after the sacking of the city by the GAULS; and were even doubtful for some time afterwards, 'till the GREEKS began to give attention to ROMAN affairs, and commit them to writing. This scepticism, however, seems to me, scarcely defensible in its full extent, with regard to the domestic history of ROME, which has some air of truth and probability, and cou'd scarce be the invention of an historian, who had so little morals or judgment as to indulge himself in fiction and romance. The revolutions seem so well proportion'd to their causes: The progress of the factions is so conformable to political experiences: The manners and maxims of the age are so uniform and natural, that scarce any real history affords more just reflection and improvement. Is not MACHIAVEL'S comment on LIVY (a work surely of great judgment and genius) founded entirely on this period, which is represented as fabulous. I wou'd willingly, therefore, in my private sentiments, divide the matter with these critics; and allow, that the battles and victories and triumphs of those ages had been extremely falsify'd by family memoirs, as CICERO says they were: But as in the accounts of domestic factions, there were two opposite relations transmitted to posterity, this both serv'd as a check upon fiction, and enabled later historians to gather some truth from comparison and reasoning. Half of the slaughter which LIVY commits on the ÆQUI and the VOLSCI, would depopulate FRANCE and GERMANY; and that historian, tho' perhaps he may be justly charged as superficial, is at last shock'd himself with the incredibility of his narration. The same love of exaggeration seems to have magnify'd the numbers of the ROMANS in their armies, and *census*.

The most prominent of the suspicious critics Hume refers to was the Dutch historian Louis de Beaufort, whose work critical of Livy and Dionysius of Halicarnassus had appeared in French in 1738 and in English translation in 1740. Cf. Gibbon's 'Essai sur l'étude de la litterature', sects. 27ff. The Gauls sacked Rome in 387 BC. Of early Greek historians of Rome, Hume is undoubtedly thinking in particular of Polybius who wrote in the second century BC. Machiavelli's *Discourses* deal with the first ten books of Livy's history of Rome, covering the period from the origins of the city to the third and final Samnite War, 298–90 BC. In the course of his account, Livy does indeed spill a great deal of the blood of the mid-Italian Aequi and Volsci, who expanded during the first part of the fifth century BC until the Romans and their Latin and Hernici allies finally threw them off the Algidus pass in the Alban Hills in 431 BC (Livy, iv. 26–9). During the Roman expansion across Italy in the fourth century the Aequi were virtually wiped out in 304–2 (Livy, IX. 45 and X.1) and the Volsci had already been subdued. The incredulity mentioned by Hume is attributed to the Romans (Livy, X.1 (8)).

8 Hume refers to the second Punic War (218–202 BC) and Hannibal's famous invasion of Italy. The eastern side-show referred to was a conference at Naupactus of the Greek and other eastern powers, attempting to find a solution to the struggle for the Greek peninsula between Macedonia and the Aetolian League of central Greece, an ally of the Seleucid Empire under Rome's enemy Antiochus III. Agelaus, an Aetolian general, addressed Philip V of Macedonia thus: 'it is evident even to those of us who give but scanty attention to affairs of state, that whether the Carthaginians beat the Romans, or the Romans the Carthaginians in this war, it is not in the least likely that the victors will be content with the sovereignty of Italy and Sicily, but they are sure to come over [to Greece] and extend their ambitions beyond the bounds of justice' Polybius, *Histories,* V.104.3. The subsequent treaty between Philip and Hannibal was made in 215 BC.

9 The reference is to three kings who all made themselves dependent upon Rome to further their own political and military ambitions. Massinissa, king of Numidia 202–149 BC, served Carthage against the Romans during the second Punic War (218–201 BC), but Scipio Africanus made him change sides, and he remained Rome's faithful ally until his death, playing a significant role in keeping Carthage subdued and in providing Rome with an excuse for the final destruction of the African power in the third Punic War, 149–6 BC, a feat that opened the way for the establishment of the province of Africa which eventually also swallowed up Numidia. Hume is suggesting that this *could* have been otherwise (the verbs 'barred' and 'preserved' are in the subjunctive mood). Massinissa is prominent in many of the eighteenth century's standard sources for Roman history, such as Livy, and Hume's

readers would immediately have associated his name with James Thomson's play *Sophonisba* (1730). The Hellenic kingdom ruled from Pergamum had a succession of three rulers called Attalus. The first allied himself with Rome to counter Macedonian power at the end of the third and beginning of the second century BC; the second continued this policy; and the third bequeathed his kingdom to Rome (133 BC). Among the rival powers of Pergamum in Asia Minor was Bithynia and, like its opponent, it tended to turn to Rome for assistance during the second century BC, especially under Prusias II (d. 149 BC), and eventually it too was bequeathed to Rome, by Nicomedes IV in 74 BC.

10 After its defeat in the first Punic War (264–41 BC) Carthage faced revolts from its mercenary troops and from dependent states and cities, for example Sardinia and Hippacritae and Utica in Libya, threatening its own existence. The ruler of Syracuse in Sicily, Hiero II, had supported Rome when it was threatened by Carthage; he now – in 237 BC – supported Carthage for the strategic reasons given by Polybius.

11 Charles I, king of Spain 1516–56, is better known as Charles V, Holy Roman Emperor 1519–56. He was of 'the house of Austria' – i.e. of the Habsburg dynasty – as paternal grandson of Maximilian I, and he was heir to Spain as maternal grandson of Ferdinand of Aragon and Isabella of Castile. His attempts to turn the empire into a universal monarchy form an important sub-plot in Hume's treatment of European politics during the reigns of Henry VIII, Edward VI and Queen Mary; see the *History*, chs. 28–37. The subsequent trajectory of Spanish power under Philip II (1556–98) until its disastrous eclipse with the *de facto* loss of the United Provinces under Philip III (1598–1621) in 1609 is pursued as part of Hume's history of the reign of Elizabeth, and the general European situation at the beginning of the reign of James I, when the balance of power was tilting towards France, as referred to in the text, is summed up in the *History*, ch. 45 (v: 6ff.).

12 Louis XIV's mother was a Habsburg (Anne, daughter of Philip III) as was his wife (Maria Theresa, daughter of Philip IV).

13 The Treaty of Ryswick ended the War of the Grand Alliance (Britain, the Netherlands and Spain) against France (1688/9–97) and secured French recognition of William III as king of England and Scotland. The Treaty of Utrecht (1713) settled the War of

the Spanish Succession (1702–13); there had been peace negotiations in Gertruydenburg in both 1708 and 1709. The Treaty of Aix-la-Chapelle concluded the War of the Austrian Succession (1740–8); there were peace overtures during the meeting of the Diet of the Empire in Frankfort an der Oder in 1743.

14 Tacitus, *Histories*, 1.37 (Loeb edn). In the old translation: 'he hath at once treated us as if we were his Subjects, with oppression; and, as if we were miserable strangers, with scorn' *Works*, II: 32. The speaker is Otho rousing the praetorian guard in a conspiracy to overthrow Galba who had succeeded Nero as emperor of Rome in AD 68. They managed to murder Galba but were themselves defeated and Otho committed suicide in AD 69.

15 The War of the Austrian Succession saw a shifting alliance led by France and Prussia and followed, among others, by Spain, Bavaria and Saxony whose respective rulers challenged the right of Maria Theresa to the Austrian crown. When Charles VI died in 1740 without male heirs, his daughter, Maria Theresa, queen of Hungary and Bohemia, claimed the Habsburg succession. At the same time, Frederick II (the Great) of Prussia successfully used this opportunity to conquer part of Silesia which was under Hungary. Faced with overwhelming opposition and poor resources, Maria Theresa managed to attract Britain as an ally and as a supplier of money and, indirectly, of troops. The troops came from Hanover, of which the British king, George II, was elector, but they were being paid for by the British, and it was – as usual in Hanoverian Britain – the transfer of funds to the monarch's other country that created opposition, first in Parliament and quickly outside. The beginning of the third parliament of George II from 1741 to 1747 was particularly 'factious' because it saw the fall of the long-serving prime minister, Robert Walpole, followed by a fragmentation of the Court–Whig interest.

16 The Bourbons were the complex Spanish–French dynasty descended from Louis IX.

20. Of taxes (1752)

1 Cicero, *Letters to Atticus*, 9.9. 'Andros' should be 'Aradus'.

2 *Account of the Netherlands*, p. 61. At the beginning of the quotation 'soil' should be 'food'.

3 Poll or capitation taxes, i.e. taxes paid by all citizens as individuals, were commonly proportioned either to the person's fortune or to his social rank. Hume considered such attempts at proportional equality arbitrary because the assessment of fortune was highly uncertain and because there was no clear correlation between rank and fortune. If however, arbitrariness were avoided by imposing the same sum on all tax-payers, one would get a situation not only of proportional inequality but of uncertainty because of the temptation on the part of rulers referred to by Hume. See the *History*, chs. 17 (II: 289) and 27 (III: 96) for discussion of historical cases of poll taxes that indicate Hume's reasoning. Adam Smith sets out the case in Humean terms in *The Wealth of Nations*, v.ii.j.

4 See Pieter Burmann, *De vectigalibus populi Romani*. Publicans were the tax-gatherers.

5 From the first edition of the *Political Discourses* in 1752 to the 1768 edition the paragraph up till this point reads:

> There is a prevailing opinion, that all taxes, however levied, fall upon the land at last. Such an opinion may be useful in BRITAIN, by checking the landed gentlemen, in whose hands our legislature is chiefly lodged, and making them preserve great regard for trade and industry. But I must confess, that this principle, tho' first advanced by a celebrated writer, has so little appearance of reason, that, were it not for his authority, it had never been received by any body.

Hume is referring to John Locke's *Some Considerations of the Consequences of the Lowering of Interest and Raising the Value of Money. In a Letter to a Member of Parliament*, pp. 87–98. The idea that all taxes ultimately were charges on land and the consequent idea of substituting all taxes with a single land tax found nourishment from every new tax invented and not least from Robert Walpole's excise scheme in 1733, which sparked further polemical and theoretical literature (cf. especially Jacob Vanderlint, *Money Answers all Things: Or an Essay to make Money sufficiently Plentiful among all Ranks of People . . .*). Somewhat similar debates were going on in France simultaneously, eventually feeding into the development of the physiocratic doctrine. But it was not until the 1760s that physiocracy was becoming widely recognised as a movement with a cause, provoking Hume to adopt fighting words like 'zealous' in later editions of the *Essays*. Mirabeau's *L'Ami des hommes* (with Quesnai's famous *Tableau économique* included as Part VI) came in 1760, his *Philosophie rurale ou économie générale et politique de l'agriculture* in 1763, Quesnai's *Analyse* in 1766, his *Problème économique*, I and II in 1766–7, P. S. Dupont de Nemours' important collection *Physiocratie* in 1768, etc.

21. Of public credit (1752)

1 The references in the footnotes are Plato, *Alcibiades* 1.122d–123b; Arrian, *Expedition of Alexander* 3.16 and 19; Plutarch, 'Life of Alexander', sects. 36, 37.

2 See 2 Kings 18:15–16 and 20:13; 2 Chronicles 32:27–9; Isaiah 39:2; etc.

3 The reference is Strabo, *Geography*, 1.13.

4 See Plutarch, *Lives*, 'Life of Caesar', sect. 35.

5 Hume is echoing Erasmus' *Moriae encomium*, which we know as *In Praise of Folly*. In Hume's time 'encomium' was commonly rendered as 'panegyric', as in White Kennet's translation, *Witt against Wisdom: Or a Panegyrick upon Folly*. In the prefatory letter addressed to Sir Thomas More (*Praise of Folly*, p. 83), Erasmus justifies his satirical work by pointing out that it had many classical precedents, among others mentioning the four cases indicated by Hume – except that Erasmus has Claudius instead of the latter's successor, Nero, an indication, among many, that Hume habitually made such references from memory. Apart from 'Folly' of Erasmus's own work, 'fever' is the goddess for fever, Febris, who is said to have been praised by Favorinus, whose work has not survived. The third case refers to the attempt by the Athenian orator Polycrates some time early in the fourth century BC to make a panegyric on Busiris, a mythical king of Egypt who, on oracular advice about how to end a drought, sacrificed all foreigners coming to his country and who was himself killed when he tried to make an offering of Heracles. This panegyric is now mainly known from Isocrates' ham-fisted attempt to better it in his 'Busiris'. Cf. Quintilian, *Institutio Oratoria*, II.17 (4). The fourth case, in Erasmus, is that of Seneca's *Apocolocyntosis* – 'gourdification' or 'pumpkinification' – *of Claudius*. This passage

in Hume is the most concrete evidence that he read *In Praise of Folly*. One would expect that he appreciated this work which is so closely modelled on one of Hume's ancient favourites, Lucian.

6 In editions from 1752 to 1768 the paragraph continues:

> And these puzzling arguments, (for they deserve not the name of specious) though they could not be the foundation of LORD ORFORD'S conduct, for he had more sense; served at least to keep his partizans in countenance, and perplex the understanding of the nation.

Hume is referring to the policy of Robert Walpole (since 1742, Earl of Orford) of using means from the Sinking Fund to keep taxes low. The Sinking Fund was established by Walpole himself in 1717 from savings on the financing of public debt when the market interest rate fell, and it was intended to be used to reduce the public debt over time. Eventually the accumulated funds proved politically irresistible, and in 1733 Walpole began using them to cover the reduction of other taxes, especially the land tax.

7 Editions from 1752 to 1768 add these paragraphs:

> There is a word, which is here in the mouth of every body, and which, I find, has got abroad, and is much employed by foreign writers, (Footnote: MELON, DU TOT, LAW, in the pamphlets published in France.) in imitation of the ENGLISH; and this is, CIRCULATION. This word serves as an account of everything; and though I confess, that I have sought for its meaning in the present subject, ever since I was a school-boy, I have never yet been able to discover it. What possible advantage is there which the nation can reap by the easy transference of stock from hand to hand? Or is there any parallel to be drawn from the circulation of other commodities, to that of chequer-notes and INDIA bonds? Where a manufacturer has a quick sale of his goods to the merchant, the merchant to the shopkeeper, the shopkeeper to his customers; this enlivens industry, and gives new encouragement to the first dealer or manufacturer and all his tradesmen, and makes them produce more and better commodities of the same species. A stagnation is here pernicious, wherever it happens;

because it operates backwards, and stops or benumbs the industrious hand in its production of what is useful to human life. But what production we owe to CHANGE-ALLEY, or even what consumption, except that of coffee, and pen, ink, and paper, I have not yet learned; nor can one forsee the loss or decay of any one beneficial commerce or commodity, though that place and all its inhabitants were for ever buried in the ocean.

But though this term has never been explained by those who insist so much on the advantages that result from a circulation, there seems, however, to be some benefit of a similar kind arising from our incumbrances: As indeed, what human evil is there, which is not attended with some advantage? This we shall endeavour to explain, that we may estimate the weight which we ought to allow it.

The references to Melon and Dutot are the same as those in Essay 13, 'Of commerce' (note 1) and Essay 15, 'Of money' (note 6). As for John Law, Hume is thinking of the incidental pieces which were collected in *The Present State of the French Revenues*.

8 Generally, East India Company shares traded higher than those of the Bank of England.

9 Melon, *Political Essay upon Commerce*, ch. 18, p. 329: 'The Debts of a State are the Debts due from the right Hand to the left, whereby the Body will not find itself weakened, if it hath the necessary Quantity of Aliments, and they are properly distributed.'

10 Archibald Hutcheson developed his scheme and the associated calculations in a number of pamphlets and speeches in Parliament between 1714 and 1719. These are gathered in *A Collection of Treatises relating to National Debts and Funds* (1721). The points mentioned are most clearly presented in 'Some Considerations relating to the Payment of the Publick Debts, May 14. 1717' (pp. 15–23), and 'A Proposal for Payment of the Publick Debts, and a Letters to His Majesty relating to the same ... January 14. 1714' (pp. 25–30).

11 Hume is referring to the financial effects of the civil war in France 1648–53, known as the Fronde. This was in large measure a

rebellion against the first minister, Cardinal Mazarin, who ruled on behalf of Queen Anne who was regent for her son, Louis XIV, during his minority. Louis succeeded to the throne at the age of five in 1643.

12 Cudgel-play was a fight with short clubs.

13 Hume must mean Louis XV's great grandfather, Louis XIV, as neither his father nor grandfather survived that monarch.

14 Tacitus, *Histories*, III.55(Loeb edn). To Hume's readers it suggested this: 'But the common herd were struck with these his acts of benevolence, so conspicuous and mighty: such as were extreamly foolish procured them at a price: with men of sense they passed for void, like all bounties which can neither be granted nor accepted without impairing the Public' *Works*, II, p. 194. Tacitus is talking of Vitellius' vain attempts to secure himself as Roman emperor; he was the third emperor to be murdered in 'the year of four emperors', AD 69.

22. Of some remarkable customs (1752)

1 The first reference is *On the Navy-Boards*, 17–22. Demosthenes' argument for reform of the taxation groups (boards) was made in 354 BC in connection with proposed preparations for war with Persia, a proposal he argued against. After the disastrous defeat, at Chaeronea in 338, of the Athenian–Theban alliance, which Demosthenes had promoted in an attempt to stem the Macedonian expansion, Ctesiphon wanted the Athenians to honour the great orator for his public services with a gold crown. Demosthenes' oratorical and political rival, Aeschines, prosecuted Ctesiphon for an unconstitutional proposal and in his charge criticised Demosthenes severely. Demosthenes' answer was the great oration in defence of Ctesiphon now commonly known as *On the Crown*. The trial was in 330 BC, and the most relevant part here is 102–9.

2 Hume's references are Plutarch, *Moralia*, 'Lives of the Ten Orators' ('Hypereides'), 849a; 'Longinus', *On the Sublime*, 15.10; and Demosthenes, *Contra Aristogeiton*, II.11 (803–4).

3 The bean senate referred to in Hume's footnote was the Athenian Council (*boulē*, as opposed to the popular Assembly), the 500 members of which were selected by lot from pre-selected mem-

bers of the city's tribes. Those who drew a white bean were elected.

4 At the end of the Peloponnesian War in 404 BC, a junta of thirty, including Critias, tried to impose an oligarchic constitution on Athens. Their design was eventually defeated and democracy restored. Three-quarters of a century later, after the defeat at Chaeronea in 338 BC and the accession of Alexander the Great in 336, that democracy was seriously at risk. Should Athens seek accommodation with Alexander, as the peace party of Aeschines argued, or continue the line of militant independence which Demosthenes had for long advocated? Were Macedon's favourable peace terms after Chaeronea to be seen as an encouragement of the former or as respect for the latter policy? Thus the choice referred to in note 1 above went to the heart of Athenian politics, and it was in this context that both Aeschines and Demosthenes tried to employ the central constitutional provision mentioned by Hume: Aeschines, *Against Ctesiphon*, 5–8. Demosthenes, *Against Timocrates*, 33 (710).

5 Plutarch, 'Life of Pelopidas', sect. 25, in *Lives* v.

6 The context of the three references is as follows. (1) When Philip II of Macedon in 349 BC attacked the Chalcidic League, the city of Olynthus in Chalcidice sought assistance from Athens. Demosthenes supported this in three speeches ('Olynthiacs') in the Assembly. In the First Olynthiac (19–20) he points out to the Athenians that they already have funds available, namely the Theoric Fund. Originally set up by Pericles to subsidise the participation of the poor in public festivals, both its social functions and its funding-base had gradually expanded until, probably in 354 BC, the orator Eubulus (a 'demagogue' in Demosthenes' and hence in Hume's eyes) managed to make it law that all the city's surplus funds should go to this fund and that it could not be used for military purposes. Demosthenes succeeded in getting the system abolished in 339 BC. (2) Athens could grant exemption from public services, including taxation, to people who had been particular benefactors of the state, and these exemptions could be hereditary. In 355 Leptines had put a law through the Assembly abolishing the system of exemptions. The following year two

315

hereditary exemptees challenged the legality of the law under the complicated legal-review system, and Demosthenes represented one of them. In the address 'Against Leptines' Hume's points are at 1–4. (3) The third case is also from the legal speeches of Demosthenes and was sparked off by a *graphe paranomon* aimed at suspending honours, promoted by Aristocrates, for a dubious political operator in Thrace. *Against Aristocrates*, sect. 86.

7 In the section in question, Shaftesbury discusses faction as an abuse of humankind's natural sociability and of the tendency to 'cantonise' in large states by creating smaller units: 'Thus we have wheels within wheels. And in some national constitutions (notwithstanding the absurdity in politics) we have one empire within another' *Characteristics*, 1: 76.

8 The registration, or *census*, of Roman citizens was the basis for both military service and taxation. In the military the *centuria* (in principle one hundred men) was the smallest unit of the legion and formed the basis for the assembly known as the *comitia centuriata* which according to tradition was instituted by the king Servius Tullius (578–535 BC). It represented the propertied classes and, with the advent of the Republic, had authority to elect the chief magistrates, to declare war, and so on. Its authority was originally subject to veto by the Senate. The *comitia tributa* (or *concilium plebis*) was the assembly of the common people (*plebs*) and excluded the patricians, though its decisions were valid for all citizens. It elected the tribunes, who presided over its meetings and the two plebeian *aediles* who administered public buildings, markets, the temples, the public games, corn supply, etc.

9 The two consuls were the supreme magistrates in both civil and military matters, while the praetors were the chief legal officers in the Roman republic. For the *aediles*, see the previous note.

10 Appian, *Roman History: The Civil Wars*, 3.27–30.

11 In the *History*, ch. 52 (V: 245–8) Hume gives an account of the trial and conviction of John Hampden for refusing to pay ship-money. Since 1634 Charles I had followed the old practice of levying taxes for the navy from coastal towns and shires, but in 1635 he extended this by decree to inland areas and Hampden, who was a leader of the Parliamentary opposition to the king, refused to pay the tax. His defence and conviction became rallying

points for the Parliamentary cause. Hume gives the character of Hampden, who fell in the Civil War in 1643, in ch. 56 of the *History* (v: 407) and modifies it in note DD to the volume (v: 574–5).

12 One of the great problems for Britain in her military and colonial efforts during the seventeenth and eighteenth centuries was to find sailors for the royal navy. While the large majority were recruited as volunteers, this never sufficed in times of crisis and war. Neither pay nor conditions attracted enough men. Successive governments therefore followed the ancient practice of 'pressing' or 'impressment', according to which the crown could force seamen to serve in the navy. The activities of press gangs from the navy's ships were always an extremely sore spot on Britain's collective conscience and led to heated debates in Parliament and the press about the justification of this blatant disregard for the liberties of Englishmen, their property in their own body, etc. Such debates raged with particular force in 1739 when the colonial war with Spain, known as the War of Jenkins' Ear, broke out, and in 1740 when the main war, that of the Austrian Succession, began.

23. Of the original contract (1748)

1 Hume's first two examples here may not be without a hidden agenda. Titus fascinated the eighteenth century because he was thought to combine exemplary virtue in his public office as Roman emperor with a character of private vice, at least before he became emperor. And Trajan, while accepted to be as nearly approaching the ideal of a constitutional monarch as the Roman imperial constitution would allow, was thought to have modified the persecution of Christians only at the suggestion of the younger Pliny, a humanity not, however, extended to the Jews. The Borgia Hume had in mind was undoubtedly Cesare, son of Rodrigo Borgia, alias the notorious pope Alexander VI. Cesare Borgia's name was as readily synonymous with the Machiavellian prince in the eighteenth century as today. Concerning Angria, see Defoe, *A General History of the Pyrates*, p. 124: 'Angria is a famous Indian Pyrate, of considerable Strength and Territories, that gives continual Disturbances to the European (and especially the English) Trade.' This century-old dynasty of pirates, about which several books were written in the eighteenth century, was finally subdued

with the defeat of Tulagee Angria in 1756; see Tobias Smollett, *The History of England*, Book III, ch. 5, sects. 41–2.

2 In the 1777 edition the following paragraph is added:

Yet even this consent was long very imperfect, and could not be the basis of a regular administration. The chieftain, who had probably acquired his influence during the continuance of war, ruled more by persuasion than command; and till he could employ force to reduce the refractory and disobedient the society could scarcely be said to have attained a state of civil government. No compact or agreement, it is evident, was expressly formed for general submission; an idea far beyond the comprehension of savages: Each exertion of authority in the chieftain must have been particular, and called forth by the present exigencies of the case: The sensible utility, resulting from his interposition, made these exertions become daily more frequent; and their frequency gradually produced an habitual, and, if you please to call it so, a voluntary, and therefore precarious, acquiescence in the people.

3 The so-called convention Parliament which was summoned by the House of Lords in January 1689 to settle the issue of the crown after the landing in England of William of Orange and the flight to France of James II is described in the *History*, ch. 71 (VI: 522ff.); see the excerpt in section I of the appendix.

4 In the *History*, ch. 17 (II: 321–2), Hume accounts for the Parliamentary 'election' to the throne of Henry Bolingbroke, duke of Hereford, following the insurrection against and the forced abdication of Richard II in 1399. In the next chapter he begins an account of the reign of Henry IV with some considerations of election versus heredity which are directly relevant to the points made in the present essay (II: 333–4). The issue recurs in Hume's account of the accession of Henry VII in 1485 at the end of the Wars of the Roses between the Houses of Lancaster and York; *History* ch. 24 (III: 3ff.). In both cases present possession was, in Hume's opinion, the real basis of sovereignty.

5 Tacitus, *Annals*, VI.14 (Loeb edn); *Works*, I: 222–3.

6 The 1777 edition adds the following paragraph:

Did one generation of men go off the stage at once, and another succeed, as is the case with silk-worms and butterflies, the new race, if they had sense enough to choose their government, which surely is never the case with men, might voluntarily, and by general consent, establish their own form of civil polity, without any regard to the laws or precedents, which prevailed among their ancestors. But as human society is in perpetual flux, one man every hour going out of the world, another coming into it, it is necessary, in order to preserve stability in government, that the new brood should conform themselves to the established constitution, and nearly follow the path which their fathers, treading in the footsteps of theirs, had marked out to them. Some innovations must necessarily have place in every human institution, and it is happy where the enlightened genius of the age give these a direction to the side of reason, liberty, and justice: but violent innovations no individual is entitled to make: they are even dangerous to be attempted by the legislature: more ill than good is ever to be expected from them: and if history affords examples to the contrary, they are not to be drawn into precedent, and are only to be regarded as proofs, that the science of politics affords few rules, which will not admit of some exception, and which may not sometimes be controuled by fortune and accident. The violent innovations in the reign of HENRY VIII. proceeded from an imperious monarch, seconded by the appearance of legislative authority: those in the reign of CHARLES I. were derived from faction and fanaticism; and both of them have proved happy in the issue: but even the former were long the source of many disorders, and still more dangers; and if the measures of allegiance were to be taken from the latter, a total anarchy must have place in human society, and a final period at once be put to every government.

7 For Augustus' testament making Tiberius his heir and successor, see Suetonius, 'Augustus', sect. 101, and 'Tiberius', sect. 23, in *Lives*.

8 The House of Lancaster, represented by Henry IV, Henry V and Henry VI ruled from 1399 to 1461, when the Yorkists (Edward IV, Edward V and Richard III) took over.

9 Paul de Rapin-Thoyras, *Histoire d'Angleterre*, 10 vols., The Hague, 1723–7. Rapin introduces the Franco-English problem

in 1328 as follows: 'Charles the Fair [IV of France] dying . . . without Male-Issue, and leaving Joanna his Queen big with Child, there arose a great Dispute concerning the Regency of the Kingdom during the Queen's Pregnancy. Edward [III of England] laid claim to it, as Nephew and nearest Relation of the deceased King: But Philip Son of Charles de Valois, and Cousin-German of the same King, maintained, he had an incontestable Right to the Regency. He founded his Claim upon the Salick-Law, which, in his Opinion, debarred the Females and their Descendants from the Succession to the Crown; whence he inferred that neither had they any Right to the Regency, in prejudice to the Male-Line' *The History of England*, vol. 1, book 10 (p. 411). After detailing the course of events, pp. 411–2 and 416ff., Rapin adds 'A Dissertation on the Salick Law, and the Dispute between Philip of Valois and Edward III' (pp. 446–52) in which he makes the sort of judgement indicated by Hume (pp. 451–2). Compare Hume's treatment of the same problems in the *History*, ch. 15 (II: 196ff.).

10 Drusus was son of the emperor Tiberius, born *c.* 13 BC; Germanicus was older, being born in 15 BC, but was not adopted by Tiberius until AD 4. Hume uses this example in the *Treatise*, III.ii.10, to make the point that the usual principles determining the 'objects of allegiance' in a state can become 'mingled and oppos'd'.

11 Hume gives a resumé of Book II of Herodian's *History*, which gives a detailed account of the bloody and confused events between the murder of the emperor Commodus in AD 192 and the seizure of power by Severus in AD 193.

12 The period is AD 238, when Gordian III was proclaimed emperor after his maternal grandfather, Gordian I. The latter committed suicide after a rule of twenty-two days when his son and co-ruler, Gordian II, was killed by the rebellious governor of Numidia. The quotation is from Julius Capitolinus, *Maximus and Balbinus*, 14 (6), and translates thus: 'In the meantime Gordian Caesar was lifted up by the soldiers and hailed emperor, there being no one else at hand.'

13 In his note Hume is drawing heavily on Boulainvilliers' 'Mémoires presentés à Mgr. le Duc d'Orleans, Regent de France pendant la Minorité de Louis XV', in Boulainvilliers, *Etat de la France*,

III: 502–90. The specific points are pp. 532–3 in Memoire IV, 'Touchant l'affaire de Mrs. les Princes du Sang'. Boulainvilliers talks of 'élection libre', rather than of contract.

14 Charles II of Spain was childless and with him the Spanish branch of the House of Habsburg died out (1700). In anticipation of this, more distant relations laid claim to the Spanish throne: Louis XIV of France (on behalf of his grandson), the Emperor Leopold I (on behalf of his second son) and the Electoral Prince of Bavaria. It was unacceptable to Britain and Holland, however, that the Spanish crown should be joined to that of either France or Austria, as this would undermine the European balance of power. In the intense diplomatic efforts to sort out this situation the will of Charles played a significant role. He first settled the whole of the inheritance on the Bavarian prince, aged seven, but he died a few months later (1699). Charles then made a new will, making the French king's grandson, Philip of Anjou, sole heir. Britain saw this as a contravention of previous treaty obligations on Louis' part, and thus began the great War of the Spanish Succession in 1702.

15 The first italicised passage is an almost accurate quotation from *Treatise of Government*, II, sect. 90, while the second is strung together, with a couple of words added, from the sections indicated.

16 *Crito* from 50a.

17 Greek and Latin, respectively, for 'to strive for novelty', meaning in general political novelty.

24. Of passive obedience (1748)

1 As so often in connection with justice – for example, in the second *Inquiry*, sect. 147 – Hume adopts topoi from traditional natural law literature, in the first case from the common discussions of the sovereign's eminent domain over the rights of citizens in cases of extreme necessity (see for example Samuel Pufendorf, *Law of Nature and Nations*, VIII, 5, vii); in the second case from the law of war relating to neutral states (see for example Hugo Grotius, *Rights of War and Peace*, II, 2, viff.). Both issues arose out of the general discussions of justice and necessity that form an important part of the background to Hume's theory of justice in the *Treatise*

and the second *Inquiry*; see esp. Pufendorf, *Law of Nature and Nations*, II, 6, vi; Francis Hutcheson, *Short Introduction to Moral Philosophy*, II, ch. 16, and *System of Moral Philosophy*, II, ch. 17.

2 Cicero said it in *De legibus*, III, 3 (8), and subsequently it has been endlessly repeated.

3 Nero's many-sided misrule led to a series of rebellions in the provinces; in Britain in AD 60, in Judaea from 66, and in 68 in Gaul, Spain and Africa. He committed suicide in 68. See Suetonius, 'Nero', in *Lives*. The Philip referred to is Philip II of Spain during whose reign the Dutch provinces began their long revolt, in 1568; the supposedly converted Moslems in Spain – the Moriscos – also rose in 1569–71; and as king of Portugal (from 1580) Philip had to fight insurrections of the Portugese in 1583 and 1589.

4 Hume is here touching on some of the leading themes of the Stuart volume of his *History*.

25. Of the coalition of parties (1758)

1 Hume is referring to the Long Parliament, i.e. Charles I's fifth Parliament which was called in 1640 and not formally dissolved until the Restoration of the monarchy with Charles II in 1660. Cf. the *History*, vol. V from ch. 54. For the hypothetical debate between Royalists and Parliamentarians in the 1640s that follows, see appendix, section II. The present essay was first published in 1758 and is thus very close to the *History*.

2 The Tudors came to the throne with the accession of Henry VII in 1485, about 160 years before this imaginary debate in the Long Parliament. A similar time elapsed between the end of the Roman Republic with the accession of Augustus as emperor in 27 BC and the reign of the emperor Hadrian in AD 117–38.

3 In the *History*'s overview of Henry's reign in ch. 26 (III: 73–4) Hume is much more willing to admit that the king extended the powers of the crown.

4 The Plantagenet dynasty, which was descended from the counts of Anjou, ruled England from the accession of Henry II in 1154 to the forced abdication of Richard II in 1399. The Houses of Lancaster and York, which vied for the crown through the fifteenth century until the death of Richard III in 1485, were branches of the Plantagenet family. The Tudors ruled from 1485

(Henry VII) until the death of Elizabeth in 1603; and the Stuarts from 1603 (James I) until the departure of James II at the Revolution in 1688.

5 Editions from 1758 to 1770 add this note:

The author believes that he was the first writer who advanced that the family of TUDOR possessed in general more authority than their immediate predecessors: An opinion, which, he hopes, will be supported by history, but which he proposes with some diffidence. There are strong symptoms of arbitrary power in some former reigns, even after signing of the charters. The power of the crown in that age depended less on the constitution than on the capacity and vigour of the prince who wore it.

This thesis proved to be one of the most controversial in Hume's reading of English history because, as he intended, it lent substance to his most central and disputed claim, that the Stuarts were not the absolutist innovators and corruptors of the English constitution portrayed in standard Whig historiography.

6 In the *History*, ch. 11 (I: 442–8) Hume gives a detailed account of the Great Charter, signed by King John on 15 June 1215 at Runnymede in an attempt to appease the rebellious barons.

7 William Camden, *Annales rerum Anglicarum et Hibernicarum, regnante Elizabetha* (1615–25); translated as *The Historie of the most renowned and victorious princesse Elizabeth, late Queen of England*, 1635. Cf. Hume's characterisation of Camden's work in the *History*, Appendix IV (V: 154).

26. Of the Protestant succession (1752)

1 Editions from 1752 to 1768 add, either in the text or in a note:

King JAMES told his parliament plainly, when they meddled in state affairs, *Ne sutor ultra crepidam*. He used also, at his table, in promiscuous companies, to advance his notions, in a manner still more undisguised: As we may learn from a story told in the life of Mr. WALLER, and which that poet used frequently to repeat. When Mr. WALLER was young, he had the curiosity to go to court; and he stood in the circle, and saw King JAMES dine, where, amongst other company, there sat at table two bishops. The King, openly and aloud, proposed this question, *Whether he might not take his subjects money, when he had occasion for it, without all this formality of parliament?* The one bishop readily replied, *God forbid you should not: For you are the breath of our nostrils.* The other bishop declined answering, and said he was not skilled in parliamentary cases: But upon the King's urging him, and saying he would admit of no evasion, his lordship replied very pleasantly, *Why, then, I think your majesty may lawfully take my brother's money: For he offers it.* In Sir WALTER RALEIGH'S preface to the History of the World, there is this remarkable passage. PHILIP II. *by strong hand and main force, attempted to make himself not only an* absolute monarch *over the* NETHERLANDS, *like unto the kings and sovereigns of* ENGLAND *and* FRANCE; *but* Turk-like, *to tread under his feet all their natural and fundamental laws, privileges, and antient rights.* SPENSER, speaking of some grants of the ENGLISH kings to the IRISH corporations, says, "All which, tho', at the time of their first grant, they were tolerable, and perhaps reasonable, yet now are most unreasonable and inconvenient. But all these will easily be cut off with the superior power of her majesty's prerogative, against which her own grants are not to be pleaded or inforced" *State of* IRELAND, p. 1537. Edit. 1706.

As these were very common, if not, perhaps, the universal notions of the times, the two first princes of the house of STUART were the more excusable for their mistake. And RAPIN, suitable to his usual malignity and partiality, seems to treat them with too much severity, upon account of it.

Ne sutor ultra crepidam is usually rendered as 'cobbler, stick to your last!' Ascribed to Apelles (*c.* 325 BC), in Pliny the Elder, *Natural History*, 35.10.38, sect. 85. Hume uses this illustration also in the *History*, ch. 48 (v: 91).
The anonymous Life of Edmund Waller first appeared in Waller, *Poems, &c.* in 1711, pp. i–lxxxii. Hume is paraphrasing from pp. viii–ix. The two bishops were Dr Neile of Durham and Dr Andrewes of Winchester, respectively, and the date is given as 30 January 1621. Hume recounts the same story in the *History*, ch. 47 (v: 60).

The reference to Walter Ralegh is *The History of the World*, I: xxvi. Cf. the *History*, Appendix 4 (V: 154) for Hume's assessment of Ralegh's *History*.

The final quotation is in the modern edition pp. 30–1. The majesty in question was Elizabeth I.

2 There were Jacobite rebellions in 1715–6 and in 1745–6, attempting to re-establish the Stuarts on the British throne. There were abortive attempts at insurrection of a similar nature in 1708 and 1719, and in 1722 the Tory bishop Atterbury attempted a Jacobite conspiracy. In 1696 a plot to assassinate William III was disclosed.

3 For Hume's account of the Parliament that invited Charles II to return from exile in France in 1660 and thus restored the monarchy, see the *History*, ch. 42 (V: 138–9). Charles II was the eldest son of Charles I; the duke of York was the second son and succeeded as James II in 1685; the duke of Gloucester was the youngest; he died at the age of twenty immediately after the Restoration. Their grandfather was James I.

4 Editions from 1752 to 1768 continue with this paragraph:

The advantages which result from a parliamentary title, preferably to an hereditary one, tho' they are great, are too refined ever to enter into the conception of the vulgar. The bulk of mankind would never allow them to be sufficient for committing what would be regarded as an injustice to the prince. They must be supported by some gross, popular, and familiar topics; and wise men, though convinced of their force, would reject them, in compliance with the weakness and prejudices of the people. An incroaching tyrant or deluded bigot alone, by his misconduct, is able to enrage the nation, and render practicable what was always perhaps desirable.

5 Editions from 1752 to 1768 continue with this paragraph:

In the last war, it has been of service to us, by furnishing us with a considerable body of auxiliary troops, the bravest and most faithful in the world. The Elector of HANOVER is the only considerable prince in the empire, who has pursued no separate end, and has raised up no stale pretensions, during the late commotions of EUROPE; but has acted, all along, with the dignity of a King of BRITAIN. And ever since the accession of that family, it would be difficult to show any harm we have ever received from the electoral dominions, except that short disgust in 1718, with CHARLES XII., who, regulating himself by maxims very different from those of other princes; made a personal quarrel of every public inquiry.

George I and George II both maintained a keen interest in their home country, the Electorate of Hanover, which made them Electors in the Holy Roman Empire. This role was occasionally difficult to reconcile with their kingship of Britain, and, even when not, the Country opposition (and others) suspected them of favouring the interests of Hanover and, not least, of subsidising Hanover with British tax-payers' money. This controversy broke out with some vehemence, especially in 1742–3, during the War of the Austrian Succession, which is the one Hume refers to. Concerning the pretenders to the Austrian crown, see note 15 to Essay 19 above. During the Great Nordic War (1700–21) Britain supported an alliance of Russia, Poland and Denmark which tried to confine Swedish dominance in the Baltic and in northern Germany, a matter of crucial importance to Hanover. British disgust with Charles XII of Sweden was particularly high in 1717–18 because the latter was involved in an imaginative intrigue to restore the Pretender by an invasion of Britain. Charles was killed on a military campaign in Norway – which was under the Danish crown – in December 1718 before anything came of this. Austria was generally considered a natural ally in Britain's attempts to counter-balance France.

6 Editions from 1752 to 1768 continue:

The conduct of the SAXON family, where the same person can be a Catholic King and a Protestant Elector, is, perhaps, the first instance, in modern times, of so reasonable and prudent a behaviour. And the gradual progress of the Catholic superstition does, even there, prognosticate a speedy alteration: After which, 'tis justly to be apprehended, that persecutions will put a speedy period to the Protestant religion in the place of its nativity.

When Augustus II, Elector of Saxony, was elected king of Poland in 1697, he converted to Catholicism, yet remained on the Protestant side in the labyrinthine politics of the Empire. He was succeeded in both positions by his son Augustus III, 1734–63. Addison concludes a discussion of the British angle on this problem – namely that the Stuart pretenders were Catholics – with the following declaration: 'In short, if there be any political Maxim, which may be depended upon as sure and infallible, this is one; that it is impossible for a Nation to be happy, where a People of the Reform'd Religion are govern'd by a King that is a Papist' (*The Freeholder*, XLIII; pp. 230–1). This was written one and a half years after the accession of the first Hanoverian king, George I and six months after the Pretender made a (futile) landing in Scotland in December 1715. By the 'nativity' of Protestantism Hume refers to Martin Luther, who was born in Saxony; and it was there, in the city of Wittenberg, that he nailed his ninety-five theses to the door of the castle-church in 1517; cf. Hume's *History*, ch. 29 (III: 138ff.).

7 Editions H to P continue:

> For my part, I esteem liberty so invaluable a blessing in society, that whatever favours its progress and security, can scarce be too fondly cherished by every one who is a lover of human kind.

27. Idea of a perfect commonwealth (1752)

1 Hume is probably referring to the debates about how to apply the study of curves defined by various forms of mechanical motions to the design of ships. In the early years of the century the *Journal des Sçavans* carried a number of contributions by Johann Bernoulli, L'Hôpital, Huygens and several others.

2 James Harrington's *Commonwealth of Oceana* was published in 1656 during the Commonwealth, i.e. the republican interregnum between the execution of Charles I (1649) and the Restoration of Charles II (1660). The work combines a number of ancient political ideas, often as interpreted by Renaissance writers such as Machiavelli, to formulate a theory and a model of republican government. The basic propositions are that citizenship depends upon man's ability to secure his independence by bearing arms and thus by owning sufficient permanent property, i.e. land, to support himself and his arms. A country

in which the people are citizens must thus be one in which property is not concentrated in the hands of one (monarchy) or a few ('mixed monarchy', i.e. aristocracy). Such a 'commonwealth' must secure a continued dispersal of property in land through an 'agrarian law' that fixes maximum landholdings and thus prevents regression to feudalism. Second it must have a constitution that guards against a corrupting monopolisation of offices; hence all members of the three layers of government must be elected and their terms of office must be limited by rotation. One third of the senate, which is to be an 'aristocracy' of talent, and of the popular assembly, which represents the citizenry at large, must be renewed every year, making each term of office three years. The members of the executive arm, the magistrates, are elected for either one or three years, and cannot be re-elected until after an interval out of office. Finally there must be a separation of powers whereby the senate alone can frame legislative bills, the popular assembly alone can vote on such bills, and the magistrates carry them into effect. During the later seventeenth and early eighteenth century these republican ideas were modified into a radical, critical reform programme for the British 'mixed' constitution, and elements of these ideas were adopted by the Country opposition.

The Lords of the Articles were a committee of the Scottish parliament stemming from the early fifteenth century. They were abolished by the Covenanters in 1640 (cf. *History*, ch. 55 (v: 333)), restored in 1661 and finally abolished in 1690.

The reference in Machiavelli is *The Discourses*, III.1. The section heading reads in the modern translation, 'In Order that a Religious Institution or a State should long survive it is essential that it should frequently be Restored to its original principles', *Discourses*, p. 385.

3 Although Hume's formulation seems to imply a reference to the Venetian senate, he is likely to have meant the Great Council, since this chose most magistrates and had an infinitely more complex system of voting than had the senate. The Venetian system was adapted by Harrington for his *Oceana*. Cf. Limojon de Saint Didier, *The City and Republic of Venice*, Pt II, pp. 110–14, and Amelott de la Houssaie, *The History of the Government of Venice*.

Wherein the Policies, Councils, Magistrates, and Laws of that State are fully related; and the use of the Balloting Box exactly described, pp. 7ff. and pp. 39–41.

4 Hume probably derived his knowledge of the Swiss system from Stanyan, *Account of Switzerland*, ch. 10, where the case of Berne's militia based on universal enrolment of all men between the ages of sixteen and sixty is described in some detail. Rousseau gives a more fanciful account in *Considerations on the Government of Poland*, pp. 240–1.

5 *Oceana*, pp. 172–3.

6 Cardinal de Retz, *Mémoires*, in *Oeuvres*, II, p. 422.

7 For the earnings of the Dutch 'burgo-masters', see Temple, *Observations upon . . . the Netherlands*, p. 31.

8 Hume describes the 'Instrument of Government' which formed the constitutional basis for the Protectorate (Dec. 1653–May 1659) in the *History*, ch. 61 (VI: 68–9). At the beginning of the eighteenth century the House of Commons had 513 members, and the Act of Union, which joined England and Scotland as Great Britain in 1707, added 45 Scots members. In England the qualification for voting was a freehold of forty shillings in the counties; in the boroughs the franchise varied significantly, ranging from voting by the corporation, through householder voting, to voting by freemen. In Scotland the vote was even more restricted, to feudal owners in the country and to corporations in the boroughs.

9 At the turn of the century the House of Lords had 220 members. The Act of Union provided for 16 Scots peers to be elected by and from the nearly 150-strong Scots peerage. These elections were generally heavily influenced by the crown, and the Scots peers were commonly considered stooges of the government, which is probably what Hume is referring to. The appointment of bishops was normally political and the appointees were expected to pay their political debts by their votes in the Upper House. Moreover, the crown's power to create new peers was a useful tool in securing the Lords' support. Furthermore, ministers in the eighteenth century often sat in the Upper House. For all these reasons Hume considered the House of Lords 'frail' as an independent force in the constitution.

10 Editions from 1752 to 1768 continue:

> It is evident, that this is a mortal distemper in the BRITISH government, of which it must at last inevitably perish. I must, however, confess, that SWEDEN seems, in some measure, to have remedied this inconvenience, and to have a militia, with its limited monarchy, as well as a standing army, which is less dangerous than the BRITISH.

> Sweden had a limited monarchy, in which the nobility largely predominated, from 1718 to 1772 when Gustavus III re-established absolutism by a military *coup*.

11 The poet in question remains unidentified.

Appendix: Excerpts from Hume's History of England

1 In this passage Hume states the fundamental principles of Parliament and of the king, Charles I, in the debates about the Petition of Right in 1628.

2 This is Hume's account of the Convention Parliament that began meeting on 22 January 1689, followed by his perspective on the consequences of the Revolution settlement.

3 This is a lengthy note which refers to king Charles I's declaration explaining his dissolution of the Short Parliament (April–May 1640) which refused to vote him the money he needed to conduct the Bishops' Wars (1639–40) against the Scots Presbyterians.

4 Hume outlines the dilemmas facing England after the execution of Charles I in 1649.

5 Hume is referring to James I and the year is 1604. Hume's references to his sources have been omitted.

6 Hume's discussion of the politico-religious situation in this and the following excerpt refers to the late 1620s and early 1630s. William Laud had become bishop of London in 1628 and became archbishop of Canterbury in 1633. Hume's references to his sources have been omitted.

Index

Index

Index

Index

Index

Index

Cambridge Texts in the History of Political Thought

Titles published in the series thus far

Aristotle *The Politics* (edited by Stephen Everson)
Arnold *Culture and Anarchy and other writings* (edited by Stefan Collini)
Bakunin *Statism and Anarchy* (edited by Marshall Shatz)
Baxter *A Holy Commonwealth* (edited by William Lamont)
Bentham *A Fragment on Government* (introduction by Ross Harrison)
Bernstein *The Preconditions of Socialism* (edited by Henry Tudor)
Bodin *On Sovereignty* (edited by Julian H. Franklin)
Bossuet *Politics Drawn from the Very Words of Holy Scripture* (edited by Patrick Riley)
Burke *Pre-Revolutionary Writings* (edited by Ian Harris)
Cicero *On Duties* (edited by M. T. Griffin and E. M. Atkins)
Constant *Political Writings* (edited by Biancamaria Fontana)
Diderot *Political Writings* (edited by John Hope Mason and Robert Wokler)
The Dutch Revolt (edited by Martin van Gelderen) Filmer *Patriarcha and Other Writings* (edited by Johann P. Sommerville)
Gramsci *Pre-Prison Writings* (edited by Richard Bellamy)
Guicciardini *Dialogue on the Government of Florence* (edited by Alison Brown)
Harrington *A Commonwealth of Oceana* and *A System of Politics* (edited by J. G. A. Pocock)
Hegel *Elements of the Philosophy of Right* (edited by Allen W. Wood and H. B. Nisbet)
Hobbes *Leviathan* (edited by Richard Tuck)
Hobhouse *Liberalism and Other Writings* (edited by James Meadowcroft)
Hooker *Of the Laws of Ecclesiastical Polity* (edited by A. S. McGrade)
Hume *Political Essays* (edited by Knud Haakonssen)
John of Salisbury *Policraticus* (edited by Cary Nederman)
Kant *Political Writings* (edited by H. S. Reiss and H. B. Nisbet)
Knox *On Rebellion* (edited by Roger A. Mason)
Lawson *Politica sacra et civilis* (edited by Conal Condren)
Leibniz *Political Writings* (edited by Patrick Riley)